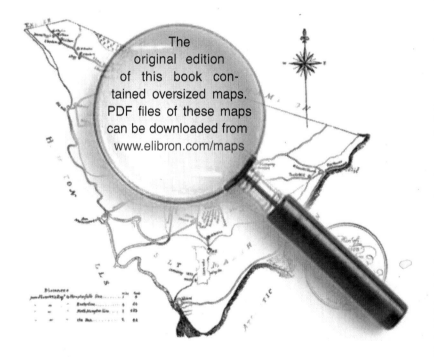

CLAUDE REIGNIER CONDER

THE

LATIN KINGDOM OF JERUSALEM

1099 TO 1291 A.D.

Elibron Classics
www.elibron.com

Elibron Classics series.

© 2005 Adamant Media Corporation.

ISBN 1-4021-5519-0 (paperback)
ISBN 1-4021-5518-2 (hardcover)

This Elibron Classics Replica Edition is an unabridged facsimile
of the edition published in 1897 by the Committee of the Palestine
Exploration Fund, London.

Elibron and Elibron Classics are trademarks of
Adamant Media Corporation. All rights reserved.

THE

LATIN KINGDOM OF JERUSALEM.

1099 TO 1291 A.D.

BY

LIEUT.-COL. C. R. CONDER, LL.D., M.R.A.S., R.E.,

Author of " Tent Work in Palestine," " Heth and Moab," etc.

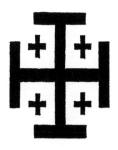

PUBLISHED BY THE
COMMITTEE OF THE PALESTINE EXPLORATION FUND,
24, HANOVER SQUARE, LONDON.

1897.

LONDON :

HARRISON AND SONS, PRINTERS IN ORDINARY TO HER MAJESTY.

ST. MARTIN'S LANE.

CONTENTS.

MAPS.

PREFACE.

THE sources on which we depend for history of the time of the great Crusades, and which have been used by Gibbon and Michaud, are well known and accessible. They include the Chronicles of Foucher of Chartres, who accompanied Robert of Normandy (1095-1124 A.D.), and of Raymond d'Agiles, who was also present at the conquest of Antioch, with that of Albert of Aix, and the great history of William, Archbishop of Tyre, which was begun in 1182 and closes in 1184.* These I have read in the great collection of Bongar's *Gesta Dei Per Francos* (Hanover, 1611), which also includes the important description of later events by Jacques de Vitry, Bishop of Acre, written about 1220 A.D.† The Moslem accounts include Boha ed Dîn's life of his master Saladin about 1200 A.D., and the later works of Kemâl ed Dîn, Mejr ed Din, Abu el Feda, and Makrizi, with El Edrizi's geography about 1150 A.D. The full details of King Richard's expedition are given in the contemporary account of Jeoffrey de Vinsauf, written about 1200 A.D.; and for the Crusade of St. Louis we have Joynville's Memoirs, the travels of Rubruquis, and Marco

---

* Continued by Ernoul, squire of Balian of Ibelin to 1228 A.D., and by Bernard the Treasurer, who wrote in 1320 A.D.

† He brings down his history to 1218 A.D.

Polo, all full of vivid pictures of the age. The pilgrim geographies now published by the Palestine Pilgrim Texts Society are equally important, and well known ; and even the later work of Marino Sanuto throws light on many questions, while the travels of Benjamin of Tudela explain the condition of the Jews in the East about 1160 A.D. I have not thought it necessary to give exact citations in every case, where sources so well known have been consulted.

The object of this volume is, however, not so much to relate the history of Crusades, as to present a picture of the curious social conditions which resulted from the establishment of a feudal society amid Oriental surroundings, and to trace the growth of civilisation and prosperity during the two centuries of Latin rule. The period is one of the most interesting in history, and the results of Frank colonisation in Palestine were far-reaching and important.

A large amount of material also exists, which has not as yet been utilised fully in treating these questions.* French antiquaries—and especially Rey—have diligently collected the contemporary documents, which relate to the tenure of land, and to the gifts and sales to the Church and to the great Military Orders. Herr Röhricht in Germany has, quite recently, reduced to chronological order a list of 1,500 documents, of the twelfth and thirteenth centuries, which relate to the

---

* *The Crusades*, by Archer and Kingsford (1894), is a *resumé* of the chronicles, and contains little that is new. It cites no authorities, and makes no use of the recent works here mentioned.

Kingdom of Jerusalem. The geography of the age was only imperfectly understood before Palestine was surveyed, and the Norman buildings—churches and castles —have now been planned and photographed, and many interesting inscriptions collected from them.* It thus becomes possible to give a picture, both of the country and of its populations, in the twelfth and thirteenth centuries, such as could not formerly be drawn ; and, though Rey has done much towards the study of social conditions, the wealth of illustration found in the works of Jeoffrey de Vinsauf,† Joynville, Rubruquis, and others, has not as yet been fully utilised, nor are the peaceful relations between Franks and Orientals generally recognised. These circumstances may perhaps excuse the present attempt to draw a picture of the Latin Kingdom of Jerusalem.

C. R. CONDER.

---

* The account of the Latin buildings within the limits of Palestine is taken from the plans and descriptions which I prepared when in command of the Survey of the country, when also I studied the mediæval topography. The details I have published in the Memoirs to the Survey (six volumes quarto) ; but the map of the mediæval topography I have since compiled from the researches of Rey and Röhricht, with additions due to the new topographical information. The map of Jerusalem which I compiled in 1883 for the Jerusalem Volume of the Memoirs is used in Archer's *Crusades*, p. 119, as well as my notes on the *Citez de Jherusalem.* In his *Crusade of Richard I* he adopts the results of my study of the march to Jaffa, first published in 1875.

† Sometimes attributed to Canon Richard, of Holy Trinity, London (who wrote in prose and verse), on the evidence of two passages quoted by a fourteenth century writer. One of the MSS., however, bears the name of the real author. In the same way an attempt was once made to show that Joynville's Memoir was not authentic.

LIST OF AUTHORITIES.

Bongar's *Gesta Dei Per Francos*. Hanover, 1611.

Guizot's *William of Tyre*. 1824.

Röhricht's *Regesta Regni Hierosolymitani*. 1893.

Rey's *Colonies Franques*. 1883.

De Vogüé's *Églises de la Terre Sainte*. 1860.

,, *Temple de Jerusalem*. 1864.

Publications of the Palestine Pilgrim Texts Society. 1886–96.

Memoirs of the Survey of Western Palestine. 1884.

Bohn's *Early Travels in Palestine*. 1848.

,, *Chronicles of the Crusades*. 1871.

Pinkerton's Travels. Rubruquis and Marco Polo. 1819.

Yule's *Marco Polo*. 1871.

Robinson's *Biblical Researches*. 1852.

Gibbon's *History of the Crusades*.

Michaud's *Histoire des Croisades*. Edit. 1877.

Besant and Palmer's *Jerusalem*. 1888.

G. le Strange's *Palestine under the Moslems*. 1890.

Journal of Royal Asiatic Society, North China Branch. 1859–86.

Chinese Recorder. 1868–86.

Green's *Short History of the English People*. 1892.

Publications of the Société de L'Orient Latin. 1885.

Hughe's *Dictionary of Islam*. 1885.

Gibbon's *Decline and Fall of the Roman Empire*. 1837.

Archer's *Crusade of Richard I*. 1893.

,, *Crusades*. 1894.

Schulten's *Boha ed Din*. Arabic and Latin. Leyden, 1732.

William's *Middle Kingdom*. 1883.

THE LATIN KINGDOM OF JERUSALEM.

1099 TO 1291 A.D.

————*————

CHAPTER I.

PETER THE HERMIT.

WITHOUT the gates of Jerusalem crowds of ragged and starving pilgrims sate disconsolate. Rude and unkempt, half-naked, sunburnt, and dusty, they lingered round the walls, where the lepers crouched on the dunghills; and waited in hopes that some goodly company of rich bishops, or courteous knights might in pity help them to fulfil their vows. For in the dark gate houses, under the towers, the savage Turkish guards were lounging—wild Turkomans and Kharezmian Afghans, in chain armour, with shining bucklers, bows, spears, and scimitars, and from beneath their steel caps looked out heavy Tartar faces, scowling in hatred and contempt on the stranger. The pilgrims had come from western Europe, by a long land journey full of perils, extending for two thousand miles over mountain and desert, through the countries of the half-pagan Hungarians, the crafty Greeks, the lawless Turks of Phrygia, the fanatic Arabs of the Syrian shore cities. Or they had endured the miseries of the sea, in crowded galleys dragged against the wind, by the labour of the hopeless slaves at the oar. The Franks, the Burgundians, the Normans and Bretons, the stolid Germans, and passionate Italians, who gathered in this famishing crowd, were scarcely less wild and lawless than the armed Turkomans who denied them entrance to the city. After enduring so many dangers and hardships, now within a short half mile of their goal, the way was barred by a toll ; and a gold piece exacted of those who had not even silver wherewith to buy bread. The sinner, the criminal, and the pious, were mingled together, all alike desiring to lay their foreheads on the stone of that Sepulchre where sins were forgiven, and guilt washed away, and vows fulfilled, and blessings granted. Only the little piece of gold was needed to secure everlasting pardon, consolation, and peace. Yet most among them were condemned to die within sight of the goal of hope, and their bodies were cast into the pits of the Potter's Field, where the dust of their bones still powders the floor knee deep.

At times some generous seigneur paced along, or a kindhearted bishop, and saved those then waiting from their fate. It was so in the year 1035 A.D., when Robert, Duke of Normandy, father of the Conqueror of England—strongest among the peers of France, came barefoot in his pilgrim's gown, with staff and scrip, followed by a long train of barons, knights, and monks,

who patiently endured the insults of the Moslem mob.*
For every pilgrim at the gate this generous prince paid a
gold bezant to the Turkish governor, and all were free
to pass within. It is said that the Moslem Emir, struck
by such devotion, sent back the money, which Robert
gave away again to the poor pilgrims he had succoured.
Their prayers went up to heaven for him when, on his
way back to his fair dukedom in the north, he died at
Nicea. It was not often that such help came to the
poor, though during all the century the nobles trooped
in ever greater numbers to fulfil their vows. Before
the Turkish conquest of the city in 1072 A.D., these
bands had yearly increased in numbers, and even noble
ladies joined these pilgrimages. The world, they said,
was growing old : the dread day of wrath was upon
them : men no longer tilled the earth, fearing the end of
all things ; and hastened to absolve their sins before the
Sepulchre. Thus, in 1054 A.D , the Bishop of Cambray
set forth leading " the Lord's host," but never reaching
Jerusalem. So in 1065 Siegfried, the lordly Archbishop
of Maintz, brought with him seven thousand rich and
poor,† camping under rich canopies of tapestry, drinking
from vessels of gold and silver, his army strong enough
to fight the brigands of Ramleh, and hand them over to
the Egyptian governor. But after this the Holy Land
became the battlefield of Egyptians and Turks from
the north, and no man setting forth could tell whom
he might find to be the Moslem master of Jerusalem.

---

* *Chronique de Normandie* (Robinson, *Bib. Res.*, I, p. 397).
† See the authorities in Robinson, *Bib. Res.*, I, p. 398.

For the last twenty years of the century the Turkomans, who took the city by siege in 1072, and pillaged
it again three years later, when the remnants of the
Kharezmian army fled from Cairo, cruelly oppressed
not only the pilgrims from Europe, but also their
brethren of the Greek Church, who had so long
enjoyed religious freedom under the wise rule of Arab
Khalifs.

Pilgrimage was not a new feature of the age or of
the faith. Among Christians it is traced to the third
century after Christ; and after the visit of Queen
Helena, mother of Constantine, to Jerusalem, it became,
in the fourth century, the practice of every rank and of
many races in Europe. Men like the Bordeaux pilgrim
had walked from France to Palestine, and had even
returned to their homes, though for one who thus
succeeded many failed or died. In the seventh century,
before Muhammad conquered Mecca, pious Arabs were
coming from all sides to see the sacred black stone, and
the red statue of Hobal at the Kaabah; and at the same
time Chinese pilgrims endured endless dangers in reaching the sacred land of Buddhists in Northern India,
adoring the holy Bo tree and the footprints of their
master. Even in Mexico the Spaniards of the sixteenth
century found the Azteks making pilgrimages to distant
temples, while in the time of St. Paul Ephesus was full
of pilgrims, who came to see the statue of Artemis, and
to carry home a silver model of her shrine. Looking
back yet earlier we find three yearly pilgrimages commanded to Hebrews by the Law; and even Babylonians

and Egyptians journeyed to famous shrines to pay their vows to the gods.

But when the gate of Jerusalem was passed the dangers of the pilgrims were not ended. The presence of the Latins was a constant peril to the native Christians. The city was crowded, and their zeal led constantly to quarrels with the fanatics of Islam, in which all Christians suffered alike. The ancient hospice founded by Charlemagne, renewed in 1048 A.D. by merchants of Amalfi, and standing south-east of the Sepulchre churches, was only for the sick and dying. Others must lodge in the Greek taverns, where vice and extortion were rampant, or sleep under archways and in cellars, hiding from Turkish and Arab bandits. Not even in the churches were they safe. A small pretext was enough for persecution. The Turkomans would then invade the sanctuary, and dance upon the altars treading on the sacred cup, dragging the Patriarch from his throne by the beard,* wreaking their fury even on the marble of the sepulchre. Happy was the pilgrim who, when his vow was paid, could escape at length from Jerusalem in peace—not held to ransom for some fancied insult to the Moslem faith. The indignation of Europe was slowly rising, as tales came back of such oppression, of sacrilege and martyrdom and general lawlessness in Palestine; but the hour had not yet struck, though Hildebrand had preached the Crusade twenty years before.

Among these luckless pilgrims, in the year 1094 A.D.,

* *William of Tyre*, I, 8, 10.

was Peter, the unnoticed monk—a knight of gentle birth from Picardy. He was then forty-four years of age, mean and insignificant of feature, low of stature, barefooted and bareheaded, clad in the rough brown robe, and girt with the cord. Yet in his heart there burned an unsuspected fire, and the voice of the soldier, who had fled from the world to a hermit's life, could ring with an eloquence born of passionate faith, which was able to persuade the hearts of men. He knelt in the poor chapels which the piety of Michael IV, Emperor of Byzantium, had raised some sixty years before on the ruins of the churches of Modestus. "Very small oratories"* they were, where once the great Basilica of Constantine, with roof of gold and pillar capitals of silver, had filled the whole space in which they were enclosed. The great wealth of Constantine's fane had been seized by Persian worshippers of Ormuzd, when they burned the building in 614 A.D. The ruins of the chapels of Modestus survived the persecution of El Hâkem, who destroyed them in 1010 A.D.; and the buildings now standing were erected in 1037 A.D., by treaty with El Mustansir, the Khalif of Egypt, grandson of El Hâkem. On the steep rock of Calvary a low arched chapel covered the altar. Beneath was the cavern of Golgotha holding the skull of Adam. A strange legend had already fixed itself to the site, telling how Seth had brought the seed from Paradise, which, placed in Adam's mouth, grew into the tree of which the Cross was made. How, on Lebanon, it escaped

* *Will. Tyre*, VIII. 3.

the Flood,* and was cut down to be used by Solomon for the Temple bridge, and trampled under feet by men until the Queen of Sheba came to rescue and adore. How, on the rock of Calvary, the Saviour's blood fell through the earthquake chasm on to Adam's skull, from this tree which had become the Cross. How Helena had found it in the pit beneath the hill, and once more the sick were healed, and the dead were raised by virtue of the sacred wood, anointed with the fragrant " oil of mercy " which came from Paradise. But no Cross now stood on Calvary, and the few fragments that were left were hidden at Lydda and Byzantium, or scattered through the Christian world. Only the crosses brought by pilgrims were strewn upon the hill.

From Calvary the pilgrim passed by steep, narrow steps down to the court-yard, and eastwards to the cavern chapel, which was lighted only from its dome, standing on heavy pillars capped with the basket capitals of the time of Modestus. It was a gloomy vault in which men said the pious Helena had watched her workmen delving for the Cross. Above and to the north they showed the Pillar of Flagellation, with finger - prints of Christ. Yet further north a colonnade led to the little chapel of the Prison, where Christ awaited execution ; and west of this the Holy Tomb itself stood in the round church, which was adorned with pictures in brocade and gold, and others painted in

* Publications of Soc. de L'Orient Latin, III, p. 158, from the Continuator of *W. Tyre,* 1261 A.D. See also A. de Gubernatis' *Mythologie des Plantes,* Vol. I, pp. 7–13 ; from the 19th chapter of the Gospel of Nicodemus, and later sources.

oil and glazed, showing the prophets of Israel, and the
Saviour riding on the ass.* In the centre rose the
chapel covering the tomb itself, adorned with coloured
marbles, and hung with silver lamps. To north and south
were other stations, of Mary Magdalen, St. John, and
Trinity, and on the outer wall of these the "Mother of
God" was painted in a fresco of Byzantine quaintness,
supporting with her long thin fingers the holy babe, and
crowned, like Him, with cross divided aureole.†

Other more terrible pictures on the whitewashed
walls presented to the pilgrim Heaven and Hell—the
day of wrath which Christians then believed to be
so soon to come.‡ Such pictures still exist in the
Armenian Church of St. James, and, in the ruins of
Crusaders' monasteries, might be seen not twenty years
ago. The saints fly up to the great throne on which
the Pantokrator sits in Paradise, and peacock-winged
angels throw upon their shoulders the resurrection
garments white and shining; while, on the other hand,
the eagle-footed demons, with tiger fangs and hairy
ears, are driving with their tridents naked souls (some
pierced with the prongs) into the gaping jaws of the
great dragon, whence issue the long tongues of fire from
Hell.

Such were the sights which Peter saw in Jerusalem.
High above the chapels of the western city loomed the
great dome of the Arab mosque, in its broad court on

---

* *Nasr-i-Khusrau*, p. 59, English translation, a description written
1047–8 A.D.
† Saewulf's description, 1102 A.D.
‡ *Nasr-i-Khusrau*.

the eastern hill, which none but Moslems might approach, and where the shield of Hamzah—rich with Persian filigree—lay beside the foot-print of Muhammad, pressed on the sacred rock in that mysterious night when angels and prophets welcomed him from heaven to heaven, until he reached the awful stillness of the veil, when naught was seen, and naught heard save the creaking of the iron pen writing decrees of fate.

From station to station Peter followed with the rest, praying in silence or wondering at the maimed rites of Greeks and Copts, Syrians, Georgians, Jacobites, and Armenians—for the city was full of Christians of the East, full also of Jews,[*] who were dyers and traders, or pilgrims to the Holy House. At night he talked with Simeon, the Patriarch, bewailing the sorrows of their common faith ; and from him first perhaps came words which served to rouse a great idea in his heart : " When the cup of tribulation is full," said Simeon, "God will send the Christians of the West to help the Holy City."

At length, either in the darkness of Helena's Chapel, or when he knelt wearied before the Sepulchre, or perhaps on the hill of Calvary, there came to Peter a voice. " Arise, Peter," it said, " the time is come. Go forth and tell the tribulations of My people. The time is come that My servants should be succoured, and that My holy places should be free."

In later days men loved to believe in more than the voice.[†] They said that Peter rested for a moment his

* *Nasr-i-Khusrau*, p. 23.
† Felix Fabri, 1483 A.D., Vol. II, Part I, p. 291. English translation of the Pal. Pilgrim Texts Society.

weary limbs before the Sepulchre, and prayed and saw the glorified body of the Risen Lord come forth from the tomb, who, looking on him, uttered the command, " Rise up, Peter, and haste to Rome, and say to Urban, Pope of Rome, thus saith the Lord, ' because of the greatness of My Name I have given My holy tomb to them of the West, that they may manifest Me to unbelievers, and worship at My holy places to the saving of mankind.' " Then the vision faded, and Peter went out to preach to Europe the Holy War.

Let us consider, then, the Asia that he left, the Europe that he reached in safety by the toilsome road through Byzantium, and the many causes which led to Peter's voice becoming powerful to change the history of Europe and of Asia alike ; for even popes in former days had preached the Holy War in vain, and statesmen had cared as little for the pilgrims' woes as did the eager traders of Italy, who were growing rich among the Moslems ; or the proud Normans who, in Sicily and in England, were carving with their swords broad kingdoms nearer home than Palestine.

The old days of peace and tolerance, and the glories of the great civilising Arab empire, had passed away two hundred years before the times of Peter. When Charlemagne, the German Emperor, had ruled nearly all Europe, and aimed at empire in Byzantium, Hârûn "the Just" was Khalif at Baghdad, swaying an united Islam from India to Egypt, trading with China, prayed for at Mecca and Cairo, spreading abroad the know-ledge of science and philosophy, which, as yet, had not

reached an university of Paris. By him the keys of
Jerusalem were sent to Charlemagne, with an invitation
to rebuild the churches of the Holy Land. Rich robes
and spices then were brought to Spain and France by
Jewish merchants. An elephant even was sent by the
Khalif to the Emperor. Venetians and Genoese
already traded by Byzantium to the Caspian and the
Oxus, and the peaceful future of civilisation seemed
secure. But when these great rulers passed away, dissensions soon arose alike in Europe and in Asia. The
old quarrel, which divided Islam ever since the death of
Omar, broke forth again. The empire of the Khalif
fell in pieces slowly, and the two sects of Shiàh and
Sunnee renewed their hatred. The mystic philosophy
of the Shiàh—followers of Àly, the prophet's son-in-law,
and mourners for Hasan and the martyred Hosein—
opposed the orthodoxy of the great Khalifs—both of
those who sprang from Abu Sofian, Muhammad's rival,
and reigned in Damascus, and of those who claimed
descent from Abbas, Muhammad's uncle, and who for
one glorious century ruled ever increasing dominions
from Baghdad. The house of Abbas decayed, and a
new power rose in Western Asia, when the Turks from
the Oxus pushed westwards under the Seljuks.* As in
the West (in 987 A.D.), Hugh, Count of Paris, protector of the degenerate Carlovignians, usurped the king-

---

* The Turks were already known to the Byzantine emperors in the
sixth century. Embassies from Justinian and his successors visited the
Chagan in the Altai mountains. Their dominions extended to the Oxus,
and to the borders of Persia. Heraclius was allied with the Khozar
Turks in the Caucasus against Chosroes, in 625 A.D.

dom, so in the East, after subduing Persia, Toghrul Bey, grandson of Seljuk, for services to the Khalif in conquering revolted provinces, was made, in 1055 A.D., Emir el Omara ("chief of the forces"), and, under the ancient Turkish title of Sultan, became the ruler of Islam.   Alp Arslan ("the brave lion"), his nephew, succeeding in 1063, had already conquered Asia Minor in 1071 A.D., taking captive Romanus Diogenes, the Byzantine Emperor.   On his assassination his son, Melek Shah, succeeded—the greatest of the Seljuks— who from 1073 A.D. (after the conquest of Syria) governed from Egypt to the Iaxartes, from the gates of Byzantium to Kashgar and the borders of India, a Turkish empire won in little more than half a century, in which El Muktadi, the Khalif at Baghdad, was no longer more than the religious head of Islam.   The Seljuks professed the strictest Sunnee orthodoxy, but the wild Turkomans whom they led from Central Asia —the Kharezmians, Kurds, and Uigurs, who commanded their armies and ruled their great provinces—cared little for the teaching of Islam, and despised its civilisation as much as they despised the creed of Greek or Latin Christians.   Wherever the Turkish rule spread, oppression and persecution followed, and the Arab tolerance was forgotten.

Egypt had already been lost to the Sunnee Khalif through the rebellion of its governor Ibn Tulun in 880, and in 910 A.D. a new leader arose, announcing himself to be a Mahdi, and claiming descent from Fatima, the Prophet's daughter.   This rebel, who had fled from

Baghdad, established the Shiàh creed in Africa, and from Kairwân the Fatimites advanced to the Nile half a century later, and founded Cairo. Their pirate fleets infested the Mediterranean, and ravaged the shores of Italy and Sicily. From Cairo Mùez advanced into Syria, and the fanatical Shiàh persecuted the Christians, until El Hâkem destroyed their churches in 1010 A.D. Sylvester II was the first Pope who attempted to rouse Europe against them, and about the beginning of the eleventh century the Pisan ships were raiding on the African coast; but the successor of El Hâkem was pleasure - loving and peaceful, and for a time the prosperity of Palestine began to revive. In the middle period of the century its cities were rich and populous*: the ships of Greeks and Franks traded on its coasts. In Tripoli the sugar-cane was cultivated; its gardens flourished with citrons, oranges, and bananas; its strong walls were guarded with balistæ. The rose gardens of Gebal bloomed in a time of peace, and paper of the papyrus of its river became famous. But the Fatimite Khalif, El Mustansir, was only a child when he acceded in 1037, and the power of the Turks pressed hard on his northern provinces. During his reign, in 1072, the Kharezmian general, Atsiz, besieged and took Jeru-salem, and invaded Egypt. He was defeated, and his scattered army massacred in Syria; but stronger leaders came to join him at Damascus, when Tutush, son of Alp Arslan, after executing Atsiz as a punish-ment for defeat, advanced to the borders of Egypt.

---

* *Nasr-i-Khusrau*, pp. 2, 5, 7, 8, 9, 20, 21, English translation.

Ortok Ibn Eksek, a general under Tutush, and himself a Turkoman, was made the governor of Syria under the Seljuk sultan, and the Sunnee once more superseded the Shiàh, though the Moslems of Palestine were in great measure followers of Aly. The cruelties of Ortok and of his sons El Ghazi and Sukmân, who ruled Jerusalem after Tutush was slain in battle by Borkiaruk, son of Melek Shah, in 1095 A.D., were among the chief causes of the first Crusade. In the year in which Peter visited Jerusalem (1094 A.D.) a new Khalif acceded in Cairo—El Mustàli, second son of El Mustansir; and during his short reign, which saw the triumph of the Christians, the government was in the hands of his strong vizir, Melek el Afdal, who played a not unimportant part in events about to be considered.

Such, then, was the condition of Asia. The death of Melek Shah, and the fall of Tutush, led to the ruin of the Turkish empire in the North. The governors of provinces—at Aleppo, Damascus, and Jerusalem—no longer recognised a common suzerain. They fought with one another and with Egypt. The Moslems were bitterly divided by the mutual hatred of Sunnee and Shiàh, and about 1096 Jerusalem rebelled, and for two years was independent of the Seljuks. Trade was paralysed, and peaceful pilgrimage became impossible, when Turk and Egyptian were struggling for Palestine ; and the Tartar Sunnee was as intolerant as the Shiàh of the South. Islam was exhausted by such conflicts, and powerless, through its divisions, to present an unbroken front to any strong power able and willing to profit by its weakness.

In Europe, on the other hand, the various rivalries of nations and of princes were held down by a central power, daily growing stronger, and one which united men by a common bond of religion. It was, moreover, an age when ambitious princes had begun to look to the East for further conquests, when the vigour of the Normans was still not exhausted, and when they had proved, in Sicily, that neither Greek nor Saracen could stand before the Norman sword. The idea of a Crusade was not a new one. Sylvester II had preached it nearly a century before; and Hildebrand had urged it* on Duke William of Burgundy, and on all Christendom only twenty years before Peter reached Europe. When Victor III succeeded Hildebrand a Crusade was preached in Italy, in 1086, against the Moslem pirates; and a Christian army raided the African shores. But as yet the idea had not taken root: the European princes were intent on other aims; and the pilgrims had not reported such cruelties as those of Ortok's sons; nor had the traders yet brought word of the death of Tutush, and of the dissolution of the Turkish empire which followed In the year 1095 A.D. the hour struck; and with the hour came the man whose voice could move the hearts of the masses.

In Italy Urban II had now been Pope six years, and though expelled from Rome in 1091 A.D., had been restored in the year in which Peter first went out to the East. He lived to see Palestine conquered, and died in the very year in which Jerusalem was recovered. The

* Greg. (VII) Epist. Lib., II, 37 and I, 46.

policy of the Latin Church aimed not only at strengthening Rome against the pretensions of the German
Emperor, Henry IV, and of his nominee—the anti-
Pope—but also at the gathering in of all the Eastern
sects, under the Papal sway, which in some small
measure actually was brought about by conquest in
Asia.   Policy and religious feeling pointed the same
way.   The Pope became protector of the oppressed
Christians of the East, and of the pilgrims from the
West alike ; and among princes his power was also
increased, by a cause which gave to him the right to send
legates, to levy taxes, and to issue commands to kings.
In Peter's zeal the shrewd Pope Urban saw an instru-
ment by which he would do more than any had before
been able to do to strengthen the power of the Holy
See.

The policy of the great trading cities of Italy, which
already had extended commerce far into the Moslem
world, tended naturally to the same ends.   Without
peace, tolerance, and strong rule in Asia trade must
suffer, and there was little prospect of stability while all
the ports of the Levant were threatened by war, and Constantinople trembling before the Turks of Asia-Minor.
But there was also in the south of Italy a still stronger
element of success, in the vigour and ambition of the
Normans.   In 1017 A.D. the Pope had invited Norman
pilgrims to conquer Apulia, from the mingled Greek
and Saracen foes of Rome.   Within half a century the
friends so invited became foes, and the Normans, under
Robert Guiscard "the Wily," had fought against Leo IX

in 1053 A.D. at Civitella. After a ten years' struggle with the Saracens, Robert had won Naples and Sicily in 1080, and, making peace with the Pope, was re-established as lawful ruler of Apulia. He tolerated the Saracens and defeated the Greeks in Italy, and twice attacked Greece itself. He died in 1085, and his sons were now at war. Half a century had passed since the "wily" Robert reached Italy from Hauteville in Normandy, with five knights and thirty men. Yet the riches of their Saracenic* dominion were such that the Normans of Sicily were among the wealthiest of European princes. Boemund of Calabria, Robert's elder son by his first wife, was a man eloquent and accomplished, standing, it is said, a cubit above most men in height, who had learned war by his father's side, following him against the Emperor Alexius at Durazzo and Larissa. But the inheritance was given to his half-brother Roger, son of a princess of Salerno, from whom he took Tarento ; and now, with his uncle Roger, he was laying siege to the trading city of Amalfi, which faces the temples of Pæstum on the north side of the bright bay of Salerno, where the Sorrento promontory runs out opposite the high peak of Capri. Instead of fratricidal war, and the ruin of Christian trade, a new ambition was offered now to Boemund by Peter and the Pope—an Asiatic principality, to be won with the sword and destined to be held for nearly two centuries to come.

From Rome, then, Peter was sent through Italy, to rouse the Norman, the Pisan, the Genoese, and the

* The Saracen conquest of Sicily, dated from 827 A.D.

Venetian; to gather armies and fleets; and to employ
the wealth which had grown from Moslem spoils, and
from trade with Asia. Ambition and desire for wealth,
no less than religion, urged the Italians to a venture
which was no longer desperate. The sailors feared
neither the Mediterranean which they knew so well, nor
the pirates whom they had already beaten. The Italian
Normans feared not the heats of Palestine, nor the
Saracens, a race from whom Sicily had been won. They
heard of allies from Provence, from Western Germany
and France, and they were eager only to be first upon
the ground. The siege of Amalfi was raised; and a
force of ten thousand horse and twenty thousand foot
was ready to follow Boemund and his cousin Tancred,
the proud, rude, but chivalrous prince, whose name has
been immortalised by Tasso as the hero of the Holy
War.

In Spain there was no hope of aid for Christendom.
The Moslems were strong there still, and the Pope as
yet was weak. The Arab civilisation, against which in
the next century the papal influence was directed, was
then civilising Southern Europe, and colouring the
thought and culture of Provence. Science was studied
in the Arabic tongue, in Andalusia and at Cordova, to
which city learned men had travelled from Baghdad a
century before. The rhyme which marks the cadence
of the earlier chapters of the Korân is said to have
first brought rhyming into poetry in France; and Arab
lyric and romantic poetry influenced the troubadours of
Languedoc. Gerbert had brought from Barcelona a

knowledge of mathematics in 1003 A.D. ; and Arab cyphers were spreading over Europe from Spain, and replacing the clumsy Roman numerals. Adelard of Bath was just about to study Arabic among the Moors ; but a century must pass before Michael Scott would be considered a wizard, because at Toledo he was able to learn not only alchemy and astrology, but algebra, philosophy, astronomy, and mathematic sciences.

We are not, then, surprised that Peter never went to Spain. The Holy War would find but few adherents in the Moorish lands : the fiat of the Pope had none to obey it where science and philosophy still flourished among Moslems. Neither went he to Eastern Europe, though Eastern Europe already, in great measure, professed allegiance to the Pope. The great quarrel with the empire had already arisen, when the nominee of Rome—Rudolph of Suabia—had been slain. The Prussians were still pagans, adoring Perkunas and other of the ancient Lithuanian gods of their earliest Aryan forefathers, though some of the Hungarian Mongols— akin to the Turks—had recently been converted to Latin rites. There was only one part of the empire whence help could come, namely, from the great state of Lotharingia, the home of Charlemagne's eldest son, where the sons of the Count of Boulogne traced descent, by the mother's side, from Charlemagne himself.*

* Godfrey the Bearded, Duke of Lower Lorraine, died in 1069 A.D. His daughter Ida married Eustace II of Bou'ogne. Her three sons were Godfrey, Baldwin, and Eustace. Her elder brother, Godfrey the Hunchback, had died in 1076. Bouillon in the Ardennes, from which Godfrey took his usually best-known title, was a lordship, which he sold to the Church for one thousand three hundred marks.

Of this family, Godfrey of Boulogne had still to do a
penance for his wars against the will of Rome.   He had
followed the Emperor when but nineteen against Rudolph
of Rhinefeld, Duke of Suabia, whom Hildebrand had
named to the Imperial Crown.   In the Imperial cause
Godfrey had even entered Rome in 1083 A.D.   Rudolph
he is said to have slain with his own hand.   But as yet
he was only thirty-four years of age—a free lance,
nephew of the ruling duke, born at Boulogne, the eldest
son of Count Eustace.   Strong, prudent, just, and wise,
even in his youth, Godfrey was loved and trusted by all.
He too, like Boemund, was taller than most men, with
handsome face and ruddy beard.   He vowed to free
Jerusalem as a penance for his sins against the holy
father ; and to supply means he sold or alienated his
estates—the principality of Stenay, bought by the
bishop of Liège, and the town of Metz, granted its freedom for the citizens, in return for funds to carry on the
Holy War.   Twenty-four thousand Franks, and ten
thousand knights, are said to have followed Godfrey
and his tall dark brother Baldwin, and his cousin Baldwin
du Bourg—a company of three kings that were to be,
besides Eustace the third of the brethren, who returned
to become Count of Boulogne after the war.

France, in the sense of a kingdom west of the Rhine,
did not exist when Peter preached the Crusade.   The
kingdom of the French king extended over the Isle
de France : his actual rule was from Paris to Orleans.
The land of France was a feudal confederacy of peers :
Eight great princes ruled eight great fiefs—Burgundy,

Aquitaine, Normandy, Gascony, Flanders, Champagne, Toulouse, and Anjou. Lorraine and part of Burgundy and Provence were not yet French. The whole land was then full of robber castles, and few were the towns which as yet had gained any charter or rights of immunity against the barons' might. Philip, the French king, then of middle age, comely and good-natured in his youth, was sinking into sloth and vice, and his gluttony already marred his powers of action. He never took the cross, and Hugh of Vermandois, his brother, although he joined in the Crusade with Robert of Normandy, deserted for a time during the early troubles, and on his way back, after Jerusalem was won, he died at Tarsus. The house of Hugh Capet had thus but little share in the triumph of the Cross : for Hugh, though brave and ostentatious, was indolent and frivolous. The men destined to be kings in Asia were made of sterner stuff.

Among the other peers were princes of greater energy than the French. Robert of Flanders led the Frisons and Flemish men. He was the first to march to Byzantium, with five hundred knights. He had usurped his nephew's place, and vowed to free Jerusalem in penitence. Raymond of St. Gilles and of Toulouse was rich and old, yet impetuous and ambitious, hated by his subjects for his obstinate tyranny, and feared as well for his violence. He owned large lands on the Rhone and Dordogne, in Gascony, Auvergne, Provence, Limousin, and Languedoc. He had fought beside the Cid against the Moors, and married Eloisa, daughter of Alphonso the Great. His wife and son went with him ; and an

hundred thousand men, who marched to Lyons and the
Rhone, crossed the Alps to Lombardy, and thence on
by land to Constantinople.

In the North the Normans had become even stronger
than in Italy.   It was not yet two centuries since Rollo
had been baptised, and settled in Normandy as one
among the twelve peers.   It was not thirty years since
William had conquered England, and but eight since he
had died, leaving to Robert, his eldest but rebel son, the
Norman fief which now he mortgaged for five years to
his brother William Rufus ; and with money thus raised
joined the Holy War, to expiate his sins against his
father.   With him came Stephen, Count of Blois and
Chartres, poet and soldier, rich and careless, who, like
Hugh of Vermandois, deserted at Antioch, and, like
him, died later in the East, leaving his son Stephen
—the grandson of the Conqueror—to become in time
the King of England.

Such were the princes who now guided the popular
enthusiasm to ends foreseen by well warned statesmen,
knowing not only their own people but knowing also
what had happened of late years in Asia.   Among them
six gained honour, power, and fame—Godfrey and
Baldwin, Boemund and Tancred, Raymond of Toulouse,
and after these Baldwin du Bourg.   A mighty host of
fighting men, well armed and well provided, followed
the princes from France and Italy.   Frenchmen and
Lorrainers, Normans and Provençals,* with Auvergnats
and Italians, and some from Spain and Burgundy, with

* *John of Würzburg*, p. 41, English translation.

Saxons led by Edgar the Atheling—nephew of the Confessor—who came with Robert of Normandy ; and Flemings and Frisons from Flanders.* The Norman element prevailed most among them, and the German Frankish race of Eastern France.

But such preparations, which brought some two hundred thousand fighting men together, under experienced leaders, were not made in a day. After the Council of Piacenza, which, in March, followed Peter's return bearing letters from Alexius, the Emperor of the East, the Council of Clermont was called in November, 1095 ; and other meetings were held under Pope Urban in Rouen, Angers, Nismes, and Tours. Not till the middle of August following were the armies set in motion, but at Clermont in the tenth sitting, after the Peace of God had been renewed among the Latins —a truce of princes to last during the Crusade—the letters from the East were read, and Peter testified to sufferings of the Eastern Christians, and Pope Urban spoke in favour of the Holy War, and all the Council echoed with the famous shout of " Diex el volt "—the war cry of the first Crusade.

For popular impatience, and for the zeal of Peter, such preparation was all too slow. His own zeal and purity of purpose we need not doubt. He underwent all the hardships, passed through all the perils, failed only for a moment at Antioch, witnessed the taking of Jerusalem, and enjoyed one short hour of triumph, when

---

* William of Malmesbury and Guibert (quoted by Gibbon, Ch. LVIII), speak of a few Scotch, Welsh, and Irish soldiers.

the Syrian Christians hailed him as their saviour ; and then reaping neither reward nor dignity returned to his cell at Hui, and was heard of no longer when his task was over. But now in France and Italy he was the popular idol. He preached in town and country, in churches, or beside the crosses in the fields. He told men of the bitter persecution in the East, and of the voice that spake to him by Calvary. His words sank into the hearts of all, and cries of wrath mingled with sobs of penitence. They crowded to touch him, and carried off the rags of his robes as relics. Nay, it is said the hairs of the very mule on which the little monk rode over Western Europe were treasured. Sinners and robbers vowed a better life, and swore to set free from Turks the land hallowed by the feet of Christ.

But many other motives wrought upon the crowd of serfs and villeins to whom he spoke, while Urban preached to princes. Such men had little interest in the land they tilled, and saw before them freedom from their slavery in Europe. Wealth and civilisation had not yet, in the West, bound the masses to their towns and fields. Many were outlaws and broken men, who owned no master who would feed them. Many for heavy crimes and sins were banned by the Church. Without the baron's command none of the villeins could leave their villages. Without the bishop's permit none might go as pilgrims. But now, when every noble seemed about to sell or mortgage his estate, the bonds of the strong narrow feudal system, which alone could hold society together in these rough times, were relaxed.

Indulgences and pardons were promised to all who took the cross, and fighting men were summoned to accompany their barons. Women and children even were allowed to follow their husbands and fathers. Criminals the most desperate—robbers, murderers, and violent men—were not denied a share in the holy work—room for repentance and for good services was given even to these. A mighty mob, equal in numbers to the army which was to follow, surged eastwards over Europe, led by Peter and by a single Norman knight, Walter Lackland—a horde recalling to mind those which in earlier times had invaded Europe, when Huns and Alans came even into Western France, or when the Gauls of Brennus overran Galatia. It was the last of the great migrations of the Aryans, and was only excelled two centuries later when the Mongols burst out of Central Asia. But it was not to these that any benefit was to come. Through Germany and Hungary they went on their tempestuous way to Bulgaria. At Belgrade they scattered, harrying the flocks and herds for food ; and here they were slaughtered by a mixed Christian and pagan peasantry. Only a remnant camped with Walter near Byzantium, awaiting the coming of a second horde which Peter led.

The second horde, entering a country where the first made enemies, suffered yet more than they had done. Forty thousand peasants entered Hungary, and sacked Semlin, and found Belgrade deserted. The German rear guards quarrelled with Bulgarians, and were slain, while women, children, and possessions were carried off.

Their comrades who turned back were massacred in turn, and half the Christian host were thus cut off and perished before the Bosphorus was reached. Twenty thousand Germans, following these, were treacherously slain in Hungary. Another "army of the Lord," as it was called, led by the priest Volkmar, slew all the Jews in Mayence and Cologne, and harrying Eastern Europe—a band of dissolute criminals, who observed no law or treaty—they were put to death like sheep by the Hungarians. Out of these various bands an hundred thousand crossed the straits at Constantinople, and ravaged the lands of Nicomedia and Nicea. Germans and Italians quarrelled for the booty gained, and the Turkish governor of Nicea drew this army of the Latins into a forest ambush, so that of all the host barely three thousand—one man for every hundred who set out—escaped to tell the tale. Peter himself fled back to Constantinople ; and long before the princes left their homes the bones of countless European peasants were blanching in the sun upon the shores of the Propontis.

Zeal and popular fury failed, where neither discipline, nor knowledge, nor money, nor arms were to be found ; and not by means of wild peasant hordes was Palestine to be won for the Christians.

It is not because of any doubts as to the faith and enthusiasm of these poor victims of a mighty movement that the story told by the early chroniclers has thus briefly been sketched. Their lawless ravages were the results of terrible need : they starved in strange lands because ill and hastily led. Yet from their fate we may learn how savage and untamed was the state of nations in that Europe which so suddenly poured whole populations into Asia, and may see that the civilisation to be learned in the East had as yet hardly dawned on Western Countries.

CHAPTER II.

THE MARCH TO ANTIOCH.

WHILE riotous mobs thus prejudiced the Christian cause in the eyes of the Eastern Church, and of the Eastern Emperor ; and while weary women and children asked, as each Hungarian or Bulgarian town appeared upon the endless road, whether that were Jerusalem, the armies of Lorraine, Provence, and Sicily were gathering towards Constantinople. Alexius seems to have little understood the greatness of the movement, or the masterful character of these princes from lands regarded by the Greeks as still barbarian. He asked for help from the West, whereby he might recover Syria and Anatolia lost to the Turks ; but behold there came an army so strong and great that its leaders took for themselves the lands which the Byzantines could not hold. He asked for restoration of the patriarchs to their thrones ; but behold they set their own Latin bishops in the vacant chairs. Alexius was weak and crafty ; his schemes were powerless against men who came not to help him, but rather to conquer for themselves. The French king's brother Hugh was shipwrecked in Epirus, and carried to the capital, where he

was held a hostage for the fealty which Alexius claimed
from the Latins.   Godfrey's answer was quickly given.
His army was marching in strict discipline, but now was
loosed to plunder as it went.   The emperor hastened
to appease the Franks, but none of the princes of Italy
or Lorraine ever did homage or acknowledged Alexius
as suzerain.   Robert of Flanders, Robert of Normandy,
and Stephen of Blois, less bold, admitted his claims,
but none of these intended to remain in Asia.

It was already autumn, or early winter of the year
1097, when the great army gathered near Byzantium.
From Normandy, Lorraine, and Southern France they
came by land, through Servia and Bulgaria ; from Italy
and Sicily they came by sea, embarking at Amalfi, Bari,
and Messina.   When the Italian galleys, sailing up the
narrow Dardanelles through the Propontis—the Straits
of St. George they called it—had passed the low white
chalk ridges, and gained the Golden Horn, a city such
as never yet most of the Latins had beheld burst on
their sight.*   Perhaps to some, coming in winter, it
first revealed itself at dawn, when the light mists had
rolled away ; and flushed with the pink haze they saw
the mighty dome of St. Sophia sprinkled with the early
snow, the strong towers, the gilded palaces, the countless sails upon the still and shining waters.   Already
Jewish Galata climbed towards the upper platform of
Pera, and Scutari, with its wooden Turkish houses,
looked across the water from Asia.   Already merchants

---

* Byzantium already contained a western force in the Varanger Guard
(see Gibbon, Ch. LV), recruited from English and Danish colonists who
fled from the Norman conquerors.

gathered in this capital, coming by sea and land, from
Egypt and Baghdad, from Media and Persia, from
Russia, Hungary, Lombardy, and Spain* dealing in silks
and furs, spices and precious stones, camlets and drugs.
Venetians, Genoese and Pisans, Jews, Arabs and Armenians, vied in a commerce which was already pushed
to Turkestan, and linked to India and China by the
Arab fleets. The men of Provence and of Italy were
not insensible to art and beauty ; but many of the
Latins came from gloomier lands—from dark castles and
small fortresses frowning over squalid wooden villages.
They were astonished at the wealth and luxury of Asia,
and their hearts rejoiced thinking of the spoils that lay
before them in the East, where Baghdad and Damascus
were said to rival Byzantium. The Greeks, they said,
were "like women," who could not fight for such an
heritage. The ancient glories of Constantine and
Justinian had passed away : the Byzantines, who once
had stayed the Huns of Hungary† on their southern
march, could now not even hold Nicea against the
Turk. The vigour of the race was sapped by luxury :
the empire had been weakened by the attacks of
Hungarians and Russians ; the trade in cloth of gold
and purple, in diamonds and rubies, had enervated those
who once had marched to Persia to bring back the stolen
Cross. But art and literature, science and knowledge,
still survived ; and many were the lessons which the

---

* Benjamin of Tudela, p. 74, Bohn's *Early Travels in Palestine.*
† Hung-ər (" Hun land ") was a name originally given to a region on the
Volga; and still existed there in the thirteenth century, as noted by Rubruquis,
but it was transferred to Europe in the time of Attila (433–453 A.D.).

ignorant Latins were destined yet to learn in the old homes of religion and civilisation.

Christmas was passed at Constantinople, and here the princes feasted and rested, flattered by Alexius, and triumphing through the city. They found the palace splendid with gilded walls and pillars, its golden throne crusted with gems, its galleries sculptured with wars of the ancients. In St. Sophia they admired the spacious galleries, the marble tracery, the mighty dome, the gates of brass. In the Pantocrator Church the monuments of Constantine and Helena rose like chapels of red jasper. The Greeks and Orientals in the streets and markets were robed in silk and cloth of gold—a crowd as gay as a garden of flowers. The city was full of relics—dried bodies of the saints—and of holy things brought from Palestine when the Patriarch fled from Omar or from Chosroes ; the fragments of the Cross, the nails, the reed, and the sponge, which had so long, men said, protected Byzantium from the infidel. At Christmas time they saw, no doubt, in the Cathedral a mystery or miracle play—perhaps that represented later, of the three children in the furnace, or the Lazarus boy dressed in flowers, or Judas who exploded in fireworks. In the At-Meidân the games no doubt were held to honour them as usual—arrow contests on horseback, the jereed throwing, and the old Roman fights of the amphi-theatre, when lions and bears, leopards and wild asses were turned into the Hippodrome, under the walls of the palace, and Alexius looked down from his gallery crowned with gold and robed in garments covered with rubies. Such was the daily life of Byzantium for even four centuries after the first Crusade.

But with the springtime came the season for war and conquest, and the army of the Latins crossed the straits to win Nicea from its Turkish master Suleiman Kilij Arslan—a descendant of the Western Seljuks. The city, so famous in Christian memory as that where first an Emperor of New Rome had presided at a Council of bishops of the faith which half his subjects held, lay in the plain east of the Lake Ascanius, under an amphithreatre of wooded hills. It had three hundred and seventy towers, three gates, and an aqueduct from the mountains. The invading army appears to have numbered at least two hundred thousand men in all, who are said to have spoken nineteen languages ; and Nicea, the advanced post of the kingdom won by Alp Arslan some twenty years earlier, had perhaps but a small Turkish garrison. Yet it stood siege stoutly, and for months the Normans were detained, hammering its walls, striving to cross its ditches, and to undermine its towers. The defenders were supplied with provisions by water ways still open, until the lighter galleys of the Normans were dragged overland into the lake, when the citizens surrendered to the small Greek force sent by Alexius with the allies, and on the 25th of June the disgusted Normans saw the banners of the Emperor waving on the walls. During the siege they visited the camp of Peter's slaughtered host, and the forest where, according to their ordinary tactics, the Turks had fallen on it from an ambush. In the ruined camp the white stones of the altar still remained, and the ground on the battle-field was strewn with bleaching bones of the peasant horde.

In the summer time, therefore, the march on Antioch began, and the success of this advance through Asia Minor astonished the world. Never before had such a march been attempted by the Christians, and never again did such attempt succeed. All the later expeditions perished in the mountains and deserts of this inhospitable land, and all future armies which gained the shores of Syria came by sea. The military wisdom of the Norman princes, and the cautiousness of their advance, with two strong leading divisions followed by the main body; the strictness of their discipline, and the genius of their generals, made this single attempt successful when all others failed.

The methods of Turkish warfare had already become known at Nicea, where a cavalry force was defeated before the siege began. The Turkish infantry was badly armed, and being partly composed of subject native tribes was unreliable. Their strength lay in the speed and valour of their horsemen. The Turkish cavalry rode on small horses famous for endurance.* They were lightly armed with coats of finer mail than that of the Normans, descending to the thigh, with skirts of silk falling below the knee. On the head they wore an iron hat, from which a conical white cap—the ancient

---

* See the account of the Burgundian knight Sir Bertrandon de la Brocquière (Bohn's *Early Travels in Palestine*, pp. 363–366), which, though written about 1433 A.D., probably applies to Turks of the twelfth century.

Tartar headdress traced back to the days of the Hittites—rose up to a high point.   Their long loose trousers were tucked into wide knee boots of red leather with curling toes.   Their arms were the mace with spikes and short handle, the scimitar, the round wooden target, and, above all, the bow and quiver on their backs.   Like Kurdish bows those of the Turks were made of horn.   They had thick strings of sinew pulled with the thumb, and short light arrows ; and though the aim was certain, the Turkish arrow had neither the force, nor could it cover the distance, of the grey goose shafts of the Norman long bow.   The horseman sat in a high hollowed saddle, with short stirrups, and knees bent forward giving little grip to the legs.   The Turkish lance was neither as long nor as sharp as that of the Norman ; and the horseman, high above his small steed, was easily borne down by the superior weight of the tall rider and the heavy palfrey, if he awaited the charge.   The Norman infantry, covered with mail and hidden behind the long shield, suffered but little from the arrows.   The bowmen and cross-bowmen who stood behind the front rank, as it knelt with spears firmly fixed against the ground, could pierce the Turkish armour and kill their horses before they came in range for their own arrows to take effect.   For steady troops awaiting attack, and relieved by a short charge of the knights upon the flanks, there was little to be feared.   The danger lay in pursuit ; and experience soon taught the Crusaders to avoid such wiles of the enemy.   The long two-handed swords and battle-axes, the slings and arrows, wrought havoc in the ranks of the

Moslem infantry, but their cavalry could only be defeated when surrounded.

The Turkish tactics were the same by which the Parthians had defeated Crassus. They made forced marches at the gallop, in perfect silence, and in well ordered ranks ; suddenly surprising a foe while camping, or on the march, they swept down in several separate bodies, keeping—as all experienced cavalry leaders have done—a strong reserve to cover those whose charge was not successful. A fierce gallop sometimes broke the infantry of their enemy ; but when these stood firm the horsemen showered arrows on them and wheeled in flight. If followed by the knights they fled, waiting the scattering of the too-confident pursuers, and at a given signal turned again, and shot the horses or smote down the riders. Sometimes an ambush waited in the woods or valleys, and single knights were soon surrounded and overwhelmed by numbers. This was the Turkish method of fighting, against which the strength, the patience, and the better arms of the Latins prevailed in many hard-fought battles.

The first of these battles—the only one of any importance till Antioch was reached—was nearly lost through the impatience of the Christians, but it ended in a victory which left a clear road to the very gates of Syria. Boemund, with his Normans and Italians, set out eastwards, along the Sangarius, to gain the highway of the plains of Dorylæum. Kilij Arslan awaited him upon the heights some twelve miles north-west of the city, by the stream of Sareh-Su, and the ravine near

Dogorganleh, which the chronicler calls "The Valley of Gorgons," where ancient cave tombs pierce the rocks of the Kara Su, or "black water." Here the Crusaders camped beside the marsh, and in the morning forced a passage, placing the sick and the women in the midst, with three brigades of mounted knights. Robert of Normandy charged the Turkish horse, whose arrows were falling fast and thick, with the war cry "Dieu le veut à moi Normandie!" and as usual they fled, drawing the unwary Normans from their camp. Another Turkish force, crossing the stream higher up, then fell upon the camp, slaying the women and the sick. Tancred, left alone, was saved by Boemund; but all the Christian host was in confusion, till Godfrey brought the main forces to their rescue, and in turn cut off and surrounded the Turks. It is said that in this battle they lost no less than twenty-three thousand slain, and all their baggage, the sumptuous tents of their leaders, and a great spoil. The Norman soldiers dressed themselves in silks and velvets, and only four thousand of their fighting men were lost, besides the sick and the women slain in camp. Kilij Arslan retreated south, wasting and burning the country; and the terror of the Norman fell on all, while news of disaster sped to Mosul and Baghdad.

The way now led along the "Royal Road," which first Augustus made from Syria to Nicea, as is attested by a still remaining milestone.* It led across the difficult Sultan Dagh ("the Devil's Mountain" they called

---

* See Prof. W. M. Ramsay's *The Church in the Roman Empire*, p. 32. There were two branches of the high road so named, the eastern of which the Crusaders followed.

it) which looks down on Antioch in Pisidia, and on the lake to its west. Thence by Isaura it passes to the lower lands west of Tarsus, leaving Lystra and Iconium to the east. The highway thus escapes the desert plateau of Galatia, with its treeless downs and salt lake, on the one side, and the deep valleys of the Hermus and the Lycus on the other. But the march was long and difficult, for it was now midsummer in Asia, and the defeated Turks had wasted the land. In Phrygia the army suffered from thirst, and many died of sunstroke. The falcons dropped dead from the falconer's perches, the hounds were lost, the horses fell and perished. But no enemy withstood them for three hundred miles from Dorylæum to the gates of Syria. Iconium, the capital of Kilij Arslan, they found deserted. Tarsus surrendered ; and further east at Adana, Guelph, a Burgundian freelance, had already captured the plains round the Gulf of Aiyas.

Still the advance was cautious and slow, and autumn was already well advanced before the army had entirely traversed Phrygia and Cilicia. Baldwin, the brother of Godfrey, followed with his Germans a day's march after Tancred and the Italians, and quarrels between the two nations began at Tarsus, when the inhabitants preferred surrender to the smaller vanguard of the Sicilian prince. The imperious Baldwin drove him out, and occupied the fort, which there looked down on the foaming falls of the Cydnus, and the gardens of oleander, orange, and palm, in a land rich with corn, wine, wood, and water, under the lofty snow-capped peaks of the Taurus.

Tancred marched eastward through these plains, with the blue Mediterranean on his right hand, to Adana upon the Seihûn river, where a great bridge spanned the stream under the walls. But the jealousies of Normans and Lorrainers were not appeased, and a small body of Boemund's men, following Baldwin to Tarsus, was refused an entry, and cut to pieces in the night by Turks under the walls. A massacre of the Moslem garrison in Tarsus followed, and here a fleet from Boulogne joined the army. Advancing to Adana the Lorrainers found the Italians furious at the loss of the three hundred of their comrades shut out of Tarsus ; a battle took place in which the latter were worsted, and only with great difficulty could Tancred and Baldwin make peace between their knights. From Adana another march brought Tancred to Malmistra on the Jihûn river, within four days of Antioch, north of the Gulf of Aiyas, and here first Christian ambassadors from the East met the Crusaders.

Thoros was prince of Edessa beyond the Euphrates, and his Armenian envoy Pancrates brought letters in November, asking Baldwin to occupy the town, and to defend it against the Turks of Mosul.* The possession of Edessa as a bulwark flanking the advance of Turkish forces from Mesopotamia, was highly advantageous to the prospects of the great task which the Latins had undertaken ; and leaving his army with Tancred, Baldwin set out, with only a hundred knights, to hold Edessa and to cover the flank of an advance on Syria.

---

* *Archives de l'Orient Latin*, I, p. 161 ; see Röhricht's *Regesta Regni Hierosolymitani*, No. 3.

The city, famous for its ancient Syriac university, was fortified with walls and strong square towers by Justinian. It stood west of the Scyrtus stream, having the slopes of the Tap Dagh to its west. A fortress on this side, upon a height scarped and surrounded with ditches, was dominated by two great Corinthian-capped pillars of victory. On north and east, and beyond the stream, gardens like those of Damascus belted in the city, which contained perhaps some thirty thousand souls, mainly Armenians, Jacobites, and Nestorians. The fountain of Callirrhoe fed the stream outside the water-gate, and the waters were full of sacred fish. Such was the first city ruled by any Latin prince in Asia.*

The possession of walled towns in such an age meant the submission of the open country round; and the counts of Edessa, for forty-five years, ruled a large province on the southern borders of Armenia. When Edessa fell again before the Turks the first great bulwark of the kingdom of Jerusalem was broken down. Among the towns and castles of this country were places as far east as Diarbekr, and north to Malatiya, and west to the Amanus. The whole region, stretching one hundred and fifty miles north and south, and three hundred east and west, was larger than the kingdom of Jerusalem and its great vassal provinces together. It reached from the Armenian mountains to the borders of Antioch and Aleppo, and from near the sea almost to the Tigris, Edessa being well seated in its

---

* *Procopius Buildings of Justinian*, II, 6 ; p. 58 Pal. Pil. Texts Society translation. Rey, *Colonies Franques*, p. 308.

centre. The whole was divided into many fiefs. Ain Tab, Daluk, Ravendah, Khyrros, were in the middle of the province west of the Euphrates. Bir was one of the chief places on the lower Euphrates, and Samosata in the regions beyond. The whole country was full of Syrian and Nestorian Christians, who cheerfully welcomed a ruler not fanatically subservient to the Roman Church. Four eastern bishoprics were included in Baldwin's great fief—at Edessa, Daluk, Jerablus, and Saruj. Its furthest towns were Amida (near Nisibis), Mardin, and Nisibis itself on the east near the Tigris, Malatiya, Besni, and Marash on the slopes of the Taurus to the north, Harran, and Rakkah on the Euphrates, to the south. Along the great river the knights of Lorraine held Jerablus (the site of Carchemish), Bir, Rum-Kalah, and Samosata. Among their fortresses in Syria were those which they called Turbessel (Tell Bashar), Tulupe (Daluk), and Ravandal (Ravandah); and at Bar Sauma on the Euphrates the Syrian Jacobite patriarch of Antioch was recognised as head of that Church. The brother of the future King of Jerusalem thus reaped the first harvest, in the first region reached after Asia Minor had been crossed; and his power seems never to have been questioned by the Greeks. But it was also the hardest conquest to maintain, and first to fall again under the Moslem rule.

Meanwhile the Christian forces advanced, and, crossing the Syrian gates, descended from the Amanus east of Antioch, and Tancred seized Alexandretta, the port which overlooks the dreary marshes of the Gulf of Ayas,

from which the Amanus rises sheer near the shore
where Issus marks the site of that renowned contest
which won all Syria for Alexander the Great. Crossing
the Iron Bridge he seized on Harenc (now Harim), an
important castle between Antioch and Aleppo, and
Robert of Flanders occupied Artesia, near the famous
church of Simon Stylites. By these various movements
Antioch was surrounded, cut off from the sea on the
west, and from the Turks of Mosul and Aleppo on the
east ; and the main body, headed by Robert of Normandy, advanced across the mountains and sat down
before the capital of Syria.

The fame of these successes spread far to the east
and south. Two policies became possible for the
princes, and remained possible while the Latins were in
Syria ; for although to the priest, the pilgrim, and the
pious Latin there seemed to be no policy needful, but
only valorous combat against every Saracen, it is clear
that from the first the leaders were statesmen as well as
generals, and owed their success to the prudence and
soldierly skill which guided the religious enthusiasm of
their army. There was the policy of aiding some of the
Turkish Emirs against the others, and so dividing their
enemies ; and the policy of alliance with Egypt against
the Turks as a whole. The Vizir of Egypt, Melek el
Afdal, tempted the leaders with offers despatched as
soon as they had entered Syria. His envoys brought a
friendly message* to the princes, advising them to join
with Egypt in fighting the Turks ; but this alliance with

* *Archives*, I, p. 162 ; *Regesta*, No. 4.

a Moslem power, then striving to occupy Jerusalem, their ultimate objective, they refused. Meanwhile Alexius, hearing of the embassy, sent in the January of 1098 to Egypt, hoping to interfere with any such plans.* On the other hand the princes wrote to Damascus asking Dokak, its governor, to remain neutral† ; and in February, Yaghi Siân, the Turkish Governor of Antioch, sent a letter to Kerboga, the Seljuk prince of Mosul, asking for help, and Kerboga in turn wrote to the Sultan Borkiaruk, son of Melek Shah, and to the Khalif of Bàghdad, the head of Islam in Asia, sending arms taken from certain stragglers of the Christian army, and boasting how easily their forces might be overcome.‡

Antioch, the famous trading city, founded by the heirs of Alexander as the capital of the Seleucid kingdom of Syria ; where first the Christians were so called ; where Chrysostom had preached later to eager congregations ; where the Romans, and the Herodians before them, had raised temples and streets of pillars, baths, and hippodromes ; where hermits had lived and died in the caves of its mountain ; where the pagan temple women had swum in the baths, and wandered in the groves of Daphne ; where Justinian had built mighty ramparts, a church of the Virgin, another of St. Michael, and hospitals for the sick ; where a great cathedral of Peter and Paul stood in the midst, and the traders of Amalfi had already a quarter of their own—a city of many memories, rich with the commerce of Baghdad

---

* *Archives*, I, p. 174 ; *Regesta*, No. 8.
† *Archives*, I, p. 171 ; *Regesta*, No. 5.
‡ *Archives*, I, pp. 167, 172 ; *Regesta*, Nos. 6, 7.

and Mosul, had now for fourteen years been subject to the Turks.

The walls of Justinian, enclosing a rude oblong south of the River Orontes, rose to the spurs of Mount Silpius, and surrounded the town and its suburbs of gardens— four mamelons in the plain, and a citadel perched on the heights. A stream ran through the gardens to join the river, and channels from the hills brought water to the houses. The circuit of the walls was over five miles in length, and on the north a single bridge spanned the Orontes at the gate of the bridge. On the east was the gate of St. Paul; on the west that of Saint George; on the south the Iron Gate and several posterns leading to the mountain. The city first became visible at some two miles distance on the east, after the Christians crossed the river, and left behind them the lake, famous in later times for its eels. Three hundred and sixty Byzantine towers and turrets are said to have strengthened the walls. Gardens of figs and mulberries, jujubes and nuts, lay within them, and the oleander groves of Daphne were near the city on the west.

The Christian army invested the town on all sides but the south, where barren crags rose up above the citadel. On the east Boemund and Tancred lay before the gate of St. Paul. Robert of Flanders and Robert of Normandy pitched between the river and the Dog Gate on the north-east, with Stephen of Blois and Hugh of Vermandois—Normans and Flemings, Bretons, and Frenchmen, were with them. Raymond of Toulouse, with the

men of Languedoc and Provence, was further west at
the Duke's Gate; and, in the centre of the northern wall,
Godfrey and the men of Lorraine besieged the bridge,
and extended to the west. But near the mountain on
the west were the Towers of the Sisters, and here,
through the gate of St. George, the Syrian and Armenian subjects of the Turks brought in provisions.

The Latins arrived late in the autumn, while the
grapes were still plentiful in the vineyards; and for a
time the great host found provision in the valley, or
obtained it from the neighbouring lands which they
harried. They discovered pits of corn—the native
metamîr—to feed both man and horse, and drove in
Turkish cattle from the pastures. But the winter was
upon them; the Genoese fleet could not approach the
open bay of Seleucia during the storms of January and
February; and the terrible necessity of wintering in the
open, before a city, strong and well supplied with food,
lay before the princes. It soon became impossible to
feed so large an army, and many deserted or were
drawn off by their leaders to other towns. An idle
army, including such rude elements, soon threatened to
fall to pieces, through want of discipline, and through
licence. Even the legate—Adhemar, bishop of Puy—
could not enforce morality upon the churchmen or the
soldiers. The Archdeacon of Metz is said to have been
caught by the Turks playing dice with a Syrian lady in
the gardens; and his head was shot into the camp from
a catapult. A monk was publicly scourged for sinning
with a nun; and when such scandals arose among

clerics the wild soldiers could not have been much better examples of the conduct fit for pilgrims of the Cross. The lands were ploughed and sown by the besiegers, but many months must pass before the crop was ripe, and meantime famine stared the Latins in the face. The winter rains swelled the Orontes, and flooded the willow marshes north-east of the walls. A Danish reinforcement of fifteen hundred men, led by a prince, accompanied by his bride, was cut to pieces at Philomelium. Flemish pirates came down upon the Syrian coast; and the Greeks, ever anxious to assert their claim to Syria, seized on Latakia, south of Antioch, to which city Robert of Normandy was sent with his division.

Meanwhile the camp-fever and scurvy ravaged the host, and Godfrey lay sick of a wound. Vice, drink, and blasphemy, became rampant; and men ate roots, and dead dogs, and horses. Out of all the eighty thousand steeds which are said to have reached Syria, only two thousand were left. It is even said by a Chronicler (William of Tyre) that the soldiers roasted the flesh of the Turks they slew. Peter the Hermit fled, and was by force brought back. Stephen of Blois deserted, as did the general of the Greek detachment, and sailing for Tarsus he found the Emperor Alexius coming with an army, to claim Antioch when the Latins should have taken it, and gave so little hope of their success that the Greek army turned again, and marched back to Byzantium. The foraging parties brought in little, and were driven back by the Turks, who also held the shores near

Seleucia. Thus by the end of the winter, though the invaders still held on, their chances of success seemed desperate enough.

But the early spring brought with it a renewed hope and also new cause for exertion when the rumours spread that Kerboga and the Turks of Mesopotamia were marching to the west. Godfrey recovered, and supplies came in from Baldwin in Edessa, from the Armenian monasteries, and by the Genoese fleet from Chios Rhodes and Cyprus. The spring, however, saw the Turks also in motion, and Kerboga menaced Edessa, while the various Emirs of Aleppo, Damascus, Sheizur and Membej gathered twenty thousand men, and fell upon the Christians, aided by a sortie of the garrison from Antioch. Arming themselves it is said by opening the graves of Turkish warriors, the Latins gathered and repulsed these two attacks ; and Yaghi Siân, anxious to gain time, proposed a truce with the besiegers, during which the Christians were free to enter the city, and the Turks to visit the camps.

This truce, however, led to unexpected results. There was little time to be lost, for it was now already late in May, and Kerboga with an army equal at least to that of the Latins was only seven days distant from the town. In such straits an offer made to Boemund by an Armenian renegade, son of an armourer in Antioch, was most unwillingly accepted by the Princes, who had hoped by force of arms to take the city. Firuz, the renegade, had charge of three towers in the strong south-west corner of the wall, high on the hill. During the truce he offered to admit the Christians to the city by night, and though the plot was suspected, and Firuz brought before the Governor, his coolness turned suspicion upon others.

On the night of the 2nd of June, 1098, the party headed by Boemund, Prince of Tarento, crept silently up to the towers, and sixty men climbed after their leader, up a rope ladder on to the wall. The ladder broke with the weight of the armed men, but another was lowered, and soon the towers were seized, the guards slain, and a postern, opened by this forlorn hope, let in the rest of the force. The flag of Boemund, the Norman who first set foot on the ramparts, waved on the walls of Antioch a few days only before the Turkish army came in sight.

A terrible massacre followed, for the city had not surrendered and the citadel still held out. Ten thousand Moslems are said to have perished, and Yaghi Siân flying to the mountain was murdered by the wood-cutters, and his head brought in to the city. The conquerors and the Christian population celebrated the capture with festivals and Eastern dances, perhaps the first witnessed by the Latins ; but the garrison of the citadel still resisted, and a huge Moslem army in turn besieged the victors, a gathering of twenty-eight Emirs, under Kerboga, with all the forces of the Turks from Mesopotamia, and levies from Damascus and Jerusalem.* It was during this concentration of the Turkish forces in the north that Melek el Afdal, the Vizir of Egypt, seized the Holy City, though Arab chronicles place the capture two years

* Albert of Aix (iv, 10) says they numbered 200,000 men.

earlier.* When Tutush was slain by Borkiaruk, the sons of Ortok in Jerusalem refused to acknowledge his sons, who were disputing the Syrian heritage ; and Rudhwân, one of these, besieged the city in 1096. Melek el Afdal sent an army from Egypt, which took possession of Tyre, and, after forty days' siege, Jerusalem passed into the hands of the Egyptian Khalifs, surrendering immediately after the great battle of Antioch in July, 1098 A.D. The troops that came against Antioch from Jerusalem were thus apparently those of Ortok's sons, El Ghâzi and Sukmân ; and when the alliance of Egypt was rejected by the Latins, Melek el Afdal took an opportunity to occupy Palestine, while the Turks were distracted by the northern war. The two branches of the family of Ortok, established on the borders of Armenia and Assyria, after the defeat of Kerboga, played their part a few years later in the history of Syria ; but the Moslems, who awaited the Latins in the south, were now for the most part Egyptian Arabs and not Turks at all.

The army of Kerboga appeared only three days too late : for three weeks they invested the city, and during that time occurred an event attested by Raymond D'Agiles, who was an eye-witness of the curious incident of which he has left an account. Peter Bartholomew, a monk, claimed that St. Andrew revealed to him in a vision where, under the altar of St. Peter's Church, lay the head of the lance which wounded Christ at the

---

* Abu el Feda and Kemal ed Din. *William of Tyre*, VII, 69, IX, 10, see Robinson, *Bib. Res.*, I. p. 404

Crucifixion. The lance head was accordingly found, as Godfrey's cousin Baldwin du Bourg also testified by letter ;* and the enthusiasm thereby roused among the war-worn soldiers secured the victory against the supreme effort of the Turkish Sultan. But the evidence can hardly have been thought conclusive, even by the Crusaders, since disputes arose soon after, only satisfied by the ordeal of fire, through which the monk passed, hardly scathed, at Arca, though not long after he died. For the moment the relic borne by Raymond d'Agiles served as the banner of the Christians, and after a battle lasting all the day on the 28th June the Turks were defeated, though attacking from both sides the Christian army sallying from the northern bridge. Fifteen thousand camels and many horses were taken, and a mighty spoil, among which appear to have been copies of the Koran in Arabic. Not long after this defeat the garrison of Antioch also fell before the assault of Raymond of Toulouse, and thus by two sieges and two pitched battles in the open, the Latins, in the course of little more than a year, became the masters of Edessa and of Antioch. The victory was announced by Tancred in a letter dated the 29th of June, and in July the princes wrote to Alexius, demanding his fulfilment of the treaty which bound him to assist their cause.†

The Latins remained four months in Antioch, organising their new possessions with the rapidity that characterised the Norman genius in this age of sudden

* _Archives de l'Orient Latin_, I, p. 177 ; Röhricht, _Regesta_, No. 4.
† _Archives_, I, pp. 175 and 177 ; _Regesta_. Nos. 9 and 13.

conquest. During this time they sent to Urban II to announce their victory, together with the death of Adhemar the legate, beseeching the Holy Father to come himself to Syria* ; but in his stead he sent at the close of the year another legate Daimbert, Archbishop of Pisa.

Alexius heard with astonishment the final success which he had so little expected, and claimed at once as his own both Antioch and Latakia. The letters only arrived after the Crusaders had started for the south. The answer sent from further south, broke off for ever the Latin and Greek alliance. Those who had failed to help in time of need could not expect to reap the fruits of victory, and so the princes refused to surrender their conquests, pleading that the Emperor had failed to carry out the treaty.†

The enmity between Franks and Greeks continued in future to be a cause of weakness to Christendom, and led to Greek alliances with the Turks, in the times of Zanghi and of Saladin. Yet Alexius profited by the Latin conquests, and drove the Turks, from Rhodes and Chios. He restored to Byzantium the cities of Ephesus, Smyrna, and Sardis ; and even for a time occupied Latakia, as well as Tarsus and Malmistra. The Sultans of Iconium were thus cut off from the Mediterranean, and the coasts between Constantinople and Antioch remained in the hands of Christians for more than a century.

---

* *Archives,* I, p. 181 ; *Regesta,* No. 14.
† *Archives,* I, pp. 189, 192 ; *Regesta,* Nos. 18 and 20.

On the Emirs of neighbouring towns the impression made by success was not less important, and served yet more to weaken the cause of Islam. Omar of Ezzaz, in the new county of Edessa, wrote in September to Godfrey, asking his aid against Rudhwan the son of Tutush ruling in Aleppo, and received a favourable reply.* This Omar had already married a Christian lady, widow of a certain Fulk. Offers of alliance came later even from Aleppo.†

Among the first to profit were the Genoese to whom, immediately after the victory, Boemund, now Prince of Antioch by right of first entry, promised the Church of St. John, a town hall or *funduk*, and thirty houses ; and two months later the Genoese nobles swore to acknowledge no other ruler in the city.‡

The new Norman province, which soon included the city of Latakia on the seashore north of Tripoli, extended over the northern Lebanon, bounded by the county of Edessa on the north-east, and by the stream near the castle of Margat on the south. Tortosa belonged to the County of Tripoli. The eastern limit was the river Orontes, dividing the Christians from the Sultan of Aleppo ; but at times they held places further east, and the castle of Harenc was the frontier fortress on the north-east, taken and retaken by Christians and

---

* In 1115, Roger of Antioch was allied to El Ghâzi, son of Ortok, and in 1116 and 1119 the citizens of Aleppo asked his help against Moslem pretenders (Rey, *Colonies Franques*, p. iv, note). Floria's offer to surrender this city to Godfrey was made in July, 1099 (*Archives*, I, p. 197 ; *Regesta*, No. 24).

† *Archives*, I, p. 183 ; *Regesta*, No. 15.

‡ Authorities quoted in *Regesta*, Nos. 12, 16.

Moslems in turn. The region extended one hundred miles north and south, by about fifty east and west, and was thus much smaller than the great county of Edessa ; but the ridge of Lebanon was cool, well watered, healthy, and fertile in parts ; and two good sea-ports, at Seleucia and Latakia, gave easy access to Rhodes and Cyprus, and to the Italian homes of Boemund's followers. The first prize had fallen to a Prince of Lorraine, the second—equally by right of first footing in the capital—fell to the Prince of Tarento.* Peaceful relations were soon established with the Moslems on the East, and in 1117, Roger, Governor of Antioch, concluded a treaty with Yaruktash, who had rebelled against Rudhwan in Aleppo, which granted to the Christian the right to protect the yearly pilgrimage to Mecca through his principality unmolested, levying a tax on the Moslem pilgrims.

There were many ancient Christian towns on the Orontes in this region, such as Apamea and El Bârah ; and the famous monastery of Simon Stylites, east of Antioch. Byzantine ruins of churches and houses, over whose doorways verses from the Psalms are carved in

---

* Boemund was afterwards captive in Cappadocia from 1101 to 1103; he left Antioch in 1104 and died in Italy in 1111. His second son, by Constance, daughter of Philip I, became Prince of Antioch in 1126 as Boemund II. Tancred, who ruled Antioch from 1101, allied himself with Rudhwan of Aleppo, defeated Javaly Secavah—an officer of the Sultan Muhammad and El Ghâzi of Mardin, at Tell Bashar, in 1107, and advanced to Edessa, where, aided by King Baldwin, he repulsed in 1110 Maudud, the Sultan's brother. Tancred died near Aleppo on 12th December, 1112, and Boemund II being then only a child, Antioch was ruled by Roger FitzRichard, son of Tancred's sister. Iorsak, of Hamadan, attacked him by the Sultan's orders, in May, 1115, unsuccessfully, but in 1119 El Ghâzi defeated and killed him on the 27th June. King Baldwin I defeated El Ghâzi on 14th August of the same year.

Greek letters, still survive to our own times. On the north-west Tancred's conquests round Malmistra were included. Ezzâz appears to have been the border on the side of Baldwin's county of Edessa. Eleven castles fortified the frontiers, of which Saone, south-east of Latakia, was one of the strongest. El Bârah, on the right bank of the Orontes, was taken by Raymond of St. Gilles on the 28th of November, 1098. Its castle still remains in ruins, and round it the sugar cane was cultivated by the Norman vassals. Apamea with its fishing lake, made by a dam on the Orontes, was also beyond the boundary river, and was the see of an archbishop of the Latin rite: at El Bârah, Artesia, Latakia, Gabala and Valenia his suffragan bishops were established. The sea ports of the Gulf of Ayas included Alexandretta (called Port Bonnel) on the south, and Ayas itself (now Baya) on the north. The port of Antioch was Seleucia, then called Port St. Simeon, or Soudin. Latakia, or La Liche, as the Crusaders called it, was one of the most important and most picturesque of all the Syrian seaside cities. It was built, like many of the old Phœnician harbours, on a promontory under the Lebanon, and was defended by two castles on a hill above the gardens. Its vineyards were famous, and its port among the safest on the coast. It was not, however, till 1109 A.D. that Tancred drove the Greeks out of the town. It is one of the very few places in Syria where a triumphal arch of Roman times is still to be seen, and a long Greek inscription of the year 214 A.D., now destroyed, described the public games.

The population of this region seems to have been mainly Christian when the Normans arrived, but the Syrians had little liking for the orthodox Greek Church, and cheerfully accepted their new Latin masters able to defend them from the savage Turk.   In the organisation of this province, and the reduction of the frontier towns on the east, the latter half of the year 1098 was employed by the Latins, who set out in autumn from Antioch, but did not actually begin the march to Palestine itself until the January of the year which followed.

CHAPTER III.

The Founding of the Kingdom.

In November, 1098, Raymond of St. Gilles appeared before Maárrah—a town on the Orontes between Aleppo and Hamath, and on the 21st of December it fell after terrible privations had been endured within its walls. But the further advance of the army was impossible in winter, when the plains were boggy, the rivers swollen, and the mountains white with snow. Not until early spring did the main forces march from Antioch, and then by two routes, along the Orontes on the east, and by the sea coast west of Lebanon. It was already April when they met at Arca, a day's march north of Tripoli, Raymond leading the van past Hamath with its giant water wheels, and Emesa with black basalt walls amid green gardens of poplar, and down the broad Eleutherus valley where the plains are dotted with oak trees between the rocky ridges, west of the long grey lake of Kades. The ground was gay with flowers springing from the basalt, with phloxes and pheasant's eyes, white narcissus and violet anemone, pink cyclamen and yellow marigold ; and the long cloud wreaths lifted only to show the snow, which loaded the branches of the cedar forests.

From Latakia along the shores the stony road led
south by Gabala and Marakia, Valenia and Tortosa,
to where the plain widens with yellow sand-dunes,
and the Eleutherus issues from its cane brake north
of Arca.

New forces from the north, among whom the Saxons
under Edgar the Atheling are mentioned, swelled the
ranks ; and, joining Raymond at Arca, Godfrey and
Tancred, Robert of Normandy and Robert of Flanders
gathered some fifty thousand fighting men. Abu Salim,
the governor of Sheizur on Orontes, had ordered the
Moslems to burn and devastate the routes by which
the Latins marched.* But such destruction was only
possible in summer time.

On the 15th of March, Raymond was already at Arca,
and on the tenth of April the Christians still besieged
its castle†, while Godfrey was encamped at Gabala to
the north. Easter passed by before the march was once
more ordered on the 13th of May, and meanwhile further
embassies were sent from Egypt by Melek el Afdal‡,
proposing terms on which the Latins might be peacefully admitted into the Holy City·; but these once more
they refused.

Although the cities on the shore were walled and
garrisoned, it is remarkable that none of them attempted
to bar the way of the Latins. The bold strategy of
marching as a flying column, flanked perhaps by the
Genoese fleet, and never again delaying to besiege even

* *Archives*, I, p. 191 ; *Regesta*, No. 17.
† *Archives*, I, p. 191 ; *Regesta*, No. 19.
‡ *Archives*, I, p. 193 ; *Regesta*, No. 21.

the larger ports, was finally successful, because the
capital was actually taken, and because the Turks would,
as the Latins knew, never join hands with the Egyptian
forces.   The risks incurred are clear ; for though the
Christian army was far too strong for any single garrison, yet if defeat had overtaken it in the far south,
after a march of five hundred miles from Antioch,
retreat past such a line of fortresses would have been
quite impossible.   It was perhaps on such final defeat
that the Egyptians, not yet ready, counted, when they
refused to meet the Latins in the open.

The route led still along the coast, under the steep
rough spurs of Lebanon, over the slippery pass of
Shakkah, where the gorge was not as yet, perhaps, closed
by the robber tower of later times : by Gebal, with its
beds of papyrus ; by the bright palm gardens of Sidon,
the sandy bay of Tyre, the white cliff at whose feet the
blue Mediterranean laps in the grottoes, and so to the
wide plain of Acre and over Belus and Kishon, to the
purple ridge of Carmel.   In May they entered Sharon,
crossing the Crocodile river, and traversing the open oak
dotted lowlands near Cæsarea ; and so passed south
to plains where, in the hot haze of the east winds, the
sand dunes flickered in the mirage, presenting ghostly
lakes and palm groves, which when reached were but
low bushes in a waterless desert.   The line of march was
pointed out by friendly Maronites, coming down from
their mountain villages to meet the princes.   It was
the safest and the quickest that they could have chosen ;
but now, as they turned inland at Lydda and Ramleh,

the stony mountains of Judæa rose two thousand feet above them.

In the plains of Lydda it would seem that three divisions were formed, advancing from north and south and west to hem in the Egyptians : for, if we may believe a later writer,* Raymond of St. Gilles marched up into the mountains not far south of Shechem, and camped at the small village which still preserves his name at Sinjil. It is at least certain that while Godfrey came up to the city by the road from Jaffa, by which most travellers now approach it, Tancred with his hundred knights moved further south, to occupy Bethlehem by the request of its Christian inhabitants. So doing Tancred was the first to set eyes upon the goal of all their hopes —the Holy City which they had marched two thousand miles to win.

It was already June when twenty thousand Latins approached Jerusalem, and when Tancred gazed upon it from the Mount of Olives. Climbing the chalky hill terraced with olives, to where the ruins of the earliest of Christian chapels enshrined the foot-print of Christ, in the rock on the summit, he saw below him on the east the shining lake of Sodom beyond the endless marl peaks flickering in the noonday haze, and the long blue ridge of Moab beyond the snaky Jordan ; and, on the west beneath him, Jerusalem lay on the slopes beyond the Kidron ravine—a grey town smaller than Antioch, without gardens, without a stream, with strong high

---

* Fetellus. (See *Memoirs of Survey of Western Palestine*, Vol. II, p. 292.)

walls and houses capped with shapeless white-washed
domes. The broad enclosure of the Templum Domini
rose close to the ravine, with Arab ramparts standing on
giant masonry of Herod's fane. The great dome of
the chapel, built by Abd el Melek from the spoils of
Christian churches, dominated the city and hid the
Sacred Rock. Its outer walls were rich with glass
mosaics, and long Arab texts proclaimed the words
of the Prophet and the pious deeds of the Khalifs.
The green bronze gates, perchance, were open, showing
the dark recesses glowing with colour. The pigeons
clustered on the dome ; the crier called to prayer from
the minaret : the Moslems gathered round the preacher
who encouraged men to die in war against the "People
of the Book," painting the joys of Paradise, the houris
stretching forth their jewelled arms, with dark eyes
smiling on the martyrs of Islam. On the south side,
between the cypresses, the women drew water from
the fountain and the hidden caverns. The Church of
Mary, built by Justinian against the southern wall, was
also now a mosque marking the Templum Salomonis.
Wild cries of *Allah-hu-akbar!* rose from the mail-
clad guards upon the ramparts, when first the glint
of Norman spears was seen on Olivet. No stately
churches rose as yet to overtop the mosque ; the Palace
of the Knights of St. John was still unbuilt ; no bells
might sound from steeples ; no Nazarene might ride in
sight of Moslem masters. A terror stricken Christian
population trembled in fear of coming massacre. Far
on the west the great square Tower of David guarded

the citadel, and further north the tower, named in after
days from Tancred himself, marked the north-west
corner of the town.   The walls were such as still enclose
the city, extending rather farther to the north, and not
as far to the west as now.   Upon the south they crossed
the higher part of Sion, excluding the Church of the
Apostles.   Deep valleys girt the city on the south and east,
burrowed with ancient caves and rock-cut monuments
of Herod's time, and of the later Christian princes of
Byzantium.   The crosses of the pilgrims were already
cut upon the rocks of Hinnom, and their bones lay
mouldering in the vault of the Potter's Field.   Upon the
north a deep wide fosse was cut outside the walls, and
only on the west, where David's Gate led to the citadel,
could the assailants reach the ramparts from the open
plateau.

Meanwhile, from Lydda, Godfrey with the army
climbed the mountains and crossed the Valley of the
Terebinth, where men believed that David fought
the giant ; and so at length, but half a mile away,
the Latins saw the goal of all their hopes—a long
grey wall, a mighty tower, a few dark cypress
trees above the rampart ; and all around grey stones,
brown rocks, a dusty soil, thistles and thorns, a strag-
gling olive grove to north, and terraces of figs
upon the south—a barren land of naked rocks, waterless and glaring under a cloudless sky.   Such the
Sacred City when they first set eyes upon it from
the west.

Bending their foreheads in the sacred dust, the kneeling

host lifted up its voice and wept. This, then, was in very deed the city of their dreams, the reality so little like that which they had fancied at home. The funnel-like cupola of the small church within the town, built over the Holy Tomb, was hidden by the towers: only the fortress wall was seen. Was this Jerusalem, the Holy City of Melchisadek and Jacob, the royal capital of David and Solomon, the place where Christ had suffered and died and risen again, the home of Saints and Martyrs, the earthly symbol of Jerusalem on high? The memory of many woes endured, of many perils past, came back into their hearts. Memories of the grim solitude of Dorylæum, strewn with bones: of the dark days of famine before Antioch: of cruel Turkish bows and yet more cruel deserts: of wives and children dropping by the way; and sons and fathers laid in roadside graves: of three years that had passed since last they saw the vineyards and the woods of Burgundy, the peaceful fields of some Italian home. All this they had endured, and had survived to reach their goal: yet still a mighty struggle lay before them ere the Sepulchre could be freed. Bishop and monk, prince and peasant, knelt together in the dust, and wept to see the long-desired city.

And yet, perchance, as many of us now think, the material object of their faith and effort was a delusion : and the site of Calvary and the Tomb of Christ both unknown. The church of Constantine was perhaps reared, not on the Golgotha where Jesus suffered: the narrow rock-cut grave, within the chapel of the Resurrection, was not a sepulchre "nigh unto the city." For eight long centuries all the Christian world had then accepted a site fixed by emperor and patriarch for reasons which no early writer has recorded. Reading the letters of Constantine, and history of Eusebius, we now perceive that in Helena's days all memory of the true sites had confessedly long been lost. Sad as it seems that so much faith and love should be lavished on an error, it is not less true that Godfrey, marshalling his host against the northern wall, may often have pressed with his mailed feet the Rock of Calvary, yet never knew the spot on which he stood. The Sepulchre was "nigh unto the city," not in its midst. The hill of crucifixion was "without the gate." Even pilgrims of the age of Godfrey found it difficult to understand how ancient Jerusalem—a city large and populous—could have been built so as to leave the sacred sites beyond its circuit ; and they gave explanations to the devout hard to reconcile with what we now know of the Herodian walls. It may be therefore that while men were striving blindly, though faithfully, for a great idea, the rock of Golgotha stood as of old, unknown like the new tomb of Joseph in the garden ; not desecrated by scenes of human hatred and wrath; and still even now, so long after Godfrey's age, only "a green hill far away beside a city wall."

The siege of Jerusalem lasted for forty days. The city was the first taken by force from Islam : for Nicea surrendered, and Antioch fell by treachery. The Egyptian garrison had not the same fierce obstinacy of resistance in its heart which made the Turk, from the first days of history, master of Syria ; but the inhospitable mountains of Judæa opposed to the Franks difficulties unknown in the well-watered and well-wooded regions of the North. Hunger and thirst, and want of wood to build siege towers, were more formidable to the army than any Egyptian enemy. Jerusalem was always hard to reach, because from of old the mountains stood round a natural citadel. Neither as a trading city, nor as a stronghold, was its possession profitable. Only as a centre of the faith was it dear to Christians, to Jews, and to Moslems alike. A century later, when faith decayed, men still fought hard for trading cities and fertile seaside plains in Palestine ; but Jerusalem no longer was desired, save by ruined clerics, and by pious pilgrims.

The first mad effort of Tancred, to win the city with a single ladder, failed ; and by the middle of June a regular siege was begun. The camp of Godfrey was on the north-east, above the valley of Kidron ; and next to the Lorrainers came the men of Flanders further west, and the men of Normandy, camping against the Gate of Damascus—or of St. Stephen as it then was called. A fosse protected the northern wall on this side, and the rampart stood on a scarp, which was highest east of the gate. Tancred with the Italians lay before the northwest tower, and Raymond of Toulouse, with the men of southern France, was on the west, over against the Tower of David ; while, later on, a portion of his force was camped on Sion, against the southern wall. By

this arrangement the Lorrainers were divided from the
Italians, whom they had fought at Tarsus, by the two
camps of Flemings and of Normans.

Within the city there was water, stored in tanks and
rocky caverns. Outside, the wells were blocked, and
some declared them poisoned. The little cave of Gihon,
in the Kidron ravine, gave only a small supply, which
flowed at times through the hill tunnel to Siloam. It
was difficult of access, and quite unfit to supply a force
of twenty thousand men. The sufferings of the army
from thirst were terrible. On the south the nearest
springs were near Bittir, three miles away; and foraging
parties, sent as far as Bethlehem and Solomon's pools,
were at times cut off by the enemy: so that water was
sold at ruinous prices; and food was also scarce for such
an army. On the north no water could be found nearer
than Bireh and Gibeon, six miles off; and here also, in
the summer, the springs and wells were soon exhausted.
Moreover, there was no wood around the city to build
the rolling towers needful for the assault. It was
fetched from the copses of Mount Joie and Gibeon; but
the trees were small, and beams from ruins, and timbers
found in a cave, with perhaps olive and fig trees from
orchards, were the best materials that the Franks could
get. The cattle died in numbers, from hunger and
thirst; and the stench of putrid corpses hung over the
Christian camps, where fever and scurvy, hunger and
thirst, wrought havoc for a month. Meanwhile, however,
the Genoese fleet, sailing from the north, reached Jaffa,
and brought skilled workmen to construct the towers.

The dead oxen were flayed, and their hides covered the timber. Three tall towers on rollers, with upper storeys for the bowmen, and drawbridges to lower on the ramparts, were slowly built; and by the middle of July all was ready for the final effort.

The Festival of the Visitation (the 12th of July) was celebrated during this time; and the army marched in long procession, headed by priests and banners, to the chapel on Olivet, where Peter the Hermit, and Arnold, the ambitious chaplain of Robert of Normandy, preached to the pilgrims. Below them, in the Temple courts, the Moslems, too, were praying in the mosques; and few were the Nazarenes then remaining in the city, for the patriarch had fled to Cyprus, and the Christians had been driven out before the siege closed in.

On Thursday, the 14th of July, 1099, the towers were rolled against the wall, the fosse was filled with stones and timbers and earth, the grey goose shafts flew from the upper platforms, the mangonels showered stones, and the rams beat against the ramparts. But the defence was stout. The desperate Egyptians, whose messengers speeding to Egypt to summon help had fallen into the hands of the Latins, fought for their lives, throwing the dreadful petroleum flames of the Greek fire upon the wooden castles, pouring hot oil and boiling water on the men-at-arms who worked the rams and mangonels, answering arrow for arrow and slingstone for slingstone. The clumsy towers rocked and creaked, dragged on by men and beasts: the wheels and rollers

broke with the strain, under the heavy weight of the
mailed knights, who held the chains of the bridges
ready to lower.   The tower of Godfrey on the east,
and that of Tancred on the west, stuck fast: the third
was burned or broken down, and night came on leaving
the city still untaken.

During this night, while (as the chronicler reports)
witches were seen weaving spells upon the ramparts,
and while the men about to die were confessing their
sins, and early at dawn receiving the sacrament of the
altar from their priests, Godfrey was hard at work
retrieving the failure.   His tower was taken down, and
moved to where, further west, near the postern called
afterwards " Herod's Gate," the ditch was shallow, and
a storming party might hope to open a gate on gaining
the wall.   Here the tower was again erected, and on
Friday, the 15th—the Moslem day of rest—the battle
raged once more: the walls tottered under the blows of
the ram: and the hides protected the tower, so that the
Greek fire failed to burn it.   At three in the afternoon
—the hour, as men remembered on which the Saviour
died—the heavy drawbridge fell at length upon the
battlement, and Godfrey, first of all the Latins, stood
fighting on the wall, and won for Germany the crowning
victory of Christendom.

The end came swiftly.   The gate was opened, the
breach was scaled, and the fierce Latins swarmed along
the narrow streets.   The Moslems fled to the mosque,
where Tancred vainly promised them their lives.   The
princes could no longer hold their savage followers back.

Without respect for age or sex, they slew and spared not.
Their arrows pierced the miserable women crowded on
the roofs, and many flying to the caverns perished in the
water. The feet of the palfreys trod deep in blood, as
the knights rode in upon the pavement of the Temple.
For seven days riot and carnage continued, and only
those who fled to David's Tower were saved by Raymond,
and sent with wives and children and baggage to seek
a refuge in Ascalon. Men forgot their vows, forgot
the Sepulchre and Calvary, hastening to gather spoil,
revelling and exulting, and claiming for their own the
empty houses which they seized. Even priests were not
slow to ask their share. Arnold, as Latin Patriarch,
claimed the treasures of the Mosque, which Tancred
and Godfrey had shared between them. Daimbert, the
Legate, declared the ruler of Jerusalem to be the vassal
of the Pope.

But meanwhile Godfrey, the hero of that day, with
only three attendants, knelt before the Holy Tomb, in
that same chapel where Peter the Hermit had prayed,
and thither he called the men of Lorraine to fulfil their
vows. Who so great among them all as Godfrey—the
blameless knight, the humble Christian, who refused to
wear a crown in the city where his Master suffered for
the sins of all? Tall, strong, red bearded and comely,
in the pride of his manhood—a hero who had fought a
savage bear in Phrygia, and had cleft a Turk in twain at
Antioch, and who first had sprung upon the wall a day
before. Yet humble, and courteous to the meanest, pure
of life, and selfless as he was strong. To all alike, during

that long and trying war, he had been the wise coun-
sellor, the true friend, the loyal comrade.   No ugly tales
of secret orgies, of sin, or licence, were recorded against
the perfect knight, the true soldier of the Cross, the
wisest of the princes.   His servants only could relate
that sometimes, lingering in the churches, he would
forget the time for food.   No province yet had come
to him, although his younger brother ruled in Edessa,
and Boemund in Antioch.   No politic scheming for
self advancement, no treachery to any comrade, no
cruelty to any foe, had stained his name.   On whom
if not on Godfrey could the choice now fall?
Who else could hold so safely the kingdom won?
Who had as sure a right as he who first entered the
city?   On whom could priest or bishop look with
greater favour, and in whom could subjects better trust?
Robert of Normandy some men said; but Robert, the
man who fought and nearly slew his own father in
rebellion, was looking to the crown of England—his by
right as eldest born.   Tancred others said; but Tancred
had failed where Godfrey had succeeded, and such a
choice was clearly unjust.   Raymond of Toulouse was
old and selfish, and men hated him and desired a leader
in the flower of his age.   He was, moreover, well contented with the fairer County of Tripoli—the cool range
of Lebanon, its rich red valleys, and the port where men
already gathered wealth.   The ruling of more barren
lands in the Judean mountains, with strong Egyptian
foes upon the south, and Turkish enemies in Damascus,
and wild Arabs over Jordan, was no such enviable task

for any man. Robert of Flanders spoke as a true knight before the Council, asking his peers to lay aside ambition and envy, and to choose from among themselves the best and strongest, the wisest and most just. His loyal words pointed to Godfrey only, and all men rejoiced when the choice was made, and the honour fell to him whose due it was. They led him in solemn procession to the Sepulchre, with psalms and hymns; but here he put away the crown, because a crown of thorns alone had pressed the brows of Christ ; and known henceforth only as duke and vassal of the Church, he took upon his shoulders the weight of anxious rule.

The vows of all were now fulfilled, the ships were ready at Jaffa to take them home, the provinces had all been given away—to Baldwin and Boemund, Raymond and Godfrey. Tancred was named Prince of Galilee — a region yet unconquered: the rest went home because no further conquests were expected ; and only one hundred knights threw in their lot with Godfrey, whose army never numbered more than twenty thousand men.

Much still remained to be done before success was secure. The northern princes held the Turks in check, but news had sped to Egypt, where the Khalif, El Mustali, was already gathering a mighty army. The emirs of Nâblus had submitted, but Galilee was still unconquered. The seaside garrisons held out for Egypt, and Ascalon was to be for many years a thorn in the side of the kings of Jerusalem. Not a moment must be lost in marching south to meet the Khalif, and even the organisation of the lands around Jerusalem was put aside, until another battle had been fought.

Scarce was the choice of Godfrey made when on the 11th August the army moved into the plains of Philistia, to meet the Egyptian host. The broad red lands had then been reaped—if, indeed, peasants had dared to sow the corn that year. Water was scarce in the pools of the "River of Reuben," which runs from the mountain vale of Sorek. The dry summer dust was raised by herds of grazing cattle, and swirled in long high columns over the plain. The heat was at its greatest, the sky a merciless blue or leaden grey for days, until the sea breeze swept again towards the hills ; and before the Latins were the walls of Ascalon, towering above the sand dunes, and the sails of an Egyptian fleet anchored off its reefs. There were only three hundred knights beside Duke Godfrey, but the spirit of the army was raised by victories over sterner foes than half-bred Arabs and sulky Nubians ; and trusted leaders— Raymond, Tancred, and both the Roberts—led the forces on the centre and wings. The Nubians charged with iron flails, and strove to maim the Norman horses ; but the dust from the herds was taken for that of new troops hurrying to the battle, and panic seized the Moslems when the dreaded Latins fell upon them. They fled to Ascalon, or hastily embarked for Egypt, and by this final victory the kingdom was secured for nearly ninety years to come. Melek el Afdal fled into the fortress, with but two thousand men, many of whom were trampled in the gate.

With songs of victory the Christians again entered Jerusalem, and Daimbert wrote to Urban II announcing yet another triumph.*

Godfrey had already sent to Boemund in the north, announcing his election; and to Europe asking for further help†; and in August Tancred reported this victory.‡ New legions soon set out, from Lombardy and Germany, with Conrad of Hohenstauffen and Wolf of Bavaria. The bishop of Milan brought the arm of St. Ambrose, and the whole army, including monks and women, numbered at least one hundred thousand souls. Their aim was not Jerusalem, but further conquests extending to Baghdad; and in the year 1101 they reached Cappadocia, only to perish near Angora, lured by the Turks into an ambush. Another fifteen thousand Latins, under the Counts of Nevers and Bourges, perished near Erekli on the way to Tarsus; and near the same town yet a third division, led by William of Poitou, was also defeated. The arm of St. Ambrose was lost, and Raymond of Toulouse, who had undertaken to lead the first of these three armies from Angora, fled to Sinope. The miserable women who accompanied the host were slain, or spared, when young and beautiful, for lifelong misery in Turkish harîms. All these chiefs died with their followers excepting Raymond, and the road by land to Syria was once more made impassable by Turkish victories.

---

* *Archives*, I, p. 211 ; *Regesta*, No. 29.
† *Archives*, I, pp. 197, 199, 205 ; *Regesta*, Nos. 25, 26, 27.
‡ *Archives*, I, p. 200 ; *Regesta*, No. 28.

Meanwhile, in winter time Duke Godfrey in Jerusalem was organising fiefs, and making laws and alliances, and giving grants to churches and to trading cities. The canons of the Holy Sepulchre were the first to gain villages and fields, orchards and vineyards, north of the city. The earliest deed in the Cartulary belongs to the one year of Godfrey's rule, when twenty villages were granted to the prior. They still retain their names, lying on the mountains* northwards, as far as Bireh and Ain Sinia—then known as Val-de-curs. In the same year the Doge of Venice set out with a fleet, to open up a new and profitable trade with all the coast, and to win privileges for his city, by aiding to conquer Cæsarea and Arsûf, Haifa, Tyre, and Ascalon. From Rhodes came letters in November, 1099, announcing the approach of these important allies ; and in the June that followed Godfrey made a treaty with them. If, from the 24th June until the 15th August, the Venetian fleet would aid his army, he promised to the Doge a third part of every city taken, and a church and market in every town, and half the spoil, and safety for the crew of any ship wrecked on the coast; and this alliance was ratified on the 18th of July, a year after the conquest of Jerusalem, and yet again by later kings.†

During the winter laws for the new kingdom, called " Letters of the Holy Sepulchre," were made—the nucleus of that famous code known later as the Assizes of Jerusalem ; and in the spring, Arsûf, the little town

---

* See *Memoirs of Survey of Western Palestine*, Vol. III, p. 11.
† See authorities in the *Regesta*, Nos. 30 and 31.

in Sharon, upon the cliffs north of Jaffa, was summoned
to give tribute ; but the Moslems closed the gates,
and bound Gerard d'Avesnes to a high cross upon the
ramparts, threatening their prisoner's death if Godfrey
stormed the walls. The prisoner boldly called to the
assailants not to regard his fate ; but Godfrey raised
the siege, and Gerard was released and came to Jerusalem, to become a little later the seigneur of St.
Abraham, as Hebron was then called. Treaties were
made by Godfrey with Acre and Ascalon, Damascus,
Cæsarea, and Aleppo ; and in the spring the army went
to help Tancred in Galilee, clearing the country up to
the borders of Baniâs. The siege of Ascalon had failed,
because Raymond had quarrelled with Godfrey as to the
spoils of a city yet untaken ; and though new hosts of
pilgrims came from Antioch and Edessa, at Christmas,
the army of Godfrey was as yet not strong enough to
subdue the cities on the shores.

It was perhaps in the Hûleh marshes, on his way to
Baniâs, that Godfrey caught the fever which caused his
early death. He was returning by the plains to Jaffa,
and meditating the reduction of Haifa—the natural
port of Galilee—when he was stricken down. They
carried him to Jaffa, where he died on the 18th July,
1100 A.D., being then in the strength of manhood, little
more than forty years of age. The long privations and
labours in the field shortened his life, and the new
kingdom met an unexpected blow, in this loss of
its first ruler—the wisest and best of all the Latin
princes.

They bore his body to Jerusalem, and buried him under Calvary. Even to our own times are shown the spurs and the long Norman sword, said to belong to this most perfect knight of Christendom ; and till the savage Kharezmians wrecked his sepulchre, it bore this modest epitaph as given by Quaresmius :—

> Hic jacet inclitus Dux Godefridus
> De Bullon, qui totam istam terram
> Aquisivit cultui Christiano
> Cujus anima regnet cum Christo.　Amen.

CHAPTER IV.

The Growth of the Kingdom.

A READER who relied solely on the contemporary chronicles, from which the main thread of this account is derived, might easily suppose that the history of the Latin Kingdom of Jerusalem was one of endless war, and of struggles hopeless from the first. The chroniclers seem to have thought that little was important beyond a record of battles won and lost, and of the marriages and deaths of kings. We might easily overlook the fact that gaps of several years occur in their annals, during which the kingdom is without a history, and the years so passed were sometimes full of other incidents. We fortunately, however, possess another class of evidence, in hundreds of documents which relate to grants and treaties, affecting the sale and purchase of land, the gifts to the Church and to the fighting Orders, the arrangements made by princes with the trading cities of France and Italy, with many other details speaking of peace and growing wealth. We have, moreover, testimony in the ruined churches, castles, and halls of Palestine which are among its proudest monuments, and nearly all of which were built in the first

fifty years of Latin rule.   For eighty-seven years no
enemy besieged Jerusalem, and for three-quarters of
a century—with exception of unimportant raids—the
battles of the Christians were fought upon the frontiers
of the kingdom, which was ever spreading and becoming
stronger.   As long as Islam was divided into hostile
camps the Franks were able to hold their conquests
safely.

Our present subject is rather that of the colonisation
of Palestine under the feudal system than the history
of Crusades, many of which failed, or had only a
transient influence.   During the period of the first five
reigns in Palestine the state of Europe was far less
peaceful than that of the new kingdom in the East.   In
England Stephen fought against a league of barons,
and all the land was desolated by the war against
Matilda.   The castles were not dismantled till 1153 A.D.,
and not till two years later was the north of England
recovered from the Scots.   The tranquillising of the
kingdom, when Ireland was occupied and Scotland
subjected, was not effected by Henry II till 1173, when
the King of Britain also ruled a third of France.   In
France Louis VI was equally hindered by the power
of barons, and the country was full of robber castles.
The freedom granted to various towns, at a time when
the same policy was followed in Palestine, strengthened
the French king against his vassals ; but the dispute
with Rome, and the wars against the Albigenses,
weakened the kingdom ; while in England the power
and pretensions of the Pope left the king almost without

subjects. In Germany and Italy the Guelphs—who aided the cause of the Papacy—were struggling with the Ghibelines, until, in the middle of the century, Alexander III put his foot upon the neck of Barbarossa. From such struggles the kingdoms of the West emerged at length ; but during this stormy time the kings of Jerusalem, and the princes of Antioch and Edessa, governed a willing people. The fame of their justice attracted even Moslems, and even a Muhammadan writer admits that the peasantry preferred the Christian rule to that of Turkish or Egyptian tyrants.*

The kingdom was divided into fiefs ruled by counts and seigneurs. The feudal system created great confederacies of princes, owning a single head, and allied for offence and defence under his direction. Such great vassals were the Count of Edessa, the Prince of Antioch, and the Count of Tripoli, to the King of Jerusalem. The latter province included Gebal, and the Mountain of the Assassins ; and on the south the smaller seigneurie of Beirût marched with Tripoli at the Adonis river, and extended east on Lebanon. The fief of Sidon was bounded by the Damur river on the north, and by the Kasimiyeh on the south, including all the southern Lebanon. The seigneurs of Tyre held all the low hills east of that city, and on the south their border was the ridge known as the Ladder of Tyre. From thence to Carmel came the royal lands of Acre, reaching inland to the higher mountains. The seigneur of Toron held a long and narrow fief upon the watershed of Upper

* Ibn Jobeir in 1185 A.D., quoted by Rey, *Colonies Franques*, p. 96.

Galilee ; and east of this the seigneurs of Maron held
the mountains and the upper Jordan valley. The fief
of Montfort was wedged between Toron and Acre, and
bounded on the south by that of St. George. All Lower
Galilee, and the hills of Safed, belonged to Tancred as
Prince of Galilee ; and on Carmel were the two small
fiefs of Haifa and of Caymont—the latter to the east.
The mountains, from the plain of Esdraelon to near
Sinjil, were ruled by the seigneur of Nâblus or Shechem ;
and to his west the seigneur of Cæsarea held the
plains of Sharon, from Carmel to the river Rochetaillie.
The small fief of Arsur (or Arsûf) divided Cæsarea from
the famous County of Jaffa and Ascalon, including
Gaza ; and here the small fief of Darum marked the
limits of the Kingdom. The hills of Jerusalem, from
Sinjil to Tekoa, were the royal domains extending
to the Jordan, and further south the seigneur of St.
Abraham owned all the Hebron hills to Beersheba.
Beyond Jordan all Moab and Gilead belonged, in the
best days of the Latin rule, to the seigneur of Kerak ;
and the fief was known as Oultre Jourdan. Bashan was
never conquered, and belonged to the Sultan of Damascus ; but all the Jaulân district, which from its black
volcanic soil was known as Soethe or the "black land,"
formed another fief of the princes of Galilee, reaching
from the Yermûk stream to Baniâs—the frontier fortress
at the springs of Jordan. Such was already the kingdom
soon after Godfrey's death, and such it remained until
the fatal battle of Hattîn in 1187. One by one the shore
towns were taken, and even Ascalon was finally subdued.

The population, girded in by chains of mighty castles, east of Jordan or west of the Orontes, enjoyed a time of peace and of prosperity greater than that of European lands ; and even a century later the western half of the kingdom still remained a Christian state. The importance of these two centuries, not only for the history of the East, but also because of eastern influence upon the civilisation of Europe, can hardly be overstated ; and nothing is more misleading than to represent the story of the Christian kingdom of Jerusalem as one long episode of war and desolation. For the moment we return to consider the main political events of sixty years of success following the conquest, but later we shall have occasion to enquire into the daily life of the Franks, and of their Oriental subjects.

Immediately after Godfrey's death Daimbert, the Latin Patriarch of Jerusalem, sent the news to Boemund in Antioch, complaining of oppression of the churches by Garnier de Grey,* who seized the Tower of David and other places, claiming to have received them from the duke. Boemund, with Baldwin, Godfrey's brother, was far away in Armenia, besieging Malatiya ; but on receiving the news, Baldwin gave over his County of Edessa to his cousin Baldwin du Bourg, and marched on Jerusalem. He had a force of four hundred knights and one thousand men, and was attacked crossing the Dog River north of Beirût, but drove off the enemy and reached Jerusalem in safety. He was crowned on Christmas Day at Bethlehem —the first Latin king—being, like his brother, unwilling

* *Regesta*, No. 32.

to receive the diadem in the Holy City; and in his proclamation to his people* promising justice and peace, he says that, like Godfrey, he submitted to be a vassal of the Church or Patriarch of Jerusalem, and received the keys from the hands of the latter, and promised to the Church the spoils of Ascalon should the city be given into his hands.   The expedition which he undertook for that purpose was, however, unsuccessful, for the city was too strong as yet to be taken.   Tancred appears at first to have opposed the new election, and difficulties arose as to the rights to the town of Haifa (not yet subdued); but in the same year we find Tancred, as Prince of Galilee, granting to the abbey of Mount Tabor lands lying in the plateaux north and south of that isolated hill, and even the village of Susieh beyond Jordan, though still unconquered,† which agreement was made with Baldwin's consent.

When Easter time approached the Holy Fire was awaited as usual, by Greeks and Latins alike.   This rite, which has survived to our own days, was already ancient.   As early as Charlemagne's time it is mentioned as a miracle occurring on Easter eve.‡   The Russian Abbot Daniel, who visited Jerusalem in the reign of Baldwin I, describes fully what was then the practice.   The church was cleansed on Good Friday,

---

* *Regesta*, No. 34.

† *Regesta*, No. 36.   Tancred was administering Antioch in March, 1101, Boemund having been taken captive by Muhammad Gumishtakin in Cappadocia.   Galilee was administered meanwhile by Hugh of Falkenberg, Lord of Tiberias, who was killed in 1107 near Baniâs, and in 1108 by Gervase, his successor.

‡ Bernard the Wise, 867 A.D., Bohn's *Early Travels in Palestine*, p. 27.

the lamps put out and filled with fresh oil, and every
candle in every church of Jerusalem was extinguished.
Daniel presented himself before the king, who called
him kindly, saying, "What dost thou need Russian
abbot?" being, as the pilgrim says, "a man of great
kindness and humility, and not given to pride." Daniel
then asked leave to place a lamp beside the rest in the
name of his Russian country, and this he was permitted
to hang at the foot of the tomb—one of the chief places
of honour in the church. On Easter eve he found the
church enclosure full of a crowd which overflowed into
the outer court, some of the pilgrims coming from
Egypt and from Antioch. "The crush was terrible, and
the turmoil such that many faint in the dense mass of
people who stand with unlighted tapers in hand waiting
for the opening of the church doors. The priests alone
are inside the church, and priests and crowd alike await
the coming of the prince and his suite: then the doors
being opened the people rush in, pushing and jostling
each other, and fill the church and the galleries." "All
the people within and without the church cry ceaselessly
Kyrie eleison! and this cry is so loud that the whole
building rings and shakes with it. The faithful shed
torrents of tears. . . . Prince Baldwin himself looks
contrite and greatly humbled."* The prince was seated,
near the high altar east of the Sepulchre, on a raised
seat. The abbot of St. Saba stood near the tomb, and
both Greek and Latin services were performed together.
A later writer says that the Fire sometimes appeared in

* English translation, pp. 74, 75.

the Templum Domini, sometimes in the Hospital of St. John, and not always in the Sepulchre.[*]   On the present occasion it was delayed for no less than three days' time ; and according to Daniel lighted only three of the Greek lamps.   The church was open above, and a fine rain fell on the close-packed crowd.   At length they began to chant the song of deliverance—

> " I will sing unto the Lord, for He hath triumphed gloriously ;
> The horse and his rider hath He thrown into the sea,"

and then, according to our pilgrim, " a small cloud coming suddenly from the east rested above the open dome of the church. . . .   It was at this moment that the Holy Light suddenly illuminated the Holy Sepulchre, shining with an awful and splendid brightness.   The bishop and four deacons then opened the doors of the Tomb, and entered with the taper of Prince Baldwin, who . . .   resumed his place holding with great joy the taper in his hands.   We lighted our tapers from that of the Prince, and so passed the flame to all in the church."   The joy bells were then rung and masses said, and the fire was carried to the Temple and to other churches.

Such fire feasts in springtime were not peculiar to Jerusalem.   It was believed that at Sinai a heavenly fire flew round the mountain every Sabbath, sometimes descending with terrible noise, but injuring none.[†] Neither was the festival purely Christian, but a common rite of ancient paganism.   In our own times the Latins

---

[*] *Theodorich,* VIII, writing in 1172 A.D., p. 15, English translation.
[†] *Fetellus,* 1130 A.D., p. 16, English translation.

declare the Holy Fire to be an imposture, and the rite is peculiar to the Eastern churches.

In this same spring the Genoese fleet also visited Jaffa, and Baldwin made a treaty with them, which was written in letters of gold and preserved in the Holy Sepulchre church. It was confirmed again three years later, and renewed by later kings* and princes. Baldwin I gave to the Genoese church of St. Laurence a square in Jerusalem, and a street in Jaffa, with a third part of Cæsarea, Arsûf, and Acre when those cities should be taken. These privileges were partly for help already given in winning Jerusalem and Antioch, and partly for later help in sieges at Laodicea and Tortosa, at Cæsarea, Arsûf, and other places. The Genoese in turn promised faithful aid to the king in war. With the assistance of this fleet in 1101 A.D. Arsûf was taken, and Cæsarea after a siege of fourteen days. The first capitulated, but in the latter case a terrible massacre of Moslems followed; and here the Genoese found a green dish which they carried home and called the " Holy Grail." It was supposed to be that mystical vessel wherein the " Last Supper " had been served, famous in our own legends of Arthur's knights. One relic of the same name had been taken to Constantinople by the Greek patriarch in the seventh century when flying from Chosroes of Persia, but that was of silver.

English and German fighting men now arrived to reinforce the army, and fought in the forest near Arsûf;

* *Regesta*, Nos. 43, 45, 46. Renewed by Amaury, No. 438, and by Conrad of Tyre, No. 704.

but at the same time a sudden raid from Ascalon
nearly led to the capture of the king at Ramleh, which
town the Moslems took. It is said he owed his safety
to the gratitude of a Moslem, whose wife this gentle
knight had succoured in distress. Escaping to Arsûf
he gathered his forces, and retook Ramleh, on the 7th
of September, 1101, after which the rest of the year was
passed in peace.

One of the most interesting letters of this reign
belongs to the year 1102,* when Anselm, the famous
Archbishop of Canterbury, wrote to Baldwin I, ad-
monishing him to rule wisely, as an example to other
Christian princes, and so that having reigned in Jerusalem on this earth, he might for ever reign in Jerusalem
above. The admonitions of the Church, bestowed upon
this just and courteous king, should, however, have
rather been directed to the Patriarch Daimbert, whose
greed and luxury scandalised the pious, and angered
Baldwin, who himself had hardly money to pay his
knights ; or else to Arnold who, disappointed at not
being confirmed in the assumed rank of Patriarch, was
intriguing against Daimbert vainly. Five years later,
in 1107 A.D., Pope Paschal II wrote to Baldwin† : for
Daimbert, openly accused of peculation, had fled to
Antioch, and a pious but ignorant monk named
Ebremar was placed in his stead. The Pope called a
Council at Jerusalem, which deposed Ebremar and
consoled him with the archbishopric of Tyre ; but

---

* *Regesta*, No. 37.
† *Regesta*, Nos. 49, 50 ; *Will. Tyre*, XI, 4.

Daimbert, who had gone to Rome, did not recover his dignity, for he died at Messina on his way to the East, and so for a few years Arnold, whom the chronicler calls "the first-born of Satan," obtained the See of Jerusalem which he had coveted so long.

After five years, in which little fighting occurred in Palestine, the ranks of the first Crusaders began to be thinned by death. In 1104 Boemund, Tancred, and Baldwin du Bourg were besieging Harrân, on the south border of the trans-Euphratic Christian County of Edessa. The Turks of Mosul came against them, and taking captive Baldwin du Bourg and Count Jocelyn of Courtenay,* spread over the country threatening Edessa and Antioch. Boemund and Tancred escaped, and the former sailed to Italy, to see the Pope, and gathered new defenders for northern Syria among the knights of Poitou, Limousin, and Auvergne ; but on his way back he visited Tarento, his old Apulian home, and here he died. It is said that he had caused himself to be taken out of Antioch, which was then surrounded by Turks, in a coffin which was placed on board at Seleucia ; and that he so escaped a Greek fleet watching for him. The policy of alliance between the Greeks and Turks, now already in existence, led to further troubles later. In the next year, on the 28th of February, 1105, died Raymond of St. Gilles fighting for the capture of Tripoli—the chief town of a county which was the last now left unorganised of all those ruled by the Christians.

---

* His mother was sister to the mother of Baldwin du Bourg, whom he accompanied to Edessa with Baldwin I.

Three years earlier Raymond had allied himself with the traders of Marseilles, promising half the town of Gebal south of Tripoli, in return for the aid of their fleet; but the city was not taken as expected in 1102 A.D.* Meantime, however, the King of Jerusalem had reduced Acre, by aid of the Genoese, who furnished seventy galleys, and thus of all the seaside cities only Tripoli, Tyre, Sidon, and Ascalon remained in the hands of the Egyptians. The Greeks were still holding Laodicea, but the Italian fleets were active in aid of the Latins. It was not, however, till 1109 that Tripoli and Laodicea fell, the first on the 21st of July by aid of the Genoese, and the latter by aid of the Pisans. Tripoli stood siege for two months, and was burned after its capitulation. It became the heritage of Bertram, son of Raymond of St. Gilles, and the capital of one of the most prosperous counties of the Latin kingdom.

Tripoli itself is said to be the safest port upon the Syrian coast, with a large harbour and strong walls, having in the twelfth century a great fortress at the south-east corner of the town called Mount Pilgrim. The city was one of the richest in Syria, and already famous for its trade. There were then, as now, two distinct quarters, separated by nearly two miles of gardens in the flat sandy plain. The port quarter stood upon a promontory: the city proper—called Mount Pilgrim from the castle—was to the east upon the river

---

* *Regesta*, Nos. 38, 44, 48, 53, 54. Bertram, eldest son of Raymond, took over the county from William Jordan, his cousin, who continued the siege of Tripoli, and who became Lord of Arca. Bertram was succeeded by his son Pons (1112–1137).

Kadisha, which, flowing from its picturesque glen in Lebanon, runs north through the town under a curious covered bridge, which, flanked by shops, may be crossed without suspicion of the river beneath. The famous fruit gardens were worth an annual revenue of one hundred thousand pounds, which in those days represented at least five times the modern value of the money. The sugar-cane was cultivated, and many industries prospered. The schools became famous, and four thousand merchants of silks and camelots lived within the walls.* Bertram, the second count, in 1109 granted to the Genoese a third of the port, and the rocks or islands near it, and free trade in the province.†
A few years later we find the Venetians settling in Tripoli, and later, in Gebal. The Pisans also owned property in Tripoli towards the close of the century.

The lands of the counts of Tripoli included the valley of the Eleutherus river, and Lebanon north and south of this natural highway, the border extending eastwards to Emesa on the Orontes, which was known as La Chamelle. A celebrated fortress, called Krak des Chevaliers, commanded the natural highway from Tripoli inland, perched on the isolated top, north of a sunken oak dotted plain, with a village nestling at its feet upon the slopes. On the east slope of Lebanon, above Emesa, another great castle, Mont Ferrand, guarded the Christian frontiers ; and near the sea Margat on the north frontier, and Château Blanc, a little nearer to the

---

* Burchard of Mount Sion, pp. 16, 17, English translation. Rey, *Colonies Franques*, p. 372.
† *Regesta*, Nos. 55, 84.

Eleutherus, were equally famous, while Akkar dominated the southern mountain, and Batrûn and Gebal
were also ports upon this side.   There is no part of
Syria which includes better lands or more romantic
mountains.   Tortosa, the most northern seaport, was
also one of the most venerated places of pilgrimage in
the East, because of the picture reported to have been
painted by St. Luke, and said to be a portrait of the
Virgin.

The eighteen years of rule of Baldwin I were almost
uniformly prosperous, and he survived all the leaders
of the first Crusade, except his cousin and successor,
Baldwin du Bourg of Edessa : for Tancred died at
Antioch in 1112 A.D.   In the following year a Turkish
inroad from Mosul followed a check experienced by
Baldwin at Edessa, and the king, falling into ambush
near Baniâs, escaped with difficulty ; while another raid
from Ascalon was carried even to Jerusalem.   The
Turks pillaged the country as far as Nâblus, but then
retreated* ; and an alliance made with Damascus seems
to have secured the safety of the kingdom while Baldwin lived.

Against this transient reverse, and the bad year of
dearth, famine, earthquake, and locusts, which followed,
we must place the reduction of all the seaports except

---

* This inroad was led by Maudud, brother of Sultan Muhammad, who
besieged Tiberias in June, 1113.   Reinforcements from Antioch reached
Baldwin.   Maudud retired to Damascus, where he was assassinated.
Rudhwan of Aleppo died in December of the same year, and the Turks
were weakened by intrigues in the north as well.   Baldwin II gained a
victory in 1119 on August 14th against the forces of El Ghazi of Mardin,
which closed for a time the wars against Antioch.

Tyre and Ascalon, and the extension of the kingdom east of Jordan in 1116 A.D., when Baldwin marched to Petra, and built the strong castle of Montreal, at Shobek on the Hâj or Moslem pilgrim road in Moab, north of the same town of Petra. This, with a fort at Petra itself, and the great castle of Kerak, frowning later from the precipices east of the Dead Sea, gave to the Christians the command of the Hâj route from Damascus to Mecca.

We have already seen that the princes of Antioch levied toll on the Moslem pilgrims; and the wealth of the caravans to Arabia was only protected by the treaty with Damascus.

Yet earlier in his reign Baldwin pushed his conquests into the Jaulan east of the Sea of Galilee. Here in 1105 A.D. he built the fort of 'Aal* which the Moslems destroyed soon after : by treaties in 1109 and 1111 A.D. half the revenues of this volcanic region were given to the Christians, and half to Damascus. The ruin of this fortress still bears the name of "Baldwin's Castle," and stands at the end of a steep promontory of the mountains, on cliffs above Wady Samak, which runs in a deep gorge westwards into the Sea of Galilee. This stronghold marked the farthest eastern limit of the Latin power in Bashan, and carried the line of frontier strongholds from Baniâs southwards, to the castles of Ajlûn and of Tibneh and to the lofty site of Kasr er Rubud, which with the fort of Salt protected Gilead. This chain of castles long defended the great fief of Oultre Jourdan.

* Arab Hist. of Crusades, quoted by Rey, *Colonies Franques*, p. 434. Schumacher's *Across the Jordan*, p. 255.

H

In the year 1107 had also been built, by Hugh of St. Omer, Lord of Tiberias, the castle of Toron in Upper Galilee—now called Tibnîn, guarding the line from Baniâs to Tyre, in a strong position on the mountains. It played an important part in the history of later wars.*

New and unexpected allies also came to help the kingdom in the middle of Baldwin's reign. The sons of Magnus Barefoot were then kings in Norway, and of these Sigurd led a fleet of sixty ships to Palestine. An ancient saga still records the prowess of these Norsemen, relating how they visited King Henry in England, and took eight galleys from Spanish pirates, and killed all the Moslems of Cintra in Portugal, and took by force a mighty booty in the cave of Formentera—an islet south of Ivica in the Balearics. After visiting Sicily they sailed on to Acre and Jaffa, and feasted in Jerusalem, where with the pride of barbarians they refused to admire the riches of the East, but gained a fragment of the Holy Cross, Sigurd promising to create an archbishopric in pagan Norway " if he could." Desiring to perform some doughty deed to help the Latins, the Norsemen aided with their fleet the army of ten thousand men which marched on Sidon and Beirût. On the 19th of December Sidon fell in 1110 A.D., Beirût having been taken on the 27th of the preceding April.† Sigurd then sailed for Constantinople, and marched by land back to Denmark. He was only twenty when he safely reached Norway after three adventurous years.

---

* See *Jacques de Vitry*, p. 18, English translation.
† *Will. Tyre*, XI, see Sigurd in Bohn's *Early Travels in Palestine*.

These conquests tempted Baldwin to invade Egypt where the Moslem Khalifs were ever growing weaker. El Mustali had died in 1101, and his vizir Melek el Afdal was no longer in power. Since the great defeat at Ascalon, the Egyptians had done little, beyond reinforcing the garrison of that city which raided at times on the Christians. The Egyptian fleet had failed to rescue any of the other shore towns, and the discredited Fatimite dynasty was represented by a Khalif sunk in sloth and luxury in his palace at Cairo. In 1118 A.D. Baldwin marched to Farama, or Pelusium, near Tanis, in the Delta, carrying the war far into the enemy's country ; but here he fell a victim to fever, and died in the retreat at El Arîsh. He must have been nearly sixty years of age, and had ruled well and justly for eighteen. He was three times married, his first wife, who was English, never reaching Palestine ; his second, an Armenian princess, having been divorced for adultery ; and his third, Adelaide, widow of Roger, Count of Sicily, being sent home after three years, although she brought a rich dower to her second husband. In the same year in which the last of the great Crusaders died, the patriarch Arnold, the Emperor Alexius, and Pope Pascal II, also passed away, and Adelaide herself did not survive her husband.

Neither Godfrey nor Baldwin I left any sons, and their third brother Eustace did not press his claim, hearing that Baldwin du Bourg was elected under the title of Baldwin II.* With him the oriental blood began

* He was the son of Hugh, Count of Rethel.

to mingle in the veins of the royal line, for his wife also was Armenian, and his famous daughters, Alice and Milicent, were hereafter to trouble the kingdom with intrigues such as the Frank and Norman ladies are not found to have undertaken. The early years of the new reign were full of strange adventures, but it was marked by the conquest of Tyre, and on the whole the thirteen years that followed were times of peace and growing strength.

This, however, could hardly have been at first foretold, for after two years, in 1120 A.D., Jocelyn, who succeeded the new king as Count of Edessa, and the Count of Tripoli, met with defeat by the Turks at Artesia east of Antioch; and, soon after, Baldwin II was himself defeated by El Ghâzi, the old enemy of the Latins and now sultan of Aleppo, who died a year later, leaving an energetic nephew Balak to succeed him.* These troubles were regarded as due to the general decay of morals among the Christians, although such decadence was not of very recent appearance. Arnold the Patriarch, who had denounced his rival Daimbert for peculation, was not himself above reproach. He was accused of sins with a Frankish lady, and even with a Muslimah, in letters received by Pascal II, from Baldwin I, and from the bishops, abbots, and priors of the kingdom; and he was deprived of his office for a time. But the accusation was pronounced by the Pope to be unproved, and Arnold was restored. On the

---

* El Ghâzi's son, Suleiman, revolted against his father, who made a truce in August, 1121, but broke it, and attacked Syria. El Ghâzi died near Mardin on 3rd November, 1122.

23rd of January, 1120, a council was, however, called at Nâblus, for the general reformation of morals.* Its ultimate effect, upon a population which was rapidly becoming half oriental though half Frank by birth, was, however, small ; and there can be little doubt that luxury, and a trying climate, were already sapping the vigour of the conquering race.

In the September of 1122 A.D. Balak succeeded in capturing Jocelyn of Edessa, with sixty knights, and on the 30th of May following, King Baldwin II also fell into his hands, at the river Sinja. But the Armenians were faithful to a prince who had married one of their race, and fifty men, who swore to set him free, penetrated in disguise into Khartpert, the town where he was held a prisoner, and massacred the garrison. Jocelyn then undertook a perilous journey, crossing the Euphrates to summon aid from Syria ; but Baldwin remained holding the fortress. Balak at once advanced and undermined the walls. The Armenians in turn were massacred, and the king was removed to Harrân, where he remained till ransomed after a year's imprisonment.† Meanwhile a regent was appointed in Jerusalem—Count Eustace Garnier—who repelled another incursion from the south. He made a new alliance with the Venetians, granting further rights in Jerusalem, promising free trade and quarters in Antioch, and in Ascalon, and Tyre as soon as they should be taken. The Doge himself came to the shores of Palestine ; the Egyptians were driven

---

* *Regesta*, Nos. 83, 89.
† *William of Tyre*, XII, 17, and Kemal ed Din.

away from Jaffa ; and the fleet and army marched on
Tyre.   Meanwhile Jocelyn had gone to help the captive
king, and slew Balak at Membej, east of Aleppo.
Negotiations for ransom followed, and from the 15th
of February to the 7th of July, 1124, the Christians
besieged Tyre, to which the head of Balak was sent.*
On the 29th of August Baldwin II was set free, and,
aided by the Damascus Arabs, he at once besieged
Aleppo.   The Turkish Sultan of Mosul marched to aid
the town, the siege was raised, and Baldwin retreated west.
The Turks defeated the Damascenes, but were in turn
repulsed from Antioch ; after this indecisive contest,
and the surrender of Tyre, we hear no more of wars in
any part of the kingdom proper for fourteen years.
Baldwin II reigned seven years after his captivity, and
yet more prosperous times succeeded.   The chronicle
of Foucher of Chartres asserts that the Latins, already
intermarrying with Armenians and Arabs, were richer
and happier in Palestine than they had ever been in
Europe.   They flocked to settle in and cultivate the
land, tilling vineyards and cornfields, and trading with
the east.   The merchants of Pisa, Venice, Genoa,
Marseilles and Amalfi lived in the cities ; and colonists
came not only from France and Germany, but even
from England and Brittany.   We now in fact approach
the zenith of Latin prosperity, under the last of those
Crusaders who had marched with Godfrey, and under
his successor, Fulk of Anjou.   Pope Honorius II wrote

---

* *Regesta*, No. 102.   Eustace Garnier, the guardian of the kingdom, was
aided in this siege by the Venetian Doge's fleet.   Tughtakin of Damascus,
and the Egyptian fleet attempted in vain to aid the besieged.

in 1128 A.D. to Baldwin II, to say that he had heard the
king's rule to be most upright and wise, and to confirm
his dignity as vassal of the church.* About this time
the Christian kingdom of Armenia was also organised
and growing strong. Maudud, brother of the Sultan of
Mosul, was assassinated at Damascus in 1114, and the
Atabek dynasty arose under Zanghi, who ruled the
Seljuk lands in Mesopotamia and at Aleppo† ; but this
new danger, which finally proved the greatest yet encountered, only showed itself clearly five years after
the death of Baldwin du Bourg.

But Baldwin had no son to be his heir. His half
Armenian daughters were Milicent, and Alice of
Antioch. Towards the close of his reign he sought a
son-in-law to succeed to the crown, and found one in
Fulk of Anjou. The House of Anjou was ancient and
famous, tracing from Tortulf the Forester, and Ingelger
the first Count in 870 A.D. Fulk the Red, Fulk the
Good, and Geoffrey Greygown, were followed by the
cruel Fulk the Black, who was an early pilgrim to
Jerusalem in the eleventh century. He is said to have
been scourged as a penitent in its streets, and on his
return he built at Loche a church resembling that of
the Holy Sepulchre. After him succeeded Geoffrey
Martel, and Fulk Rechin, and at the age of eighteen
Fulk, the future King of Jerusalem—the last pure-

* *Regesta*, No. 122.
† Imad ed Din Zanghi became governor of Mosul under the Sultan in
1127. He took Aleppo in 1128, and Hamah in 1129. He first attacked
the Franks in 1130. The Turkish term Atabek signifies a " guardian " of
the Seljuk Sultan.

blooded Latin ruler—became Count of Anjou. He was already nearly forty when he married Milicent, and had a history of no little importance. Baldwin du Bourg, like the two former kings, was tall and strong, fair, with a long beard streaked with silver ; but Fulk was small of stature, and red haired. Like the other kings he was, however, brave and generous, courteous and prudent ; but troubled, as no others had been, by a turbulent wife. He had already been married, and his son, Geoffrey Plantagenet the Handsome, wedded the widowed Empress Matilda, daughter of Henry the First of England, some five years before his father's second marriage. Their son was Henry II, and thus, through Fulk, the Kings of England inherited Anjou, and, on Henry's marriage with Eleanor of Guienne and Poitou, the Angevine dominions, including the kingdoms of England, Scotland, and Ireland, with Anjou, Normandy, Touraine, and Maine, Poitou and Guienne stretched over nearly half France down to the Pyrenees. The reign of Fulk marked the zenith of the Latin power in the East, although Ascalon resisted till nine years after his death ; Edessa was lost the year after Fulk was killed in hunting—the first ominous sign of the growing power of Islam, though twelve more years of peace were yet to follow even then.

In 1130 A.D. Baldwin II had attacked Damascus, but the campaign failed owing to the winter storms. In the next year he died at Jerusalem, shortly after his return from Antioch. Troubles had there arisen with his second daughter, widow of Boemund II, who determined to keep the principality in her own hands, although the heiress was her daughter Constance, as yet a child and ward of King Baldwin. For this purpose Alice entered into treaty with the new Turkish Sultan Zanghi, and in this revolt against the suzerain she was aided by Pons of Tripoli, grandson of Raymond of Toulouse, who had married Tancred's widow Cecilia, the daughter of Fulk's mother Bertrade, born after she had become the mistress of the King of France, Philip I. The ambitious Alice was not supported by the citizens of Antioch. Her treaty with Zanghi was discovered, and the wrath of her father perhaps shortened his life. Jocelyn, the stout Count of Edessa, died however at the same time as Baldwin II, and Alice again intrigued with his successor, Jocelyn II, and with Pons of Tripoli. Fulk's first troubles were thus with his sister-in-law, and with the husband of his illegitimate half-sister. This disgraceful intrigue led to a refusal, on the part of Pons, to allow King Fulk to pass through his county of Tripoli. The king embarked therefore at Beirût, and went by sea to the port of Antioch, where Pons attacked him but was defeated. Renaud of Margat was then made regent of Antioch, but, immediately after, Zanghi raided over the Euphrates, and besieged Pons in the castle of Montferrand. King Fulk attacked and defeated the Turks in 1133 and sent as far as the court of King Henry I, for Raymond of Poitou, whom he married to Constance—a child of twelve. Her mother Alice retreated to Latakia, and so at length the troubles in the north were settled.

But hardly was this scandal silenced when another
trouble arose, due to the elder of the two half Armenian
sisters, Milicent, King Fulk's own wife, the heiress of
the Kingdom of Jerusalem.   Hugh of Jaffa was the
son of the seigneur of Puyzet, who had rebelled against
Louis VI of France ; and his estates being confiscated
he himself was banished.   His relations with Queen
Milicent were suspected, and his own son-in-law, Walter
of Cæsarea, denounced him as a traitor.   Summoned to
try the cause by ordeal of battle, Hugh fled to Ascalon,
and made alliance with the Moslems.   He then fortified Jaffa, and declared his decision to resist the king.
Hugh was the cousin german of the queen, a man
handsome, brave, and strong.   King Fulk perhaps did
not believe the charge, and entered into an agreement
whereby the Count of Jaffa promised to suffer exile for
three years.   He came to Jerusalem, and there while
playing at dice in the streets was stabbed by a Breton
knight, and left for dead.   He was cured however of
his wounds, and sent to Sicily, where he died.   Queen
Milicent became a zealous benefactress of the Church,
and in the last year of the reign of Fulk obtained, from
the Canons of the Holy Sepulchre, the lands of Bethany
giving Tekoa in exchange.   She built the strong tower
which still dominates the Bethany village, and founded
a nunnery.

Four years passed away, and in 1137 other troubles
arose in the north. John Comnenos the Emperor of
Byzantium, allied with Zanghi—although the Christians
of Asia Minor are said to have preferred the rule of

the Turkish Sultan of Iconium to that of the Greeks—
advanced on Antioch, which was still claimed by the
Emperors, and occupied Tarsus, Adana, and Malmistra,
while Zanghi once more besieged Mont Ferrand. Pons
of Tripoli was here slain, and King Fulk shut up in the
castle was forced to cede it to the Turks. Raymond of
Tripoli was taken prisoner, and forced to do homage for
Antioch to John Comnenos, who then aided the Latins
against the Turks, the joint forces of Byzantium and
of King Fulk besieging Sheizur on the Orontes, which
belonged to Aleppo. A truce was made, and John Comnenos, marching back across the Taurus, was slain in 1143,
by a poisoned arrow. This was almost the last attempt
made by the Greeks to regain their old ascendancy, and
for the next half century the history of Byzantium was
one of ever-increasing weakness.*

It is worthy our notice that about this time (1137-8)
the Kurdish Governor of Tekrit on the Tigris—between
Mosul and Baghdad—was a certain Eyûb, son of Shadi,
much trusted by Zanghi the Atabek Sultan; and in
this town was then born to him a small baby destined to
fill a large page in history half a century later—Yusef
called Salâh ed Dîn.

Five years later the Franks, allied with the Damascenes, took Baniâs once more from Zanghi, and the last
year of King Fulk's reign was passed in peace. This
monarch left his kingdom stronger and more secure
than ever. On the south-west he built three castles,

* In 1159-60 Manuel Comnenos seized Renaud of Chatillon, and
entered Antioch, but he was then father-in-law of Baldwin III.

as a defence against Ascalon, and put an end to the
Egyptian raids into his kingdom. The first of these
was at Yebna, or Ibelin, on the shores south of Jaffa,
which place the Latins wrongly thought to mark the
site of Gath. A citadel with four towers was built of
ancient masonry at Ibelin in 1142, and a small church
—still standing as a mosque—within the town. The
second castle, on a white chalk cliff called Tell es Safi,
south of the valley of Elah, was erected in 1144. Here
also the square fortress, which was called Blanchegarde,
had four corner towers. The foundations of its walls may
still be seen, and it stood on the real site of ancient
Gath. Another and earlier fortress closed the highway
to Hebron, in the fertile olive yards of Beit Jibrin, south
of Blanchegarde. This town was fortified by King
Fulk as early as 1134, and the remains of its walls are
also still traceable.* On the east of the kingdom Fulk
also added the strong and important castle of Kerak,
in Moab, to that of Montreal already noticed. Hardly
were these various works finished, during a time when
building was going on in all parts of Palestine, than the
king fell while coursing a hare on the sands near Acre,
and was killed while as yet he was not more than fifty-
three years of age. He left two sons by Milicent, the
eldest—Baldwin, afterwards Baldwin III—being about
thirteen years of age, and Amaury his brother four
years younger.

During the reign of King Fulk Jerusalem attained to

---

* *William of Tyre*, pp. 362, 437, 439, Vol. II, Guizot's translation,
1824; *Memoirs Survey West. Palestine*, Vol. II, pp. 414-5, 440-1 ; Vol.
III, pp. 257-8, 267-72.

its highest pitch of prosperity, and was filled with stately buildings of Italian Norman architecture, none of which existed when it was first besieged by Godfrey. Entering the Gate of David from the west the pilgrim found an open market under David's Tower, filled with a busy crowd of peasant traders ; for the wisdom of the rulers had remitted tolls to all those pilgrims who brought provisions or merchandise. Plunging into the narrow lane of David Street, he saw the money-changers sitting in their shops, before the piles of bezants and marks ; and jostled with the eager mingled mob of Latins and natives. The swarthy peasant, white shirted, red slippered, with brown striped cloak and yellow turban ; the page gorgeous in brilliant silks and velvet ; the red cross knight in mail; the bowman and the man-at-arms; the pale Moslem in his purple robe with the green turban of the sherif ; the dusky Arab from over Jordan in flying headdress ; the blue robed peasant woman with her basket ; the shrinking Jewish dyer—stained with indigo ; the black eyed Greek ; the sturdy mountaineer in felt and camlet, with broad red sash and baggy breeches —a pilgrim from Armenia or the Caucasus—even the Russian with his greasy gaberdine, long locks and beard ; the Italian trader and the Frankish freeman ; all these met in the streets in peaceful intercourse. The Norman seigneur, in furs and scarlet, rode his Arab courser down the market; the Patriarchs of Latin or Eastern rites passed by in long processions ; the palmer with his grey gown and cockle-shell, his staff and scrip and flapping hat, purchased his palm branch in the

Street of Palmers east of the church.   Bright cloths
and wooden pent-houses shaded the ill paved lane, and
further east, in Temple Street, the purple and amber and
crimson of the merchants' dresses mingled with green
and russet of the fruits piled in the open shops ; and the
smell of musk, and sandal wood, and rosewater, filled
all the street where the perfumers dwelt.   The peasants'
asses were pushed through the crowd, the camel swung
along with loads of grain ; and under the ribbed vaults
of Norman roofing, which still cover the streets, the
butchers and herbalists plied their trades ; and the odour
of food cooked for the pilgrims filled Malquisinat.

A great cathedral now enclosed the ancient chapels,
and a strong tall belfry rose above the southern courtyard of the Church of the Sepulchre.   Here Philip
D'Aubigny reposed under his tombstone, daily trodden
by countless feet of those who entered under the pointed
arches, between the slender clustered pillars of the
southern doorway, where boldly carved reliefs presented
scenes from the last days of the Saviour's life—the ass
and foal on Olivet, the raising of Lazarus, the Last
Supper, and allegoric figures of the bird and centaur,
with delicate arabesques, running along the cross beams
of the arches, with cornices and pillared windows above,
all wrought in the same perfect style of Norman
Romanesque.   East of the plain Gothic chapel of the
Sepulchre, in its rotunda open to the air above, was now
erected the great choir of the canons, with apses to the
east ; and on the vaults, and dome above, the vine of
David was painted.   Here stood the Patriarch's throne,

while for the Greek bishops humbler seats were left
between the choir and the rotunda. The abbey of the
Canons of St. Sepulchre was on the east, above the
cavern chapel of Helena. On the west another pointed
arch led from the level of the Patriarch's street, into the
gallery of the round building enclosing the Tomb. In
other respects there was but little change. The older
chapels were left untouched ; but north of Calvary the
tombs of two more rulers stood by Godfrey's, and figures
of kings and saints in glass mosaic here adorned the
church, including Constantine, Heraclius, and Queen
Helena, with pictures of the Resurrection, the Last
Supper, and Elijah fed by ravens.

West of the covered street, and south of the Sepulchre
Cathedral, a great quadrangular block of noble buildings
had arisen. It was reached by the broad arched portal,
on which the twelve months were carved, each represented by a human figure with Gothic lettering for the
month name over it. The church of Ste. Marie la Grande
occupied all the north-east corner of the block, and south
of this a convent stood, with mighty reservoirs, sinking
to the rock of the deep valley beneath. The Hospital
was to the west, divided by a narrow lane with shops,
from church and convent. It also had its chapel, with
bells whose ringing was a cause of quarrel with the
canons opposite ; but of this famous Hospital we as yet
know nothing, hidden as it is beneath the mounds of
rubbish which are not cleared away.

Baldwin I had made the Templum Salomonis his
palace, but when the Burgundian knights were there

established, the Kings of Jerusalem fixed their abode
where now the Greek Patriarch resides, to the west of
the cathedral, and separated from it by the " Street of
the Patriarch," which ran north and south. This palace
appears to have extended over the vaulted street, so
that a window looked down into the church itself; a
garden inside its courtyard was adorned with orange
trees and pomegranates. It included many vaulted
rooms, and could with comfort contain a hundred
persons.*

Passing eastward, and leaving on the right two other
churches of St. Mary, the pilgrim gained the covered
street of St. Stephen, leading to the northern gate ; and
further yet to the north-east, entered the Ghetto or
Juiverie, where also churches stood—St. Mary Magdalen
and the small chapel of St. Peter, and—near the eastern
wall—St. Anne, with the covered pool, then called
Bethesda or Piscina Interior. On Sion, to the south-
west, the great Armenian church of St. James stood by
its cypress garden, and within, rich carpets covered the
floor, and the chapel of St. James was, perhaps, already
covered with tortoise-shell and mother-of-pearl, while in
the southern corridor, a fresco represented the fate of
sinners in the gaping jaws of hell. In this quarter there
were other Latin churches—St. Giles and St. James the
Less among them ; but it was a cause of bitter complaint
by Germans that as yet no street or hospice in the city
belonged to them. The German Knights' hospital, and
the German lake (outside the city to the west) were not

---

* *Felix Fabri*, Vol. I, Part II, p. 394 English translation.

yet in existence, but in Jerusalem there were at least fifteen Latin churches, within the walls, and nine on Olivet and near the city on the other sides, not counting older buildings of the Greeks, and Syrians, Armenians, Georgians, and Copts.

The great enclosure of the Temple itself was also changed. No longer a mosque it had become, first the royal palace, and then the Hospice of the Templars. These white-robed figures, with the long red cross upon their breasts, tonsured, but clad in mail beneath the robe, are brethren of the Temple—knights who have sworn to keep the Holy Land for Christendom, and to aid their brethren the canons of the Templum Domini. The Order, founded by Baldwin I in 1118 A.D., is destined to become the richest and the proudest of all the half-lay, half-religious, Orders. They have their gardens and houses round the courtyard : their horses are stabled in the great vaults to the east.* The long basilica of St. Mary, built by Justinian on the south wall, is called by them the Templum Salomonis ; and apses with carved pillars have been added to its east, while on the west a Norman building, lately finished, is the great refectory of the Order ; beneath are baths, and granaries, and stores for wood, and cisterns ; and to the north are courts and vestibules and gardens.

The central building in the great enclosure is Àbd el Melek's chapel of the Rock—eight-sided and domed standing on a higher platform, the model of future temple churches not only in Palestine, but in France and

* *Theodorich*, 1172 A.D., pp. 24, 31. English translation.

I

England also. The golden Kufic letters, in glass mosaic, with a rich blue ground, still attest the age and character of this most beautiful chapel, but were unread by the Latins though thought to refer to Omar.* The smaller Chapel of the Chain to the east—the model of the Templum Domini—was called by Franks the Chapel of St. James. The outer walls of the Templum† glowed with mosaics of glass, and long inscriptions in Latin ran beneath the upper arcade, invoking peace for ever on the Holy House. The vaulted dome of painted wood was covered with lead, and on its apex was the golden cross, hateful to Moslems. The Sacred Rock beneath was covered with marble, and on it stood an altar. The footprint of Muhammad was shown as a footprint of Christ. A beautiful screen of hammered iron work, with finials of the lilies of St. Joseph, ran between the pillars of the inner circle which supported the dome. There were small altars with curiously carved twisted pillars on the walls ; and frescoes, painted between the gates and windows, recalled the legends which grew up around the spot. Here Jacob was depicted laying his head on the stone of Bethel, which some ignorantly recognised in the Sacred Rock of the Templum, and angels walked upon the ladder above him. Here Simeon held the Holy Babe ; and Mary sat as a child with seven maidens reared in the Temple. To the Old and New Testament stories thus was added, one from Jerome's Latin Gospel of the Nativity of Mary, or from

* *William of Tyre*, I, and VIII 2.
† *John of Würzburg*, IV, 1160–70, A.D. pp., 12–20, English translation.

the Gospel of St. James—then held as part of Scripture.
The legend told how Mary span true purple and scarlet,
fed by the angels, and guarded by the priests ; how
Joseph was chosen from her suitors by ordeal of the rod
which bloomed with lilies, and from which a dove flew
forth. The faded relics of these frescoes still remain
beneath the marble flags with which Saladin covered
them later.

Such was Jerusalem when Fulk of Anjou died ; and
so it remained for more than forty years after his body
had been placed by that of Godfrey. His son, a gallant
boy as yet, succeeded him, and Milicent, the scheming
mother, was crowned beside him in the new cathedral ;
another reign of broken peace followed that of Fulk,
and lasted eighteen years. Edessa fell to Zanghi, and a
new power rose, threatening the future loss of Palestine
and the reunion of the Moslem world. The days of the
last pure blooded Frankish king were the best days of
the Latin rule.

The kings of Jerusalem seemed to have always
opened their reigns with some campaign, in which they
showed their prowess and won their spurs. The new
king—tall and brave like his ancestors—prepared,
though yet a boy of thirteen, to lead his army over
Jordan, attacking the plains of Bashan south of Damascus. Meanwhile, the Count of Edessa, Jocelyn II
de Courtenay, was besieging Aleppo, while Sultan
Zanghi with a large army advanced on Edessa, and
mined the walls, and slew the defenders on the 14th of
December, 1144 A.D. In September, 1146, he was

I 2

assassinated, and Jocelyn II, entering the city by the
water gate, strove to re-establish his power ; but Nûr ed
Dîn—" Light of the Faith,"—the Sultan of Aleppo and
Damascus, succeeded to the western dominions of his
father Zanghi,* and Jocelyn fled from Edessa to Samosata. Thus Edessa was lost for ever, and Jocelyn II,
taken captive at Aleppo about 1149, there died in a dungeon nine years later. He was not friendly with Raymond
of Antioch, and received no help from Jerusalem. The
first great bulwark of the kingdom was broken down,
and the alarm was felt not only in Palestine, but in
Europe also. The young king, Baldwin III, had raided
eastwards, by Edrei, to within sight of Bostra ; but the
Bashan plains are waterless, and the heat was great, and
Nûr ed Dîn was approaching. Thus, in the south as
well as in the north, the Christians experienced a check.
Envoys were sent to France, where Louis VII—a pious
king—had ruled for seven years, and was still only
thirty-five years of age. St. Bernard—then Abbot of
Clairvaux—preached a new Crusade in 1145, and
though already growing old,† and within two years of
his death, he traversed France, and prevailed even on
the Emperor Conrad III to take the Cross. In
England the civil wars of Stephen and Matilda made
it hopeless to expect assistance. In Germany a fanatic
monk named Rudolph proposed to murder all the Jews
which St. Bernard, to his lasting credit, opposed. Segur,
the wise minister of Louis, opposed the new adventure ;

---

* Zanghi's other son, Kutb ed Dîn, ruled Mesopotamia from Mosul.
† He was about fifty-four. In 1145 Pope Lucius II was killed in the
riots at Rome.

but at the Council of Bourges, the step was decided, and a bull of Eugenius III confirmed the measure. The forces of Germany gathered at Ratisbon, and Frederic Barbarossa, nephew of the German emperor, took the cross. The French forces also gathered at Metz, and Bernard wrote to the Patriarch of Jerusalem, counselling amity with the Templars in presence of the common danger.* The relics of John the Baptist had just been found in Samaria, and this no doubt encouraged the Christians, who were ordered to observe a penitential period of forty days.†

The new Crusaders met with troubles in Thrace, and massacred the Greeks at Adrianople. Manuel Comnenos, the grandson of Alexius, was Emperor at Byzantium : he did little to assist the Latins. The Germans crossed the straits to Cappadocia, passing Nicea in October of 1147 A.D. They marched in two divisions— one along the old route to Iconium, and the second further west towards Laodicea. Famine, thirst, and want of discipline prepared an easy victory for the Turks : the western division lost its road, and fell before the onslaught of the Moslems ; the eastern also perished near Iconium. Conrad escaped to Nicea, with Frederic who was destined to attempt the same adventure nearly half a century later. Meanwhile the French were struggling on along the coast route, by the Cayster and valley of the Meander, forcing a passage over this river, and reaching, after disastrous conflicts, the seaport of

* Epit. 175, see *Regesta*, No. 238.
† *Regesta*, No. 235.

Satalia, across the Cadmus range. King Louis embarked at this place to go by sea to Antioch, deserting all who could not gain a passage with him. The plague appeared among the French : the Greeks refused to help them : a small force of about 3,000 or 4,000 men strove to march on Tarsus, but perished on the way ; and thus with but a quarter of his army, the pious monarch, with his gay queen, Eleanor of Guienne, at length arrived in Antioch.

Raymond of Poitou, husband of the heiress Constance, feasted the French, and so enchanted Eleanor—destined hereafter herself, as wife of Henry II, to feel the pangs of jealousy for Rosamond Clifford—that she declared her wish to be divorced from Louis for his sake. She was therefore carried off by night, and the remnant of the French Crusade, diverted from its proper aim of regaining Edessa, was directed to uncertain objects further south. With Louis VII came also Renaud of Châtillon, whom Constance of Antioch chose as her second husband, and who was to be in future the chief cause of Christian misfortunes, through the injustice and violence of his acts against the Moslems. A great Council was held on June the 24th, 1148, by all the allies, at Acre.* Conrad and Frederic, Louis and Baldwin, the legate, the Masters of the Temple and the Hospital were present, with many counts and other magnates of Europe and Syria, including all the bishops, and Manasseh, cousin of Queen Milicent, constable of the kingdom. Europe was once more united

* *Regesta*, No. 250 ; *Will. Tyre*, XVII, 1.

by a common fear, for the loss of Edessa threatened not
only loss of Palestine, and of the commerce of the East
yearly growing more important, but it threatened the
possible invasion of Europe by the Turkish race, already
pushed westwards by the growing power of the Mongols
in Central Asia. Palestine and Byzantium had become
the frontier lands of the western civilised world, and
statesmanship, no less than religion or Papal policy,
was bent upon maintaining all that had been gained.
The decision reached, after this important Council, was
to march against Damascus; but the result of the
enterprise unfortunately weakened rather than aided
the Christian cause. The city was held by Eyûb, the
Kurdish Emir from Tekrit, already mentioned, who had
become Governor of Baalbek: his son destined to be
distinguished as the "honour of the faith"—*Salâh-ed-
Dîn*, was probably with him as a child of ten.

Damascus stood as now amid its gardens, with
minarets out-topping its poplars; beside the rushing
Barada, which flows into the plain from desert gorges
on the west; and under the shadow of the snow-
crowned Hermon. The Christian army marched by
Baniâs, south of the mountain, and reached the city in
the heat of summer. The first attack was on the west
close to the river, but here the mud-built garden walls
were held by bowmen, hidden among the trees and
hedges. The Templars are said to have counselled
attack upon the south and east, where no such outworks covered the ramparts; but this was found
impracticable, since the army was too far from water to

maintain its camp ; and rumours reached the princes of a
general levy of the Turkish armies under Nûr ed Dîn,
advancing from Aleppo and Mosul.   Having failed to
take Damascus by surprise the Franks retreated: the
French declared themselves betrayed, and all the blame
was laid upon the Templars,* whose ambition was
already suspected, and who, according to the vulgar
belief, had taken casks of gold from Eyûb to betray the
cause.   Louis VII remained a year in Palestine, and
left donations to the monastery of Milicent,† but no
further warlike attempts were made.

On his way home by sea King Louis was nearly
captured by the Greeks, but saved by a Norman fleet.
King Roger of Sicily, nephew of Robert Guiscard, was
then at the height of his power.   After having lost
Apulia for a time—on the fall of Anaclete the anti-Pope
—he had regained it by agreement with the new Pope,
and had successfully raided on the Moslems of Tripoli
in Africa.   He had renewed the old contest against the
Byzantines, and his fleet attacked Corfu and Athens in
1146.   Two years later it even threatened Constantinople.   Manuel Comnenos in revenge attacked southern
Italy in 1155, but his alliance with Venice was finally
broken, and a truce between Sicily and Byzantium
lasted for thirty years, from 1156 A.D.   The royal
Norman house in Sicily did not, however, retain its
conquests as long as did the descendants of Boemund in
Antioch.   The last male heir died in 1189, and Con-

* *John of Würzburg*, Ch. V, writing in 1160-70 A.D., p. 21, English
translation.
† *Regesta*, No. 296.

stance of Sicily married Henry VI, son of Frederic Barbarossa, who claimed for Germany, through her, the Italian kingdom of the Normans.

In the year 1149 A.D. Nûr ed Dîn arrived from Mosul, and many castles of the Prince of Antioch were taken, and Raymond of Poitou slain with several barons, on the 27th of June. Parthians, and Persians from Khorassan, came in the Sultan's army, and from Iconium came other Turkish bands raiding the country and carrying off the crops.* In the south there was also trouble : for Manasseh de Herges the Constable, cousin of Queen Milicent, rebelled, and seized on Mirabel, a fortress in the plains near Lydda, standing beside the reedy springs of Antipatris. He, however, surrendered when besieged by the king. The ambition of Milicent was one of the early causes of dissension in Syria, and during a great part of her lifetime she appears to have governed the south, King Baldwin III, remaining in Tyre and Acre for a while. He afterwards seized Nâblus and besieged his mother at Jerusalem in the Tower of David. The mediation of the Patriarch led to an agreement at last, and Milicent retired to Nâblus, where she died on the 11th September, 1161. Meanwhile the energies of the Latins were turned once more towards Ascalon, and in 1153 A.D., after seven months' siege, it fell.

The wisdom of King Fulk, in forming a base from which this city could be safely attacked, was now evident, and the increasing weakness of Egypt made its

---

* *Regesta*, No. 261, *Will. Tyre*, XVII, 9.

garrison at Ascalon an easy prey. New pilgrims came
to swell the Christian ranks in spring, but a fleet was also
needful, for the city stood upon low cliffs above the reef
which made a landing place—not indeed a port—for
Egyptian reinforcements. There was but little water in
the city, which depended on its wells and cisterns ; but
at the town of Mejdel to the north, supplies were avail-
able for the Christian army. The walls, which William
of Tyre compares to a bow with its string to the west,
were built of small stones set in hard cement, and overlooking lower outworks. Four gates existed on the
four sides of the city, and many towers (of which the
two largest flanked the western entry) strengthened
the ramparts. All round were sand dunes, but on the
north were vines and fruit trees and fertile valleys.

Neither the Venetians, the Genoese, nor the Pisans
aided the Latin army. The first two cities were intent on
quarrels at home between themselves : the Pisans were
negotiating for free passage to the East through Egypt,
and bound themselves by treaty, neither to attack the
Khalif nor to help the Franks to do so ; and in return
their prisoners were released, and town-halls granted
them in Cairo and Alexandria, with promises of safety
and free trade.* King Baldwin had, however, made
a league with Marseilles, in the autumn of 1152, and
promised to this city streets and churches in Acre
and Jerusalem, and part of Ramleh, with free trade in
Palestine.† The Marseilles fleet apparently was that

---

* *Regesta*, Nos. 288, 289.
† *Regesta*, No. 276.

which anchored in the roadstead of Ascalon, and warded off the Egyptian galleys. The siege was undertaken on 25th of January, with, as usual, wooden towers higher than the walls. The Moslems cast down wood soaked with oil to burn the towers; but the wind was in the east, the flames calcined the walls, and the fire spread into the city. The breach so formed was stormed by the Templars, who hoped to add the city to their other fortresses. The town seemed won for the moment, but the Moslems drove the Christians out, and barricaded the wall. The siege was well-nigh raised, but Ascalon surrendered to a second attack on the 12th of August, 1153 A.D.,* and the inhabitants, safely conducted through the desert, retired to Egypt, leaving the last Egyptian stronghold in the hands of Christendom, in the tenth year of Baldwin III.

Secure on the south, the king next turned to the north, and three years later advanced to help the Hospitallers in Baniâs, which Nûr ed Dîn was besieging. The siege was raised; but in retiring King Baldwin fell into an ambush south of the Huleh Lake, and fled to the castle of Safed, his scattered followers, including eighty-seven Templars, submitting to become the slaves of the Saracens. In revenge a wedding party of Saracens was surprised, and many were taken, no doubt for exchange of prisoners.† New Flemish forces under Theodoric, who married Baldwin's half sister Sibyl, arrived during this year to strengthen Antioch; and the frontier

---

* Boha ed Dîn says on 19th September, 1153.

† *Will. Tyre*, XVIII, 14, gives the date 18th June, 1157. The details are from a letter of Adrian IV. See *Regesta*, No. 326.

fortress of Harenc was retaken and Sheizur (or Cæsarea) on the Orontes. These successes led to fourteen years of peace in Palestine, marred only by a fruitless efforts to conquer Egypt. Alliance with the Greeks also resulted from the marriage, in September, 1159, of Baldwin III with Theodora, a girl of thirteen, niece of Manuel Comnenos the emperor ; and she brought a rich dowry to aid the kingdom. Thus the last five years of Baldwin's reign were passed in peace, which was not less secure when Milicent died five months before her son and when Renaud of Châtillon was taken prisoner by Manuel Comnenos at Malmistra, on the 23rd of November, 1160,* and afterwards by Nûr ed Dîn. During this period, however, the quarrels of the Church, and the jealousies of the fighting Orders, troubled the country. The Orders became a source of weakness rather than strength, being mutually envious, and independent also both of the king and of the Church, owing allegiance only to the Pope, and to the Masters. In 1155 the Knights Hospitallers openly opposed Foucher, the Patriarch of Jerusalem, refusing to pay tithes, and protecting all who lay under the ban of the Church, which had no power to lay an interdict upon the lands of the Order. They rang their chapel bells to the annoyance of Amaury, prior of the Holy Sepulchre, and demanded as their right alms and possessions which the Church retained.† The Patriarch went to Rome, but got little satisfaction ; another quarrel of the canons with the monks of Olivet,

* *William of Tyre*, XVIII, 29 ; *Regesta*, 383.
† *Regesta*, Nos. 316, 318.

as to the service on Ascension Sunday, was, however, set at rest during his absence.* The Church was divided against itself in Syria, and also quarrelled with the ruling princes. The quarrels of the patriarchs of Jerusalem and Antioch began even in the reign of King Fulk, when Innocent II intervened, placing the bishops of Acre, Tyre, Sidon, and Beirût under Jerusalem†. The villeins in villages belonging to the canons of the Holy Sepulchre were discontented with their masters, but got little pity from Milicent.‡ Raymond of Aquitaine, and Renaud of Châtillon, in Antioch, created further troubles with the Church; and through these discords the king found little help in dangerous times from either priests or military monks. Renaud of Châtillon had been harrying Cyprus, after King Louis left him in the East, and had married Constance, heiress of Antioch, after Raymond of Poitou was slain. This was the cause of quarrel with the Patriarch, to whom perhaps the restless and dangerous character of Renaud was better known than to the king. After seventeen years of captivity at Aleppo and after the death of Constance, Renaud married again, his second wife being widow of Humphrey of Toron, constable of the kingdom. Thus, about nine years before the fall of Jerusalem, he was perhaps the most powerful of the barons, for by this second marriage he became Seigneur of Kerak and Montreal, the great fief of the family of Philip of Nâblus, called Oultre Jourdan. The family held lands in Upper Galilee near Maron, Toron, and Tyre.

---

* *Regesta*, No. 323.
† *Regesta*, Nos. 171, 178.
‡ *Regesta*, Nos. 278, 307.

On the east they afterwards owned the country from the Zerka Valley to the Red Sea, including the castles of Ahamant, Petra, Montreal, and Kerak, and the deserts to Sinai, given by Baldwin III in exchange for the fiefs in Galilee and at Nâblus, in the last year but one of his reign.* In 1162 A.D., coming back from Antioch, the king died, on the 16th February, of fever in Beirût, being little over thirty years of age. He left the kingdom to his younger brother Amaury—less capable and less well educated than himself, and he left, in Reñaud of Châtillon, an ambitious and unscrupulous soldier, whose faithlessness in dealing with the Moslems was the prime reason of the coming downfall. He left two great Orders jealous of each other, and with interests at variance with those of their suzerain. He left a Church ill-governed, and hated by the peasantry of Palestine, and powerful parties of Greek and Syrian Christians, to whom the Latin clergy were equally detestable. He left also an army diminished in numbers and courage, and filled with half-caste natives, who had failed before the Turks. The vices and luxury of the second generation alike weakened the Christian state ; and all the elements of catastrophe had appeared under the rule of Milicent, his mother. While strong statesmanship, close union, valour and justice, were needed to save the kingdom, the successors of Baldwin III were weak and obstinate, and the Latins were divided by civil quarrels just at the time when Islam once again became united.

* *Regesta*, No. 366.

CHAPTER V.

THE LOSS OF THE KINGDOM.

WE have now considered sixty years of growth and prosperity, during which three generations of kings succeeded each other, and the walls of Jerusalem grew old and ruinous, because no enemy appeared before them. Then followed a quarter of a century of misfortune, and increasing weakness, ere a Moslem conqueror once more entered the Holy City, and the kingdom was lost; though Palestine remained, with diminished boundaries, a Christian possession for even a century more.

When in the winter of 1162 Baldwin III died in his youth, El Ádid, the last of the Fatimites, was Khalif in Egypt, having acceded two years earlier. He was the fifth successor of El Mustali, who had seen Jerusalem taken by Godfrey ; and each Khalif was weaker than his predecessor, while Egypt groaned under the tyranny of viziers, and the intrigues of rival emirs. There were now two parties in the country—that of Dargham the vizir, and that of his rival Shawer, whom he had defeated and banished. The latter fled to Damascus, and allied himself to the great Sunnee power of the North, pro-

posing to Nûr ed Dîn* an union of Islam, in which Egypt
should become a province under the Baghdad Khalif, of
which no doubt Shawer was to be the sultan.   The danger
was a great one, not only for Egypt, but for the Christian kingdom of Syria also : for the Turkish power was
steadily increasing, and the Atabek brothers ruled, from
Mosul and Damascus almost to the Afghan borders.
It was not unnatural, then, that Egypt and Palestine
should unite against the Sunnee Moslems : for Nûr ed
Dîn had chosen the bravest of his generals—Shirkoh the
Kurd, brother of Eyûb and uncle of Saladin—who
marched through Moab, past the Christian castles, crossing westwards over the deserts of Sinai.   At first Shawer
and Shirkoh were unsuccessful ; but Dargham, having
routed them, was slain by an arrow in the battle, and
the Syrian allies occupied Cairo on 8th May, 1163, but
refused apparently to give it over to Shawer.   The
latter, whose sole aim was self advancement, then sent
secretly to King Amaury asking his aid.   It was clearly
dangerous to Palestine that Nûr ed Dîn should have the
power to attack it on all sides by holding Egypt ; and
Amaury in 1163 besieged Bilbeis which Shirkoh held.
The town was not taken because, as Amaury explains in
a letter to Louis VII of France, a sudden rising of the
" River of Paradise " occurred, by which phrase the
autumn rising of the Nile was meant, the springs of
that great river being then thought to flow from some
mysterious Eden.†   Shirkoh, however, entered into treaty

* Nûr ed Dîn had entered Damascus in 1154 A.D.
† *Regesta*, No. 382.

with Amaury and with Shawer, and withdrew his forces in November to Damascus. The first attempt of Nûr ed Dîn thus failed in its real object, and he himself suffered a check in Northern Syria while attacking Tripoli. But in the following year the tide again set against the Christians, and Amaury sought alliance with the Greeks, and wrote for help to France, lest Antioch should become a Greek possession. In April he wrote again, to say that many of the Antioch castles had fallen ; and urgently besought immediate aid.* Nûr ed Dîn pressed on, and took the frontier fortress of Harenc ; and Boemund III of Antioch, and Raymond of Tripoli, grandson of Bertram, with Prince Thoros of Armenia, and the Greek Governor of Cilicia, were routed, and all the leaders save Thoros taken prisoners, while the Christian army fled. But for the sudden arrival in Syria of Thierry, Count of Flanders, with a few stout knights, the whole of Northern Syria might have fallen even then : for its leaders were captives, with Renaud of Châtillon, at Aleppo on the 12th of August, while in the July of the same year Amaury was invading Egypt aided by the Templars. A new and fatal policy was about to be followed by the king, and one which the Templars soon discountenanced. They wrote to Louis VII to tell how, while Bilbeis was captured in the south, the lands of Antioch were falling to the Turks and Arabs : and on the 17th of October Baniâs—the mighty frontier fortress guarding the Jordan springs— was betrayed to Nûr ed Dîn.† Amaury himself, at the

* *Regesta*, Nos. 394, 396. † *Regesta*, Nos. 403, 404, 405, 406, 407.

close of this year of mingled success and defeat, addressed a letter to the Master of the Hospital in Europe, and to all clergy and sons of the Church in the West, describing the miseries of the Holy Land, and telling Louis VII how Baniâs was lost.*

King Amaury was then not more than twenty-seven years of age, and was neither loved nor respected in his kingdom. He, like his ancestors, was tall and handsome, with well-formed features and brown hair; but the Armenian blood perhaps accounted for the corpulence which marred his figure, and the frank and generous manners of the former kings were not inherited by this unfortunate monarch, whose avarice betokened the Armenian, and whose gloomy reserve was not accompanied by austerity of life. Not only was he licentious in morals, but he was also suspected of religious scepticism, nor was the sanctity of treaties any reason in his sight against changing the usual policy of his predecessors, and fighting the same Egyptians whom he had just been aiding against Shirkoh.

In 1165 the Holy War was preached in Baghdad, by order of the Sunnee Khalif; and Shirkoh, with his nephew Saladin, was sent once more to Egypt in the autumn. Shawer the vizir sent in haste to Amaury, and the Christian army was despatched to Gaza to watch the Syrian advance. With such a road to traverse it was no light matter to carry any force from Damascus to the Delta, and in the present instance the Turks and Syrians met with burning winds, and men and camels

* *Regesta*, Nos. 410, 411.

perished in the deserts of Moab, or in the waterless and
rugged wilderness of Sinai. But Nûr ed Dîn was
not to be gainsaid ;* and once again in 1167 ambassadors from Egypt summoned Christian help, offering
a sum of some £140,000, which we must reckon to
have then been worth five times as much as now.
Amaury consented, and Hugh of Cæsarea, with Foucher,
a Templar, were sent as envoys, and even admitted
to an audience with the Khalif, insisting on the
treaty being ratified by a grasp of the naked hand,
which the religious head of the Shiàh faith was very
loth to grant. The splendour of his palace at Cairo,
his golden throne and rich robes, his mysterious retirement and many wives, the jewelled curtains which
concealed his audience hall, the Nubian guards, the
marble courts and cool fountains, the strange beasts and
gaudy birds in his pleasure grounds, and the abject
prostration of Shawer before his master, seem to have
much impressed the Frankish knights ; the Khalif—a
young and handsome man, but like his predecessors a
mere sacred figurehead in Egypt—was forced to tolerate
his Christian allies, and a treaty was made which, to the
Templars at least, if not to Amaury, was binding.†
When Shirkoh next advanced from Syria in the spring
of 1167, a battle was waged near Cairo, and Alexandria
was taken from the Syrian invaders. The second

* Boha ed Dîn does not mention the disaster in the Sinaitic desert, but
speaks of Shirkoh's leaving Damascus in January, 1167, and being in Egypt
till April. Nûr ed Dîn was attacking the Franks in Syria during this year,
and joined forces with his brother Kutb ed Dîn, near Hamath. In July-
August he assaulted the castle of Hunîn in Upper Galilee.
† *Will. Tyre,* XIX, 17, 18.

attempt of Nûr ed Din failed like the first, and the Christians returned once more to Palestine.

But Amaury was pondering another policy, and in the same year 1167 A.D., allied himself with the Greeks, marrying Maria, a grand-niece of Manuel Comnenos, who promised in return a fleet, by aid of which the Christian king proposed to conquer Egypt for himself. To this violation of the recent treaty the Templars were steadily opposed. Their views were sound in policy, as well as honourable. They held that while the forces of the Turks were yearly pressing harder upon Antioch, and Shirkoh and Saladin gathering all the Syrians and Arabs at Damascus, it was folly to attempt an enterprise which was always difficult, because of the intricacy of the irrigation channels in the Delta, protecting Cairo, and rendering attack peculiarly perilous ; and an attempt which would raise against the Christians, guilty of breaking faith with the Khalif, the whole mixed Shiàh population of Nubia, Palestine, and Egypt. But Amaury was obstinate, and covetous of the prize which seemed so ready to his hand, while Egypt was unable to resist invasion. At Tyre he met the Greek Emperor, and concerted his plan during the marriage festival.* It was an ill-omened alliance, and led to no results. Amaury had already been married, and by his first wife had a son, afterwards Baldwin IV, then but six years old, and a daughter Sibyl, children of Agnes, daughter of the younger Jocelyn of Edessa. Isabelle, his second daughter,

---

* Manuel Comnenos, one of the few Greek Emperors allied to Franks, had twice married, first, a sister-in-law of the Emperor Conrad, and secondly, a daughter of the Prince of Antioch.

was the child of Maria Comnena. The education of
Baldwin was given, three years later, to William, the
famous Archbishop of Tyre, who wrote the history on
which mainly we depend for knowledge of these later
days of trouble. The terrible discovery made by the
tutor saddened the later days of Amaury. His son was
a leper ; and the dread disease, which usually appears in
children only about the age of twelve at earliest, had
already withered the right arm which should have held
a sword, and gradually spread to both the hands and feet.

In the year 1168, Nûr ed Dîn was occupied with the
affairs of the Aleppo province, but prepared once more
to send Shirkoh (called Asad ed Dîn "the lion of the
faith") to Egypt in December. Saladin confessed in
later years that he went unwillingly with his uncle—
preferring perhaps the pleasures of Damascus. " Well
may we apply," says his friend Boha ed Dîn, " the words
of God—' Perchance ye may hate a thing that is for
your good.'" (Korân II, 213.)

On the 11th of October, 1168, King Amaury signed
a treaty with the Master of the Hospital, to aid him in
his unjust war on Egypt. It promised to the Order the
lands, both cultivated and untilled, round Bilbeis, to
the value of about £35,000 of annual rent, and £20,000
additional from ten Egyptian cities, including Cairo and
Damietta, Alexandria and Tanis. In every town they
had the right to build a hospice, and half the spoil of
conquered cities was to be for them. On these conditions the Order of St. John promised the aid of a
thousand knights, and of an equal number of Syrian

horsemen called Turkopoles,* under experienced leaders;
stipulating that if more could be sent, more money should
be given, but if fewer then less ; but that whenever the
king himself was not with the army all they could seize
by force should be for the Order.   " O blind cupidity of
men," says William of Tyre, " there was no foe for us in
the south : the Egyptians brought their merchandise,
and spent their gold in our country, and now all is
changed . . . the avarice of one man has done
this : his cupidity has clouded the clear bright sky
which the goodness of the Lord had given us."

The somewhat doubtful allies chosen by Amaury—
Greeks and Egyptians and Armenians—were forced
upon him however by the state of Europe.   His letters
to the West were many and urgent, but they met with
no response.   Louis VII was then fifty years of age. and
had just married his third wife, Alice of Champagne.
He was at war with Henry the Second of England.   The
Pope had fled from Italy to France, and the Italians
were distracted by quarrels of the Genoese and Venetians, the Guelphs and Ghibelines.   The Greeks were
unreliable, and failed to send their fleet, and though the
Hospitallers took Bilbeis by assault on November 3rd,
1168 A.D., Amaury hastily retreated to his kingdom on
hearing that Shirkoh was again advancing with a mighty
army.   In the end of the year the Syrians were in Cairo
and threw off the mask.   Saladin, now thirty years of
age, himself arrested the deceitful Shawer, and by order
of the Khalif he was beheaded, while Shirkoh succeeded

* *Regesta,* No. 452.

to the dignity of Vizir and of Sultan in Egypt, on the 18th January, 1169. He did not long live to enjoy his conquest, for on the 23rd March he died of some internal complaint, and Saladin was appointed his successor. The jealousy of Nûr ed Dîn was roused, and he resumed Shirkoh's fief of Emesa in Syria, and strove in the spring to seize Kerak, the key to Egypt and to Mecca, which Saladin had already been attacking from Egypt.

Manuel Comnenos, now roused too late, sent in 1170 a fleet of 150 galleys, with sixty transports and a dozen larger vessels to help his son-in-law. With these a final effort was made, and Damietta was besieged.* But Saladin held out boldly, and half the Christian army perished from famine or in battle before the walls, while all the fleet was lost. On the 21st of December a truce was signed, and Amaury left for Constantinople returning later to Jerusalem. Meanwhile a terrible earthquake ruined Antioch, and shook the walls of Latakia, Tripoli, Emesa, Hamath, and Aleppo. These various disasters brought upon the kingdom all the evils that the Templars had foreseen. King Amaury in vain had promised to the Pisans† all that they owned in Egypt, and in vain had sent ambassadors to Europe, including the Bishop of Acre and the Masters of the Temple and Hospital. They set out in 1169 and were wrecked at sea,‡ and in their stead William of Tyre was then despatched, not

---

* Boha ed Dîn speaks, however, of an attack by sea on Alexandria by the Franks in 1174.
† *Regesta*, No. 467.
‡ *Regesta*, No. 480.

only for aid, but to find a husband for the king's daughter—presumptive heiress of the kingdom, one able to defend the state should the unhappy leper heir be taken away.

The star of Saladin was rapidly rising to its culmination. He was already called Melek en Nâsr, "the Conquering King," and began from Egypt to raid upon the southern borders of the Latin Kingdom.

Whatever may have been the intentions of Nûr ed Dîn regarding his too successful general, he was unable to attack him, for his brother, the Atabek prince of Mosul, Kutb ed Dîn, died on the 6th September, 1170, and Nûr ed Dîn departed to the Tigris to settle the family affairs. He met with opposition, and was engaged fighting in Mesopotamia till 22nd January, 1171, when he made a treaty with his nephews, Seif ed Dîn Ghâzi, who governed Mosul, and 'Imad ed Dîn of Sinjar. It was not till May that Nûr ed Din got back to Aleppo.

The Egyptian Khalif El Adid died without an heir on 13th September, 1171, and Saladin being a strict adherent of the Sunnee sect called Shâfài, proclaimed the Khalif of Baghdad—El Mustadi—to be the one religious head of Islam, he himself remaining Sultan of Egypt.[*] The jealousy of Nûr ed Dîn was increased by such a policy, and he entered into alliance with one of the rival heirs of Thoros of Armenia. The Latins were driven for a while out of Armenia and Cilicia, and Nûr ed

---

[*] Jacques de Vitry accuses Saladin of killing the Khalif (p. 95, English translation).

Dîn took Arkah, Besni, and Marash in North Syria, and advanced on Kerak in Moab, where, however, Humphrey of Toron defeated him. On May 15th, 1174 A.D., he died at Damascus, the last of the Atabeks to rule in Damascus, leaving as successor Melek es Saleh, a boy of fourteen. King Amaury no sooner heard of this event than he set out to retake Baniâs, but the Damascus Moslems bought him off with gold and by surrender of prisoners ; and falling ill of dysentery he too died on the 11th of July, 1174. By this astonishing series of events following each other in quick succession, Saladin, who had already taken Akabah—the seaport of the Franks upon the coast of Arabia—and had plundered all the plains near Ascalon, found himself without a rival, and confronted only by a leper king thirteen years of age among the Franks, and by a boy, as Sultan of Syria. King Amaury's last letters in the summer of the year 1173 A.D. were written to Henry the Archbishop of Rheims, beseeching him to make a peace between the Kings of France and England, that both might come to help the Holy Land, and telling how the conquest of Antioch was threatened by the Moslems for the following Easter.* The death of Nûr ed Dîn prevented such attack, but in the following year (1175) Saladin married the widow of his former master, and Damascus, Emesa, and Hamath welcomed the hero of Islam as their ruler. Aleppo only remained to the Atabek princes, and Saladin was now the single authority from Hamath to

Cairo, over all the lands beyond the Jordan and Orontes, in Sinai, in Yemen,* and in the Delta.

Such was the outlook when the leper boy, Baldwin IV, ascended to the throne of Amaury, his father. Islam was united under a man of genius and experience, respected for his orthodoxy and strict observance of religious custom, brave and generous, just and courteous like a Christian knight, descended from the sturdy Kurdish stock, and in the flower of his strength—thirty-six years of age. And on the side of Christendom was a distracted Europe, and a cripple of fourteen ruling a seditious state, with Templars and Hospitallers jealous of each other, quarrelling with the Church, foreseeing clearly what was soon to come, and anxious rather to preserve their own broad lands in the shore plains, or far north in Syria and Asia Minor, than to prevent the loss of regions where the king and Church held all the towns, or to protect the Holy City from the Saracens. In 1170 internal dissensions had also arisen among the Hospitallers themselves. Gisbert, the Grand Master, was excommunicated, and Amaury, with some of the brethren in council, wrote to Pope Alexander III asking him to settle the dispute.† While Christendom was so distracted, the name of Saladin was mentioned in prayer in all the mosques of Western Asia, Arabia, and Egypt. The first concern of Raymond of Tripoli, elected regent to advise the leper King—a man brave and able but harassed by cares and dangers—was to make peace with

---

* Turân Shah, Saladin's brother, overcame the heretic Abd en Nebi Ibn Mahdi in Yemen in 1174.   Boha ed Dîn.

† *Regesta*, No. 480.

the new Sultan of the Saracens; and Saladin, not yet
ready for the conquest of Syria, agreed to make a truce
which lasted for three years.

Amid these troubles a new hope arose in a new policy
advocated by the Pope himself.* The possession of
Palestine was becoming more and more important to
the Papacy. Its church was the richest that owned
obedience to Rome. The capture of Jerusalem had
greatly increased the Papal power, and hopes were entertained that all the Eastern churches would be gathered
to the bosom of the Church of St. Peter. The demands
made on the Easterns were wisely moderate, and in
1180 A.D. the Maronites submitted, being allowed to
keep their married priests—for priestly celibacy indeed
was hardly yet fully established even in the West.
Great hopes were entertained that the Syrian Jacobites
would follow, and active measures were taken to convert
the Armenians. In 1170 A.D. a book on the " Procession
of the Holy Ghost " was sent to Antioch, and received a
year later.† During the next twenty years the Popes
all strove to convert the Armenians, and attained to some
success in the thirteenth century. But Alexander III,
who was Pope for the unusual space of twenty-two years
(dying in 1181 A.D.),‡ had even wider views; and sought
for allies against Saladin in countries ruled by Turks and
Mongols. The Sultans of Iconium belonged to the old
Seljuk family, and had not even their nationality in

---

* *Regesta*, Nos. 264, 544.
† *Regesta*, Nos. 480, 491.
‡ Under Lucius III (1181–1185) the Romans were again in violent
conflict with the Papal party.

common with the Kurdish master of Egypt and Syria.
They were shut in on. the west by Greeks, and on the
east by Armenians ; and the majority perhaps of their
subjects were Christian, while they themselves were
thought to be "philosophers," perhaps as belonging to
the philosophers of Islam, whose influence was wide, but
hateful to the Sunnee orthodoxy.   The Papal attempts,
by means of letters and missions, were unremitting, and
aimed at conversion of the Sultans of Iconium.   The race
was no longer purely Turkic ; and to our own times the
language of the Osmanlis testifies to the many centuries
of Persian, Arab, and Greek influence upon the stock in
Asia Minor.   As now but one word in ten in the
Osmanli vocabulary is really Turkish, so in the middle
ages these Sultans, intermarrying with Greek and
Armenian, Georgian, and Circassian wives, ruled provinces
in which perhaps only one in ten of their subjects was
a Turk.   Alexander III wrote to the Sultan of Iconium,
who had already it appears expressed some interest in
the Christian creed ; and two years after the triumph of
Saladin at Hattîn, Kilij Arslân of Iconium offered help
to Frederic Barbarossa.*   Yet he was secretly allied to
Saladin.

But Alexander III looked even further, and sent a
letter to Prester John, as King of India in the year 1177
A.D.†   The name of this ruler has become so mingled
with myths and legends that some detail of explanation
is required to show why Christians looked so far away

* *Regesta*, No. 544, Note and 686.
† *Regesta*, No. 544.

for allies who might draw off the energies of Saladin from the doomed Latin Kingdom. Already in 1145 A.D. the Syrian bishop of Gebal had written to Eugenius III about this mysterious Christian Tartar.* His information came perhaps from the Nestorians of Persia, or from the Venetian traders on the Oxus. He stated that Prester John had conquered the Medes and Persians, and was himself descended from one of the Magi who came to Bethlehem. According to the famous Syrian writer, Bar Hebræus, the country of Prester John, lying north-east of the Turks, had been converted in the eleventh century to the Christian faith. In 1150 A.D. a letter was shown in Europe, from Prester John to Manuel Comnenos and Frederic Barbarossa and every Christian Prince, which boasted of the power and riches of his empire.† To understand the facts which underlay these vague but flattering reports, on which the policy of popes and kings was founded for a century or more, we must turn to the history of Central Asia during the times of which we now are speaking.‡

The map of Ptolemy, about 150 A.D., shows in Kashgar above the Pamirs a people called the Khatæ. When in the seventh century the Nestorian priests from Persia reached Kashgar, the Khatæ or Khitai were still there, and had become yet more important. They tolerated the Eastern Christians, and in the eighth

---

* Yule's *Marco Polo*, I, p. 205.
† *Regesta*, 264.
‡ *Journal Royal Asiatic Society*, XIII, II. Do. North China Branch, X, pp. 76-108, XIX, Part II, Article 2. *Chinese Recorder*, Vol. VI and Vol. IX. Taylor, *Hist. of Alphabet*, Vol. I, p. 299.

century there were archbishops at Herat and Samarcand and even in China.   In the sixth century the
great wall of China was built to keep the Khitai out;
but by 916 A.D. the terrible weapon of Greek fire was
known among them, and their civilisation had so greatly
increased, by contact with the Indian Buddhists and
Persian Nestorians, that they began to be supreme in
Central Asia.   They had already an alphabet, and a
literature of many thousand volumes, including works
on medicine ; and they were skilful painters, and had
arts and knowledge then quite unknown to the Chinese.
In 1101 A.D. they founded the Liao dynasty, which
lasted till 1125 A.D. in China, when it was overthrown
by the Kin Tartars.   From the tenth to the twelfth
centuries their power increased ; and their ruler became
known as the *Gur Khan* or "universal monarch."   They
entered into close alliance with the Uigurs, and conquered Turkestan in 1128–9 A.D.   Even in the eleventh
century their rule extended south beyond the Oxus.
Their language shows them to have been of Turko-
Mongol race ; and, though they tolerated Christians
and Buddhists, they were not themselves converted,
and continued to believe in all the myths and superstitions of the Mongol animism.   Towards the close
of the twelfth century, Ung Khan was ruling the Kara
Khitai, or " Black Chitans," and was in truth a powerful
monarch who had defeated the Eastern Turks.   He is
said by Rubruquis to have been succeeded by a Nestorian priest, named John, but this is not a certain fact,
and probably his name of Ung was that which Christians

of the West converted into Yohan. His daughter married the son of Genghiz Khan—a Mongol from the Altai—but with this marriage the power of the Khitai passed away. The Altai Mongols fought and conquered them, and while the popes were hoping for their aid against the Turks, the centre of Asia was plunged in civil war, and the last remnants of the race of Prester John fled, early in the thirteenth century, to southern Siberia and to Manchuria. The tradition of a Christian king survived long after ; and its great influence on the history of later times we must consider again in speaking of the Tartars. But the settlement of the vexed Eastern question was brought about, not by such shadowy alliances, nor by the efforts of Louis VII, or of Guy of Lusignan, but by the wisdom and valour of the English king, Richard Lion Heart. Meanwhile, the fortunes of Saladin were ever growing brighter, and neither the Papal zeal, nor the efforts of the leper king, nor any danger from the Mongols on the east, were enough to frustrate his great design of freeing Syria for the Moslem, and so uniting Islam under his sway.

In 1174 A.D. Raymond of Tripoli was already free from his captivity, and regent of the kingdom. Three years later Renaud of Châtillon was ransomed, after seventeen years of prison, and in November,[*] having married his second wife, this "quondam Prince of Antioch," as he calls himself, was granting lands as Seigneur of Hebron, and of Montreal in Moab. The

[*] *Regesta*, No. 551..

dangerous province over Jordan which he boldly held,
cut off the road to Egypt and Mecca from the Syrians
of Damascus.   But the wisdom and moderation which
might have made this position valuable to the Christian
cause, were not to be expected of Renaud, whose
adventurous and hostile spirit, embittered by his long
captivity, led to the final ruin of the kingdom.

In order to understand the many expeditions of
Saladin, after he had been received in Damascus on
27th November, 1174, it is necessary to remember that
a successful attack on the Franks could not be made
while there was danger of an invasion by the Atabek
cousins of Melek es Saleh, from whom Saladin had
usurped the rule of nearly all Syria.   It must also be
remembered that communication with Egypt was very
difficult, while Kerak and Shobek (Montreal) were
occupied by the Christians.   On 26th January, 1175,
Saladin defeated Ezz ed Dîn, the younger of the
Atabek brothers ruling in Mesopotamia, near Hamath ;
and on the 22nd April, 1176, he defeated Seif ed Dîn
Ghâzi the elder brother, Prince of Mosul, who had come
himself to help his cousin Melek es Saleh.   This second
battle also occurred near Hamath, and immediately
after Saladin overran Northern Syria.   Membej fell on
15th May, Ezzaz on 24th June, Aleppo was approached,
but not taken, and while Saladin was obliged to revisit
Egypt in October, Melek es Saleh remained its prince.
His rule appears to have been unsuccessful, and revolts
had to be quelled at Harenc and other places.   He died
on 22nd November, 1181, leaving his diminished

possessions to his cousin Ezz ed Dîn, who had become ruler of Mosul on the death of Seif ed Dîn Ghâzi, his brother, on 29th June, 1180.

In 1177 A.D., when the truce with the Franks expired, Saladin was in the South, and marched his army northwards far past Ascalon, to where the Castle of Gezer defended the road from Jaffa to Jerusalem, the most southern of a group of fortresses, at Toron (Latrûn), Beit Nuba, Château Arnaud, and Mirabel, which stood at the foot of the mountains, north of Blanche Garde and Beit Jibrin. The terror of his coming caused the Latins to rebuild the crumbling walls of Jerusalem, which had so long been unneeded ; but victory declared itself for Baldwin IV, and the Egyptian army was pursued to the " Canebrake of Starlings,"* a marshy spot, which seems to have been near the site of Lachish, where the Moslems held a fortress in the plains. This repulse saved the kingdom for ten years, and Saladin never again advanced from Egypt. The frontier on the south was strong and easy to hold, for Ascalon was faithful, and King Amaury had built in 1149 A.D. a castle at Gaza, which was given to the Templars, who raised the beautiful Cathedral of St. John, which still attests their wealth and piety preserved as a Moslem mosque.†

The battle of Gezer was fought on the 25th of November, and gave great satisfaction to the Christians. A letter of Roger de Moulins, Master of the Hospital, announced the victory to Christendom.‡ But confidence

---

* *Itin. Ric. V*, ch. XLI. *Will. Tyre*, Vol. III, p. 353, French translation. Clermont Ganneau, *Recueil*, No. 8, pp. 350–391.
† *Will. Tyre*, XX, 20. ‡ *Regesta*, 264.

was not restored, and sales of land to the Military Orders became frequent and large in the years that followed. As early as 1158 a knight is found selling his property to pay his ransom from the Turks, and between 1164 and 1166 large properties were sold to the canons of the Holy Sepulchre and to the Hospital. A year after the victory of Gezer, Boemund III of Antioch gave to the son of Jocelyn II of Edessa, lands to the value of three thousand bezants, in fief; and many other documents attest the general mistrust in presence of the power of Saladin.* It is remarkable also that the lands acquired were mainly in the seaside plains, which Christians held for more than a century after Jerusalem fell.

Meanwhile, a husband able to defend the kingdom was sought for Sibyl, the elder sister of the unhappy leper king. William of Tyre had gone to France to find him, but the good archbishop was singularly unfortunate in his choice. He had returned during the lifetime of King Amaury, bringing with him Stephen, son of Thibaut, Count of Blois; but Stephen, after some months spent in scandalous licence in Jerusalem, returned to Europe. The choice then fell on William of Montferrat, related to the King of France, who came in 1178, and died three months after he reached the country, leaving Sibyl about to bear a child. A second husband was provided for her within a year in Guy of Lusignan; her child Baldwin being declared the heir of a kingdom which had as yet only twice descended from a father to a son.

* *Regesta*, Nos. 335, 409, 416, 420, 425, 426, 555.

The northern borders of the kingdom were now a source of anxious thought, for Baniâs was the key to Galilee. The Franks had striven to reconquer it, and early in the reign of Baldwin IV had raided into the lands of Damascus, and from Sidon up to Baalbek. In 1178 a fortress called Château Neuf was built in ten months' time, to guard the Jordan bridge south of the Hûleh Lake. It stood on rising ground—an oblong fort 420 feet by 200, defended on the east and south by the river, and by a ditch on north and west, and had four gates and four towers at its corners.* Humphrey of Toron, seneschal of the kingdom, was its builder, but four years later it was given to Jocelyn, brother of Queen Agnes and uncle of Baldwin IV, who was appointed seneschal after Humphrey's death, and granted many lands in Galilee, extending from Carmel to Maron, and from Acre to Jordan. At the same time the Castles of Hunin and Safed were strengthened, and the Knights Hospitallers bought lands in Galilee, even as far east as Tiberias, near which they built the Castle of Belvoir in 1182, while, before 1179, the Templars had erected the Castle of Belfort between Baniâs and Tyre. A tax, moreover, was imposed upon the kingdom generally—on money and on lands, on churchmen and laymen alike ; and in 1180 a new truce was made with Saladin.

About this time 'Ezz ed Dîn, Kilij Arslân, the Sultan of Iconium—who ruled from 1155 to 1192—was allied

---

* *Will. Tyre*, XXII, 22 ; *Memoirs of Survey W. Palestine*, Vol. I, p. 250 ; Rey, *Colonies Franques*, p. 478 ; *Regesta*, 587, 588, 608, 614.

to Saladin and joined him in 1178 in an attack on Kara Hissar in Armenia. His mediation with the Atabek princes of Mosul and Sinjar was accepted and peace signed with them by Saladin on 2nd October, 1180. In 1182, however, when Saladin failed in a raid on Beirût from Damascus he heard that the Atabeks were negotiating with the Franks against him. He marched at once over the Euphrates, taking Edessa, Rakkah, Nisiba, and Sarûj. Taking part with Imâd ed Dîn, the third of the Atabek brothers, against Ezz ed Dîn, who had occupied Aleppo but exchanged it for Sinjar, which his brother found that he preferred, after experience of the unruly Syrian emirs, Saladin succeeded in making peace once more in November at Mosul.

But Renaud of Châtillon was busy in the south, and broke the truce while Saladin was in the east.

Ailah, now Akabah, was the Christian port of the Red Sea, occupied by Baldwin I in 1116 A.D., and taken by Saladin in 1167. It lay east of the head of the gulf with palm groves near the shore, and steep mountains rising behind. A small fortress in the sea occupied what was called the Isle de Graye. The place was a station of the pilgrims on their way to Mecca. This town Renaud of Châtillon seized in 1182, and besieged the Moslems in the castle, which he failed to take. Ships were taken to pieces at Ascalon, and carried by the Bedouin over the Sinaitic desert, and launched again at Akabah. Five galleys and many smaller boats were so collected, and while two remained to aid the siege, the rest were sent to harry the Hejâz shores, and went even to Aden, burning all the Arab trading vessels, and carrying ruin amid their commerce. But Saladin was swift to make reprisals, and by his order all Christian pilgrims in Egypt, and all vessels wrecked on its coast were seized, and he caused ships to be carried on camels and rebuilt at Suez, manning them with Moorish sailors. On the 2nd March, 1183, the first of Renaud's galleys was captured by this fleet.[*]

Meanwhile, assisted by the Templars, and with an allied force of three hundred Bedouin, Renaud set out to march from his sea base at Haura on Medina, in the heat of summer. This city, sacred as the burial place of Muhammad, lay on the upper plains behind a mountain range a hundred miles inland. There was little water on the way, until the pools of the date gardens were reached. The land was bare and rocky, with dark desert ranges. The town was guarded by a castle, with walls and ditch, and watered by a subterranean aqueduct. Yet in this mad and useless enterprise Renaud persisted till within a day's march of Medina. Saladin, furious at an insult to the faith, sent the Emir Hishâm ed Dîn Lulu in pursuit. The ships at Haura were burnt, and the retreat of the Christians cut off. The Moslem force came up behind, and stormed the heights on which the Christians took refuge. The greater number were seized and carried in chains to Cairo, where fanatics were permitted to torture them to death, and two were reserved—as human sacrifices—

---

[*] Chronicles of Ernoul and Bernard the Treasurer, quoted by Rey, *Colonies Franques*, p. 156.

and taken to Mecca, where their throats were cut on the day of sacrifice in the Valley of Mena. Renaud himself escaped by land to Kerak with great difficulty, but Saladin never forgave the outrage and the breaking of the truce.

This defeat was not the only adverse event of the year to Christians. In the spring Saladin was returning to Syria, from Mosul, where by agreement with Imâd ed Dîn he became ruler of Aleppo on 11th June. He occupied Harenc on the Antioch frontier a fortnight later, and thus strengthened his position against the Latins. He reached Damascus once more on 24th August, and prepared to attack Lower Galilee.

A raid, beginning on 29th September, 1183, was then pushed across the Jordan up the Valley of Jezreel. The Christian forces camped not far from the small fort of Fûleh, south of Tabor, which was a post and depôt; and fed for several days on fish from the Fountain of Tubania, which flowed towards Beisân. The pool still bears its ancient name, and still is full of fish, but these so small that the hard living of the frontier guard may be imagined, although in numbers the supply is said to have been miraculous.* The exact site of this incident has remained thus far unknown to writers on the wars of Saladin. Failing to surprise the post, Saladin withdrew to Tabor and finally to Damascus.

Saladin had written as early as April, 1182, to Frederic Barbarossa acknowledging an envoy.† In

---

* *William of Tyre*, XXII, 27.   Boha ed Dîn.
† *Regesta*, 598.

1183 his brother, Seif ed Dîn, wrote to Pope Lucius III, to say that Saladin's empire stretched from Nineveh to Damascus, and warning him to force the Christians who obeyed him to keep the peace, if captives were expected to be ransomed. Saladin himself also addressed the Pope as to the captives, and claimed to reckon the exchange of prisoners according to rank, since, while he held at Cairo nobles of Christendom, the Christians, as he argued, had only captured peasants and low-born Moslems.* In October, 1183, he sat down for a while before the impregnable walls of Kerak, for Saladin's main object now became the defeat of Renaud and the opening of the trade route from Damascus to Mecca, and to Egypt, by the capture of Kerak and Montreal. On the 5th July, 1184, he again left Damascus, and reaching Heshbon found the Franks encamped at Wâdy Wâleh north of the great stronghold of Oultre Jourdan. Saladin came on to Mâin, and finally began the siege of Kerak on the 13th August. On the 4th September he, however, retired, and sending troops to make a sudden raid on Nâblus and Jenîn in central Palestine he was back at Damascus within ten days. And here the chronicler relates a story which casts a strong light on Saladin's chivalrous character, and on the manners of the age.† Humphrey, the step-son of Renaud of Châtillon, was just married to Isabelle, the half-sister of Sibyl and of Baldwin IV, and Renaud sent out to his enemy presents of wine and meat to celebrate the

---

* *Regesta*, 626, 635.
† Ernoul, quoted by Rey, *Colonies Franques*, p. 20.

wedding. Saladin received the gifts with thanks, and asked the messenger which tower of this gloomy desert fortress above the Dead Sea cliffs was that in which the bride and bridegroom were then living. Having been shown the tower he ordered that none in assaulting Kerak should shoot upon it or attack. Yet Renaud was himself the only Christian to whom Saladin refused his life at Hattîn.

While these incursions wasted the kingdom the leprosy of Baldwin IV grew more and more painfully advanced. The toes and fingers wasted off, the sight failed, and the king was unable to move. The general dissolution of society was evident in public manners. Templars and Hospitallers quarrelled and appealed to Rome.* The Patriarch led a life of open sin: drinking and dicing and vice disgraced both nobles and knights, and William of Tyre laid down his pen in disgust, unwilling further to record the annals of the fated kingdom. Guy of Lusignan, the new husband of Sibyl, was elected regent by the barons, but showed no energy and refused to obey the king. His character has been variously given, and some declare that he was brave and honest; but of his weakness and incompetence the history of his single year of rule seems to give evidence. He neither resisted Saladin in Galilee, nor aided Renaud at Kerak, but shut the gates of Ascalon, and refused to open them even when the helpless and dying Baldwin was carried down to claim admission. The regency was given, in 1184, to Raymond of Tripoli, and Guy disgraced.

* *Regesta,* 572.

Meanwhile, appeals to Europe were fruitless. The Pope was driven from Rome, the King of France promised no help. Henry II was troubled by the coming rebellion of Richard and John his sons, and though he promised and prepared to take the Cross the vow was unfulfilled. Manuel Comnenos, the ally of Amaury, and friend of the Franks, had died, and against his weak successors, accused of favouring the Latins, the people rose in 1185, and placed Isaac Angelus on the Byzantine throne. Two years earlier a terrible massacre of Franks had taken place in Byzantium, in which the Pope's legate was beheaded. The new emperor entered into treaty with Saladin, and opposed later the march of Frederic Barbarossa on Antioch. The Patriarch of Jerusalem, the Masters of the Temple and Hospital, were sent from Palestine as envoys to Europe; and in September, 1184, King Baldwin IV wrote to them, while on their way, to tell of the latest raids made in the summer by Saladin.* In the next year Heraclius the Patriarch wrote to Frederic Barbarossa the Emperor, beseeching instant help; but he, like others, was either unable to leave his dominions, or perhaps regarded the alarm as needless.† The kingdom was abandoned to its doom, and in the same year, 1185 A.D., Baldwin the Leper died, followed a year later by Baldwin V, the child of Sibyl‡: they were the last whose bones were laid beside those of Godfrey under Calvary; and to the danger from without was added

---

* *Regesta*, 638.
† *Regesta*, No. 647.
‡ He died at Acre in September, 1186.

that of civil war within, between the parties of the two
half-sisters Sibyl and Isabelle. The barons saw that
with the rightful heiress Guy, her husband, must be
taken for king. They called a Council at Nâblus,
refusing to be present at the coronation of Sibyl, which
the Patriarch and both the Masters of Temple and
Hospital supported. Renaud of Châtillon was busy
with intrigues, and the crown was offered to his step-son,
Humphrey of Toron, as husband of the younger sister.
But meanwhile, in September, 1186, Sibyl was crowned,
and gave a second crown to Guy. Humphrey was still
a youth, unwilling to take so desperate a task upon his
shoulders. He fled from Nâblus by night, and came to
offer his allegiance to the rightful queen.

A short respite due to Moslem dissensions occurred
about this time. The Mosul Atabeks broke the peace,
and while Saladin was at Kerak, in 1184, an army from
Mosul was defeated by his forces near Aleppo. He was,
however, obliged again to turn his steps to the east. On
the 15th April, 1185, he was on the Euphrates, and stayed
a month at Harran. Reaching Mosul in the hot summer
he fell ill in July and retreated, but negotiations at length
resulted in a final peace signed on the 3rd of March,
1186, and by the 23rd of May Saladin was once more in
Damascus, and free from any fear of attacks from Mosul.

The end had come; and Renaud was the cause.* He

* Boha ed Dîn says that there was a truce with Saladin at this time.
It appears to have been made by Raymond of Tripoli in 1186 without the
consent of King Guy, which may have served as Renaud's excuse. (See
William of Tyre, XXII, 28 ; *Jacques de Vitry*, p. 99, English translation.)

seized a caravan of Moslem pilgrims coming from Mecca and took them prisoners near Montreal; and in the March of 1187 A.D. Saladin went out again to beleaguer his castle. Meanwhile, the unwilling barons were called, in the winter time, to join King Guy at the Fountain of Sepphoris in Lower Galilee, and Raymond of Tripoli, who was then in his Castle of Tiberias, made peace with the king. A small advance guard of the Moslem hosts, under command of Melek el Afdal, son of Saladin, raided as far as Nazareth; and near Kefr Kenna on the 1st May met the Masters of the Templars and Hospitallers advancing from Fùleh in the plain south of Tabor with only a hundred and forty knights. Surprised or outnumbered the Templars were defeated; the Grand Master escaped; but Jacques de Maillé, the Marshal of the Order, was slain, with the Master of the Hospital. A holy war had been proclaimed by Saladin throughout his empire, and forces came from Egypt, from Arabia, and from Mesopotamia. When the defeat of the Templars was known to Saladin, he turned his course to join his son, and a great army soon reached Tiberias,* while Renaud also hastened to the king in Galilee. The Patriarch brought the Holy Cross, and fifty knights were sent from Antioch. After six months of preparation an

---

* The Survey explains much of the topography of Boha ed Dîn. Thus in 1183 Saladin marched from Damascus by *Fuàra* to *Wady Kuseir* on Fùleh : the former place at the head of the valley being twelve miles east of Jordan, and the valley eight miles north of Beisân. In 1187 he crossed Jordan by the Jisr es Sidd, immediately south of the Sea of Galilee; and in 1189 the Diarbekr troops fled by this same bridge to Fîk, east of the Sea of Galilee, by the plain of Kahwâneh immediately east of the bridge. The Arabic text reads *Fakhwâneh*, the second dot of the K having been written over the H, changing them to *F* and *Kh*.

army of fifty thousand men, including all the forces of
the fighting Orders, assembled round the Fountain of
Seffûrieh; and all the money sent in charge of the
Templars, by Henry II of England, in preparation for
his own appearance in Palestine, was given to Guy by
the Master to pay the troops. Two thousand knights in
all led with them eight thousand foot-men. The rest
were Turkopoles, light armed troops, and archers.

Saladin had, according to Boha ed Dîn, made a truce
with Antioch, so that by mutual consent the duel was
to be fought in the south, and the forces of Aleppo
were, like the knights of Antioch, set free to join their
respective chiefs. On the 26th of June the Moslem
army left Ashtaroth in Bashan, and marching south of
the Sea of Galilee over the Jordan bridge it ascended
north-west by Sennabris, leaving Belvoir to the left, and
reached Hattîn on the fourth day. Tiberias was sacked,
and only the castle held out for Raymond of Tripoli.

Seffûrieh was an unwalled town, on the low hills north-
west of Nazareth. The Church of St. Anne stood in its
midst, and a strong tower on the hill above overlooked
the brown cornfields, which stretched towards the
rugged mountain chain of Upper Galilee, and eastwards
to the plain over Tiberias—an open and waterless
plateau. The Fountain of Seffûrieh lay a mile towards
the south, in an open valley full of gardens, with a
stream which now drives eight mills, and which, therefore, was sufficient for so large an army as that which
gathered round King Guy. The surrounding lands also
were full of villages, and gave ample provisions.

Saladin's camp was ten miles to the east, upon the plateau near the little village of Hattîn. The place was surrounded with olives and fruit trees, and a good spring —copious and fresh—flowed, on the south-west, into the gorge of Wâdy Hammâm. There was plenty of water in the valleys beneath, and near Tiberias, where the wife of Raymond of Tripoli was shut up in her castle, upon the margin of the sacred lake. Just south of Hattîn rises the dark and rocky hillock, famous in history as the "Horns of Hattîn," six hundred feet above the low-lying village, and overlooking the western plain a hundred feet below. The highway from Acre led over this plain, and not a single spring or stream of any size existed between the camps. It was the hottest season of the year, and a long march for infantry divided the hosts of Christendom and Islam.

From the peak of Hattîn the watchman looked, towards the west, over a sunburnt plain, with long grey ridges dotted with bush to north and south. Behind him lay the Lake of Galilee seventeen hundred feet below, shut in with precipices mirrored in its shining waters, with Hermon on the north rising snow-streaked over the Valley of the Upper Jordan. Far east the craters of the Jaulân ridge stood up against the plains which stretch towards Damascus. The towers of Safed rose above the northern shores of the lake, and to the south the black walls and ditches of Belvoir frowned upon the rolling plateau. Defeat in such a position meant disaster to the Moslem forces, hurled down the slopes and driven into the lake ; but in order to attack,

the Christian army must cross the waterless plain, and
after a long march would find the enemy covering all
the springs and streams that flow into the lake.

When we remember that the Franks possessed two
strong outposts, at Fûleh and at Belvoir; that an advance down the Valley of Jezreel to Beisân could have
been made without any difficulty as regards plentiful
supply of water, and that Saladin's position was also
strategically most dangerous, being at an angle to his
line of retreat, it appears strange to a soldier that part,
at least, of the Christian army was not despatched to
attack the Jordan bridges, and to cut off the Moslem
retreat, which could then only have been accomplished
by the northern bridge guarded by the fortress of
Château Neuf. A general like Godfrey would not have
failed to take so evident a precaution, but probably the
Franks were afraid of the summer heat in the Jordan
valley.

A Council was called by King Guy, upon the night of
the 1st of July, 1187, at Seffûrieh, in order to decide the
fatal question whether a march should now be made
to raise the siege of Tiberias, or whether to await the
Moslem onslaught. Raymond of Tripoli was most
concerned of all, because his wife and children were
in danger; but his advice was sound and soldierly.
" Between this place and Tiberias," he said, " there is no
water. We shall all die of thirst before we get there."
But the Templars were burning with shame and anger
for their recent defeat, and the Master of the Temple
denounced his counsel as shameful to the army. The

decision taken was in accordance with the better wisdom of Raymond; but in the night the Master came to King Guy's bed, and bade him strike his tents and march on Hattîn. The weak king yielded,* and the barons had but just lain down when suddenly the trumpets blew, and in the darkness of the dawn the army set forth in silence to its fate. It was a Friday morning, the sacred day of Moslems,† the 23rd of Rabiâ eth Thani, or 2nd of July.

The sun in early hours, and in a treeless plain, is more terrible when its rays strike level at the face than even in midday when the breeze begins to blow. All that long morning the Christians marched, their heavy mail heated by the July rays, without water, without shade, without daring to halt for food. Raymond of Tripoli led the first division, and in the centre the bishops of Acre and Lydda bore the wood of the True Cross. The Templars came in rear. The light armed Turks and Arabs hovered on the flanks, and harassed the army with their arrows. They fired the sun-scorched grass and stubble, and long tracks of flame swept across the plain, and smoke obscured the way, and parched the throats of the Christians. In the afternoon they reached the village of Lûbieh, standing on a limestone ridge, with a few olives and fig trees, but without a spring, and watered only from cisterns which perhaps were dry.

---

* Gerard de Ridford, the Grand Master, had been chosen in 1185, and had supported the king at his coronation.

† Many of Saladin's victories occurred on Friday, a day he chose because the dervishes were then praying for his success in all the mosques. Jacques de Vitry makes the defeat occur on 4th July (Feast of the Translation of St. Martin), not on 3rd. See p. 101, English translation.

Nine miles of road they had traversed, and Hattin still lay two miles further to the north-east. Furious assaults continued to be made upon them, and utterly exhausted they halted for the night. They passed that night under arms, with smoke and fire around them, and saw at dawn the barren plain before them, and the enemy holding the springs. Many deserted and went out to beg for water from their foes, and one of these is said to have brought the news of the distress they suffered to Saladin. "Fall on them," he said; "they cannot help themselves: they are dead already."

The battle began at dawn, and the old Turkish tactics were repeated. Wherever the knights charged down, the horsemen fled, and turned upon them when disordered. Templars, Hospitallers, and bowmen fought on with desperate courage, but many of the foot-men broke their ranks, and cast away their arms, fainting with thirst and heat. The Moslem forces fell upon them, and half the army was slain, and half was taken captive. The leaders, with only an hundred and fifty knights, gathered on the Horns of Hattin to protect the Cross, and strove to rally the flying army; but the arrows fell thick upon them, and the knights of Raymond of Tripoli raised the cry of " Sauve qui peut ! " and with his few followers, and Balian of Ibelin, he cut his way through the Turks, and brought the only remnant of the great army safe to Tyre. And so at length there were none left to fight, and the survivors of the little group on Hattin surrendered to Saladin. Among them were King Guy and Amaury his brother,* Odo, seigneur of Gebal, Humphrey of Toron, Renaud of Châtillon, the Masters of the Temple and the Hospital, the Bishop of Lydda, who had lost the Holy Cross.

Saladin was sitting by the tent, which was being hastily pitched, and one by one the captive princes were brought before him. King Guy received a cup of iced sherbet, and gave it to Renaud of Châtillon. "It is thou, not I, who hast given him to drink," said Saladin, and all men knew that Renaud's fate was sealed. What Moslem could forget the march on Medinah, the capture of the Mecca pilgrims, the broken truce? To all but Renaud food was given, and when refreshed they were brought again to rest in the tent. Then, turning on the arch enemy of Islam, Saladin reproached him with his cruelty, his insolence, his broken pledges, and offered to him the choice of infidels—the Korân or the sword. But Renaud would not even then renounce his Christian faith, and Saladin rose, and the sharp scimitar clove Renaud's shoulder, and his head was laid before his conqueror's feet in sight of all the princes. Two hundred knights of the Temple and Hospital—all that were taken—also were beheaded, as being priests of Christendom; but the king and Humphrey, with the other nobles, were treated with courtesy, and taken prisoners

---

* Boha ed Dîn calls King Guy Geoffrey, and his brother Guy. Ibn el Athîr calls the brother Geoffrey. Ernoul, and Raoul Coggeshale (who was present at the battle), speak of the brother being captured, and Ernoul calls him Amaury, constable of Jerusalem. Jacques de Vitry, who mentions both Geoffrey and Amaury, speaks of the former as with King Guy at Acre in 1189 (pp. 107, 117, English translation).

to Damascus.*   The Castle of Tiberias surrendered the
following day, and Raymond's wife departed to join her
husband at Tyre.   The fragments of the Cross—en-
cased in gold and adorned with precious stones—were
also brought to Saladin, and held, like the princes, to
ransom.

Such was the fatal battle of Hattin, in which the Latin
Kingdom of Jerusalem was lost.   The cry of treachery
was raised as soon as the astounding news was sent
to Europe—treachery of the Templars in advising the
march, treachery of Raymond in counselling a halt at
Lubieh, and in leaving the field.   But the latter did
good service afterwards at Tyre, and the Templars, after
all, were only too eager to fight.   A great mistake had
been made, and the blame lay equally on King and
Council ; but that any among the leaders meant to sell
the victory to Saladin is most unlikely.   Many another
battle has so been lost, when the defenders fought on
their own ground, against a wearied and disorganised
assailant.

Six months of the year remained in which to push
yet further the victory, and to take Jerusalem before the
news could bring a new Crusade from Europe.   Letters
were speeding to the West, from the princes and the
barons, from the Templars and Hospitallers, from Raymond of Tripoli, and Conrad of Montferrat, and Boemund III of Antioch, to the Pisans promising new
concessions, to Pope Urban III, to Frederic Barbarossa,
to Henry II of England, to Philip II of France, and

* Boha ed Din.

even to Bela of Hungary. They told of defeat and loss
of cities, but that Tyre and Tripoli and Antioch still
held out, and many other castles.* The news aroused
the whole of Europe. The Pope† made peace between
the Genoese and Pisans, and Frederic wrote to Saladin
to say that he was coming. Not a moment was to be
lost, and the series of military movements that followed
was astonishing for rapid execution. Acre opened its
gates within five days of the victory. In three weeks'
time the strong castle of Toron, in Upper Galilee, surrendered to Saladin. The Egyptian army occupied Jaffa
and Mejdel Yaba. Haifa, Cæsarea, and Arsûf, Nazareth,
Sebastieh, and Nâblus, submitted to detachments sent
against them. The forts south of Seffûrieh (which was
found deserted) were occupied, including Fûleh and
Debûrieh, Lejjûn, and Beisân. From Toron Saladin
marched to Sidon and took it, after subduing Sarafend.
Within a month the walls of Beirût were mined, and it
capitulated on the 8th of August. Gebal was given up
to a Moslem force a week later, as ransom for Odo its
seigneur; and Humphrey of Toron was given to his
mother, in exchange for Kerak and Shobek, where, however, the garrisons refused to carry out her compact.
Saladin next marched south, taking Ramleh, Yebnah,
and Darum south of Gaza, and besieging Ascalon,
which refused to open its gates till, after fourteen days,
King Guy himself gave the command to the defenders

---

* *Regesta*, Nos. 658–670.
† Matters were complicated by the death of Pope Urban III October
11th, 1187; Gregory VIII died December 17th of the same year; Clement
III died March 27th, 1191.

and on the 6th of September it passed again into the hands of Moslems.* Meanwhile Gaza, Beit Jibrîn, and Latrùn fell before detachments of the army of Islam.

On the 20th of September Saladin appeared before the west gate of Jerusalem, and swore to take the city by assault; he fixed his camp on the north at the east angle of the wall. Balian of Ibelin, who had escaped with Raymond, had gone there under safe conduct to fetch his wife, but yielded to the prayers of some twenty thousand Christians, left without a leader, and who had fled from all the country round; and so he stayed to hold the city. He made fifty knights—for all the men of war had gone to Hattîn—and paid them with treasure of the Hospital, and with the silver stripped from the Holy Sepulchre. Saladin offered a truce, and even to pay for entry to the city, but Balian refused. The walls were mined: the countermines of the Christians failed; and on the following day a breach was made and occupied. But the assailants were driven back, and an agreement for capitulation was signed on the 2nd of October. The ransom was fixed at £10 for each man, and £3 for every woman and child, and 30s. for the poor; but this was afterwards halved, and many were set free by Seif ed Dîn, or given to Balian, or set at liberty by Saladin. Queen Sibyl and her sister were allowed to leave unransomed, and all the exiles were conducted safely to Tripoli, where, however, Raymond refused to add them to the numbers he must feed in case of siege. There was no massacre, no plundering, no

* Boha ed Dîn.

violence. The entry of Saladin was like that of Omar, rather than that of Godfrey.

On the 1st of October the Moslems entered the Holy City, and on the Friday following a sermon was preached in the Temple enclosure before Saladin, and the Haram was purified and became again a mosque. The great gold cross was dragged from off the roof of the Dome of the Rock : the walls which the Templars had built before its *mihrabs*, or ancient Moslem prayer niches, were taken down. The images and altars were removed : the carved faces on the pillar capitals, and the crosses, were hammered out. The pictures on the walls were defaced or covered over. The whole building was washed and sprinkled with rose water ; and carpets were laid, and lamps hung up, and a beautiful wooden pulpit—still remaining—was sent from Damascus* ; and two years later the woodwork of the Dome of the Rock was repainted, and the proud titles of Yusef, son of Eyûb, Salâh-ed-dîn, were written round it. Thus soberly and mercifully the greatest of the Moslems reaped the fruits of his victory.

The reconquest of Jerusalem on the very night when the Prophet was believed to have ascended thence to heaven sent a thrill of joy through Islam. Dervishes and Ulema hastened to visit the second holy city of the Faith so long closed to them by the Christians. All such learned and pious men Saladin received with

---

* This *mimbâr* bears the date 1168, with the names of Nûr-ed-Dîn and his son Melek es Sâleh, and was made, as it records, by Hamed ben Thafir of Aleppo.

honour, giving them costly gifts, and establishing them
in the ancient Haram of the first Syrian Khalifs.

Meanwhile, the army of Islam gathered against Tyre,
where Conrad of Montferrat was holding out, having
escaped from Acre, whither he had come by sea, not
knowing of the victory at Hattîn. On the 30th of
December the first turn in the tide of success was
witnessed by the conqueror at Tyre, for Saladin's fleet
was utterly destroyed by Christian ships off the harbour ;
and winter coming on the siege was raised four days
later. Hunin, one of the chief fortresses of Upper Galilee,
had fallen on 26th December, and early next year the
Moslem army, which had suffered much from cold and
snow, appeared before Belvoir, south-west of Tiberias.
It was, however, found too strong to be taken, and the
siege was raised on the 12th March, 1188. On the 10th
of May the untiring Sultan was again in the field, to
join new forces coming from the east. He left Damascus,
and by Baalbek and Lebweh made forced marches
without baggage, taking Latakia and Gabala, Saone and
other places further north ; but finding Antioch strong
and well prepared, he granted a truce to its defenders
for seven months.* Leaving his northern army, and
joined by his brother, who had just succeeded in taking
Kerak in October, Saladin next besieged the Hospitallers'
fortress of Safed in Upper Galilee, which was surren-

---

* Boha ed Dîn gives the following dates :—Tortosa stormed 3rd July,
1188 ; Gabala, 16th ; Latakia, 22nd ; Saone, 29th ; Bekas (on the Orontes),
5th August ; Shoghr, 12th ; Sermanaya, 19th ; Berzieh, 23rd ; Durbessac,
16th September ; Baghras, near Antioch, 26th. Margat (Merkeb), the
castle of the Hospitallers, escaped (Abu el Feda, ch. 29).

dered on the 6th December. Belvoir, south of Tiberias, held out till 5th January, 1189 A.D.; Shobek (Montreal) resisted till May of the same year, and Belfort on the mountains north-west of Baniâs, negotiated for a twelve-month, and only yielded on 3rd May, 1190.* Thus, in less than three years of rapid movement, the whole of Palestine and of Syria, which had been won in sixty years, fell before Saladin; and only Tyre, and Tripoli, and Antioch remained in Christian hands. When we remember that Saladin was fifty years old at the time of the battle of Hattîn, and had been actively employed for twenty years; that he had been very ill in Harran in 1185, and suffered from exposure during the winter campaigns, we cannot but marvel at his energy. His dominions in Syria stretched five hundred miles north and south; and from Aleppo to Mosul was a distance of three hundred and fifty miles. Yet we find him constantly traversing his dominions by bad roads, on horseback, in heat and cold, east wind or mud, taking but a few days' rest in Damascus or Aleppo, and always present at the important point, whether at Mosul or Kerak, Cairo or Tyre. We can hardly wonder that he died six years after the conquest of Jerusalem worn out by care and hardship. His last success at Belfort marks

---

* The Lord of Belfort diplomatised and gained much time, professing to be willing to surrender. He thus kept Saladin employed, and relieved the pressure on Tyre, and assisted the landing of forces at Acre ; but he was arrested on 22nd July, 1189, and taken to Baniâs. The defenders then refused to carry out his agreement for surrender. Belfort was a Templar castle, and this châtelain is said to have been a very able man, who could speak Arabic and had studied Moslem books. He discussed questions of religion with the besiegers " with great moderation and courtesy."—Boha ed Dîn.

the end of the first age of Latin rule in Syria, and the culmination of his power in the East, just ninety years after Godfrey's death.　The story of the thirteenth century which follows belongs to another order of events. The third Crusade was being already prepared, and its results settled the Eastern question for a hundred years.

CHAPTER VI.

THE FRANK LIFE IN PALESTINE.

FROM the preceding account it will be seen that the Latins in Syria enjoyed, for nearly a century, an amount of peace and prosperity greater than that of most European lands during the same period, and that often for many years they were untroubled by war, while for the first sixty their contests were all on the boundaries of the kingdom, which were ever growing wider and stronger. We may therefore now consider the daily life that they led in the East ; and afterwards the condition of their native subjects, Christian or Moslem. The picture so presented also, in part, applies to the conditions of the thirteenth century, after the Eastern question had been settled by agreement between King Richard and Saladin. In two main features there was a difference between the two periods—namely, in the ownership and organisation of the country, and in the increased trade, which made the later merchant population more important. As regards the nobles and the lower classes the habits of life remained but little changed, excepting in regard to increased education, and better understanding of the East.

The organisation of the kingdom, with its great fiefs of Tripoli, Antioch, and Edessa ; its four chief baronies of Jaffa, Hebron, Galilee, and Montreal; and its lesser seigneuries of Darum, Arsûf, Caymont, Cæsarea, Beisân, Sidon, Beirût, Toron, Maron, Suethe, St. George, and Haifa, has been already described,* with the boundaries dividing these from the lands of Damascus and Aleppo, owned by Turkish sultans.   The same feudal organisation which bound the provinces to the Royal Domain also regulated the holdings of the knights, in the subordinate divisions of the country, and in part controlled the trading communes in the seaport cities, save in so far as self-government was granted, by their charters to the Genoese and Pisans, Venetians, Marseilleise, and merchants of Amalfi.

Each of the greater vassals had a court with officers like those of the king—a constable, a marshal, a baillie (or treasurer), a seneschal, a grand butler, and a chancellor. Each prince had his chamberlain, each castle its châtelain.   The great Orders also had their various officers under the Grand Masters ; and under the Viscount or president of the Court of Burgesses were officials with native titles, and dragomans or interpreters.   The trading communities had their consuls responsible to the home authorities ; and the jurisdiction of the Church was organised under the Latin patriarchs of Antioch and

* Jacques de . Vitry (p. 26, English translation) speaks of Jerusalem, Acre, and Tyre as directly under the king, and enumerates the chief vassals as including the Count of Tripoli, the lords of Beirût, Sidon, Haifa, and Cæsarea, the Prince of Galilee and Tiberias, the Count of Jaffa and Ascalon, the Lord of Montreal (beyond Jordan), and the lords of Arsûf and Ibelin.

Jerusalem. The smaller fiefs in towns and villages owed to the barons military service according to their size and value ; and rendered to their owners certain shares of produce, and a certain number of horses and mules. The land was divided into carucates, which might be separately sold ; and by their number the values were assessed.* Thus John of Margat's fief was valued at two hundred bezants and fifty measures of wheat, twenty of barley, ten of lentils, and fifty of oil. He furnished four horses in time of need. Eudes of Seleucia owed two hundred bezants, fifty measures of wheat, one hundred of barley, five of lentils, and fifty of oil, also providing four horses. John of Arsûf was valued at five hundred bezants, bringing the same number of horses ; and John of Beit Jibrîn at three hundred and fifty bezants, and the produce of two carucates, for the same service. Three pack animals were equal to two horses ; and smaller owners, not being knights, provided each his beast when following his lord. The seigneur in return provided sustenance for his knights, and through them for their followers, in a degree which was to the less wealthy seigneurs often a terrible burden : his own income was derived from customs and rents, but these left not less than half the produce of the soil in the hands of the Moslem peasants. The duties as well as the rights of property were fully understood by these great seigneurs, living on their lands amid their people, defending and guiding them in times of war, doing

* *Codex Diplom.*, I, p. 171, quoted by Rey, *Colonies Franques*, p. 24. The bezant was from about seven to eight shillings.

justice in times of peace, and helping the poor and unfortunate in times of famine, earthquake, or locust visita-
tions.   In States that were small and thinly peopled, in
days of war and ignorance, while trades and profes-
sions were yet in their infancy, the feudal system was a
blessing to the people, holding them together with a
strong hand, under experienced rulers trained from
childhood to their duties.   Tyranny, in Syria at least,
was checked by laws which were common to every
province : liberty was protected by courts and juries ;
and public opinion demanded from the seigneur a
generosity and justice, a courtesy and kindness, which
were part of the religion of a gentle born knight, whose
fair name was the patent of his rank.   No doubt this
character for upright dealing was lost in the last years
of social dissolution ; but under kings like Godfrey and
his brother, Baldwin du Bourg, and Fulk of Anjou, the
example set from above seems very generally to have
been followed ; and most of the barons and seigneurs
were respected for their courage and firmness, and loved
for their justice and kind courtesy.   Some of the deeds
by which the fiefs were held* describe the boundaries
with completeness, running from some fixed point—
a tree, a cave, a rock marked with crosses—and they
stipulate that the holder shall himself appear " whenever
the king orders out the army."   Some fiefs only owed
a single knight out of a village.   In the agreements
with communes it was stipulated that murder and
homicide, treason and theft, were cases only to be judged

* *Regesta*, Nos. 341, 499, 517, 680.

by the king or by his courts. The levying of forces, and equality of law, were thus made equally simple, through a self-acting system of tenure. Joynville informed St. Louis that the maintenance of a single knight, with those who followed with him to the war, amounted to four hundred livres for six months, with double that sum for his own equipment with horses and armour, and to keep "a table for my knights."[*]

The population of the country was very much mingled, including elements from many parts of Europe and Asia. In the middle period it included[†] Latins and Germans, Hungarians, Scots, Navarrese, Bretons, English, Franks, Ruthenians, Bohemians, Greeks, Bulgarians, Georgians, Armenians, Syrians, Nestorians from Persia, Indians, Egyptians, Copts, Maronites, and people of the Delta. The ruling race was Norman, Italian, Frank, and Provençal, with knights from Lorraine and Auvergne, Burgundy and France. The Germans were less numerous, most of them having returned after the first Crusade. The English were few, though Queen Theodora gave a house to an Englishman in Jerusalem as early as 1161 A.D. In the next century poor English pilgrims became so numerous as to need a special home of refuge, in the "English Street" of Acre[‡]; but we hear little of those Saxons who came with Edgar the Atheling. In the second generation intermarriage with natives began to be common, and even from the first the Norman princes took Armenian wives.

---

[*] Joynville in Bohn's *Chronicles of the Crusades*, p. 468.
[†] *John of Würzburg*, ch. xiii and xxviii. English translation, p. 41 and p. 69.   [‡] *Regesta*, Nos. 367, 1216.

The native language of Palestine was an Arabic dialect of Aramean character ; and Syriac—the tongue of native Christians some centuries earlier—was still spoken in the North.   Turkish was a foreign speech, little known ; but Greek, which had for a thousand years been the official and commercial tongue of Western Asia, was also commonly spoken by the townsmen. The language of Law and of the Church among the Franks was mediæval Latin, full of words taken from the Italian, the French, and the German tongues.   In time also many Arabic words were incorporated, and others that were Greek, or that came from the Greek through an Arab medium.*   A curious instance is the word *fondacum* for a town hall, derived from the Arabic *funduk*, which was but a corruption of the Greek *Pandokeion*, " an inn."   The names of weights and measures and coins used by the natives were in like manner Greek in origin, but adopted under their Arabic forms by the Latins.   The Latins called a fowl market *soqueddik*, from the Arab *Sûk ed Dîk*, "market of the cock" ; and many similar instances might be given, out of a vocabulary of some two hundred spurious terms, occurring in chronicles, letters, and deeds of the age, which mark the peculiar character of Crusaders' Latin.

The common tongue of the knights and nobles was, however, the ancient Norman-French, something of which may still be heard spoken in Guernsey.   It was a vigorous and terse idiom, preserved to us in some of the chronicles and pilgrim diaries, in the *Chanson du*

* See Röhricht's Glossarium in the *Regesta*, pp. 513-516.

Voyage de Charlemagne (about 1075 A.D.), and in similar lays and gestes. Many Arabic words found their way into the speech of the ruling race, converted into strange shapes by Norman tongues. But Arabic itself was gradually acquired by the more polished seigneurs, and the names of villages and castles are often Norman translations of the native titles. It is remarkable to note that the speech of the conquerors has left no impression on the language of those whom they ruled so long. The only Crusaders whose memory still lingers in Palestine are Raymond of St. Gilles (*Sinjil*), Baldwin (*Bardawil*), and King Richard Lion Heart (*Melek Rik*): the few traces of the Lingua Franca, or trading patois, which survive, are found in Italian words, taken perhaps much later than the twelfth century from the merchants of the coast. Greek, Persian, and Turkish have tinged the speech of the modern peasantry far more than Norman French, or Latin, though even these foreign elements are still comparatively insignificant. On the other hand, the languages of the West were greatly influenced by contact not only with the Moors, but with the natives of Syria. When we remember such words in English* as azimuth, nadir, admiral, elixir, shrub, sofa, amulet, chemise, sarcenet, artichoke, alcove, magazine, alcohol, cipher, lute, mattress, mohair, camlet, and saffron, to say nothing of terms denoting Eastern dignities or customs, we perceive the influence of Arab trade and civilisation and science upon the Western mind. The

---

* Skeat, *Etymological Dict. English Language*, p. 760.

mingling of so many nations, the knowledge gained of
so many religions, and habits of thought, strange to the
West, hastened the advance of European culture.   It
was Europe, not Asia, which profited most in the end,
and the result of the Crusades was the Renaissance.
The Turks had little or no part in the education of the
Latins.   No Turkish words found place in their daily
speech ; and the Seljuks themselves fell under the same
great spell of an ancient civilisation, which was Greek
and Persian and Arab in its origin.

The influence on the Latins of their Syrian education
was not less remarkable in questions of religion.   To
the first Crusaders there was but one true Faith—that
which the Normans had accepted under Rollo, and of
which the Pope, as spiritual ruler of Europe, was the
head.   They supposed that the Saracens (*Sharkiyin*, or
"Easterns") were idolaters adoring a mummy image
called Baphomet or Mahound : it took many years to
convince them generally that the Moslem worshipped
only One God, and that the Korân taught, in Muhammad's own words, that he was an "unlearned prophet"
from among his Arab brethren.   Yet within a very few
years their princes were making alliances with Moslems ;
and after Hattîn the very Master of the Temple—a
tonsured monk—was suspected not only of treachery,
but even of apostasy.   Moslem philosophy attracted
many, and renegades began to be numerous.

Moreover, the Eastern churches were found to steadily
deny the Papal claims, and to represent themselves as
more ancient in foundation and orthodox in tenets

than any western church. They said that Peter never went to Rome, that Cyprian withstood the Papal claims to authority in Africa, and that Chrysostom wrote to Innocent only as to a bishop of the West. The Latins learned that nearly all the fathers were Syrians or African bishops, and that the memory of Origen and Chrysostom, of Cyril and Basil, of Athanasius and Gregory represented greater traditions than those of the West. They found that Jerome had fled disgusted from the court of Damasus, and had been the first to call the city of the Popes the " Scarlet Woman." The influence of learned priests and monks of the Jacobite church was strongly felt by the more enquiring Normans, while the ignorance and bad conduct of many of their own Latin clergy destroyed their authority. King Amaury distressed the good and able William, Archbishop of Tyre, by asking for proof of immortality outside the Scriptures. The answer, we are told, was after "the Socratic method." No doubt the arguments found in the Phædo and the Crito are those intended.

Nevertheless the piety of the nobles was deep and unquestioning as a rule, and the gifts to the Church were numerous. They included oil and wine, and lamps to burn forever before the Cross and the Sepulchre and Calvary, and wax for candles, and incense. Even the whole of a man's property was bequeathed after his death to some church, and the prayers asked in return were for father or brother, wife or child, who had died, or for the soul of the pious donor himself.* Some of

* *Regesta*, Nos. 161, 209, 348, 494, 656, 809.

these gifts were the issue of vows, if God were pleased
to grant new conquests such as that of Ascalon ; but it
is suggestive that the existing documents recording
them belong, for the most part, to the earlier years of
Latin rule.*   Yet the belief that the world was "waxing
old" survived even in King Richard's time.†   In the
middle of the thirteenth century the Western clergy
complained to St. Louis that no notice was taken of
excommunication, suggesting as a remedy the seizure
of the property of the offenders.   This the just king
refused ; and Queen Blanche, his mother, protected
peasants against priestly tyrants, although the same
good king refused even to speak to a renegade.   Some
bishops were found who would absolve men even from
the Patriarch's ban ; and the Knights Hospitallers, on
whose land none but the Pope could lay an interdict,
protected those whom their bishops had cursed.   Moreover, it mattered little to a knight or noble, whose
peasantry were Moslem, whether an interdict was proclaimed or no, because it did not touch his powers, or
interfere with his income.   The Church waxed rich, and
the good fathers received wine and tithes down to the
very year of Hattîn ; but the yoke of their authority
was broken in the East.

The earlier Normans were ignorant and superstitious.
We hear nothing of books bequeathed or bought, but
the Chronicles are full of appearances of saints and
angels—not indeed within the writer's own experience,

---

* *Regesta*, Nos. 113, 141, 342.
† Jeoff. De Vinsauf, II, 5.   Joynville (Bohn's *Chron. of Crusades*),
pp. 365, 489.

but in the days of an earlier generation of which he speaks. Many of the pilgrim diaries are written by ignorant monks, and notice superstitions of the age common to East and West, such as the " Egyptian," or unlucky days for setting sail,* and the half-eaten fishes which the Saviour threw into the Sea of Galilee, where they still swam alive, and the holy oil of the Sardenai image, and the ambrosial liquor of St. Catherine's tomb on Sinai.† Legends from the Apocryphal Gospels, and from the lives of the saints, were firmly credited, and relics devoutly reverenced. The Rock of Calvary was covered with the crosses brought by pilgrims,‡ and the Patriarch sent a fragment of the True Cross to Germany, to be adored by all who were too weak or poor to travel to Jerusalem.§ Relics were also eagerly demanded from the Holy Land, including remains of St. Thaddeus, and of the mythical King Abgar, from Edessa.‖ In the thirteenth century, on the other hand, the relics came from West to East. The arm of St. Philip was sent to Acre in 1268 A.D. from Florence,¶ where it had been adored for sixty years ; and English soldiers were protected, in King Richard's time, by " a certain writing hanging from the neck,"** better than by the coat of mail, or thick pourpoint beneath. The natural history of Palestine was well known in the thirteenth century, but

---

* *Saewulf,* English translation, p. 2.
† *Ernoul,* English translation, pp. 45, 47, 55.
‡ *Theodorich,* English translation, p. 20.
§ *Regesta,* No. 317.
‖ Ditto, Nos. 99, 103.
¶ Ditto, Nos. 1361, 1365.
** *Jeoff. de Vinsauf,* I. 49.

in 1130 A.D. it was believed that no bird was able to fly across the Dead Sea.*

Perhaps the most remarkable feature of the Latin rule was the great Code of laws, framed to meet the peculiar conditions of the Syrian government.   The Assizes of Jerusalem,† as now extant, belong to the thirteenth century, and were edited by John d'Ibelin for the new kingdom of Cyprus ; but the core of the Code is of much earlier date, and was founded on the *Letters of the Sepulchre*, drawn up by Godfrey himself.   The basis of these laws was found in Justinian's Code, and they presented features as yet quite unknown in Europe, especially in their careful provision of justice for the bourgeois and the peasant, and for the trading communes whose fleets were so necessary to the king.   Three courts existed—for nobles, burghers, and villeins respectively. Over the first, or High Court, the king presided, aided by judges chosen from the liege knights, and before the king and his assessors, barons and knights were judged. The Court of Burgesses, to judge the townsmen and Franks not of gentle birth, was under a Viscount appointed by the king, but with a jury of citizens, who did judgment upon all freemen of their own rank, or even upon knights who chose to come before it.   Over these burgesses the High Court had no control.   The third, or Native Court, was under a *reiyis*, or native " head," with a council or jury of twelve natives— modelled on the village *mejlis* surviving to our own

---

* *Fetellus*, English translation, p. 12.
† Beugnot's edition, Paris, 1841, 1842, 2 Vols. folio.

times. The native customs were administered to the
villeins, or peasants bound to the soil, who, like serfs in
the West, were sold with the property. The only cases
reserved were blood feuds, murder, and other crimes of
violence, and the same reservations governed the com-
munal rights. In later times this court was changed,
because it would seem the corruption, never rooted out
of Oriental tribunals, increased under the *reiyis*. In its
place the Cour de la Fonde was constituted, under its
baillie, mainly for commercial cases. The jury then
included four Syrians and two Franks. The Court of
the Chain was, in fact, the Custom-house, named from
the chains which closed the mouths of harbours like
Acre, Sidon, or Tyre.* In spite of many immunities the
Customs appear to have been an important source of
revenue to the State. The regulations of the markets
were under an official called a mathessep, from the
Arabic *matahaseb* or " accountant." He had charge of
the standard weights and measures, inspected streets and
bazaars, and regulated the trade of bakers, butchers,
cooks, and corn merchants, dealers in fried fish, in pastry,
in butter, oil, and in various drinks, and also the native
schools, the native doctors, oculists, and chemists, the
horse surgeons, grocers, money changers, and hawkers,
the cloth merchants, tanners, shoemakers, goldsmiths,
blacksmiths, and tinsmiths, the slave market, and the
market for horses and mules.†

An Arab writer has described the Custom-house of

* Benjamin of Tudela (Bohn's *Early Travels in Palestine*, p. 80).
† Rey, *Colonies Franques*, p. 63.

Acre about 1184 A.D.,[*] under its native title of *dîwân*
whence the French "douane." The scribes, assisting
the farmer of the Customs, though Franks, could write
and speak in Arabic. The baggage of travellers was
examined, and the imports of merchants taxed according
to regulation. The caravans paid certain imposts for
safe conduct, and posts were garrisoned along the roads
to levy these, with bars or turnpikes closing the way in
certain defiles. The tariff of the Templars in Armenia
in the thirteenth century is still preserved.

The right of anchorage in harbours and roadsteads was
also paid for; but the main revenue was raised from capitation taxes—on the Moslems, on the Jews, and even on
the Syrian Christians. Baldwin II took off, at the Patriarch's request, a tax from which the pilgrims suffered at the
Jerusalem gates, for all who brought in corn and vege-
tables; but this, apparently, still was levied on others
who were not pilgrims.[†] The privileges of free trade,
granted to the Italian cities, were thus of very high
advantage in a country full of local imposts. All this great
system fell to pieces at Hattîn, and Joynville commends
Sir Gautier de Brienne because "he kept possession of
his county of Jaffa for many years, although continually
attacked by the Egyptians, and without enjoying any
revenues but what he gained in his incursions against the
Saracens."[‡]

The dress of the Franks was not less influenced than
were their manners by living in the East. The armour

---

[*] Rey, *Colonies Franques*, p. 258, quoting Ibn Jobeir.
[†] *Regesta*, 91.
[‡] Bohn's *Chronicles of the Crusades*, p. 488.

of Crusaders we still find sculptured on monuments of our own country. It consisted of the hauberk, or coat of chain-mail, with leggings of the same, and iron shoes, and a hood of mail or a round cap, often with a nose piece, and a neck piece of mail. The hauberk came to the knees, and was divided into tails behind for riding, and under it was worn the gambison, bliaud, or pourpoint, which is described as "a tunic of many folds of linen difficult to pierce, and artfully worked with the needle":[*] it is also said to have been stuffed with wool soaked in vinegar, which was believed to resist iron, and similar quilted protection was also worn by Saracens[†] under the Persian name of *khazagand*. Scale armour was worn in King Richard's time,[‡] and the helmet became gradually pot-shaped, covering the face with bars, as shewn on the seal of John d'Ibelin.[§] The shield was of wood covered with leather and braced with iron, some two feet in length, with a point ; and on this the arms of the knight were painted. The mail was covered with a robe of linen or of silk such as that of the Templars—white with a red cross—and the horses were also protected from heat and flies by similar coverings, and even with mail. The cuirasse and greaves, with other pieces of plate armour, did not appear till late in the thirteenth century.

The bearing of blazons began in Syria during the Crusades, and appeared among Turks and Latins alike. It was no doubt as necessary for the knight, who could

---

[*] *Jeoffrey de Vinsauf*, I, 49.
[†] Joynville (Bohn's *Chron. of Crusades*, p. 487), and Boha ed Dîn.
[‡] *Jeoffrey de Vinsauf*, III, 5.
[§] Rey, *Colonies Franques*, pp. 28, 29.

not speak the native tongue, and whose face was hidden,
to bear some distinguishing mark by which his followers
—especially the natives—might know him, as it is necessary even now to make use of uniforms and badges.   The
antiquity of a coat of arms is shewn by its simplicity.
The red shield and the white are among the oldest in
France.   The Count of Jaffa bore a gold field with a
cross patée gules.*   The arms of Jerusalem were older
than heraldic rules which made them false heraldry, as
shewing metal upon metal.   The Turks had also their
badges, on banners or bucklers, and in the twelfth century
the family of Ortok bore the two-headed eagle, which
they may have noticed carved on the rocks of Asia
Minor by the Hittite tribes four thousand years earlier,
and which came to Russia, and to Austria, to be thus
adopted finally by two Christian emperors.†   In the
thirteenth century the Egyptian sultans bore the lion,
which equally appears on the seal of John, Viscount of
Tripoli ; and Kelaun bore the duck according to the
Mongol meaning of his name.‡   The lambrequin, or roll
round the helmet, was perhaps taken from the Arab headdress.   The heraldic furs all came from Asiatic trade.

---

* Joynville (*Chron. of Crusades*, p. 399).

† The two-headed eagle, supposed to represent the mythical *hamka* or
rukh, is found as early as 1217 on coins and standards of the Turkomans,
and is represented on the walls of Diarbekr.   It occurs in 1260 on coins of
Otho, the Flemish Count of Gueldres ; of Arnold, Count of Looz ; and of
Robert de Thoureth, bishop of Liège.   In 1345 it became the arms of the
Holy Roman Empire : in 1497 it is found on the seal of Ivan III, Czar of
Moskow, after his marriage, in 1472, with Sophia, daughter of Constantine
Palæologus.   It is found also on coins of the Arsacidæ in Persia (third
century A.D.), and on Indian coins, where it represents the mythical *garuda*
bird.   The oldest examples are on the Hittite monuments of Pteria and
Eyuk.   (See Count Goblet D'Alviella's *Migration of Symbols*, pp. xii, 22.)

‡ Rey, *Colonies Franques*, p. 51.

Henry of Champagne even deigned to wear the turban and the Arab robe which Saladin sent him.[*]

The infantry of the Franks had a short shirt of mail, and leather breeches mail covered, with helmets and long shields. They carried the spear, and Danish axe, and club, the sling, and dagger. The lance and sword were used by horsemen. The Frisons had a javelin with a thong[†], but the bows and cross-bows of the archers placed between the spearmen did most execution.[‡] The native troops, light armed and irregularly marshalled, must be considered later. The army marched round its standard, which was sometimes drawn on a truck, and ambulances for the sick were not forgotten,[§] with provision waggons, and pack horses. The music of the army included horns and trumpets, the pipe, the timbrel, the harp,[||] and the *nacaires* or metal drums[¶] borrowed from the East.

The dresses worn in time of peace were rich and gay, and increased in magnificence as wealth increased. They were often inherited, and all men were expected to dress according to their rank, and not to ape their superiors. The hair was worn long except by Templars, and the beard was grown. King Richard shaved the beards of the Cypriotes " in token of their change of masters."[**] The dresses also appear to have been long

---

[*] Rey, *Colonies Franques*, p. 12.
[†] *Jeoff. de Vinsauf*, I, 18.
[‡] Ditto, VI, 22.
[§] Ditto, I, 19 ; IV, 10.
[||] Ditto, III, 2.
[¶] Pietro de la Valle (Bohn's *Chronicles of Crusades*, p. 389, note).
[**] *Jacques de Vitry*, p. 68, English translation ; *Jeoffrey de Vinsauf*, II, 36.

and loose, with wide sleeves, and lined with fur, which
has always been prized in the East, though the short
cloak of Anjou also belongs to the twelfth century.
The costume of the French knights in Palestine is
described, in the time of the third Crusade, in quaint
terms :—

"For the sleeves of their garments were fastened with
gold chains, and they wantonly exposed their waists,
which were confined with embroidered belts, and they
kept back with their arms their cloaks, which were
fastened so that not a wrinkle should be seen in their
garments . . . and round their necks were collars
glittering with jewels, and on their heads garlands inter-
woven with flowers of every hue : they carried goblets not
falchions in their hands."*

King Richard's own dress was specially magnificent
at the time of his wedding in Cyprus. He rode on a
red saddle spangled with gold, and having the peak behind adorned with gold lions. His vest was rose coloured,
with crescents of solid silver ; his hat of scarlet embroidered with beasts and birds. His sword hilt was gold,
and the scabbard, bound with silver, was attached by a
woven belt. His spurs were also of gold.†

In the thirteenth century Joynville describes equally
magnificent costumes. His own squire was dressed in
scarlet striped with yellow. The surcoats at festivals
were often of cloth of gold ; and broidered coats of arms
and rich saddles became commoner, and in the East

---

* *Jeoffrey de Vinsauf,* V, 20.
† Ditto, II, 36.

St. Louis wore black silk lined with squirrel skins, and with gold buttons. The surcoat was sometimes of "velvet in grain," and the hats lined with ermine for kings. The knights were clad in silk, and the coverlets on the beds were of scarlet lined with minever—the fur of the Siberian squirrel; in which mantles also the dubbed knights were wrapped after the bath.* The merchants were more soberly dressed—in camlet with rabbit's fur, or in the woollen tyretain named from Tyre. The monks and palmers wore the roughest dress, but the array of the higher clergy was rich and costly.

The Latin ladies were equally magnificent, in long trained dresses with long wide sleeves. The tall slight figures, with plaited locks hanging to the waist from either shoulder, are known from the monuments. The grey Norman eyes, and fine small features, most admired, were very different to the ruddy and black browed Armenian beauty, or to the fine olive complexion and long black lashes of the pure Arab women, whom, however, the knights seem also to have admired, though less attracted by the dead-white hue of the stout Greek ladies, who painted their faces, as they still continue to do. The baronesses were decked in samite and cloth of gold, with pearls and precious stones. Ibn Jobeir describes the bride he saw at Acre in 1184 A.D.,† in a sweeping robe of cloth of gold, with diadem and veil also of gold: who walked preceded by

---

* Joynville (Bohn's *Chronicles of Crusades*, pp. 353, 357, 364, 397, 440, 459, 461, 515).
† Rey, *Colonies Franques*, p. 13.

seigneurs in their festal dresses, and accompanied with music and with song.

The laws of chivalry gave to these ladies from the West a very different position to that of their Eastern sisters. Though faithless dames and recreant knights were found, the creed of the gentle embodied the truths of their faith, whatever they thought of its dogmas. To be brave and true was not enough unless a man were also humble of heart, and courteous to all, and pure of life, and kind and merciful. It was no idle saying that "next to God all honour came from ladies," for the deeds of the age shew us how all that was done was by the dame's consent. When she was an heiress she made her own agreements, by consent of her husband. Whether the manners of modern society are preferable to those of houses which, from one generation to another, trained up the young who lived in the castles of their seigneurs in all that was fair and gentle, as well as in all that was manly and adventurous, we may perhaps doubt; in a time when many of the clergy were ignorant and self-seeking, and the lower classes brutal, such education was the very salt of the earth; and the influence of ladies was a softening restraint on violent and daring men. Venetian traders might immure their women in palaces not unlike the harims of the East,[*] but the Norman lady was not only free, but was the queen of all who stood before her. For Salique law, named from a Frankish tribe, was never binding on

---

[*] Jacques de Vitry (p. 64) speaks with contempt of the Poulains or half-castes who shut up their wives.

Normans, and the fiefs descended not only to the heiress, but to the second husband of the widow without a child. The age of majority was fixed for boys at fifteen, and for girls at twelve, by the Assizes, yet mothers of princes sometimes kept their sons in ward till twenty-one,[*] and Milicent exacted obedience from her son for many years, having herself been crowned. The courage of ladies who went out on long campaigns with their husbands to the East, who held their wedding feasts in beleaguered castles, and bore children on crowded galleys (like Queen Margaret of Provence), obliged to set to sea again with infants of a few weeks old, will not be questioned. The degeneracy of the later generation is traced to marriages with native women, and not to be laid to the account of Latin ladies. Queen Theodora was served by eunuchs—but she was a Greek.[†] In the early days of Baldwin I a Christian knight did not fail to care for a Moslem's wife even when fighting against her lord ; but when the Syrian dancing women began to appear in the castles, and delighted the French at Acre, the spirit of chivalry was already dead.

The life of both knights and ladies in the castles was perhaps less dull in Palestine, where the winter nights were not so long, than in Europe. Gloomy and bare as the great halls and turret chambers now appear, they were at least cool in summer and warm in winter, because of the thickness of their walls. The light of the wax torches, tapers, and lamps, was dim ; but few read,

---

[*] Joynville (Bohn's *Chron. of Crusades*, p. 487).
[†] Abu el Faraj, quoted by Rey, *Colonies Franques*, p. 106.

and usually they went to bed early, and so enjoyed the
early dewy dawn.   Knights and ladies played chess
with huge pieces on heavy boards.   The men gambled
at " tables."   The ladies sewed and embroidered, they
played the milder games of draughts and backgam-
mon, and made wonderful cates, and distilled waters,
and said their prayers from jewelled breviaries, and
taught their daughters all a dame should know.   There
were, moreover, rich Oriental hangings, and wondrous
Persian carpets, and pillows of silk and down, to beautify
their bowers ; and all the glorious art and colour of the
East was at their service.   They drank from chaced
goblets of silver and gold crusted with gems, and
enjoyed the baths of the castle, and the noonday siesta.
They went out to hawk and hunt, or to wander in
gardens and orchards ; and merchants came to them
with rich stuffs and jewels, and works of exquisite
Oriental art ; and jongleurs, troubadours, musicians, and
readers of romances paid their lodging with perform-
ances at evening, in the great dining hall of the castle.

The tables were spread with fine white linen.   The
food included game and fish—the roebuck of Carmel, the
fallow deer of Tabor, the gazelle of the plains, bears'
feet from Hermon, Greek partridges, and quails, wood-
cock and snipe, and desert grouse, as well as mutton
and beef, wild boar and fowls.   The fruits of Syria—
oranges and lemons, damsons and pears, apricots and
quinces, apples and nuts, dates and bananas, grapes
and melons—were followed by spices and preserves ;
and flowers of orange or violet, crystallised in sugar.

The sauces, learned from the Arabs, with vinegar and
lemon juice, seasoned the dishes. They drank the
heady wines of Lebanon and Hermon, and beer spiced
with nutmeg and cloves, and sherbet cooled with snow.
They had butter and cheeses in spring, and the sour
delicious *leben* of the Arabs.   There were flowers enough
in the plains and valleys—tulips and anemone, narcissus
and cyclamen ; and roses, at Gebal and Damascus and
growing wild on Hermon ; and fragrant gardens often
lay within the city walls.   William of Tyre speaks of
the dances of natives, celebrating family festivals* ; and
for music they had harps and lutes, organs and rebecks
cymbals and nacaires, flutes and guitars.†

For amusements they had the tournay, and feats
of skill on horseback, and the quintaine, and hunting
and hawking.   There was plenty of game: even bears
and leopards, as well as gazelles : and King Fulk was
killed chasing a hare with a lance.   The boar was also
noble sport, and the hounds were excellent, as were the
Arab *slughis* or greyhounds.   They also hunted with
cheetahs and lynxes‡ ; and Arab emirs were as fond of
hawking as the knights who lost their hawks and hounds
in Phrygia, or Philip of France whose falcon flew into
Acre.   King Richard went boar hunting near Ascalon
in the midst of the war, and was nearly killed by an
ambush when hawking.§   The life of the Normans was
gay and pleasant, but for the fever in the lowlands, and
the mosquitos, and fleas, and heat, and, in a lesser

* *Will. Tyre*, quoted by Rey, p. 49, *Col. Franques.*
† Ditto, p. 47.   ‡ Ditto, p. 55.
§ *Jeoffrey de Vinsauf*, IV, 28 ; V, 31.

degree, the snakes and scorpions which sometimes gave trouble. The two curses of the nobles were wine and dicing ; and the latter especially was a crying evil. The temperance of the Normans was naturally greater than that of Germans, but the natives of Palestine saw with astonishment the mighty eating of the English.* Fishing was perhaps not an amusement, but the Latins ate fish in Lent, and the monks were fond of eels. Among other rights we find noticed that of eight days fishing between Septuagesima and Easter in the Sea of Galilee—which swarmed with fish—and of keeping a ship on the lake, granted by the Patriarch. Boemund of Antioch gave the monks of Tabor a thousand eels each year, from the lake of Antioch ; and the brethren of St. Lazarus gained the same privilege in 1216 A.D.†

The monuments which the Latins left behind them in castles and churches attest their mastery of the art of building. The masonry was far more truly cut than that of the Byzantines : the slender clustered pillars : the bold and sharp relief of the foliaged capitals : the intricate designs of cornices, witness their skill as masons and sculptors. The mighty rusticated stones of the ramparts rival the Roman ashlar in size and fitting. Their mortar, with powdered shells and pottery, was harder than stone : their arches and ribbed groins were superior to the Arab workmanship. The finer finished masonry is signed with masons' marks, including Norman letters and mystic signs—the bow, the fish, the

---

* Richard of Devizes (Bohn's *Chron. of Crusades*, p. 58).
† *Regesta*, Nos. 142, 629, 888.

hour glass, the trident, and fleur de lys, Solomon's seal
and the shield of David ; and the same marks so found
in the twelfth century in Palestine, where the builders
were Italians and Sicilians, recur in the thirteenth and
fourteenth centuries on the walls of cathedrals in France,
in England and in Scotland.

The houses in the cities were yet more noble than the
castle halls. The towns were small, at least within the
walls, though suburbs sometimes stretched among gardens beyond, as unwalled hamlets also climbed the steep
slopes to the scarped rock and deep ditches of the castle.
The château of Beirût* close to the sea, looked out on
the bay on one side and on the gardens round the city
on the other. A floor of mosaic in the hall represented
waves: the walls were veneered with marble: the
vaulted roof was painted like the sky. A marble
fountain stood in the midst, and a dragon disgorged a
stream from its mouth. Large windows let in the sea
breeze, and the coolness of the chamber was delightful
in summer.

Acre, and Tyre, and Antioch were full of palaces, on
whose roofs the noble ladies walked in crowns of gold.
The streets were covered with coloured awnings, after
the Italian manner ; and the ceilings of the Sidon
palaces were of cedar brought from Lebanon.† Antioch
was full of fountains, fed by a great reservoir on the
heights in the north-west corner of the city. The houses,
as at Damascus, were on the outside of mud, but they

* Will. of Oldenburg, quoted by Rey, *Colonies Franques*, pp. 8, 326.
† See authorities in Robinson's *Biblical Researches*, II, p. 482.

O

enclosed courts paved with marble, with tanks and gardens of orange-trees; and underground channels carried running water through the houses.

The castles were perched on heights, or raised on hillocks in the plain. The outer walls ran along the precipices, often scarped, and the approaches were cut off by rock cut ditches difficult to undermine, in which were rock cut stables with rocky mangers for the horses. The inner baily was fortified with a second wall, and led to the courtyard into which the chambers opened; while great outer towers often replaced, or else were added to the keep. The Templars built round chapels in their towns and castles. The Hospitallers had also chapels in their inner courtyards. The best remaining examples, at Toron, Baniâs, and Krak des Chevaliers, still remain almost intact, and at Krak, north-east of Tripoli, the battlements of the towers are standing, and the heavy oaken door, studded with nails, leads to the stepped and vaulted passage, by which the horseman rides into the inner court.

Yet more remarkable are the Latin churches still either standing in ruins or preserved as mosques. In the earlier age the masonry is heavy and half Byzantine, with classic pillars and round arches; but about 1140 A.D. the pointed arch—at first low and broad—begins to be associated with clustered shafts, ribbed vaults with groins, and delicate tracery. The Norman dog-tooth moulding also then appears, and a peculiar arch with voussoirs like the backs of books in row. In addition to cathedrals and priories churches were raised

by foreign princes, as when Conrad III of Dachau
vowed as a pilgrim to build one.[*]   The earliest erected
was the choir of the Holy Sepulchre, and the church
of Tabor was built in 1110 A.D., St. Mary Latin in
Jerusalem was standing in 1103 A.D., and Ste. Marie la
Grande in 1140 A.D.   The small but beautiful church
of Bîrch was built in 1146, St. Samuel of Mountjoy in
1157, and the Nazareth church was the latest in 1185.
They all included fonts, superseding the Greek baptis-
tries, and that at Bethlehem bore the modest inscription
that it was given by those "whose names are known to
the Lord."   The beautiful church of St. John at Gaza,
and that of St. Mary at Ramleh, stand almost intact as
mosques.   At Hebron a Gothic church occupies half of
the ancient Herodian enclosure, round the tomb of
Abraham.   In Cæsarea only foundations of the great
cathedral remain, and not much more at Tyre.   At
Samaria the church of St. John is half ruined : at Nâblus
the principal building dating about 1150, is now a
mosque.   The ruins of the large churches at Tabor and
Nazareth are traceable, but those of Acre have perished.
In Syria the best preserved example is that at Tortosa
with its added minaret.[†]   The plan is nearly always the
same, St. Samuel being the only cruciform church of
the age.   A nave and aisles ended in three apses, built
for the Latin rite and not divided by walls.   In one case
(at Kubeibeh north of Jerusalem) the stone altar stands
yet against the central apse wall ; and the piscina is

[*] *Regesta*, 623.
[†] Boha ed Din says that Saladin destroyed the church at Tortosa in
1188.   The existing church may have been built in the 13th century.

often traceable. The nave rose to a second tier, with clerestory windows above the roofs of the aisles, and a barrel vault is usual to both aisles and nave.

For the adornment of churches and monasteries pictures in glass mosaic, or frescoes, were sometimes made. They existed in the cathedral of the Holy Sepulchre, and in the Templum Domini, but are only extant now at Bethlehem. These latter mosaics were given by Michael Comnenos, whose portrait the artist Efrem introduced among the saints. The groundwork was of gold, and from the fragments left we know them to have represented half lengths of the ancestors of Christ, with Greek inscriptions, and buildings with curtained altars and arabesque foliage, referring to the councils of the church ; while quaint Byzantine figures of angels stand above between the windows. On the west wall Joel, Amos, Nahum, Micah, Ezekiel, Isaiah and Balaam were figured with a "tree of Jesse" whence they sprang. In the choir the subjects represented were from the life of Christ and of the Virgin. In the Jordan Valley, near Jericho, the ruins of the Latin monastery of Hajlah were till recently covered with Byzantine frescoes of the twelfth or thirteenth century, now destroyed by the vandalism of Greek monks. The subjects included the Resurrection, and the Last Supper, with figures of Pope Sylvester, Sophronius of Jerusalem, John Eleemon, and Andrew of Crete, and a smaller picture of the Annunciation. This monastery appears* to have been the famous Calamon of the middle ages.

* Phocas.

Near Tripoli also a rock, with hermits' graves, is covered with pictures over which coarser pictures were painted by the Greeks in later times. The earlier designs represent Christ as the carpenter, the Annunciation, the Salutation, Christ enthroned between Joseph and Mary, and a figure on a tree perhaps intended for Christ on the Tree of Paradise (taken from the gospel of Nicodemus), with other subjects connected with the legend of some saint or Latin abbot.

The Latins were mainly influenced in their art by Byzantine models, and probably employed Byzantine artists. The miraculous pictures of Tortosa and Sardenal were already ancient when they came with others bearing Syriac inscriptions. At Beirût was a picture of Christ, which was said to have bled when the Jews pierced it with a spear,* and a drop of this blood healed the sick. The Latins had statues as well as pictures in their churches, such as the full-sized silver statue of Christ above the Holy Sepulchre itself.† Their seals and coins were also influenced by Byzantine art A special coinage was however struck at Acre, in the thirteenth century, for use with natives, bearing the cross on one side and the Arab legend " God is One " on the other, and round the centre, also in Arabic, the words " Father, Son and Holy Ghost," " Struck at Acre in the year 1251 of the Messiah." Similar coins were struck at Antioch, and they were called Saracen bezants, and contained about seven shillings in gold. One of

* *Jacques de Vitry*, p. 6, English translation.
† *Fetellus*, p. 52, English translation ; *Abbot Daniel*, pp. 15, 55, English translation.

the most remarkable relics of twelfth century art is the breviary of Queen Milicent, now in the British Museum, with its covers of carved ivory and silver, and silk back embroidered with a cross of gold all in Byzantine style.

The Latins were at first extremely ignorant of literature, and Theodorich remarks that, being strangers, they knew the names of few places.* They indeed carried hopeless confusion into topography when they placed Beersheba at Beit Jibrin, Bethel at Jerusalem, and Ashdod at Arsuf. The ancient Bible towns were much better known in St. Jerome's time, and often preserved by the Greeks while the Latins invented new sacred sites. They could not read Arabic as a rule, and when Tripoli was taken they burned the valuable library of the Kadi Abu Thaleb Hosein.† Yet the Normans were not all illiterate, since Henry Beauclerk already had translated Æsop's fables. A knowledge of Greek was attained by churchmen like Geoffrey, abbot of the Templum Domini; and Renaud of Belfort studied Oriental sciences under native masters in Saladin's time.‡ Jurisprudence was also much studied, and a theologian was expected to understand grammar, logic, and rhetoric. Early in the thirteenth century Jacques de Vitry gives a good account of the fauna of Syria and Egypt, describing such animals as the lynx and jackal, the cheetah and cerastes, the hyena and hippopotamus. He had heard from traders of the elephant and rhinoceros, the caiman, the boa, and the beaver. He

---

* *Theodorich*, p. 2, English translation.
† Rey, *Colonies Franques*, p. 165.
‡ Ditto, pp. 172, 173, and Boha ed Dîn.

knew the ibis, and might have seen crocodiles in the river north of Cæsarea, where they had been for a thousand years at least (being noticed by Pliny and Strabo), though tradition said they came from Egypt. He had also seen parrots brought from India, and knew that the pearls of the Persian Gulf came from oysters. But such learning spread rather among laymen than in the Church, and few of the clergy had studied at the University of Paris, as William of Tyre had done for ten years.*

The corruption of the church is recognised and lamented by more than one chronicler himself a priest. Richly endowed, and with bequests constantly increasing through the piety of kings and nobles, the bishops, abbots, and priors lived in luxury, feasting and exacting tithes from all, and often oppressing the villeins till they appealed to king or viscount. They drank good wine, and sometimes led scandalous lives, till Saladin swept away their glebe lands, and left them destitute exiles, or subjects of the Moslems, who gave their lands to the mosques.

In Europe the Papal power increased and reached its culmination while the rich Syrian church obeyed the fiat of Rome. In the time of King Fulk, Louis VII was entangled in disputes with Pope Innocent II, who claimed the right of investiture to benefices in France. Thirty years later the Papal power was at its height in England, as represented by Thomas à Becket, when

---

* This university is traced to 1150–70 A.D. Its four nations were however, not recognised by the Popes till 1231.

bishops usurped the rights of king and people. After the third Crusade, in 1208 A.D., came the quarrel with Innocent III as to Stephen Langton, when King John was forced to receive his crown anew from the Pope, and interdict and excommunication followed each other, and tribute was levied on England by Rome. About the middle of the twelfth century Alexander III made the proud Frederic Barbarossa prostrate himself before him, and set his foot on his neck. But heresy already troubled the court of Rome, in Languedoc, and an emperor was to arise who cared not at all for excommunication: the Eastern churches were slow to be reconciled when their bishops had been dethroned by the Latins. Even in the presence of a disaster like Hattîn it was difficult to rouse the ancient spirit, and when King Richard came to aid the cause of the Church his settlement of the East was only improved on—for a few short years—by an adversary of the Pope, and the Crusaders' zeal died out never to be revived. The fortunes of the Church of Rome waxed and waned with the fortunes of the Latins in the East.

In 1113 A.D. Pascal II placed the bounds of the patriarchates of Antioch and Jerusalem at the River Eleutherus,* having exhorted the clergy to obedience two years earlier, and approved the parishes in the same year.† Councils were held under the Legate at Jerusalem, in 1107 and 1111 A.D.,‡ and to depose the Patriarch in 1115; in 1120 there was a council at Nâblus for reform

---

* *Regesta*, 72, 73.
† Ditto, 60, 61.
‡ Ditto, 50, 62, 81, 89, 171, 203, 208.

of morals: in 1137 the encroachments of the Patriarch of
Antioch were annulled by Innocent II: in 1141 there
was a Council at Antioch; and in the next year, on Sion,
to warn the Armenian Catholicus against his abhorrent
heresies; and many references to Rome served in
addition to confirm the Pope's authority over the Church
in Syria. Most of the bishoprics were at ancient
centres, established in the fourth and fifth centuries, but
in Palestine some new sees were established, including
Hebron, Nazareth, Bethlehem, Baniâs, Jaffa, and Es
Salt. Nazareth was so raised in 1160, and Hebron in
1167 A.D. The Church of St. Peter became a cathedral
at Jaffa in 1169, and Baniâs was reconstituted in the
same year. The four Metropolitans, under the Latin
Patriarch of Jerusalem, were the Archbishops of Cæsarea,
Tyre, Tiberias, and Montreal or Petra. Jericho and
Livias were under Petra with Sinai (a Greek convent);
and the northern regions, including Acre and Baniâs,
were under Tyre. Nazareth afterwards gave a suffragan
to Tiberias, to which the churches east of the upper
Jordan belonged.* This division differed therefore from

* Jacques de Vitry, writing about 1220, gives the following organisation
(pp. 33-34, English translation), under the Patriarch of Jerusalem, of the
four Metropolitans: 1. Archbishop of Tyre, with four suffragans at Acre,
Sidon, Beirût, Baniâs; 2. Archbishop of Cæsarea, with one suffragan at
Samaria; 3. Archbishop of Nazareth, with one suffragan at Tiberias (the
see being changed from Beisân to Nazareth); 4. Archbishop of Petra, with
the Greek bishop of Sinai as suffragan. The Patriarch had directly under
himself the bishops of Bethlehem, Hebron, and Lydda, with the priors of
St. Sepulchre, Templum Domini, Mount Sion. and Olivet (Augustines)
and Abbots of St. Mary Latin, Jehosaphat, St. Anne, and Bethany
(Benedictines). The Benedictines of Mount Tabor were under the Archbishop of Nazareth. Jaffa had then no bishop, but was under the Prior and
Canons of the Holy Sepulchre. Nâblus had no bishop but was under the
Temple.

the old Greek Patriarchates of Palestina Prima, Secunda, and Tertia, in the introduction of a second metropolitan in Galilee. The bishops of the various Eastern rites—except the Greek Orthodox—consented to become suffragans of the Latins, but during the succession of the ten Latin Patriarchs who actually occupied a throne in the Holy City, the Greek Church enumerates a parallel list of eight rightful heads of the see.

Some of the churches and monasteries were more famous, and received more donations, than any of the cathedrals; but the Church of the Holy Sepulchre was the richest and most important of all. Godfrey bestowed twenty-one villages on the canons, and the number increased to seventy through the donations of other kings and of barons. These lay mainly in the mountains round Jerusalem within the Royal Domain; but in 1165 five villages in Galilee were purchased, and land in the plain north-east of Cæsarea.* They had also a church in Rome in 1179 A.D., and possessions yet earlier in Sicily. The loss of Jerusalem was a terrible blow to this church, but the canons were in part consoled by grants in and near Acre, and by new lands in Cyprus, and even in Poland.

Next in wealth to the Sepulchre cathedral appears to have ranked the church of the Virgin's tomb—Our Lady of Jehoshaphat. In the Bull of Pope Alexander IV, dating 30th January, 1255, no less than forty-eight villages are enumerated as its property, and thirty

---

* *Regesta*, No. 420–425, see *Quarterly Statement, Palestine Exploration Fund*, January, 1890. There are fifty documents in the Cartulary of the Holy Sepulchre, referring to property in Palestine and in Europe.

documents refer to their gradual acquisition. This church also had lands in Calabria, Apulia, and Sicily. It stands yet unharmed in the Kidron Valley near Gethsemane, with a Norman façade, and a long flight of steps within, leading down to the cave chapel, where Queen Milicent, who rebuilt it in 1161, was buried; but it has passed from the hands of Latins to those of the Greeks.

The church of Bethlehem also attracted the piety of many donors, and the possessions which belonged to it, enumerated in Bulls of Gregory IX in 1227 A.D. and Clement IV in 1266 A.D., amounted to forty in all ; but the names were so badly transcribed that many are doubtful. They were, however, scattered all over Palestine and Syria. The abbey of Tabor owned thirty-four villages in Lower Galilee, and twenty-two beyond Jordan or in the Jordan Valley. It was one of the oldest foundations, as shown by the Bull of Pope Pascal II, dating from the 29th July, 1103 A.D. Another important abbey was that of St. Sion, outside Jerusalem to the south ; and the Bull of Alexander III, in 1179 A.D., enumerates twenty-eight villages belonging to this ancient church. These also were scattered in the lands of Ascalon, Cæsarea, Nâblus, Samaria, in Lower Galilee, near Tyre, and Sardenai ; and in addition lands were granted in Sicily, Apulia and Calabria, Lombardy and France. The church of Nazareth likewise owned property in Europe, and, among other churches concerning which documents have been preserved, are those of Tyre, Shechem, Bethel, St. Mark in Acre, St. Mary Latin, and the Quarantania chapels.

Queen Milicent also founded a famous nunnery of St. Lazarus at Bethany, where she built a tower. It was built in 1147; and two years before her death (1160 A.D.) she gave two villages near Nâblus whither she had retired. Many other donors presented vineyards and hamlets, but, in 1256 A.D., Pope Alexander IV was obliged to ask that the Benedictine abbess and the nuns should receive necessaries from the Premonstrant abbot in Acre, their nunnery at Bethany having been destroyed by the Saracens.* There was another St. Lazarus outside Jerusalem on the north, close to the Lazarus Postern, west of the Gate of St. Stephen. It received, from King Amaury, in 1171 A.D., an annual sum of £25 from the tolls of the Gate of David, to support certain lepers ; and in 1174 he added £14 from the customs of Acre. There is a pathetic significance in these donations, when it is remembered that King Amaury's son was already known to be a leper.†

The tithes of the church were levied not only on crops but on beasts and many other things titheable, and even on the spoils of war ;‡ disputes as to these tithes often arose even within the Church itself, as when the Abbot of Mount Tabor appealed to the Patriarch against the Prior of the Holy Sepulchre, concerning the tithes of Sinjil and two other villages in the Nâblus hills.§   By the reformation of morals, in 1120 A.D., appears to have

---

* *Regesta*, No. 1244.
† Ditto, Nos. 487, 512, 995.
‡ Rey, *Colonies Franques*, p. 270.
§ *Regesta*, No. 234.

been understood the regular payment of tithes. The power of the ecclesiastical courts, as settled by the Assizes, was considerable. They judged the clergy on questions of heresy and sorcery, and pronounced decrees of nullity of marriage. In four cases the wife was obliged to enter a convent, and her dowry was restored, either in a capital sum or by annual payments. All questions of wills and bequests, of tithes and churches, were also judged by this court.*

The earliest religious order of the Latins in Palestine seems to have been the Benedictine, established in the Amalfi hospice in Jerusalem by 1023 A.D. The Bethany convent was also Benedictine.† The grey monks, or Premonstrants, are said to have originated at St. Samuel —the hill called Mount Joie by the Franks—north of Jerusalem‡ ; they lived under the rule of St. Basil. In the thirteenth century they are found in Acre. The Minorites or Franciscan friars, who were sent out for conversion of the infidels, belong also to this later century, and in 1350 were still settled at Jerusalem, when amid many dangers they buried the dead in Aceldama. The brethren of St. Lazarus, who tended the lepers, bore a green cross and were under the rule of St. Augustin.§ In 1272, we find a monk relinquishing the order of St. Damian, to join that of St. Augustin.‖ The most celebrated however of the Syrian orders were the Carmelites. Cluny monks had settled at Tabor in 1113, and arrived at

* Rey, *Colonies Franques*, p. 269.
† *Regesta*, 1275-7-8.
‡ *Theodorich*, 38, see p. 58, note, English translation.
§ Rey, *Colonies Franques*, p. 280.
‖ *Regesta*, 1385.

Haifa in 1170 A.D.,[*] and one who came from Calabria—an ordained priest—had there built a tower and a chapel, and had gathered ten brethren, by 1185.[†] About 1209 they obtained a rule, for "Brocardus and the other hermits," from the Patriarch of Jerusalem.[‡] There was then a monastery of St. Margaret about two miles to the south of their hermitage;[§] but four of the Cluny brothers were still found in the church of the Palm Grove north of Haifa; and another chapel of St. Denys seems to have existed at the foot of Carmel.[‖] The hermitage of St. Brocardus was apparently near the present monastery on the Carmel promontory, where was a cave supposed to have been inhabited by Elijah, which was the real motive of these anchorites in selecting the mountain for their retreat. Baldwin IV gave to their ship a right of free anchorage.[¶] In 1248 A.D. their rule—which excluded all use of meat—seems to have been found too severe for the climate; and it was mitigated by the bishop of Tortosa[**]; two years later the Seigneur of Haifa mentions them, in connection with vineyards on the mountain given to the Abbot of Mount Tabor.[††] They became numerous in Palestine, but were cruelly massacred by the Moslems in 1291. St. Simon Stock, of Kent, was General of the Order in 1245, and

---

[*] *Regesta*, 484.
[†] Phocas, p. 35, English translation.
[‡] *Regesta*, 489.
[§] *City of Jerusalem*, p. 31, English translation.
[‖] *Regesta*, No. 495, *City of Jerusalem*, p. 30, English translation.
[¶] *Regesta*, 606.
[**] Ditto, 1165.
[††] Ditto, 1189.

they were visited by St. Louis and by Edward the First
of England. Such was the origin of a celebrated Order,
which traces even to 1163 A.D., when Benjamin of
Tudela found a chapel by the cave. The Greek hermits
preceded them, and received a rule as early as 412 A.D.
Simon Stock was the first to wear the scapular among
them. When they fell, chanting the Salve Regina,
under the swords of the cruel Egyptians, the Order
became extinct for three centuries and a half, and twice
after that were they massacred, yet still remain in
possession.*

Although the payments made to churches were a very
heavy charge on the kingdom, it is not to be forgotten
that the clergy maintained the poor and aided the
pilgrims, though not to the same degree with the Military
Orders of monks. They also paid taxes, and led troops
in some cases to war, like the aged Archbishop Baldwin,
with Richard Lion Heart, or the valiant Bishop of Soissons, who charged the Saracens single-handed in the time
of St. Louis.† Some churchmen were of high character
and ability, like William of Tyre, who was born in
Palestine about 1127 A.D., and went to study at the
University of Paris for ten years. He was the tutor of
Baldwin IV, and Archbishop of Tyre in 1173 A.D. After
writing his famous history he busied himself in preaching
the third Crusade in Europe. His elevation to the
Patriarchate of Jerusalem was defeated by an intrigue,
Queen Maria, the Greek wife of Amaury, preferring the

---

* *Tent Work in Palestine*, Vol. I, p. 176, from the history of the Order
found in the monastery in 1873.

† *Jeoff. de Vinsauf*, I, 62 ; *Joynville*, p. 457, Bohn.

dissolute Heraclius of Cæsarea, whose life scandalised the Church. William of Tyre appealed to the Pope, but was poisoned by a doctor in the pay of his rival.[*]

The pilgrims were an annual source of strength and of revenue to the State and to the Church. The Italian fleets which brought them, came yearly from Easter to June and left in August. They landed at Acre, where indulgences and pardons began, and journeyed along routes protected, at regular stages, by fortified posts, towers or castles. The palmers are mentioned in the earliest times of Baldwin I, and they bought their palms in the Street of Palms, leading east south of the Sepulchre.[†] The Knights Templar were their bankers, and led them to the Jordan under escort. They also visited Sardenai near Damascus, by special treaty with the Saracens in the thirteenth century, to obtain the oil which flowed from the breast of the miraculous picture of the Virgin, painted on wood; and Tortosa with its portrait of the Virgin. The oil of Sardenai was a precious relic in French churches,[‡] as was the hay from Bethlehem, sent to Rome it was said by Helena (three hundred years after it had been used as the bed of the infant Jesus).[§]   But all relics were not equally reliable: in the fifteenth century bodies of the Innocents were bought from the Saracens, which were manufactured for the purpose with appropriate gashes, and

---

[*] Rey, *Colonies Franques*, p. 272.
[†] *Saewulf*, English translation, p. 8.   *City of Jerusalem*, p. 7.
[‡] Rey, *Colonies Franques*.
[§] *John of Würzburg*, p. 54, English translation.

embalmed in myrrh.* Those who were unable to make the pilgrimage sent rings, with which their friends—or persons paid for the service—touched the sacred spots and relics. So Louis VII sent his ring by a Templar ; and even in the fifteenth century the custom survived, Felix Fabri being entrusted with many such jewels of great value.† The pilgrims also ate the red earth at Hebron, of which Adam was made‡ ; and the Pisans carried the earth of Aceldama to the Campo Santo.

One of the most curious features of Church society, though not peculiar to the East, was the making of alliances of brotherhood between various religious bodies. This was no doubt a result of the chances of war, which might ruin one monastery but leave another untouched, as when the abbot of St. Paul's in Antioch swore brotherhood with the abbot of Mount Tabor, that he might be received should Antioch fall, which was only too probable in 1183 A.D.§ The relations with the Greek Church were also friendly at first, and Daniel, the Russian abbot, was kindly received by the rich Latin bishop of Nazareth|| ; but they grew bitter later, when the Orientals refused to enter the Roman fold.

The most remarkable result of the conquest of Syria was, however, the formation of new Orders of chivalry, which were religious, and bound by vows of celibacy very contrary to the creed of knights who sought a lady's love. Of these the Knights of St. John were the

---

* *Felix Fabri*, Vol. I, p. 566, English translation.
† *Regesta*, 398 ; *F. Fabri*, Vol. I, p. 93, English translation.
‡ *John of Würzburg*, 21.   § *Regesta*, No. 634.
|| *Abbot Daniel*, p. 71, English translation.

first, and the Templars followed five years later. The Teutonic Order belongs to the thirteenth century, although as early as 1143 A.D. Celestin II approved the separation of a special German hospice, set apart by the Knights Hospitallers,* which stood in the south quarter of the Holy City, where a few remains of its foundations and ribbed vaulting may still be seen near the tiny chapel of St. Thomas, now the house of a Morocco Jew.

The canons of the Templum Domini were established by Godfrey, and in the last year of his reign, 1118 A.D., Baldwin I associated with them eight Burgundian knights under Hugh de Payen, vowed to poverty, chastity, and obedience, and tonsured as monks, granting them his palace—the Templum Salomonis—where half a century later they had erected a large refectory and other buildings. In 1126 A.D. Baldwin II asked for a rule to guide them, which Pope Honorius granted. Two years later St. Bernard was their advocate,† and by his aid the regulations of the Templars were drawn up at Troyes in 1128 A.D. Gradually they increased in power and wealth, and obtained lands in Palestine and in Europe ; but their greatest expansion was in the century after the kingdom fell. Unfortunately, the Cartulary of the Order is lost, and the dates at which they obtained their lands and castles are unknown. Valenie, Tortosa, and Arca were among their Syrian possessions, Belfort in Upper Galilee,‡ and Gaza in the extreme

* *Regesta*, No. 214.
† *Jacques de Vitry*, p. 51, English translation.
‡ *Burchard of Mount Sion*, p. 13, English translation.

south, with Château Arnaud and Emmaus-Nicopolis, concerning which their dispute with the Hospitallers was settled by the Pope in 1179 A.D.* There was great jealousy, leading later to actual war, between the Orders. Tortosa became the Templar centre after Hattîn, where their archives and treasure were stored. Their famous banner "beauseant" was black and white, and their robe, after 1145 A.D.,† white, with the red cross. The seal of the Order represented the Templum Domini. At Hattîn they are said to have lost two hundred and thirty knights in all, besides those slain shortly before at Nazareth. They then became very unpopular, and even much earlier were suspected of treachery at Damascus in the second Crusade. Conrad of Montferrat—not a very reliable witness—accused them in England of malversation of the funds sent out by Henry II, and to Frederic Barbarossa of being more dangerous to Christendom than even the Saracens. Yet they were not allowed to hold personal property, though each knight provided three horses and a squire.

Of the Knights Hospitallers of St. John of Jerusalem much more is known, and they retained their popularity none the less because they opposed the tyranny of bishops. They had a great reputation for charity, and far outwent the Templars in their care of the poor and in their doles. The Order originated in one already existing when the Crusaders entered Jerusalem. The hospice of Charlemagne and its library were destroyed

* *Regesta*, No. 572–3.
† *Jacques de Vitry*, p. 51.
‡ *Regesta*, Nos. 653, 676.

in the eleventh century, but, soon after, the Benedictines were established by the Amalfi merchants,* and by leave of the Egyptian khalif. The firman of the Sultan Mudhaffer still exists in the Franciscan monastery in Jerusalem, which established the new hospice in 1023 A.D. The first church of St. Mary Latin was standing south-east of the Holy Sepulchre in 1103 A.D., with the smaller establishment for women called St. Mary Parva† ; and Gerard Tunc was superior of the Benedictines when the Christians won the city.‡ Pascal II took under the protection of Rome all the property of the hospice in Syria and Europe, as early as 1113 A.D., when a new additional building had arisen near the new church of St. John Eleemon south of the Holy Sepulchre ; and Gerard Tunc became the first Master of the military monks from that year until the death of Baldwin I. He was followed by Raymond du Puy, who erected the great buildings, still standing in ruins, about 1130 to 1140 A.D. The patron saint then became St. John Baptist. Seven other Grandmasters followed after 1159 A.D., including Garnier de Nablus in the year of the battle of Hattîn. A third church, St. Mary the Great, stood between the older hospice and that of St. John,§ and a nunnery lay to its south.

The hospital was intended for the use of sick pilgrims, and St. Mary Latin for services in Latin. In the middle

---

* *Jacques de Vitry*, p. 47, English translation.
† *Saewulf*, p. 14, English translation.
‡ *Albert of Aix*, VI, 25 ; *William of Tyre*, IX, 18 ; *Regesta*, No. 71.
§ *John of Würzburg*, p. 44, English translation ; *Theodorich*, *p.* 22, English translation.

of the twelfth century more than two thousand men and
women were admitted at one time.* The seal of the
Order represented a sick person so tended. The dead
were buried in the charnel house of Aceldama, over
which a vault was built about 1143 A.D.† It lay on the
hill south of the Valley of Hinnom. In addition alms
were distributed to the poor, and knights sworn to
defend the holy places. The hospice outside the north
gate of St. Stephen at first belonged to the Order, but
later to the Temple,‡ and the Leper Hospital seems also
to have grown out of the same organisation.§ When
Saladin desecrated the churches, and built a minaret
near the hospital, he respected this charitable institution
and the pilgrims still occupied its beds.

The Order of St. John was at first supported by
certain tithes granted by the Church‖ in the diocese of
Cæsarea, in Tripoli, Nazareth, Acre and elsewhere down
to 1141 A.D.; but the brethren had a large grant of
property as early as 1110 A.D. from Baldwin I,¶ in all
parts of the kingdom; and their possessions grew
steadily in Syria, as well as in Palestine,** especially in
the western plains. By 1167 A.D. they had large lands
near Antioch, and in 1179 bought property at Nâblus,
where their hospice is still inhabited by lepers. No less
than one hundred and forty documents of the twelfth

* *John of Würzburg*, p. 44, English translation.
† *Regesta*, No. 215.
‡ *Theodorich*, pp. 22, 42, English translation.
§ *City of Jerusalem*, p. 16, English translation.
‖ *Regesta*, Nos. 65, 78, 106-7-8, 117, 155, 205.
¶ Ditto, No. 57.
** Ditto, Nos. 118, 164, 293-4, 428, 583, 637.

century are extant, referring to their affairs ; they spread
to Turbessel near the Euphrates, and to Edessa beyond
it : they took charge of Emesa (La Chamelle) in 1184,
besides their hope of properties in Egypt.   Gebal,
Valenia, Tortosa, Gabala, were among their stations, with
Latakia, Saone, Beirût, Marakia, and Margat.   After the
defeat of Hattîn the Grand Master fixed his habitation
at Krak des Chevaliers, where the beautiful chapel still
bears the modest legend on its door

> Sit tibi copia
> Sit sapientia
> Formaque detur
> Inquinat omnia
> Sola superbia
> Si cometetur.

The Hospitallers also begged for alms in Europe,* and
were granted the taxes on certain Bedouin tribes newly
subjugated.†   All along the sea plains in the lands of
Ascalon, Cæsarea, and Jaffa, round Acre and Tiberias,
in Upper Galilee, and at Scandalion north of Tyre, they
bought properties and built castles and towers.   By the
thirteenth century they held more than one hundred
and eighty villages, and to King Amaury they promised
the help of a thousand knights.   They would seem to
have been more numerous than the Templars, and more
trusted.   Their dress was the black Dominican robe,
with the white cross well known as that of Malta.
Remembering the liberality of princes, the doles of
Latin and Eastern churches and monasteries, and those

---

* *Regesta*, Nos. 374, 422.
† Ditto, 355, 568, 593.

of the Temple and Hospital, we may suppose that, in a country not thickly populated, the poor were well tended, and that none need die of want. The lepers were no longer allowed to wander and die in misery at the town gates, but had special care devoted to them, at least in the later years of the century. It is remarkable, however, that leprosy was becoming a crying evil in France during the reign of Philip II, Augustus (1180–1223 A.D.), when lazar houses were established in every town. The disease is a sure companion of misery, bad food, and uncleanly habits, but that it is hereditary is certain, and that it is sometimes contagious appears also to be established.

As with the Military Orders, which finally became the masters of the remainder of Palestine, after the destruction of the older organisation, so with the trading communes, the chief development of power belongs to the thirteenth century; but the movement begun soon after the Latin conquest. The Amalfi merchants not only appeared in Jerusalem, but had also their street in Antioch before the first Crusade. The mother city was engrossed in trade, and free from war, in the middle of the century, with lands covered with vines and olives, gardens and orchards* : the men of Amalfi had also a cemetery in Acre, and free trade in Latakia, and houses in Tripoli. In 1171 they obtained immunity from tithes in five villages of the low hills near Lydda. The Pisans also settled in Latakia, Joppa, Acre, Tyre,

---

* *Benjamin of Tudela,*' p. 69 Bohn's *Early Travels in Palestine. Regesta,* Nos. 372, 388, 453, 690.

and Tripoli ; and Baldwin III gave them rights, which
however excepted the iron, pitch, and other articles,
of the Egyptian trade which they developed.   Saladin
confirmed their treaty with Egypt, as did his brother
Seif ed Dîn.*

The treaties with the Genoese have been already
noticed.   They were established in Antioch, Tripoli,
Gebal, Jerusalem, and El Arish, under consuls† ; and
made engagements for limited periods, in return for
which they claimed a third of some towns such as
Tripoli.   The Pope supported them even against
Baldwin III and Amaury, when their rights were
ignored ; and their aid in the defence of Tyre, after
Hattîn, was most important, leading to the loss of
Saladin's fleet.   In Jibeil (Gebal) there were seven
Genoese counsellors in 1163 A.D., under Julian
Embriaco, who belonged to one of the oldest patri-
cian families of Genoa, being a descendant of William
Embriaco, who aided the princes to take Gebal in
1109 A.D., and who was very jealously regarded at
home.

The Venetians, who in the thirteenth century acquired
eighty villages near Tyre, already claimed a third of
that city in the twelfth, and quarters in Haifa, Acre,
Sueidiyeh, Tripoli, and Ascalon‡ ; but their power was
yet further to be increased, by the conquest of Byzan-

* *Regesta*, Nos. 53, 292, 322, 324, 449, 500, 541, 585, 591, 617, 621.
† Ditto, Nos. 12, 35, 43, 55, 153, 224, 247, 285-6-7, 312, 438, 659 ;
William of Tyre, XI, 9 ; *Benjamin of Tudela*, p. 79, Bohn's *Early
Travels.*
‡ *Regesta*, 31, 84, 102-5, 139, 197-8, 282, 434, 632, 639.

tium itself. Finally, the merchants of Marseilles failed at Gebal in 1103 A.D., but were specially serviceable at the taking of Ascalon. Baldwin II gave them bake-houses in Jerusalem; King Fulk a yearly sum of £140 from the customs of Jaffa; Baldwin III added grants at Ramleh, and the Bishop of Bethlehem sold them, for £420, a property near Acre.[*]

The Latin relations with Moslem princes were not less calculated to strengthen the State than were their alliances with the seafaring cities of Italy. The Turkish governors, jealous of one another, began, as we have seen, very early to call in the Christians to their aid. Roger, Governor of Antioch, was allied to the very El Ghâzi, son of Ortok, whose tyranny in Jerusalem led to the Crusade, and this as early as 1115 A.D. In 1116 and 1119 A.D. the people of Aleppo appealed to the Franks against Moslem princes.[†] In time of peace invitations to hunting and hawking were freely interchanged, and in 1192 A.D. King Richard actually knighted Saladin's nephew.[‡] Godfrey himself made treaties with Moslem governors of Ascalon, Acre, Cæsarea, Damascus, and Aleppo. The intermarriage with native women even included Saracens, who renounced their creed. Hence arose the mixed race called Poulains,[§] who were specially numerous among

---

[*] *Regesta*, Nos. 38, 85, 163, 276, 386.
[†] Rey, *Colonies Franques*, p. iv, note.
[‡] *Jeoff. de Vinsauf*, V, 12.
[§] This word Poulains has been variously explained to mean *Fellahîn*, "ploughmen," or *Falaniyûn* "anybodies." Perhaps it is more probably to be connected with *Pouloi*, "offspring," as in the case of the Turkopoles. Jacques de Vitry (p. 58, English translation) derives the name from their Apulian mothers   The Poulains were reputed to learn witchcraft from

the bourgeois class. Joynville tells us of a Turk knighted by the Emperor, who bore as arms those of Aleppo and Cairo, combined with those of the empire.* The offspring of Frank fathers and Greek women were known as Gasmoules. The most despised class were, however, the renegades, who were often prisoners of war, but trusted neither by Christians nor by Moslems.

The caravans protected by the Latins were both Moslem and Christian, travelling from Mecca with the Moslem pilgrims, or coming from Baghdad and Mosul or from Christian Armenia. Fairs were held annually near the frontiers, such as the Meidan fair near the sources of Jordan, and that on the River of Reuben near Yebnah. King Richard captured a caravan from Cairo near Beersheba,† consisting of horses, mules, and camels laden with spices, gold and silver, silk cloaks, purple and scarlet robes, arms and weapons, coats of mail, cushions, pavilions and tents, biscuit, bread, barley, grain, meal, conserves, and medicines, with basins, bladders, chess boards, silver dishes, candlesticks, pepper, cinnamon, sugar, and wax. The camels and dromedaries numbered four thousand seven hundred in all, with innumerable mules, and one thousand seven hundred horses of the Turkish guards.

The army of the Kings of Jerusalem also included native troops. The Maronites were reputed good

the Syrian women, and to live on the pilgrims, charging them extortionate prices, and calling them "fools" (p. 57). See opposite, Turkopoles.
　* Joynville, p. 404, Bohn's *Chronicles of the Crusades.*
　† *Jeoff. de Vinsauf,* vi, 3, 4.

archers. The Turkopoles* were light armed native horse,
with long cane lances such as still are used by Arabs.†
The Royal Domain, according to the Assizes, could
raise five hundred and seventy-seven knights and five
thousand and twenty-five men-at-arms—the latter provided by the churches and the burghers. Tripoli sent
one hundred knights, and Antioch the same. The
Prince of Edessa mustered five hundred knights ; the
total force, including the Templars and Hospitallers, and
native auxiliaries, did not exceed twenty-five thousand,
not counting the armies sent from time to time from
Europe in the various Crusades.

A register was kept of the horses and mules which
could be mustered for war. The supply came not only
from Syria and Cyprus, but from Armenia, where a
small but hardy breed has always been famous. These
could not have supported the later heavy armed knights,
but were efficient for light armed men in mail. King
Richard, however, brought all his horses from England.
High prices were given for blood horses of the Kurds
and Persians.

The siege towers and mangonels have already been
noticed. They could be taken down, packed, and removed to other towns. The towers received names like
" Mauvoisin," " Mategriffen," and " Berefred." The
parties undermining or battering the walls worked under
cats and cercleia, which were galleries or shields of
hurdles covered with hides.‡ The Greek fire, which

---

* That is, Turkopouloi or " Turk-sons."
† Rey, *Colonies Franques*, pp. 32–44, 109–10.
‡ *Jeoff. de Vinsauf*, iii, 8.

seems to have been regarded as very mysterious because it could only be put out with sand, and would float burning down stream, was destructive to these machines. It was carried in bladders, and sometimes apparently shot from arrows, or thrown in barrels, and in bombs of earthenware, with a detonating fuse. The main component was petroleum, brought from the wells of Baku, to which orpiment and sulphide of arsenic were added. It had long been known to the Mongols of Central Asia and the Greeks. Philip II took some of it home from Acre, and therewith destroyed the English fleet at Dieppe ; but the composition was long a secret to the Franks, whose siege towers, balistæ, and mangonels were also borrowed from the Greeks, and traced back with little change to those employed for instance by Alexander the Great against Tyre.

A few words on the Navy* will conclude the present enquiry. The Mediterranean was full of pirates, both Christian and Moslem, and the trading fleets encountered great dangers, unless escorted by fighting vessels. Of the great Venetian passenger-galleys, in the thirteenth century, some account will be given later. The earlier ships were small, and as many as eighty could anchor in the small port of Acre.† The rights of shipwrecked persons were secured by the laws of the kingdom, and by special grants. The ships built in Syria were mainly of European wood, as suitable timbers were not easily found in the East. The Templars and Hospitallers had

---

* See Rey, *Colonies Franques*, pp. 150–164.
† *Theodorich*, p. 60, English translation.

ships, and the latter a commander of the sea. Light-
houses, with beacon fires, were established at Latakia,
Gebal, Tyre, Acre, and other ports. Signal fires were
indeed much used, and even carrier pigeons by besieged
towns, as well as divers (who were sometimes caught
in nets), and ships sailing under false colours, to throw
provisions into the ports.

Among the earlier trading or passenger vessels are
mentioned galleons, dromonds, and cats.* The galleons
were from an hundred to a hundred and thirty feet long,
and about twenty in greatest beam ; they had one bank
of oars, and a crew of one hundred men. The cats were
smaller, and the saities were swift vessels, about fifty
feet long, with ten to fifteen pairs of oars, drawing little
water, and built of pine, elm, or cedar, for coasting. The
dromons, or dromonds, were large, heavy, and slower
than galleys,† but, like the galleys, had square sails, as
well as two rows of oars : twenty-five pairs of the latter
—each manned by two men—propelled the dromons.
Barges and smacks carried provisions and munitions of
war ; and barbotes were used in 1188, which were very
flat-bottomed, and built in the harbour of Tyre, to run
close to land inside the Egyptian fleet. Other vessels
called gameles (or camels), nefs (navis), busses, and buze
nefs, were used for merchandise and for passengers—
the busses having two or three masts, and some 500
tons burden : the tarides and salandres were also ships
for commerce ; and the huissier, or urser, was a horse

---

* *Saewulf*, p. 8, English translation.
† *Jeoff. de Vinsauf*, I, 34, 61 ; II, 26 ; IV, 5.

boat. In the thirteenth century the French ships carried, in some cases, five hundred persons on board.[*] The Latins had also boats on the Sea of Galilee, and on the Dead Sea crossing to Kerak. The European fleets included not only those of the Italians, Marseilleise, and Danes, but in the third Crusade those of the Frisons and English.

The fighting galleys, with outriggers for the oars, sometimes had from fifty to ninety oars each side, in two banks, and the fighting men stood on deck above, protected with shields. Like the galleys with which the Carthaginians defeated the Romans, the Frank galleys had iron beaks. At the sound of the trumpet they charged the enemy, and sank it, or grappled with it, and, by diving under, the sailors bound the rudder with ropes. Arrows, sling stones, and Greek fire poured on the assailants : the latter was extinguished with sand ; many heavy armed men, unable to swim, were often thrown into the sea ; and hand-to-hand fighting on deck decided the victory.

This, briefly sketched, was the life of the Latins in the East, in peace and war, among high and low, clerics and laymen ; but we must not forget that they were always few among the many native subjects of the King of Jerusalem—a ruling caste among strangers ; and to the life and customs of the natives our attention is equally due.

---

[*] Joynville, p. 508, Bohn's *Chron. of Crusades ; Jeoff. de Vinsauf*, I, 34 ; II, 41.

CHAPTER VII.

THE NATIVE LIFE IN PALESTINE.

FROM the earliest age of Christianity the traditions of Italy had differed from those of the East, and open rupture would have occurred in the second century, concerning the question of Easter, but for Irenæus. Thenceforth the two great Churches went on their own ways, and the schism grew ever wider : in the fourth century the customs of the East and West already differed greatly. The fierce Trinitarian controversies then rent the Churches, and Arian and Orthodox prevailed alternately in the empire ; but the Filioque clause—though added by the third Synod of Toledo in 589 A.D.—was still unnoticed by the Creed of Gaul in the seventh century. Half a century before Charlemagne's accession Gregory II defended the use of images, and Greece and Italy fought the question out at Ravenna. The separation of the two Churches was complete before 800 A.D. ; and for a time—when Saracen fleets entered the Tiber in 846 A.D.—it seemed as if Islam were destined to destroy both alike ; but Franks and Greeks united, under the Eastern emperor who ruled all Southern Italy in 871. Meanwhile the contests of the Iconoclasts had resulted in the triumph of the Empress Irene, who defined the adoration to be paid to pictures, with incense, salutations, and candles, but forbade carved images, or pictures of the Deity. Thus the Church of Byzantium denounced the Church of Rome as idolatrous, because it still used statues, such as Leo the Isaurian had cast down from the Gate of Byzantium in 726 A.D. Yet St. Augustine had held that those who paid religious reverence to pictures were condemned by the Church at large. In 1054 A.D. the Pope had hurled his anathema at the Church of Constantinople, and by Godfrey the Greeks were dis-established for a century in Syria.

But separation had not rid the Papacy from home troubles caused by Eastern heresy. The later followers of Paul of Samosata—expelled from the Patriarchate of Antioch in 270 A.D.—nourished the Sabellian heresy, which taught that Christ was but a man inspired, and they were persecuted by Greek emperors after their establishment in Armenia and Pontus in 660 A.D. Transplanted to Thrace, in the eighth century, they reached Sicily and even Rome ; they influenced the Bulgarians, and spread to Milan, and beyond the Alps ; and, as Albigenses, they diverted the zeal of Western Christians, and often occupied the attention of the Popes, almost to the exclusion of more important efforts in Asia.

The rigid dogmatism of the Greeks had caused the separation, in Western Asia, of the various churches. Though united against Rome, as to the nature of the

Holy Spirit, they were divided among themselves as to the nature of the Son. The minds of Asiatic Christians were long influenced by two opposite teachings : that of the Nazarenes of Bashan, who believed that Jesus was a human prophet ; and that of the Gnostics of Syria and Alexandria—Saturninus and Basilides—who regarded Christ as not truly human at all. The Church decided that both views were heresy, and that Jesus was both human and divine. The question then raised was whether this nature was single or double, and whether actuated by a single or double will. Each question was answered in turn by the Church, in favour of the complex nature. Nestor, a Syrian, but Patriarch of Constantinople, doubted if the Virgin might be called the "Mother of God." The zeal of Cyril of Alexandria induced the Council of Ephesus to condemn him unheard in 431 A.D. The followers of Nestor withdrew to Nisibis, not far from Nineveh, and established a centre of learning which eclipsed that of Edessa two centuries later. Their missionaries carried a knowledge of letters into Central Asia ; they spread to North India, Ceylon, and Malabar ; and the Nestorian Church was found in China as early as 636 A.D. They, like the Sabellians, taught that the human Jesus, born of Mary, was distinct from the Spirit Christ who dwelt within Him.

The enemies of Nestor, led by Eutyches, flew to the other extreme, and preached a single nature, which the Council of Chalcedon, in 451 A.D., declared to be equally heretical. Some of the Syrians, obeying this decision, remained in communion with the Greeks, and were known later as Melchites, or those of the "king's party." But the majority followed Eutyches; and Jacob Baradæus, Bishop of Edessa in the next century, converted Armenians, Copts, and Abyssinians, to monophysite doctrines. Meanwhile a new solution of the problem was proffered in the Lebanon, where the Christians of Apamea taught that though the nature of Christ was double His will was single. In the seventh century they were known as Maronites, from Maro their first bishop.* Their dogma was decreed heretical by the sixth General Council in 680 A.D.† Thus when the Latins entered Syria, in the twelfth century, they found the native churches divided into four great bodies. The orthodox Greeks of Byzantium, and the Syrians called Melchites, were separated from the Nestorians of Persia, and of Eastern Mesopotamia ; the Monophysite Jacobites of Syria followed Jacob Baradæus, and, with the Armenians, relied on the decision of the Council of 449 A.D., which confirmed the views of Eutyches, and which was revoked at Chalcedon : while the Monothelite Maronites formed yet a fourth communion.

The influence of the Popes was directed to the reconciliation with Rome of these churches denounced by the Greeks. In 1182 A.D. the Maronites renounced their

---

* The Maronites claim to be named from Mâr Mârûn (about 400 A.D.) a saint whose relics were shown at Apamea, and whose hermitage is on the east bank of the Orontes, south of Emesa, a rock-cut monastery. The patriarch John Maron (686–707 A.D.) claimed the see of Antioch. The Emperor Heraclius had favoured the Monothelite doctrine, but the Maronites were known later as *Mardi* or "rebels." The present patriarch resides at the monastery of Kanobîn.

† *Jacques de Vitry*, p. 79, English translation.

special dogma, and being allowed to retain their married clergy they accepted the Papal protection. In 1237 A.D. Gregory IX was informed that a Jacobite patriarch at Jerusalem, and an archbishop from Egypt, with another who was Nestorian, had been converted.* Yet earlier, in 1206, the Armenian King Leo II accepted the Latin rites, and asked for plenary indulgence from Innocent III; but seven years later the same Pope had to complain that the same king drove out the Latin priests. This was the utmost that missionary zeal, and papal policy, effected.† The eastern Churches, all except the Maronites, remained independent of each other, and unreconciled with Rome. Armenians, Copts, Georgians Jacobites, Abyssinians, and Nestorians, still taught that Christ did not receive His body of the "substance of His mother." Greeks, and Orthodox Syrians, still held their separate Easter, and condemned what they called the image worship of Rome.

In the estimation of the Latins the Jacobites‡ held the first place, as the most important opponents of the Greeks, and the most learned of Orientals. They were the native Christian Church, and their apparent conformity was rewarded with recognition of their bishops as suffragans of the Latin hierarchy; but they retained the ancient rite of circumcision, which the Nazarenes had so strictly observed: they still blew their rams' horns like the Jews at festivals.§ Their Patriarch of

---

* *Regesta*, Nos. 1075.   † Ditto, Nos. 817, 862.
‡ Rey, *Colonies Franques*, pp. 75-82.
§ *Theodorich*, p. 14, English translation. *Jacques de Vitry*, p. 72, English translatoin.

Antioch lived at the Bar Sauma monastery, on the Euphrates, named from the zealous disciple of Nestor, who was ejected from his chair at Edessa, and founded the great school of Nisibis.   In Jerusalem they held the Chapel of St. James, under the belfry of the Holy Sepulchre Cathedral.   Their vestments are no doubt but little changed—the Patriarch wearing cloth of gold, with a cowl of the same.

The Nestorians were chiefly found in Persia, and further east, but also in Cyprus and at Tripoli, Gebal, Beirût and Acre.   Their famous school in Tripoli produced Bar Hebræus, who will be mentioned later.   As the Syrians preserved Syriac for their sacred language, so the Nestorians preserved an Aramaic dialect, then known as Chaldean.   Their Sacrament was according to the Greek rite, and their archbishopric of the west included Syria, Palestine, and Asia Minor, Cilicia, and Cyprus.

The Armenians were mainly known to the Princes of Edessa and Antioch, and became important allies in the thirteenth century, when the Latin power increased in their country.   Their priests were bound to marry, yet they were highly esteemed in Rome ; and some of their leaders advocated union with the Latin church.   The Assizes of Jerusalem were translated, in 1265 A.D., into Armenian ; and, as early as the middle of the twelfth century, the influence of the Normans was so strong in Armenia that the Court of the King was organised in imitation of that of Edessa.   The power of the Templars increased in Armenia, through the royal favour, until their own want of moderation led to their expulsion. The gigantic mitre of an Armenian patriarch, robed in silver cope lined with rose satin, dwarfed the small and angular Norman mitre of the Latin bishops, in the great ceremonies in which all Christians joined ; the nasal chanting—unaccompanied by music—of their masses, was perhaps hurried and irreverent even as now ; but the long white beards, and portly persons of their priests, gave them a venerable air of Oriental dignity. Their great church in Jerusalem was St. James on Sion.

The Armenians were distinct from other Christians in not mingling water with the wine of the Eucharist, and they observed the Nativity of Christ as a fast not as a feast, keeping the Epiphany instead as a festival. These customs still distinguish them, and though derived by them from Eutyches, were based on the early Gnosticism which regarded Christ as having only a spiritual body— a belief against which many of the Fathers wrote, although it was in a measure supported by Clement of Alexandria. The mingled cup is traced among Christians of the East to the second century, but Cyprian allows that the practice was not then universally followed.*

The Coptic monophysites from Egypt were also represented at Jerusalem ; but in small numbers. Their bishop wore a crown like the Greek patriarchs ; their monks wore white pointed cowls. They still preserved the ancient " kiss of peace," which was not

---

* *Jacques de Vitry*, p. 82, English translation. This practice of the Armenians was condemned in the Council of Constantinople in 691 A.D.

yet extinct in the West; and like the Armenians they
sprinkled the congregation with rose-water from silver
vessels. The Georgians from the Caucasus formed another
small community in the Holy City,* which their pilgrims
had visited already in the eleventh century. They
possessed the Abbey of the Cross, west of Jerusalem,
where ancient mosaics still remain, perhaps as old as, or
older than, the twelfth century. The legend of the
Cross they localised there, and claimed to show a
fragment of the Sacred Wood. They were said to come
from the "Land of Feminie," where Amazons were
believed still to ride out to war. In Northern Syria
sixty Georgian monks dwelt in the ancient monastery
of St. Simeon; and after Hattîn they took the place of
Latin hermits, in the caves and chapels of the Quarantania precipices over Jericho. A monastery of these
Iberians, as they were otherwise called, was built on the
banks of Jordan, and washed away by floods before
1185 A.D. Here they still practised the old penance of
standing on pillars, like St. Simon Stylites, as well as in
Northern Syria, and at Satalia in Asia Minor†; further
west at the monastery of St. Chrysostom—now Tell el
Kursi, south of Jericho—other Iberian ascetics gathered,
living side by side with the Greeks of St. John on Jordan,
and the Latins of Calamon. The Latins called the
Georgians "Christians of the Girdle."

The Abyssinian Christians are not noticed by the
mediæval writers but were found in Jerusalem in the

* Rey, *Colonies Franques*, p. 93; *City of Jerusalem*, p. 22, English
translation; *Jacques de Vitry*, p. 83, English translation.
† Phocas, p. 27, English translation.

fifteenth century by Felix Fabri. Like the Georgians they circumcised ; and they are said not to have baptised but to have branded their children on the face. This African custom is still preserved among them. It is to them probably that Jacques de Vitry refers, though confusing them with the Syrian Jacobites.*

These were the native churches separated from the Greeks. The Syrian Greeks had little of the Aryan blood in their veins, being mainly of Arab or Syrian race: they shut up their wives like other Orientals, and their daughters were veiled† ; but they were Greek by religion, and Greek in language, as regarded their clergy at least. They bitterly resented the intrusion of the Latin clergy, and obeyed their own patriarchs of Jerusalem and Antioch. But the Greek monks of Sinai were more subservient, and their abbot was a suffragan of the Latin Archbishop of Petra and Kerak. The Princes of Antioch‡ were willing, but unable in face of the Legate's opposition, to restore to the Greeks their possessions ; but about 1240 a Greek Patriarch who professed submission to the Pope was established for a time. A small sect of Greek Catholics was gradually formed, and still remains in existence with Catholic Armenians. This was, however, not the triumph aimed at by the Roman policy, and in 1187 the Greeks regained their power, tolerated by Saladin, and appropriating Latin churches left deserted. In 1160 the Latin Patriarch asked the commands of Alexander III as to these

* *Jacques de Vitry*, p. 75, English translation.
† *Jacques de Vitry*, p. 18, English translation.
‡ Rey, *Colonies Franques*, p. 89.

schismatics,[*] who were placed in an inferior position to
the Jacobites. In the reign of Baldwin I they had still
a monastery and an abbot, side by side with the Latins
on Tabor,[†] where the cave of Melchisadec was shown,
and the supposed site of his meeting with Abraham.
Their monastery of St. Saba, in the Judean desert, was
hallowed by the bones of John of Damascus, and the
same order had its house in Jerusalem.[‡]   South of
Bethlehem also their monastery of St. Chariton held the
remains of seven hundred fathers, which exhaled " a
wondrous perfume."   The abbot of St. Saba was
allowed a lamp in the Sepulchre for the Holy Fire, with
other Greek dignitaries whose altar was west of the
Tomb.   The caves on the eastern cliff of the Kidron
were inhabited by Greek, as well as by Armenian and
Jacobite hermits.   The hermitage of St. Euthymius, east
of St. Saba, was restored from ruins in 1185 A.D., at the
site now called *Mird;* and in the Kelt Valley was St.
John of Chozeboth, with a small chapel, the frescoes of
which still remain.[§]   These, with the larger monastery of St. John on Jordan, are all the buildings
mentioned by Greek pilgrims ; and the Latin writers
generally abstain from any notice of schismatic holy
places.

* *Regesta*, No. 357.
† *Abbot Daniel*, p. 68, English translation.
‡ Ditto, pp. 3, 18, 34.
§ *Phocas*, pp. 14, 20, 25, English translation.   These frescoes (see *Mem.
Survey West. Pal.*, III, p. 192) at Deir Wâdy Kelt represent St. Athanasius
of Mount Athos, St. John of Chozeboth, St. Gerasmius of Calamon,
Joachim the Virgin's father, and pictures of the Entombment, the death
of the Virgin, the Last Judgment, and the Washing of the Disciples'
feet, as I ascertained from the inscriptions in 1873.

The greater number of the native Christians lived in the Lebanon—even as far east as Sardenai near Damascus—and in the Principalities of Antioch and Edessa, as well as in Armenia. In Palestine itself the population was mainly Moslem in the villages, with Greeks and Jacobites in the towns. The Moslems also were divided among themselves, by differences of religious faith ; and the few Jews who dared to live among the Normans were equally divided from the Samaritans scattered throughout Palestine.

Religious divisions had arisen in Islam as soon as the Prophet died. After the conquest of Syria, and the death of Omar, the Khalifs of Damascus maintained the simple orthodoxy of Islam, although descended, not from the Prophet, but from his conquered enemy Abu Sofian, of the Omeiyah family of the Koreish. They reigned in Syria till 749 A.D., when the last of them was defeated by the Baghdad Khalif Abu-el-Abbas es-Suffah, descended from the prophet's uncle ; but by the Abbaside family the true creed was equally maintained. Among Persian Moslems who had followed Âly (Muhammad's cousin german and son-in-law) and who did not accept the first three great Khalifs, preceding him, but fought for his son till he resigned in 660 A.D., strange philosophic views developed, and mysticism gathered round the names, not only of the Prophet or of Âly, but of Hasan and Hosein, and of the eight Imâms whom the Shiâh acknowledged as true successors, down to El Mahdi the Muhammadan Messiah, who is yet expected to appear again on earth.

The schism was political and racial as well as religious, and the Shiàh or "followers" of Àly were mostly Persians, who hated the Arab conquerors, and rejected their Sunna or "customs," in favour of their own mystic comments on the Korân, which finally raised the unhappy Àly to the rank of a deity. The doctrine of a future Saviour was not taken from Christian teaching, but from the Persian expectation of a mystic future hero ; and just as the earlier Manicheans of Persia had mingled, in a strange eclectic system, the teaching of Buddhists and Mazdeans with their own Gnostic beliefs, so too the Moslem philosophic and mystic sects mingled Buddhism, and Mazdeism, and Gnostic Christianity, with the plain teaching of the Arab prophet. It resulted from a belief in the coming of the Mahdi—the "guided one" who was to be also the Guide—that Moslem sects, time after time, split off from the main body of believers, because in some Khalif or Imâm they held that the Mahdi had at last appeared. It is the same cause which, in our own age, separates the Bâbis of Persia, and the Soudan Moslems, from their orthodox brethren.

But another tendency underlay the heretic teaching of other thinkers. Educated Arabs were attracted by the Greek philosophy, preserved in Syriac translations by the learned Nestorians of Nisibis and Edessa. The reign of El Mamûn, the seventh Abbaside Khalif, was the palmy age of Arab literary culture : science, philology, poetry, music, history, and archæology, flourished equally : Greek and Persian, as well as Arab, books were stored in libraries : Sanskrit, Aramaic, and Syriac writings, were translated: the philosophy of Aristotle and Plato became known to Moslems; and though free thought was discouraged by the tenth Khalif of Baghdad —El Mutawakkil—in the latter part of the ninth century, it was not extirpated; the companions of the Epicurean Omar Khiyam, whatever their public teaching might be, were Moslem sceptics of the eleventh century. In the time of El Mamûn Aristotle, as preserved by the Nestorians, was translated into Arabic, and the Neo-Platonic speculations became familiar; while the Sufis, or Sophists, were attracted by the Buddhist doctrines, at the same early period of cultured thought. In El Ghazâli both influences were combined, but the scep-ticism of this Persian disciple of the ancients, who died in 1111 A.D., led to the revolt of the orthodox against philosophy, which, henceforth dying out in Asia, flourished only in Spain. The Arabs added little that was new, but they became imbued with the spirit of the Greek, Persian, and Indian culture, just as their architecture was founded on that of the nations they conquered, and their numerals borrowed from India and given to Europe.

Like the Buddhists they believed that philosophic truth could never be attained by the masses of the people, and that some form of creed was necessary for the many, from which the few were free. This was the basis of the various systems which organized an initiation in various grades. The Batenin, or "Esoteric" teachers, appeared as early as 700 A.D., in the followers of Hasan of Basrah. Mutazali, Khatebi,

Karmathians, Ismàiliyeh, and other sects which followed, while teaching a syncretic dogma, were at
heart sceptics, who believed in neither God nor
prophet.   Islam cast out these heretics, and persecuted them ; but their influence was sufficient to rend
the Moslem world.   From the orthodox centre of
Baghdad they fled to Syria and Egypt, and so dis-
seminated schism in the west.

Among the earliest of these sectarians were the
Ismàiliyeh, who arose among the Persian Shiàh, and
recognised as their reincarnate leader Ismàil the sixth
Imâm.   In the ninth century they became established
in Syria, and the Fatimite Khalifs of Egypt descended
from a firm believer in their system.   Thus over Africa,
and all the Egyptian dominions, their heresy flourished ;
and in the eleventh century the townsmen of Syria were
mainly Shiàh.   Abdallah, their great teacher, was a
sceptic, well versed in many religions, and he taught a
system which aimed at attracting men of every faith,
and at leading them, through seven grades of initiation,
to the final result of the denial of all belief.   Only two
realities existed—so he taught the favoured few—the
active and the passive, the male and female principles of
nature which were the source of being.

Side by side with the Ismàiliyeh rose the Nusciriyeh.
They sprang from the powerful Karmathian sect of
Persia, which for a while, in the ninth century A.D.,
reduced to tribute Arabia, Syria, and Egypt ; and they
took their name from an Imâm El Faraj, of the town of
Nasrâna, whom they called El Nuseiri.   In the wild

glens of Lebanon their adherents still found shelter, when their power was overthrown.

The eleventh century witnessed the appearance of two other heresies far more formidable—that of the Assassins, and that of the Druzes. Three ambitious sceptics swore brotherhood in Persia. The first was Omar Khiyam the poet, the second was Nizâm el Mulk, who became the vizir of the Turkish Sultan Melek Shah, the third was Hasan el Homeiri, founder of a secret sect which, in the twelfth and thirteenth centuries, was feared in Syria by Christian and Moslem alike—followers of the Sheikh of the Mountain, called Hashshâshîn, "hemp smokers" or Assassins. All these three comrades were initiated into the highest order of the Ismàiliyeh, and as such had no religious belief at all.

This alliance did not long continue, when the Assassin strove and failed to supplant the vizir. Melek Shah and Nizâm el Mulk were among his first victims, for in 1090 he seized the Castle of Alamut in Irak, and gathered disciples. Near the impregnable cliffs of Alamut, " the Eagles' Nest," were fair gardens in a valley watered by springs and conduits, and peopled by the fairest of Persian girls. Among the wild youths of the region, Hasan sought for such as seemed to be daring and reliable, and promised them the joys of Paradise as the reward of obedience. They drank the drug he offered them, and waked to find between the mountains fair lawns and flowers, and shady trees, and pleasant kiosques with pictures, and gilded bowers, and tapestries of silk, and pillows of down. Wine and fruits lay on the tables, and beautiful women gaily dressed sported, and sang the songs of love, with instruments of music in their hands. It was Paradise, with living Houris waiting for the brave ; and so a few short days of happiness passed swiftly by, and the initiate woke again in the grim castle at the valley mouth. Was it a dream, due only to the hemp he smoked, or a reality ? It matters not; though nothing now remains to show that such a fairyland existed, yet Marco Polo firmly held it did. The new disciple or *fedawi*, "the devoted one," from whom a blind unquestioning obedience was exacted, was promised that he once again should enter Paradise when his desperate task was done. The secrets of Hasan were known only to the *rafîk* or "companion ": the intelligence needful for political schemes was supplied by the *dai* or "missionary," who sought converts in distant regions, preaching the strange mysticism which the leaders knew to be only delusion. The *fedawi* neither knew nor cared for anything save Paradise—the secret confided to him by his master. Thus an unscrupulous sceptic organised murder. He died in 1124 A.D. ; but the sect lived on until suppressed in 1254 A.D. by Mangu Khan. By the middle of the twelfth century their Sheikh was established in the rugged Lebanon, east of Tripoli, and was known to the Latins as the "Old Man of the Mountain " ; and their first victim was the Khalif of Egypt in 1149 A.D. Raymond of Tripoli, and Conrad of Montferrat also fell their victims, with two other Khalifs, and various Arab and Turkish Emirs.

They attempted Saladin's life in 1174, and at Ezzaz in Syria in 1176, and that of Edward of England in 1272. Bibars, the cruel conqueror, was not loth to use their daggers; and neither creed nor race protected the victim of their evil designs.

The Druze heresy, if yet wilder in its teaching, was far less dangerous in its moral aims. El Hâkem, the Fatimite Khalif in Egypt, born in 985 A.D., was not twelve years old when he acceded, and his early years were marked by revolts in Syria, and intrigues of the provincial governors. After fourteen years he beheaded the eunuch Barjewân, his tyrannical vizir, and began to rule for himself. He belonged, like his ancestors, to the Ismâiliyeh sect ; but symptoms of insanity soon showed themselves in the fantastic character of his regulations. Many of the most respected Sunnees were put to death, and Jews and Christians were persecuted, until a revolt in 1007 A.D. for a time induced some moderation. Three years later, however, the Jerusalem churches were destroyed by his order ; and in 1014 all women were ordered to remain in their houses, and shoemakers forbidden to make them shoes. It was about this time that Persian mystics began to trade upon his crazy fancies, and Muhammad ed Derâzi persuaded El Hâkem that he was not only Khalif of Islam, but an incarnation of deity—the Mahdi himself. The Egyptians drove out Ed Derâzi, who fled to Mount Hermon ; but his master Hamzah of Khorassan, had followed him when he established himself in El Hâkem's service, and he continued to influence the crazy Khalif. The pilgrimage to Mecca was discontinued, and Moslem customs disregarded. At length at the age of thirty-six, after twenty-four years of evil government, the manias of El Hâkem became intolerable, and he was strangled by his sister's order, in his retirement on Jebel Mokattam near Cairo.

Hamzah and his followers, persecuted by the new Khalif El Hâkem's son, fled to join Ed Derâzi in Syria, where the Ismàiliyeh dogmas had attracted many among the rude and ignorant mountain tribes. Hamzah denounced Ed Derâzi to these, and preached that El Hâkem would return once more. The year following he too disappeared, leaving a new heresy in Islam having its centre in the glens of Hermon.* The religion of the Druzes was a mystery to the uninitiated; and Jews and Christians told strange stories about them; but it is known to us as explained in works attributed to Hamzah, and contains little to distinguish it from Ismàiliyeh beliefs, except the dogma of El Hâkem's divinity. It aimed at gathering in Jew, Christian, Manichean, and Moslem, in one great body—to each proclaiming that his faith was but a part of truth. Muhammad himself had so regarded the partial revelations which preceded him; but Muhammad was sincere, and the leaders of the Druzes accepted all men because they believed in no form of faith themselves. So vigorous was the preaching of the missionaries, sent out from Hermon by Boha-ed-Dîn, successor of Hamzah, that in the twelfth century the sect had spread through Syria and Persia, to Ghuzni and India, to Arabia and Egypt, and even

* See Sylvestre de Sacy's *Religion des Druzes*, and Churchill's *Lebanon*.

to Constantinople. It is not impossible that the
Templars were influenced, either by Druze teaching,
or by some other form of the Ismàilîyeh doctrines,
while they held the Assassins of the Lebanon to tribute.

The doctrines of Hamzah were founded on the
Platonic teaching of the phenomenon and the idea.
His professed belief was in a series of incarnations of
the Deity in historic persons accompanied by incarnations of the Spirit in contemporary prophets. Abraham, Moses, Jesus, Muhammad, and El Hâkem, were
the Divine incarnations: Ishmael, Aaron, Simon Peter,
Àly, and Hamzah, were the human beings in whom
the Spirit had dwelt. To the Jew the Druzes spoke
of Abraham and Ishmael, Moses and Aaron: to the
Christian they spoke of Jesus and Simon Peter; to
Moslems of Muhammad and Aly: and to their own
chief disciples of El Hâkem and Hamzah—the last and
greatest manifestations on earth. They inculcated on
the uninitiated obedience to the seven commands of
Hamzah—prayer, sacrifice, tithes, fasting, pilgrimage,
the holy war, and submission ; and every mystic idea
found in any system then known in Asia was incorporated. Transmigration of souls was borrowed from
the older philosophies of Greece and India, with the
attainment of the Imâmat, when the perfect are no
more born in the flesh—the Buddhist Nirvana. All
former faiths were but types and allegories : yet the
Resurrection was to reward the pious after a time of
trouble, such as Hebrew prophets and Persian followers
of Zoroaster had foretold.

There is much in the Druze system to connect it with the Buddhism of Central Asia. They said that El Hâkem would re-appear, leading an army from their Holy Land in China, to which the good Druze was carried by angels when he died : a judgment of the wicked, and a temporal reign of El Hâkem, were then to follow. They taught that the Evil Spirit had also been incarnate in the various ages, to oppose the divine persons and prophets ; and that his last appearance was in the very Ed Derâzi from whom the name by which they were called by others was taken, but who among themselves was cursed as Hamzah's enemy, and called El Ȧjal, " the Calf," by a play on the title of El Ȧkal, " the Doctor," which he claimed. This was the origin of the brazen calf—perhaps a relic of older paganism—which they kept in their *Khalwehs*, or solitary meeting places, only to treat with insult and contempt. Ed Derâzi was the incarnation of Satan and Iblîs, the Antichrist, and the Rival. Hamzah was the Imâm, the Mediator, the Book, the Kiblah, the flower, the trumpet, the banner, the Spirit, the camel, and John the Baptist. Such wild symbolism was based on the dogma of re-incarnation. The details are of little interest, because the teaching was not a real belief. They included Persian archangels, cabalistic values of mystic numbers, parables, and philosophic speculations, quotations from the Gospels, and allegoric explanations of the Korân. It was a mighty mingling of every form of dogma known in Asia, with the new figures of El Hâkem and Hamzah ; but it was designed to be a solvent which, by admitting all to the lower degrees of knowledge, should lead the few to the " Concealed Destruction," which was the real and secret teaching of Hamzah and his heirs.

The Book of the " Concealed Destruction " also exists, teaching a very different doctrine from the openly avowed Druze catechism of the ignorant. Hamzah believed that no religion of any kind was true ; and to the leaders he gave the Seven Laws, which abrogated those prescribed to their followers. These were : Truth, its Concealment when needful, Mutual Aid, Renunciation of all Dogma, the Oneness of God, Submission to His Will, and Resignation to Fate. Hence it arose that the Druze was commanded to agree with each sectarian— Jew, Christian, Moslem, or Buddhist—in turn : to deny his faith : to use no ceremonies or prayers : to be chaste and sober : and to do no evil : but to despise in his heart the errors of the ignorant.

This system was not of Arab origin, nor were the Hermon Druzes of Arab race. They were in great measure of Persian stock ; and their women wore the silver horn beneath the veil, projecting forward from the forehead, a costume which was usual among tribes of the Oxus and Caspian.* They were secluded as among Moslems, but the secrets of initiation were not confined to men. There were women among the leaders of the sect, to whom the final teaching was also imparted. The Druze ascetics dwelt in solitary hermitages, lying on mats with stone pillows, dressed in wool with girdles like the monks, and eating dry bread and raisins. The

* *Journal Royal Asiatic Society*, April, 1886, p. 202.

secret symbol by which the Druzes recognised each
other was the fig, which was also a Manichean emblem*
of a secret and abominable worship. The Christian
dogmas of the Druzes appear indeed to have been
mainly based on the teaching of Manes.

These, then, were the mystic and sceptical sects which
the Crusaders found in Syria. The Shiàh Moslems were
mainly found in the mountains east of Tyre. They
awaited the return of Àly, and mourned for Hasan and
Hosein like their Persian brethren. They carried with
them sacred earth and stones from Persia, and they wore
the long side locks like the Pharisees, which still distinguish them. They broke the platter which a Christian
might have touched, and refused to give even a draught
of water to any not of their own creed. But they
were few among the many, seeking refuge in the
higher mountains, and hating the Sunnee as well as
the Christian. The Druzes dwelt among them east of
Sidon, and on Hermon, and fought the garrisons of
Belfort and of Château Neuf in Galilee. Nûr ed Dîn
confirmed their sheikh in the government of Hasbeiya.
Benjamin of Tudela relates the vulgar opinion as to
their beliefs, and accuses them of immoralities connected
with the phallic worship which appears to have really
prevailed among the Ismàilîyeh, and which is charged
against Druzes even now.

The Nuseiriyeh were found in the country of Tripoli,
at Akkar on the south and Safita on the north. Many
of them were slain during the first advance in 1098 A.D. ;

* Cyril, *Catechetical Lect.*, VI, 23.

but their mysterious tenets are mentioned in 1234 A.D. by Alberic de Trois Fontaines. Jacques de Vitry, who confounded them with the Essenes, or Jewish hermits of the time of Christ, does not distinguish them from the Assassins, who held ten castles in the mountains east of Tortosa in 1140 A.D.* The phallic worship of the Ismâilîyeh, who are the last modern remnant of the Assassins, in this same region—on the mountains west of Emesa—is generally credited among natives of Palestine. If we may believe Clement of Alexandria and Tertullian, the final symbol of the Eleusinian mysteries denoted the same worship of the creative energy.† In each case the reason was the same, whether among Greeks and Romans, or Assassins and Templars—scepticism and materialism were the real facts, concealed by vows of secrecy and by mystic language.

But these wild and dangerous sects did not represent the majority of Moslem peasants and wandering Arabs, who paid tribute to the Latins.

The Fellahîn, or " ploughmen," were Moslem by name, but not of Arab race, and not instructed in the Arab faith. They were descendants of the ancient Hittites and Amorites, of the Assyrian colonists from the East, and the old Nabathean tribes also transplanted by Assyrians to Palestine; and an infusion of later Arab blood had only in part modified their race and their language, which still presented a dialect mainly Aramean.

---

* *Jacques de Vitry*, p. 85, English translation ; Rey, *Colonies Franques*, pp. 98–100 ; Benj. Tudela, p. 80, Bohn's *Early Travels in Palestine.*
† Cohortat II, and *Against the Valentinians.*

Their religion was the ancient worship of local spirits, called indeed Nebys or " prophets," but essentially the same with earlier Baals adored on mountain tops or under green trees.   They piled up memorial pillars in their honour, and fastened rags of their clothing to the branches to call attention to their visits, and swore by sacred stones and dolmen altars in the woods, and lighted lamps for the sick, and sacrificed kids and lambs, and held their ancient harvest feasts, and cast bread on the waters, and feared the malignant spirits—ghouls, and jân, and ghosts, and afrîts, and goblins.   All that they asked was bread to eat, safety from the cruel Turk, and justice.   These three things the Latins gave them, and they were content as serfs under Latin lords.   But after half a century the favourites of the half-Armenian Milicent, the vassals of the avaricious Amaury, and of his leper son, began to oppress.   New taxes were levied, and justice was sold.   Then arose a Sunnee leader just and merciful, able to defeat the Franks in battle, pious and not given to wine—a sultan who united all Islam under his sway.   The Fellahîn were zealous to follow Saladin, yet had been content to live under the just and merciful rule of Godfrey.

The old land law of the East was a " village tenure," which distributed the lands according to the numbers of each family and of their ploughs ; so many strips divided off by stones being assigned to every plough, and each tiller receiving some of the good land and some of the bad.   This arrangement was not disturbed by the Latins.   The carucates remained as units of sale, and the serfs or villeins were handed over when a village was given or sold. Thus the peasants were never displaced, and, as they rarely went more than a few miles from the village, their servitude was unfelt, although the law forbade masterless men to wander through the country unless as pilgrims. When the tithes, and capitation tax, and rights of the seigneur were paid, there yet remained half the produce for the peasant—more, probably, than Turkish governors had granted. Neither Pope nor Patriarch heeded the Saracen villein, and while robbers and murderers were hanged by the king's constable, the native customs were adjudged by the native jury under the baillie. There was little, therefore, to cause complaint among the peasantry, as long as the seigneur was just, or the appeal was justly decided.

The cultivation of Syria and Palestine—lands in which the soil is often very rich and productive—was fully developed by the Latins. The existing records of the twelfth century are full of references to vineyards and olive - yards, orchards, cornfields, and watered gardens. In the north* there were forests of oak, pine, and cedar : the sandstones and upper limestones of the Lebanon were hidden by the bright green of the vines, trailing over the drystone terrace walls. The sandy shore of Beirût had already its pine plantations, and at Haifa and other seaside towns were palm groves by the streams. In Oultre Jourdan the roebuck wandered among the glades of oak by running brooks, and hid

* Rey, *Colonies Franques*, pp. 236–252.

also in the copses of Carmel. The hills of Palestine
were covered with brushwood, the plains of Cæsarea
dotted with oaks. In the more open lands wheat and
barley, oats, Indian corn, durrah, rice, millet, lentils,
beans, and sesame, were grown. Cotton, and flax, and
indigo, were cultivated in the plains, and in the Jordan
Valley. Madder grew at Tripoli and Damascus. The
flax of Nâblus was as good as that of Egypt. Chick
peas, and lupines, fennel, peas, cucumbers, and melons,
flourished in the irrigated gardens.

The Casale was a hamlet of at least an hundred
houses, taxed at about seven shillings each a year.*
The carucate was a plot of twenty-three cords in
length by sixteen in breadth, each cord being of
eighteen toises (not quite two yards in length), giving
an area of about eighty English acres.† The tithes
were paid at St. Martin's Day in November. The
angaria, or feudal service, did not, in the Royal
Domain, amount to more than one day's labour for
every carucate. The seigneur gave out seed when
needed, and demanded only one fowl per carucate in
return. The fruits in the gardens were the same as
now—figs, olives, pomegranates, and apricots, oranges,
bananas, and almonds. The olive-yards covered the
lower hills, and the vineyards flourished in the higher
mountains.

The cultivation of the sugar-cane was not confined to
Tripoli. The old Crusaders' sugar mills still stand in

---

* *William of Tyre*, pp. 271, 423, 434, French translation, Vol. III.
† The *Feddân* of the modern Syrians is about forty acres.

ruins near Jericho, and others existed at Acre, El Bassah, and Tyre, Yanuh, Byblos, and Engedi.* The growth of cotton was especially developed in the lands of Antioch, Edessa, and Lesser Armenia. The wines of Latakia and Batrun were famous, and that of Engedi was prized in Jerusalem ; but the vineyards were spread throughout the country, and each had its watch-tower and its rock-cut press. The present culture of Palestine does not, perhaps, attain to a tenth part of that which enriched the Latins in the first century of their rule.

In the deserts to the east the wandering Arabs lived at peace tending their countless herds of wild unsaddled camels, driven in droves like oxen. Amaury of Nâblus in 1178 A.D., sold to the Master of the Hospital "all his Bedouin of the Beni Karka" for a sum of twelve hundred pounds. Baldwin IV gave them a hundred tents of Bedouin in 1180 A.D.; and twenty years earlier they obtained from Baldwin III "fifty tents of Bedouin, namely those who had served neither himself nor his predecessors."† The Arabs, however, were among the first to join Saladin, and to shake off all semblance of serfdom.

Slaves, not attached to the land as serfs, were owned not only by Saracens but by Christians also. The Moslems made slaves of Christians taken in war, and brought them also from Nubia, by the old route through Jeddah. The Latins often set free their slaves,‡ whose rights and liabilities were regulated by the Assizes. By

* *Regesta*, Nos. 644, 1082.
† Ditto, Nos. 355, 567, 593.
‡ Rey, *Colonies Franques*, p. 107.

the agreement of King Amaury with the Church of St.
Lazarus, north of Jerusalem, every tenth slave taken in
war was to be given to the brethren.[*]

Two other small elements of the mixed population of
Syria are still to be noticed—namely, the Jews and the
Samaritans. The Jews are hardly noticed at all in
extant documents, though in 1274 and 1286 A.D. we
find a Jew banker, named Eli, noticed by Agnes of
Scandalion.[†]   The Crusades were often begun by
murder of the European Jews, and in the East they
were forbidden, by the Latin law, to hold any land,
and were classed as inferior to the Moslems.[‡]   It is
from Benjamin of Tudela, the Jewish traveller of 1160
A.D., that all we know as to their fortunes in Asia during
this age is gathered.

Rabbi Benjamin travelled for nearly fourteen years :
from Saragossa he went over Europe to Rome, where
he arrived about 1160 A.D., and reached Constantinople
next winter. He was in Antioch in 1163, and then
passed on to the south, and reached Egypt, returning
to Sicily about 1169 A.D. He appears to have gone to
Baghdad and Persia, Arabia and Nubia, and he distin-
guishes his own experience from what he heard of more
distant lands. His information is valuable except as
regards the ancient sites of his fathers' land ; but he is
hopelessly wrong in most of what he says as to Bible
geography. He found the Genoese powerful at sea,
and at war with the Pisans. The trade of Byzantium,

[*] *Regesta,* No. 397.
[†] Ditto, Nos. 1399, 1435.
[‡] Rey, *Colonies Franques,* p. 104.

which he describes in detail, was partly in the hands of the Jews of Galata and Pera, including two thousand Rabbinical, and five hundred Karaite Jews, whose quarters were divided by a wall. As soon as he entered the Latin dominions he found the Jews few in number and poor. In Antioch, under Boemund the Stammerer, he found only ten Jewish glass makers; but in Gebal, where the Genoese were settled, there were two hundred; and fifty in Beirût. The Jews of Tyre, four hundred in all, were shipowners and glass makers. In Jerusalem two hundred Jewish dyers lived under the Tower of David. The Juiverie, or Ghetto, in the north-east quarter of the city, he does not notice, and it was perhaps established later. The " mourners of Jerusalem" who, in all ages since the Temple was destroyed, have been maintained by Jewish charity, seem, then, to have been still wailing at its outer wall, among whom was Rabbi Abraham, a pious ascetic. Twelve Jewish dyers lived in Bethlehem, and a few in Hebron, where the bones of others were brought in coffers, to be left near the site of Abraham's sepulchre. At Beit Jibrîn there were only three Jews, but at Toron on the Jaffa road (now Latrûn) there were three hundred. Three who were dyers lived at Beit Nûba, and three others at Ramleh. In Jaffa, where he saw the ancient Jewish cemetery of the second century A.D., which has yielded so many early Hebrew texts, there was, in 1163 A.D., only a single Jew—a dyer. Ascalon was then a trading port, and two hundred Rabbinites had ventured there from Egypt. From the south Benjamin travelled back to Jezreel, where another

Hebrew dyer lived, and so reached Tiberias, famous
from the second to the fifth centuries of the Christian
era for its great Talmudic school.   Only fifty Jews
remained in this sacred city.   In Upper Galilee he
found twenty at El Jish, and fifty at Alma ; and finally,
at Acre, four hundred from the south of France.   These
details seem to represent the Jewish population of the
Latin Kingdom, numbering only one thousand nine
hundred in all.   Not one is mentioned as being rich,
and it is the more clear that the Latins would have none
of Jews because in Moslem regions around they were
found to be numerous and highly prosperous.

In Damascus, under Nûr ed Dîn, Rabbi Benjamin
found three thousand Jews, "many of whom were rich
and learned men."   In Palmyra two thousand warlike
Jews were independent of both Christians and Moslems.
They were equally numerous in the Edessa region, now
already lost by the Latins, and at Nisibis and Mosul ;
but Baghdad was the centre of the Eastern Hebrews,
under the "Prince of the Captivity," who claimed
descent from David.   Side by side with the Abbaside
khalif, this religious leader appears to have been
honoured by even Moslems.   He wore a diadem on his
turban, and rode through the city robed in embroidered
silk, while men shouted before him "Make way for our
Lord, the Son of David !"   His authority extended from
beyond the Caucasus, over Armenia, Persia, Mesopotamia, and Arabia, to Yemen.   All Rabbis and ministers
were appointed by him, and a tax levied for him on
Jewish markets, merchandise, and inns.   Many costly

gifts were brought him, and he was rich, learned, and hospitable. The Baghdad synagogue had pillars of coloured marble plated with silver and gold, and the city seems to have been the Paradise of Israel during an age of persecution in Europe.

At Hillah, on the Euphrates, the Jews also were many ; and the College of Pombedatha, which had existed for several centuries, was still maintained. In Arabia the Jews—who had been powerful in Muhammad's time— were independent, holding the cities, tilling the land, rearing cattle, and fighting the Arabs. In Persia they dwelt near the Assassins, who were independent, and near the frontiers of Media twenty-five thousand Jews were congregated. In 1155 David el Roy, a Jewish mystic, had here claimed supernatural powers, and had stirred up sedition till his own father-in-law killed him in his bed. Yet further east, at Khiva on the Oxus, eight thousand Jews lived in alliance with the Tartars, and throve as traders. In Samarkand there were fifty thousand Jews. The trade of Eastern Asia was thus secured by the Hebrew influence over the Turks and Mongols ; and in Khuzistan the merchants of India met, on the Tigris, with those of Arabia, Persia, and Mesopotamia ; and the Jewish brokers dealt with them all. The black Jews of India, and others in Ceylon, had pushed their way yet further ; and they had also entered China,[*] where a synagogue at Pien appears to have been built in 1164 A.D.

In Egypt the Israelites, settled at Assuan and Chalua, commanded the trade of inner Africa, in gold and precious

[*] Yule's *Marco Polo*, I, p. 30.

stones, iron, and copper; and in Egypt generally they were very numerous. Alexandria was already a meeting place of all nations, where Spaniards and Italians, Germans, Danes, Saxons, English, Normans, and Frenchmen, met with the Moors, the Indians, the Arabs, and Abyssinians. Three thousand Jews lived in this city, and the Pisans found its trade of great importance.

From this description it is clear that, though excluded from Syria, the Jews in great measure commanded the trade of Asia and Africa with Europe. It is still more remarkable that they had established a Jewish kingdom beyond the bounds of Norman influence. The legend of the Lost Ten Tribes, living in the mountains of Gog and Magog, was, like the legend of Prester John, much talked of in the West, and, like the latter, it had a foundation in truth. As early as 1175 Petachia of Ratisbon travelled to the East to find the ten tribes, and "reached the tribe of Issachar" in the mountains beyond Persia and Media.* The Jews of this region regarded the Tartars as descendants of the Canaanites, the Khitai being Hittites, and the people of Khiva Hivites. Rabbi Benjamin himself speaks of four Jewish tribes in Bactria; and the Sabbatic river, beyond which the lost tribes were to be sought, had been displaced from its true site under the Castle of Krak in Syria, to be variously identified with the Oxus and the Ganges. The belief originated in the story of the land Arsareth, never before inhabited, and beyond a river which should be

---

* Carmoly, *Itinéraires de la Terre Sainte*, pp. vii–xiii ; *Jacques de Vitry*, p. 86, English translation.

dried up when the ten tribes returned, which is found in the second book of Esdras (xiii, 41–50).

North of the Caspian lived the Turkish race of the Khozars, among whom were many Alans and Georgians, Armenians, Jews, and other refugees from the south. The Khozars held the Volga, and the Caspian itself was called the Khozar lake.* The terms *Bak, Ilik*, and *Khakhan*, which denominated their chiefs, are sufficient evidence of the Turkish character of Khozar language.

The Karaite—or non-Talmudic—Jews had reached the Crimea in the second century A.D., and early appeared among the Khozars. The later Sassanian monarchs of Persia fought against them, and Kobad built the wall near Derbend in the Caucasus to shut them out. When the Moslems conquered Persia they also fought in vain against the Khozars. In the time of Harûn-er-Rashîd, according to Arab writers, they were converted to Judaism, and a Jewish king ruled over the mingled population, which included many Moslems. At Ismid also an allied Jewish king ruled in the tenth century, amid a population mainly Christian; and a Jewish general commanded the army. Masûdi says that most of the Khozars accepted Jewish beliefs, though some were pagans. The trade in furs—fox skins and ermine and minever—was carried through their country. The Jewish minister of the Khalif of Spain is said to have written to the Khozar king in 958 A.D., and Yusef, the Jewish monarch of this mingled people, sent an answer. Their power then extended

* Carmoly, *Itinéraires de la Terre Sainte*, pp. 3–104;

even to the Crimea, and to the Sea of Asov; but in
1016 A.D. the Byzantines had already broken up this
kingdom ; and in the twelfth century the Jews of the
Volga and the Oxus remained only as trading communities among the Turkic tribes.   Frederic II wrote
to Henry III of England, in the thirteenth century,
calling the Tartars descendants of the ten tribes shut
up by Alexander the Great in the Caspian mountains ;
and the legend survived, as did that of Prester John,
long after the reality had ceased to be.

The Samaritans of the twelfth and thirteenth centuries
were tolerated by the Latins, and were found in more
than one city of their kingdom ; but they did not
possess the power of the Jews, and were already a
dying sect.   Benjamin of Tudela says that they numbered a hundred in all at Shechem, their original
centre, with a synagogue on Mount Gerizim, where they
held the Passover.   They had been very turbulent in
the time of Justinian, and were far more strict in the
observance of the Law, both in the sixth and in the
twelfth century, than were most of the Jews—especially
as regarded defilement by the dead, and the purifications
of Levitical custom.   There were also two hundred
Samaritans in Cæsarea, and three hundred in Ascalon.
In Damascus four hundred Samaritans lived as friends
with the Karaite Jews, who most resembled them in
their beliefs: but the two sects never intermarried.
Probably there were others in Gaza and Alexandria,
where they had synagogues till quite recent times.

The Samaritans have a chronicle of their own, begun

by Eleazar ben Amram in 1149 A.D.,* and continued two
centuries later by its copyist Joseph ben Ismail ; but it
gives little information as to their history in the twelfth
and thirteenth centuries beyond the High Priests' names.
They had suffered from the Turks, who took five hundred
of them captive to Damascus ; and some who claimed
to be of the tribe of Benjamin fled to Gaza. In 1244
the Kharezmians invaded Palestine, and, after the great
Christian defeat at Gaza in that year, the Samaritans
suffered cruelly from these barbarous tribes from Eastern
Persia. A great many were slain in Shechem, and men,
women, and children were again led captive to Damascus, where their settled brethren helped them. Very
few, however, returned to their ancient home ; and less
than two hundred survivors now assemble on Gerizim,
whereas in the time of Muhammad their settlements
were scattered in all parts of Palestine.

The sum of the mingled native populations ruled by
the Franks is thus completed ; and with the manners
and beliefs of all they became fairly familiar. Syria was
the centre towards which the populations of Europe and
Asia seemed to turn their faces, where Aryan, Semitic,
and Turanian peoples came together in peaceful intercourse—Greeks and Russians from the North, Turks,
Tartars, Armenians, Jews, and Arabs, from East and
South, Egyptians and Nubians and Copts from Africa,
and every European nation from the West. Even in the
Isle of Skye a Viking treasure has been found, including
coins of Arab Khalifs of the tenth century, and in 1248

* Neubauer, *Journal Asiatique*, 1869, pp. 365-447.

A.D. letters in Mongolian reached the Pope in Rome. There was perhaps no period in history when nations of the far West and East were more closely connected by a constant intercourse, than they became during the age of Latin rule in Palestine, and in the trading period of the thirteenth century which followed.

CHAPTER VIII.

THE THIRD CRUSADE.

AFTER the fall of Jerusalem in 1187 William of Tyre sped to preach the third Crusade in France, where Philip II, Augustus—then only twenty-three years of age—had already reigned eight years, and had become absolute in his kingdom over his feudal lords. He had cut down the frontier tree of conference at Gizors, on the Norman border, to vex Henry II ; and Richard and John had joined the French against their own father, who, after his long and important reign, died on the 6th of July, 1189, at the age of fifty-seven, afflicted by the ungrateful rebellion of his favourite younger son. Richard took the cross in penitence, but more than a year passed by ere he was ready to leave Europe. The great disaster of Hattîn had spread dismay in the west, and the defeat of Saladin became a pressing necessity for peace and commerce ; but money and armies could not be raised in a moment.

In February, 1188, Frederic Barbarossa wrote to Saladin. He had been warned by the Patriarch of Jerusalem, as early as 1185, of the impending evil, and had heard the news from Hattîn immediately after the battle was lost.* He now addressed "the illustrious Saladin formerly ruler of the Saracens, may he take warning by Pharaoh, and not touch Jerusalem." He demanded the surrender of Moslem conquests, on pain of war in Egypt, and threatened the anger of Germany, boasting the power of his warriors from Bavaria, Suabia, Saxony, Franconia, Thuringia, and Westphalia, the Brabantines, Lorrainers, Burgundians, Swiss, Frisons, and Italians, the Austrians and Illyrians, whom he summoned to his banner. But Saladin, who had received and sent envoys to Frederic, as early as 1182,† was then already master of Jerusalem, and offered very different terms. "In the name of God—merciful and pitying," he wrote, and signed himself Hâmi-el-Haramein, "guardian of both sanctuaries"—of Mecca and Jerusalem. He too could call on many nations to assist, and even the Khalif would obey his order. Only Tyre, Tripoli, and Antioch were left to Christians, and nothing, he said, "remains but that we should take these also." If peace were desired these towns must be surrendered; and in return Saladin offered the Holy Cross, the freedom of all Christian captives, liberty for one priest to serve before the Sepulchre, and all the monasteries to be left open which Christians had held before the conquest by Omar, with freedom for pilgrims to come and go in peace.

For now the church bells rang no more in Palestine; and minarets were rising over churches; and in the

---

* *Regesta*, Nos. 646, 658, 671, 672 ; *Jeoff. de Vinsauf*, I, xvii.
† *Regesta*, No. 598.

early dawn the cry of the mueddhin rose in sleeping
cities :—

> " God is most great ! God is most great !
> I testify there is no God but God.
> I testify Muhammad is God's messenger.
> Come ye and pray, come ye and pray,
> For prayer is better than sleep,
> There is no God but God."

But it was not the Cross, nor the Sepulchre, nor right
of pilgrimage, nor freedom for Greek churches, that
Europe now desired. It was no longer the age of
Godfrey, but the age of trade, and of landed interests in
Syria. Those who could not leave their country were
called on to subscribe the " tithe of Saladin." A priest,
a Templar, a Hospitaller, a king's man, a baron's man,
a bishop's clerk, and an accountant, were appointed in
every parish to receive the money. Yet, when it was
given, Philip and Richard used it for the war in Normandy, and the Pope excommunicated the latter, and
threatened Philip with an interdict. The French king
bade the Pope not to meddle in the affairs of Princes ;
and Henry II was forced to sign a treaty, and left his
curse upon his sons.

The fame of Saladin had spread far and wide in Asia,
and Asiatic Christians, bitterly estranged from the Latins,
were ready to make terms with so moderate a ruler even
though a Moslem. Not only was Isaac Angelus of
Byzantium his ally, but even Basil, son of Gregory, the
Armenian Catholicus at Ani, wrote to him as an humble
slave to report the march of Frederic Barbarossa.

In 1189 Queen Sibyl announced to Frederic that the

Emperor Isaac of Byzantium had made a treaty with
Saladin. She had met Guy, the vanquished King of
Jerusalem at Tortosa, and was now in Antioch, the king
being free, but under promise not to fight for his kingdom.
Isaac Angelus sent to Saladin, to say the Germans could
not reach Syria, and if they did, could do him no harm.
His letter was in Greek and Arabic, and sealed with an
enormous figure of himself in gold.   But Kilij Arslan,*
the Turkish Sultan of Iconium, was now jealous of the
rising power of the Kurdish conqueror, and offered aid
to Frederic.   He was "of the sect of Philosophers,"
and Pope Alexander III had hopes of his conversion.†
The German army gathered at Ratisbon, and marched
through Austria and Hungary, where King Bela helped
them.   Crossing the Danube they fought the Huns, and
Alans, and Bulgarians.   They took Adrianople, where
new mosques were being built by permission of a Chris
tian Emperor ; and here they wintered, and Isaac released
their captive envoys, fearing their vengeance.   Prince
Henry, son of Frederic, was sent to bring ships, from
Venice, Genoa, and Ancona, to blockade Byzantium ; and
already in 1188 the Doge of Venice had ordered all his
navy to be ready by next Easter, to help the Holy Land.‡
Fifteen hundred smaller ships, with twenty-six galleys,
were ready to carry the Germans to Asia : for Isaac had
submitted, and the Pope was no longer asked to preach
a crusade against him.   But the expected ally at Iconium

---

* As a Seljuk he must have regarded the Atabeks, the Ortoks, and
Saladin equally as usurpers of the empire of Melek Shah.
† *Regesta*, Nos. 681, 685, 686, 688 ; *Jeoff. de Vinsauf*, I, 11.
‡ *Regesta*, No. 679.

proved a traitor—"a deceitful man, thirsting for Christian blood." Frederic—" an illustrious man, somewhat tall, with red hair and beard," already streaked with grey—followed the route of the second Crusade, by Sardis and Philadelphia, Tripoli on the Meander, and Laodicea ; he reached Philomelium on the Octave of the Ascension, but was harassed by Turkoman flying troops. After more than a month of toilsome march, a thousand knights fought their way to Iconium, and took the town ; and thence the Germans marched through Greek territory, to Tarsus, and on to the Gueuk Su, the borders of Armenia. The Armenians looked coldly on the Germans and sided with the Greeks of Byzantium. It was June, and Frederic, though no longer young, was strong and bold ; but the river was cold, and in swimming across he caught a chill of which he died, and with his accidental death his army melted away. Some got to Antioch, many died of fever, others wandered towards Aleppo, and were taken captive. Thus one more effort to cross over Asia Minor failed, and half the strength of Europe was spent in vain. Not more than five thousand followed Frederic of Suabia by the coast road to Acre, out of some 200,000 who left Germany.*

Meanwhile the Norman King William of Sicily had sent fifty galleys, and five hundred knights, who escaped the pirates from the Greek islands, and came safe to Tripoli ; but he died soon after, and thus in him another Christian bulwark was lost. The clergy of Syria

---

* *Jeoff. de Vinsauf,* I, Chs. 14-17 ; *Jacques de Vitry,* p. 103, English translation.

absolved King Guy of his oath to Saladin; and in 1189
A.D. he gathered an army, and appeared at Tyre.   Conrad of Montferrat—son of the Marquess, then a prisoner
in Damascus—had won credit by his defence of this
seaport, but if we may believe the English chronicler,
who hated this Italian noble allied to Philip of France,
he was a man selfish and treacherous, "surpassing
Sinon in devices, Ulysses in eloquence, and Mithridates
in variety of tongues";* who had seen his father brought
in chains before Tyre, and vowed he would rather be the
son of a martyr than surrender the city.   He refused to
let King Guy enter Tyre; and gave little help to those
who were in sore straits besieging Acre.   All this might
be explained in his favour; but his ambition became
clear when, in the following year, he took Isabel, younger
half-sister of Queen Sibyl, from her husband, Humphrey
of Toron, with whom she had lived three years since
their wedding feast at Kerak; and, though related to her
within the prohibited degrees,† for he had himself married
the Greek Emperor's sister, who as some said was still
alive, he claimed through Isabel the throne of Jerusalem,
Queen Sibyl having died soon after her sad meeting
with King Guy at Tortosa.

In the summer of 1189 the main forces of Saladin
were still near Belfort and Baniâs, but on the 4th and
5th of July skirmishes took place on the River Leontes
between Tyre and Sidon in which the Moslems were
defeated; forays were also made from Tyre towards

---

* *Jeoff. de Vinsauf*, I, Chs. vi, vii, x, xxvi.
† *Regesta*, Nos. 860, 867.   She was by her mother's side related to
Conrad's first wife.

Toron in Upper Galilee, perhaps to ascertain Saladin's position before the landing of the expected Crusaders. Conrad seems to have been not entirely inactive in the cause of Christendom, although he usually remained in Tyre during the war. Among other means of rousing popular enthusiasm, he is said to have caused a great picture to be painted, representing a Moslem on horseback defiling the Holy Sepulchre, and this was taken to Europe and shown in towns and markets.

Without his aid, therefore, the Christians beleaguered Acre ; they landed to join King Guy at Scandalion (Iskanderûneh) south of Tyre, and marched along the coast by the " Ladder of Tyre," reaching Basse Poulaine (el Bassah) and Achzib north of Acre on the 26th of August ; and on St. Augustin's day, in the end of the same month 1189, began a long and difficult siege, which lasted two years, and would have failed but for the armies of King Philip and King Richard, which followed each other to Syria.* The army of King Guy numbered nine thousand men, and the Pisans of Tyre, who took his part as rightful king, brought fifty galleys. The Danes and Frisons added a force of twelve thousand, and an English and Flemish fleet preceding King Richard arrived later at Tyre on the 16th of September and at Acre on the 12th of October, 1190, with Archbishop Baldwin of Canterbury. The first Crusaders landed, and made an entrenched camp on Mount Turon, to the east of the town, nearly a mile from the sea, and close to the River Belus. Saladin, whose forces were at

---

* *Jeoff. de Vinsauf*, I, Chs. xxv–lxxii.

first not strong enough to withstand this army, camped on the 29th August, 1189, at the foot of the hills at Tell Keisân, five miles to the south-east,* having a well supplied country behind him, and protected on his right flank by the Belus marshes.

French, English and Germans joined the invaders, but in the first encounters on the 14th and 15th of September, 1189, the Christians were routed by Saladin, who himself entered Acre and walked on its walls during this battle, while the Franks fled into their camp, leaving Andrew of Brienne and the Master of the Temple slain. King Guy was only saved by Jacques d'Avesnes, who gave him his own horse. After this the Christians—themselves besieged—carried a wall of turfs, with deep ditches, round the promontory of Acre from sea to sea. Saladin being reinforced had crossed the Belus northwards to el Àyadîyeh nearly five miles east of Acre, his left resting on the river. Fighting continued from the 21st of September to the 4th of October with varying success. On the latter day the Moslem troops from Diarbekr were defeated and fled even beyond Jordan, and though the Franks were driven back Saladin retreated on the Nazareth road some eight miles to the south-east. Tidings had reached him of the advance of Frederic Barbarossa. He was himself ill, suffering from painful boils on the lower parts of the body, and his men were discouraged. He sent urgent appeals to the Atabek Prince of Mosul, to come to his aid in the common cause, and meantime only watched the Franks

---

* Some writers have confused Tell Keisân with the River Kishon.

with reduced forces during the winter. At Easter time of the year 1190 the Marquess Conrad brought provisions, men, and arms, from Tyre ; and a sea fight was won by his ships. The Christians attacked Acre from their camp, which caused Saladin to advance to his old position at Tell Keisân on the 25th of April. In May reinforcements reached him from Aleppo and Sinjar. On the 12th of June a fleet of fifty galleys from Alexandria entered the harbour and provisioned the town. The siege dragged on till autumn, and on the 4th of October the Moslems, who communicated with the garrison by fires and pigeon messengers, made a combined attack, but were driven back from the camp.

A second winter found the two armies still facing each other ; three siege towers had been built during the summer, but were soon destroyed by the Greek fire. Three vessels with provisions again entered the port, while others were wrecked on the reef at its mouth. A mighty shout of joy, with clashing of cymbals, and music of pipes, arose in Acre ; but famine soon again threatened the town, which was again relieved. On the 25th July, 1190, the Latin army had made a sortie for food, and met with further disaster while feasting in Saladin's camp. Further reinforcements reached them later, and among other leaders came Henry of Troyes, Count of Champagne, to whom the command of the army was given. Duke Frederic of Suabia, son of Barbarossa, followed, but " proved a cause of disagreement ; for the French had an old and long standing quarrel with Germany, since the kingdom and the empire contended for supremacy." Frederic died, however, of fever on the 20th January, 1191.

Moezz ed Dîn of Sinjar deserted Saladin with his troops in November and was brought back from Fîk east of the sea of Galilee, but the Mosul men were sulky and anxious to go home. In the autumn and winter of 1190 very few Moslem troops remained, and these were quartered at Haifa and Shefa Àmr. The final struggle was put off to the spring, and time gained by King Guy and his allies, who awaited the Kings of France and England.

Curious ancedotes are preserved by Boha ed Dîn of the siege of Acre. He records the kindness of Saladin to the poor Frank woman, whose baby girl had been taken in a Moslem attack on the camp. The small ransom was paid for her by this gentle prince, and she departed blessing him in some unknown Western tongue. Saladin's friend, who was present all through the siege, tells us how the two armies would at times cease fighting to rest and talk, or would make the boys on both sides fight for their amusement ; and how a horse from the Frankish horseboats insisted on swimming into the harbour of Acre, and so was captured by the defenders. Yet more he relates the iron fortitude of Saladin, sitting in pain on his horse in the battles, and passing sleepless nights in seeking to retrieve defeats. He relates the attacks by sea on the " Tower of Flies " ; the raids of renegade pirates on the Christian commerce. The Moslem ships stole, he says, through the besieging fleet disguised with crosses, and carrying pigs on board, while the sailors were dressed as Franks; and so provisions were carried to the town. He speaks also of Saladin's release of an aged prisoner who had come only as a pilgrim; of the King of France, whose white falcon flew away to the city, and was valued at a thousand pieces of gold; and of Aisa the swimmer, drowned in carrying gold and messages into the town, whose body was cast on shore —" never before," he adds, " have we heard of a dead man delivering a message entrusted to his care."

Other incidents of this long episode, which contrasts with the former rapidity of Saladin's movements, are also vividly described by Jeoffrey de Vinsauf. He tells of the soldier safe-guarded by an amulet: of the woman who zealously aided, with others, to build the parapet, in which, when slain by a dart, she desired to be buried: of the Turk whose horse was caught in a net: and of another taken in a foot trap: of the fishers who caught, in their nets, the Saracen swimming into Acre with a bladder of Greek fire: of the Christians scourged on the walls: of the Welshman and Parthian shooting at each other for a wager: of the towers on the Pisan galleys, which were burned; and the ram—a ship's mast shod with iron—also destroyed by Greek fire: of the defeat of fifteen galleys and dromonds, dashed on the rocks, and boarded by the Italians outside the chain of the port: of Archbishop Baldwin of Canterbury, leading the charge in his old age, with his two hundred knights, when Saladin fled to the hills. The Christians, under Geoffrey, brother of King Guy—sent out a force to bring in a convoy of provisions, landed at Haifa on the south of

the bay. They met the Saracens at Tell Kurdâneh,
near the Belus springs half way along the sandy plain
towards Haifa ; and retreating east of the river, forced
the bridge at Dâûk, and brought their charge safe back
to Mount Turon. But idleness and discouragement told
on the Latin forces, and Archbishop Baldwin died,
lamenting the dissolute manners, the drunkenness and
dicing of the army. Famine began to be severe ; and
eggs and chickens were sold for fabulous sums ; and the
marquess sent no help. Horses were eaten, and grass
and offal ; and scurvy carried off great numbers of the
soldiers. They fought fo bread, and gnawed bare
bones ; and even knights and nobles stole food ; and
many men became apostates, and deserted. The beans
of the locust tree were sold—thirteen for a denier ; and
flesh was eaten in Lent if it was found. And worse
still, wine was not lacking, though bread and meat were
scarce. It was among the poor that this scarcity was
most felt ; and the Bishop of Salisbury made collections
for them ; and at length a ship arrived with provisions,
and the greedy Pisan, who had stored his corn for a
year, lost it by fire, and all the army rejoiced ; and after
Easter of the year 1191, the French king came on the
13th of April, and found the Latins cursing Conrad of
Montferrat, who, after all, had perhaps little to spare to
feed so large a host.

The discipline of the army had been sorely taxed by
its long inaction. On the 21st of October, 1190, the
chaplain of Baldwin, Archbishop of Canterbury, wrote
home, to describe with horror the dissolute and drunken

manners of the Crusaders. "The Lord is not in the camp," he wrote, "there is none that doeth good. The chiefs envy one another, and strive for privilege. The lesser folk are in want and find none to help them. In the camp there is neither chastity, sobriety, faith, nor charity—a state of things which I call God to witness. I would not have believed had I not seen it. The Turks are besieging us, and daily do they challenge us, and persist in attacking us; while our knights lie skulking within their tents, and though they had promised themselves a speedy victory, in slothful fashion, like conquered men, let the enemy affront them with impunity. Saladin's strength is daily increasing, whereas our army daily grows smaller. On the Feast of St. James (25th July) more than four thousand of our choicest foot soldiers were slain by the Turks, and on the same day many of our chiefs perished . . . the Kings have not yet arrived, nor is Acre taken."* Such was the condition of affairs before King Richard arrived, and also after the French king had failed in his first attempt on the town.

Richard Lion Heart, acceding in 1189, had met Philip Augustus at Gisors on the Norman frontier; and both had taken the cross, and gathered forces. The Pope had granted plenary absolution to all who would set out for the East; and men were told of relics desecrated and Christians martyred in Palestine. Richard had been promised by his father to Adelais, Philip's sister;

---

* See Archer's *Crusade of Richard I*, p. 18. This agrees with Boha ed Din, Part II, Chap. lxxiv.

but broke the bond in favour of Berengaria, daughter of the King of Navarre ; paying ten thousand marks of silver, and giving towns in compensation.* The friendship of the English and French kings was hollow, and the masterful ways of Richard roused dislike and jealousy in the mind of Philip Augustus. He marched with perhaps sixty thousand men to Genoa, and went to Sicily in Genoese ships, while some of his forces set out from Venice, and others from Balata, and Brindisi, after the meeting with Richard (then newly crowned) at Vezelai. Philip reached Messina on the 16th of September, 1190 A.D.

In England the preparations for a Crusade began while Henry II was yet alive. Money was sent to the Templars in 1187, and in the next year King Henry wrote to the Patriarch, to say that he had taken the cross with his son.† In the year of Richard's accession the usual murder of Jews preceded his departure. On the day of his coronation (the 3rd of September) "a sacrifice of the Jews to their father the devil was begun in the city of London." In Winchester the old accusation was revived, that they had murdered a Christian boy at the Passover, and great dissatisfaction was felt because "gold contented the judges," and the Jews escaped.‡ The same accusation was brought in 1144 and 1179 against other Jews, and in the case of Hugh of Lincoln, was renewed in 1255 A.D. Chaucer puts the

---

* *Richard of Devizes*, Sect. 31.
† *Regesta*, No. 673.
‡ *Richard of Devizes*, Sects. 3, 9, 10, 12, 79 83.

scene of another instance in Asia, and reflects the popular prejudices against Jews who were—

> " For foul usure, and lucre of vilanye,
> Hateful to Crist and to his companye."*

The funds for the new Crusade were raised by selling dignities, and leave to stay at home. William, Bishop of Ely, bought the king's seal for three thousand pounds of silver; and King Richard declared "I would sell London if I could find a chapman." The custody of castles was so arranged, and security taken from the kings of Wales and Scotland, that they would not annoy England while King Richard was absent. Nevertheless, troubles soon arose, through the tyranny of William, the chancellor, Bishop of Ely. In the year following the king's departure Prince John, his brother,† was received as a liberator, after the scandalous imprisonment of Geoffrey, third son of Henry II, Archbishop of York, by the Constable of Dover; and the chancellor fled. Only the influence of his mother held back Earl John from usurpation of the throne of England.

King Richard's fleet sailed by Gibraltar, after encountering, on the 5th of May, 1190, a storm which scattered it off the Spanish coast, and on the 22nd of August it reached Marseilles—one hundred galleys and fourteen busses. Each galley held forty horses, forty soldiers, and fifteen sailors, with a year's provision for man and horse; and the busses had a double number of each. The army marched from Normandy, through the

---

* Prioresses Tale, 1681-2.
† *Richard of Devizes*, 46-50.

Angevine possessions, to Lyons, Avignon, and Marseilles; and sailed by Stromboli to Messina, where
other ships awaited them.* William of Sicily, lately
dead, had married Richard's sister Joan in 1177 A.D.;
but now Tancred, natural brother of Constance, wife
of the Emperor Henry VI, who had just succeeded
his father Frederic Barbarossa, had seized Apulia and
Sicily, and held the dowry of Queen Joan in ward.
King Richard left France on the 16th of August,
1190 A.D., and reaching Messina on the 23rd of
September,† found the English already quarrelling
with Griffons, as they called the Greeks, and Saracens,
who called them in contempt the "Englishmen with
tails." A riot, begun about the weight of a loaf, gave an
excuse for storming Messina, and on the walls of the
city the English flag was hoisted, to the wrath of the
French. The dowry of Queen Joan was demanded,
and a great wooden tower, called Mate-Griffon, was
built upon the hill commanding the town. Tancred
made peace, and paid the dowry; and the plunder
of Messina was in part restored. But it was now too
late to sail for Acre before the spring, and Christmas
was celebrated in Sicily with splendid festivals. On the
25th of March, 1191, Philip set out for Palestine; but
Richard waited for his mother Eleanor, who was
bringing Berengaria with her, to be placed in charge
of Queen Joan, while Eleanor returned to Normandy.
On Wednesday after Palm Sunday, the 10th of April,

---

* *Richard of Devizes*, 20 ; *Jeoff. de Vinsauf*, II, xi.
† He coasted by Genoa, Pisa, and Naples, where he landed on 28th
August, and rode to Salerno on 8th of September, staying there till the 13th.

the English fleet set sail. The two queens went in front, with three ships holding treasure. Thirteen busses and galleys followed in a second line, and the five next lines numbered one hundred and four in all after which came the king's ship, burning a signal light.[*] The whole fleet was thus one hundred and twenty-one sail, but contrary winds scattered the ships, and twenty-five were missing at Crete. It seems doubtful whether the English force could have exceeded ten thousand men in all.

Of King Richard himself we learn that, unlike King Philip, he was as gay at sea as though he stood on firm land.[†] He was thirty-four years of age, and thus the senior of Philip, who was only twenty-six. Richard was tall, with long limbs, and ruddy auburn hair; of great personal strength, and much respected and admired. Of Berengaria we only hear that she was virtuous, but plain. Richard had seen her at the tournay of Pampeluna, and preferred her to the fair but frail Adelais. In later years they were estranged for a time, but reconciled before his death. She gave no heir to the Crown of England, but survived her husband thirty years.

On the 1st of May the English fleet, scattered by a storm on the 12th of April, left Rhodes; and the adverse gales drove the buss on which the two queens sailed near to the port of Limousin on the south coast of Cyprus, while three other ships were wrecked on the

---

[*] *Richard of Devizes*, 59 ; *Jeoff. de Vinsauf*, II, xxvii.
[†] Of King Philip, Richard of Devizes says, *Francus mare nauseans.*

rocks, and the crew taken captive by the Cypriotes, who also seized the wreckage. On the 6th of May King Richard brought the whole fleet into port, demanding satisfaction for the outrage. Cyprus was then under an " Emperor " named Isaac Comnenos, who was allied to Saladin: he had declared his independence of Andronicus of Constantinople.* He failed to entice the queens on shore, and is said to have scorned to deal with one " merely a king." The Greek army, assembled to oppose Richard's landing, were clad in "costly armour and many-coloured garments." Richard was first to spring on shore, and catching a horse he charged the emperor, challenging him to single combat. But this was not the manner of Greek emperors, and the Byzantines fled, and left Limousin in the hands of the English. In a second combat near the town (now Limasol) the Emperor did not so succeed in escaping ; for Richard charged and bore him from his horse ; and he fled yet further to the " strong fort called Nicosia," on the mountains.

Whether by design or accident this descent on Cyprus, and the appearance of King Guy coming, with three ships, to ask advice and aid against the French, who had proposed Conrad of Montferrat as King of Jerusalem, led to important political results. King Guy had been defeated at Hattîn : Conrad had saved Tyre from

---

* Manuel Comnenos, whose grand niece Maria had married King Amaury of Jerusalem, died in 1180. His son Alexius was murdered in 1183 by his cousin Andronicus, who in turn was murdered in September of 1186 A.D. Andronicus had sent Isaac Comnenos, a nephew of Theodora (wife of Baldwin III), to Cyprus before his own death : Isaac's daughter seems to have been sent to England with Berengaria.

Saladin. The better soldier was by some thought fitter for the crown; and Sibyl was dead and had left no heir. It might be a fair question whether Isabel was not now the rightful queen; but there was no doubt as to what was thought at Acre by the army, which had expected things perhaps impossible of Conrad. It was said, too, that he had a wife in Europe, and one at Constantinople, besides Isabel; and Humphrey of Toron was certainly alive, and Archbishop Baldwin had excommunicated Conrad, and declared that the clergy were coerced to dissolve the former marriage, though Isabel had said that she never consented to the strange wedding in Kerak, and had willingly followed Conrad: "for a female," says the Norman monk Jeoffrey—called de Vinsauf because he wrote as to the keeping of wine—"is always variable and changeable, her sex frail, her mind fickle, and she delights in novelty. So she lightly rejects and forgets those whom she knows . . . and willingly receives evil advice"—questions concerning which a monk had, we may suppose, no personal knowledge. In spite, then, of King Guy's failure, the cause which King Richard advocated against the French was the popular opinion.

The wedding of King Richard and of Berengaria was now solemnised on the 12th of May, 1191, in Limousin, where she was crowned Queen of England. The king, we learn, was "very jocose and affable." King Guy meanwhile led the army to Famagusta, and fought the so-called emperor near Nicosia. The Greeks disowned him, and the English flag was hoisted on the walls; and

Isaac submitted, and was bound with silver fetters, but permitted to see his daughter who was taken captive.[*] So began the first English occupation of Cyprus, seven centuries ago. The country was rich and prosperous : the spoil included much treasure, and many precious stones. Thus King Richard held in his gift, even before reaching Acre, a kingdom nearly as large as that of Jerusalem, to be given as he might see fit.

Design or accident having so given to Richard a conquest which the less daring Philip missed, seneschals and justices, sheriffs and constables, were appointed, " just as in England " ; and King Guy received a share of the booty.[†] A rumour came that Acre was taken; and King Richard hasted to prepare his fleet, to cross to Syria. " May God delay the taking of Acre till I come," he said ; and sailed with his swiftest galleys from Famagusta. Soon the dark Lebanon was sighted, the Castle of Margat, Tortosa, and Tripoli ; and here a three-masted ship, full of arms and bottles of Greek fire, was taken ; and, coasting to Tyre, the fleet sailed south past Scandalion, and Casal Imbert, and sighted the " Cursed Tower " over Acre.

It was the week of Pentecost, 1191 A.D. The peaceful Mediterranean lapped on the yellow sands of the shallow bay ; the long grey ridges of Upper Galilee ran up

---

[*] Ernoul says she was taken to England, but escaped after King Richard's death, and stopped at Marseilles, where she was forced to marry Raymond VI, of Toulouse, who divorced her later to wed the sister of the King of Aragon. She married a Flemish knight, who claimed Cyprus, but was expelled from the island, by Amaury II, as being mad. (Archer's *Crusade of Richard I*, p. 69.)

[†] *Richard of Devizes*, Sect. 61.

towards Hermon streaked with snow. To the south was
the dark shoulder of Carmel, with palm groves at its
feet. On the low hills were the black tents, and gay
pavilions of Saladin; and in the great entrenched camp
of Turon, above the Belus gardens, a famine-stricken
Latin army lay between the city and the Saracens.
The town stood on a promontory, with a small port to
the south, closed by a chain, and guarded by the "Tower
of Flies." The sound of trumpets, horns, and pipes,
timbrels and harps, rose from the camp, as the besiegers
mustered to welcome the English galleys, which on the
8th of June set their square emblasoned sails towards
shore; and at night-time they welcomed Richard with
wax torches and lights, until "the Turks thought that
the whole valley was on fire."*

The Christian army now numbered about one hundred and twenty thousand men in all; and Richard
outbid King Philip, offering four aurei per month as pay
for a soldier, instead of three. The Pisans, who were
faithful to King Guy, swore allegiance to King Richard,
and the siege towers of the French were burnt by the
besieged. But "Mauvoisin," the Duke of Burgundy's
great mangonel, was the first to breach the wall of the
Cursed Tower; and Richard bought the petrariæ of the
Count of Flanders, who died during the siege. French
miners were sapping the walls, and the French repelled
a furious assault from Saladin's troops, who stormed the
camp, fighting with axes, and daggers, and clubs that

* *Jeoff. de Vinsauf*, III, ch. i–ii.

bristled with spikes. The mines, supported by logs of timber, were fired ; and the wall so sapped fell down in ruins. The Christians pressed into the breach on the 3rd of July and set their scaling ladders ; and the banners of the garrison were crowded on the wall, while the Greek fire poured on the Latins. At length the Cursed Tower—at the north-east corner of the city— was mined, and the Turkish counter-mine met the French gallery. King Richard was ill,* but carried on a bed of silk he encouraged his men, who crossed the ditch under a hurdle screen, and sapped a tower which fell. The siege had dragged on, till only six thousand Turks remained in Acre, and the besieged at last con- sented, on the 12th of July, to surrender the city, to give back the Holy Cross, and to free two thousand nobles and five hundred other Christian captives, if only the garrison were allowed to leave the town. The Turks marched out, after a stubborn defence of one year and eleven months ; and the Latins, entering the open gates with songs and dances, occupied Acre in the last days of July. Saladin, anxiously watching from the plain, beheld the Christian banners placed on the " Bloody Tower " at the north-east angle of the inner wall, on the Castle further west, on the mosque itself, and on the Templars' Castle in the south-west angle of the city. The grief of the Moslem army was great, as they sullenly withdrew to the hills of Shefa Àmr on the road to Nazareth.

---

* Boha ed Dîn describes fruitless negotiations for peace with Saladin during this period.

The quarrel of the two factions, one favouring King Guy and the other Conrad of Montferrat, now burst forth afresh. It was settled for the present, however, by compromise, the former being accepted as king for his lifetime, and Conrad appointed his heir, and meanwhile Governor of Tyre, Sidon, and Beirût. King Philip was ill, angry with Richard, eager to seize the lands of the Count of Flanders, who had died at Acre, and weary of the war. He left most of his army in Palestine, and returned on the 1st of August to France, where, in revenge for real or fancied injuries, and in spite of an agreement from which Pope Celestin III would not release him, he harried Normandy, and stirred up John to seize the throne of England. Richard Lion Heart remained unquestioned chief in Palestine, and all Europe rang with the fame of his exploits, in Sicily and Cyprus, before the walls of Acre, and after his march to Ascalon. But the month allowed to Saladin for restoring the Cross expired, and neither this nor any of the principal captives or money were sent. In our eyes the fair fame of King Richard is dimmed, whatever may have been his treaty rights, by his cruel severity to the hostages he held. On the 15th of August two thousand seven hundred Turks were killed by his order : " his soldiers came forward with joy," says the chronicler, " to fulfil his commands, and to retaliate, by Divine Grace, taking revenge on those who had destroyed so many Christians with missiles from bows and arbalists."*

* *Jeoff. de Vinsauf*, IV, 4. The arbalist or cross bow was unknown in the East. (*Anna Comnena*, X.)

Such was the fate of nearly half the brave defenders of a surrendered city.*

On the next day the preparations for the march to Jaffa began, but it met with such resistance that it was already the 10th of September before they reached the ruined town.† Three weeks were occupied in traversing a distance of three days' march, along the road which Godfrey had followed. Saladin, who had retreated to Shefa Âmr and thence marched to join reinforcements at Caymont east of Mount Carmel, crossed the downs south of the mountain and lay on the flank of the Christians with his brother Melek el Âdel at the Âyûn el Asawîr in the plain south of Carmel.

Acre‡ had become a scene of very riotous living since its capture. Wine and dancing women abounded, and King Richard found difficulty in withdrawing the disaffected French force from these attractions. The army is said to have now numbered three hundred thousand men, and it camped for some days in the plain south of the Belus stream. It marched with the standard on its truck, guarded by Normans, in the centre. The king led the van: the French brought up the rear: a fleet of barges and smacks carried provisions along the coast;

---

* According to Roger of Howden's *Chronicle,* Saladin had beheaded his Christian captives two days before. Boha ed Dîn also says that Richard's order was reported to be a reprisal for the Christians slain by the Moslems. According to him the treaty was made by the besieged, and not accepted by Saladin himself. Saladin declined to give up the Cross or pay the first instalment of money demanded till the Moslems were handed over. After this massacre Saladin put to death all prisoners falling into his hands, even including women.

† *Jcoff. de Vinsauf,* IV, 24.

‡ Ditto, IV, ch. 9–25.

and wagons as well as pack animals were used. They halted two days at Haifa under Mount Carmel, watched by the Turks ; and on the 27th of August advanced to the little fort of District,* ten miles from Haifa, being much impeded by the long grass and copses, and finding the country full of game. The vanguard was close to Kefr Lâm—a small castle, then in ruins, five miles south of District, and like it within a mile of the shore. Each night when they camped a herald was appointed to cry aloud, "Help, help the Holy Sepulchre!" and the army took up the cry, and prayed with tears, being "much refreshed" by the exercise. They suffered from the scorpions which infest these plains, and tried to drive them away by clashing shields, helmets, basins, and cauldrons.

Two days later, being supplied from the fleet, the main body marched to Merla, which seems to have been the Tour des Salines†—*el Melât*—on the Crocodile River, eleven miles from District; and the king with the vanguard was three miles further south at Cæsarea. The Turks still harassed the march from the slopes of Carmel, but lost an important emir. Many stragglers from Acre joined in ships at Cæsarea. The next stage was the "Dead River," now called Nahr el Mefjir, "the gushing stream," only three miles from Cæsarea. It is a

---

* District was not Athlit as some have supposed, since that castle was built by the Templars in 1218, but the older post to the north now called Dustrey, where there are remains of a fort with a stable cut in the rock of the fosse. (See *Memoirs of Survey Western Palestine*, Vol. I, p. 3C9, where I have given a plan and full account.)

† Rey, *Colonies Franques*, p. 424. It was so called from the salt pans of the Hospitallers, which still exist.

perennial brook crossed by an ancient bridge, with a
sandy bar at its mouth, and marshes above. The banks
are high and steep, and the country to the south wooded
with oak.

After three days* the advance continued, through
rocky country with long grass and trees ; and the
Templars lost many of their horses by the Turkish
arrows. The King of England himself was wounded
by a dart, and only five miles of road were traversed
to the "Salt River," now called Nahr Iskanderûneh—
a sluggish marshy stream. Three days later the whole
force, in battle array, marched through the oak glades
to the Nahr el Fâlik, or "River of the Cleft," which the
Latins called Rochetailie. It is formed by a cutting
through the low hills near the shore, which the Romans
made to drain the papyrus marshes within. This was
a ten mile march, partly over sand dunes. The forces
which arrived are reckoned at only one hundred thousand
men, so that great part of the army must have been left
in garrison, besides the losses by sickness, wounds, and
desertion on the way. It was now the 7th of September,
a time when the heat in the shore plains is at its height ;
and a distance of five miles still separated the camp from
the town of Arsûf, on the shore to the south. The main
battle of the campaign was fought along this stretch of
road, which had the sand dunes and shore precipices on
its west, and the oak forest of Arsûf on its east.

The spies brought word that a Saracen force of three

---

* Boha ed Dîn (II, 119 120) says that negotiations for peace went on
during these three days, both sides wishing to gain time for the arrival of
reinforcements.

hundred thousand men was approaching from the east
The army of Richard was now divided into five divisions,
each of two companies—or brigades—of ten thousand
men. The Templars led the van: the Bretons and
men of Anjou—the king's subjects—followed: King
Guy came next with the men of Poitou; the fourth
division was Norman and English with the Royal
standard: the fifth was the rearguard of Knights
Hospitallers. The whole army was closely mustered,
stretching from near the shore to the forest; and a
flanking party, under Henry of Champagne, marched
on the east, with bowmen and cross-bowmen. The
baggage and provisions were near the shore. At nine
in the morning a body of ten thousand Turks appeared,
on the left flank, charging with loud shouts, and shower-
ing darts and arrows. Some of them were Nubians,
some Bedouin from the eastern desert, with bow, quiver,
and target. A support of Turks, well ordered under
many banners, followed these lighter troops, and numbered some twenty thousand men. The Arab emirs,
through clouds of dust, led the onset to the sound of
clarions and trumpets; but the saddles were emptied
by the steady fire of English bows. Suffering from
the heat of their mail, and the arrows of the Moslems,
the European force moved steadily on. All the forces
of Saladin, from Damascus and Mosul, from Egypt and
Syria, pressed them towards the sea.

The Knights Hospitallers now became impatient, as
one by one they lost their horses in the rear, and they
sent for reinforcements to the King. The signal for

attack was to be given by six trumpets—two in rear, two in the centre, and two in the van ; but Baldwin de Carreo, Marshal of the Hospital, with another brother, precipitated the crisis ; and all the knights of the Order charged in troops, followed by the flanking force. The second and third divisions became engaged, and the dismounted Turkish bowmen were butchered by the foot-men. King Richard came to their aid and broke into the Turkish infantry.

"Oh, how different," says the monkish chronicler, "are the speculations of those who meditate amidst the columns of the cloister, from the fearful exercise of war !" Richard was conspicuous in the *mêlée*, hewing a wide path with his sword. Amid the blinding dust, the cries and groans and shouts of battle, were seen at times glimpses of fallen banners, slaughtered horses, and dying men. The ground was strewn with scimitars and long cane lances tufted with black ostrich feathers. Some Moslems fled to the west, and fell from the sandy cliffs into the sea. The English and Norman reserves followed slowly, inland, the scattered divisions which pursued the fugitive Saracens. A kinsman of Saladin led the last charge, with seven hundred of his chosen household troops, under a yellow banner ; but King Richard on his bay Cyprian steed charged again so furiously that the victory was decided. The Christian force was double that defeated at Hattîn, but that of the Moslems was perhaps the largest yet encountered by the Latins since the battle of Antioch. King Guy thus lived to aid in a terrible defeat of his former conqueror ; and at the battle of Arsûf that of Hattîn was avenged by Richard Lion Heart.

In the evening Arsûf was reached, and a Turkish force, sallying from the town, was defeated ; and here the wearied troops camped in safety. Thirty-two Turkish chiefs were found on the field, splendidly armed and arrayed. Seven thousand dead, of lesser rank, were carried away by the Moslems ; but the loss of the Christians was small. Jacques D'Avesnes, the Flemish leader, fell in one of the charges, and was buried next day—a Sunday, September 8th, on which the Nativity of the Virgin was celebrated by solemn masses and large thank-offerings in the Church of Arsûf. The defeated Moslems marched south to Mejdel Yaba.

The steps taken by Saladin after this crushing defeat were curious. He gave orders to dismantle the walls of Ascalon, Jaffa, and Gaza, the castles of Galatia, Blanche-Garde, Plans, Maen, Lydda, Ramleh, Belmont, and Toron —the latter two on the Jerusalem road—and Château-Arnaud, Beauvoir, and Mirabel* ; reserving only the fort of Darum on the Egyptian frontier, and the fortresses of Jerusalem and Kerak. The reason was that he had no longer forces enough for so many garrisons. These

---

* Galatia appears to have been *Jeledìyeh* (not Keratiyeh, which is too far from Tell es Sâfi), and Blanche-Garde was *Tell es Safi*. Plans, or the "Castle of the Plains" as otherwise called. is probably the Castle of *Kalensâweh* in the plains. Maen is *Bîr Mâîn ;* Belmont is now *Sôba* west of Jerusalem (see *Memoirs Survey of West. Palestine,* Vol. III, p. 19, where I have cited the authorities, and p. 157 for the ruins). Toron is now *Latrûn,* and Château Arnaud appears to have been at *El Burj* (*Memoirs,* III, p. 15). Beauvoir is probably the castle near Tabor : Mirabel (*Memoirs,* II, p. 263) is now *Râs el Âin,* the ancient Antipatris. There are remains of mediæval castles at all these sites, which led me to these identifications in 1875. Blanche-Garde was already known.

places would fall into Christian hands, and would become—as intended when they were built—strong posts on the line of advance, or for guarding the lowlands. On the 10th of September King Richard's infantry reached Jaffa, ten miles from Arsûf, and found the town in ruins. Here the two queens—of England and Sicily—came into port, and the victorious army rested, and enjoyed the shade of the gardens, and the abundance of figs and grapes, citrons and pomegranates. The discipline of the force was however soon undermined, as at Acre, by idleness and luxury, though the rebuilding of the walls, and clearance of the ditches, afforded plenty of work.

Several small skirmishes followed, while the army recruited ; and a galley was sent to reconnoitre Ascalon, which was being dismantled, and which would, but for the rebuilding of Jaffa, have been at once attacked. The castles of Plans (Kalensâwch) and Maen—three miles east of Ramleh—were rapidly repaired, by the Templars and the King respectively, and thus the whole of the plains of Jaffa were cleared of enemies. Towards the end of the autumn an embassy was sent to Saladin to treat of peace. King Richard demanded the surrender of all that Baldwin the Leper had ruled in Syria, and the tribute that King Amaury had required of Egypt. Saladin offered in return to make the Jordan the boundary of the restored kingdom, if Ascalon was left an unwalled town. Seif ed Dîn, Saladin's brother, was honourably received ; and the son of Humphrey of Toron acted as interpreter, in interviews at Yazûr and Jaffa, being well versed in Arabic.* King Richard then demanded that Kerak and Montreal should be dismantled, and on this point the treaty failed to be concluded. The English army advanced on Jerusalem, but lingered seven weeks at the foot of the hills between Ramleh and Lydda. A foray into the mountains gave the Templars two hundred head of oxen, and a skirmish occurred in which the Earl of Leicester had two horses killed under him.

The winter was now beginning, and the advance was only pushed as far as Beit Nuba, in the plain, eleven miles south-east of Lydda. Here storms of hail and rain deluged the camp, and violent winds upset the tents. The bacon and biscuits were spoilt, the arms and armour rusted. The Templars, Hospitallers, and Pisans counselled delay, and urged that Ascalon should first be fortified. Had they known the deep dejection of Saladin at this time, and the fears of his counsellors who would not let him leave Jerusalem, a very different decision might have been reached. When to their surprise the Moslems saw the Franks retreat, Saladin believed it to be the answer to his prayers when, in despair, he had thrown himself on the mercy of God as his last refuge. The argument of the knights on the other hand was that no water could be found for the army outside Jerusalem. Early in January the Franks retreated a day's march to Ramleh, where cold and rain and mud disheartened the soldiers. Most of the French departed to Jaffa and Acre, others with the Duke of Burgundy

---

* *Jeoff. de Vinsauf*, IV, 31. *Boha ed Dîn*, II, 123, 126, 128–9, 133–144, 158–161.

to Plans. King Richard, much displeased, marched over the boggy plains to Yebnah, and camped on the 20th of January in the dismantled fortress of Ascalon. The Saracens also went into winter quarters, and the rebuilding of Ascalon now engaged the English. According to the Arab account of Boha ed Din, Richard and Henry of Champagne on the one hand, and Conrad of Montferrat on the other, were negotiating against each other with Saladin. When, however, he says that Richard wished his sister Joan to marry Melek el Àdel, Saladin's brother, and that she refused, even if he became a Christian, and she was made Queen of Palestine, we may well doubt such statements, which are not supported by the Christian accounts. The new walls of Ascalon were no doubt only a renovation of the old ones, but in some cases solid foundations were only found by digging deep. Fifty-three towers had been overthrown, and among these are named the Tower of Maidens, that of Shields, the Bloody Tower, the Emir's Tower, and the Tower of Bedouin, as being the five principal. King Richard reconnoitred the fort of Darum, south of Gaza, and set free a convoy of twelve thousand Christian prisoners then on their way to Egypt. Easter fell on the 5th of April, and found him still in Ascalon ; but the climate of Palestine is unfit for campaigns before that season, and very little time of any value was lost.

Meanwhile the quarrel with the French became a source of weakness, very important because so large a part of the force was French by birth, if not by allegiance. Conrad of Montferrat refused to come to Ascalon, but met the king at Casale Imbert, north of Acre. The Duke of Burgundy demanded money, and retired to Acre with his men, where the Pisans and Genoese— taking opposite sides in the quarrel—fought each other in the streets, until Richard came himself to pacify them ; he returned to Ascalon after the conference with Conrad on the Tuesday before Easter. The remaining Frenchmen, occupied in building the walls, refused to continue in his service—probably because money now began to fail—and departed to Tyre under an escort of Templars. In Jerusalem the Holy Fire appeared at Easter, but Saladin said it was " a fraudulent contrivance." After Easter came the Prior of Hereford, bringing letters from the chancellor whom Earl John had driven out of England, and with a message that no more money remained in the treasury at home.

King Richard neglected nothing that could further his enterprise ; the negotiations for peace, the winter, the want of money, the bad news from England, the French defection, the fatigues he had experienced in the most unhealthy season of the year, were worries telling on his health ; yet none could have been avoided, since an agreement had already been made with King Guy. But there was Cyprus in reserve, and Richard showed no obstinacy in his conduct, for much against his own wish he consented to give the Kingdom to Conrad, as the price of French assistance. Hardly, however, had this decision been announced in Tyre when Conrad fell a victim to the Assassins.*   On the 28th of April, 1192, he returned from a feast given by the Bishop of Beauvais, grandson of Louis VI, in that city, when two young men attacked him near the custom house, and he fell from his horse with their daggers in his heart.   One of the murderers was slain at once, the other, dragged from a church, declared that he had obeyed the orders of the Sheikh of the Mountain : both had been in Conrad's service awaiting their time.   A letter written to the Duke of Austria, by the Sheikh, in the following year is said to have absolved King Richard of all knowledge of the plot ;† but the French suspicions were fatal to his enterprise, and they refused to follow him further. Henry of Champagne hastened to Tyre, and married Isabel, the heiress of the kingdom—Conrad's widow— though Humphrey of Toron was still alive.‡

The spring being now advanced, reconnaissances were pushed from Ascalon to Darum, and even to the walls of Jerusalem.§   Henry of Champagne‖ was chosen king of the half-conquered kingdom, and joyfully received at Acre, whither he brought Isabel.   The citizens came out with songs and dances, burning incense in procession, and decking the streets with silken awnings.   Sixty thousand men in armour went out to meet him, and the clergy brought a fragment of the Holy Cross, with other relics, which he kissed.   King Richard bestowed on Guy a better kingdom—that of Cyprus—in which the house

* According to Ernoul (289–290) Conrad had previously pillaged a ship belonging to the Assassins at Tyre.
† *Regesta*, No. 715, it is thought to be a forgery.
‡ *Jeoff. de Vinsauf*, V., 6–31.   § Ditto, 32–41.
‖ Henry was half nephew of Richard, and of Philip Augustus.

of Lusignan long ruled in peace, "there was not another king found," says the chronicler, "of more royal habits or character than he . . . he was simple-minded, and unversed in political intrigue." The Templars had offered to buy Cyprus for their Order, but Richard gave it as a royal gift, and one more valuable than the kingdom which Guy had lost.

The siege of Darum next occupied the English army. It was a fortress on the road to Egypt, south of Gaza, built about 1170 by King Amaury, with a deep ditch, and seventeen towers—the only walled post garrisoned by Saladin in the plains. The walls were mined and after four days the place was taken by assault on the 27th of May. The garrison was a small one, and Darum is now an open village with palms and ruins of a chapel. It however commanded the road to Egypt, and after it fell all the plains round Ascalon were cleared of Saracens to the foot of the hills. In this enterprise the French took no part, and King Richard's army was now less than half that which fought at Arsûf. They marched to Beit Jibrîn, on the way to Jerusalem, suffering much from the mosquitos and the summer heat, but eager to reach the Holy City. After the capture of Beit Jibrîn they returned for a time to Ascalon, but on the 9th of June reached Toron, at the foot of the hills on the road from Jaffa, and regained their former camp at Beit Nûba, twelve miles from Jerusalem. Here it would seem that some of the French from Acre, with Henry of Champagne, joined the force, and a council was appointed of five French nobles,

five Templars, five Hospitallers, and five Syrian Franks.
They advised a march on Egypt; and it is remarkable
that on these two occasions none but the English seem
to have cared for the conquest of the Holy City.   The
king—who meantime had captured a great caravan near
Beersheba*—accepted the advice, which was perhaps
politically sound, since the strategic value of Jerusalem
was small compared to the destruction of Saladin's base
in the Delta; but the English soldiers murmured, and
returned much discontented to Jaffa on the 6th of July.
Richard himself lost heart; and heavy news came yet
again from England.   With most of his force he
retreated to Acre, and began to prepare for the voyage
home.

These signs of weakness encouraged Saladin, who,
marching swiftly from Toron at the foot of the Jerusalem
hills, fell on Jaffa, and undermined the wall.   The Turks
poured into the town, massacring the citizens, staving
in the wine barrels, and killing all the pigs.   Wine and
blood flowed in the streets, Christians and pigs were cast

* The accounts of Jeoffrey de Vinsauf (vi. 4) and Boha ed Dîn of this
capture on the 23rd of June quite agree.   The former says King Richard
marched by night to Galatia (Jelediyeh) sending to Ascalon for provisions,
and made a second night's march to where the caravan had halted by a
"Round Cistern."   Boha ed Dîn (ii. 155) says it was one of three caravans
from Egypt coming by Kerak, the desert, and the sea plain : that King
Richard's army stayed the night at Tell es Sâfi, and marched by El Hesy
to Khuweilfeh, which is evidently the "Round Cistern," since it has a
well like those at Beersheba (Memoirs iii, p. 397.)   Probably the English
writer is best informed as to where Richard slept.   Jelediyeh is only six
miles west from Tell es Sâfi, and thence to Khuweilfeh is twenty-three
miles.   From Jelediyeh to Ascalon is eleven miles.   The old proposal to
place Galatia at Keratîyeh does not assist the question, as it is further from
Tell es Sâfi.   Tell el Hesy was on the route to Khuweilfeh, fourteen miles
to the north-west.   Boha ed Dîn mentions the King's arrival at Tell es
Sâfi separately.

together out of the gates. Only the citadel held out, and a swift ship was sent to fetch King Richard from Acre. The French refused to march, but Templars and Hospitallers hastened south by land, and the English went by sea, delayed three days by contrary winds at Haifa. The last day granted to the garrison of the citadel had well nigh come when King Richard leapt from his red ship into the surf at Jaffa, and fought his way on shore.

Once more, on the 1st of August, 1192, the terror of Melek Rik, and of the English bows, fell on the Turks ; and in a mighty fight they were worsted and fled. The king returned covered with arrows, but victorious. To Saladin's envoys he spoke, as Boha ed Dîn says, " half seriously, half joking," saying " This Sultan is mighty, and there is none greater in this land of Islam. Why did he fly at my coming ? By God, I was unarmed and unready to fight. I have my sea shoes on still. Why did you fly ? " " God's goodness ! Jaffa, I should have said, could not be taken in two months, and he took it in three days." Henry of Champagne, who was ever loyal to his leader, also arrived at Jaffa, but only mustered fifty-five knights mostly mounted on mules, with bowmen and retainers. Both Pisans and Genoese assisted in this final effort, but the French remained in Acre. Saladin, unable to rally his forces, retired to Yazûr, four miles from Jaffa.

Thus the contest waged for four years in Palestine resulted in a drawn game, in which both players were wearied out, though new forces came from Mosul, and further fighting occurred near Jaffa. The king was ill with fever, anxious to leave the country, and without money to prolong the war. Saladin had failed in every battle against him; his resources were exhausted, and his troops refused to face the English, while all the plains from Antioch to Ascalon were strongly held by Christian troops. Thus at length both the great leaders were willing to conclude a truce, accepting what was done; and Templars and Hospitallers alike advised the treaty.*

It was agreed that Ascalon should be dismantled, and so remain for three years from the 2nd of September, 1192: that Jaffa and the plains up to the mountains should be held by the Christians; and pilgrims allowed to visit the Holy Sepulchre. Two Latin priests, and two deacons, were to remain in Jerusalem, and an equal number in Bethlehem. The terms were all that could be fairly asked, and the chronicler says—alluding to unfriendly critics—"Whosoever entertains a different opinion concerning this treaty, I would have him know that he will expose himself to the charge of perversely deviating from the truth." It will be found, in considering later events, that the settlement made by Richard and Saladin was in effect the settlement of the whole Eastern question for a century after. A new Latin Kingdom was founded in Cyprus,† and every

---

* *Jeoff. de Vinsauf,* VI, 1-38, Boha ed Dîn, II, 170. The latter finds it equally necessary to excuse the peace to Moslems; but Saladin feared an alliance of his great nephew el Mansur at Hamah with other rebels against him.

† The history of Cyprus does not concern us. Amaury of Lusignan, Guy's brother, the last and fourth husband of Isabel, the half Greek

important seaport was regained in Syria, with almost
all the lands owned by the military orders. This was
no small result of four years of constant effort, and the
credit of such success was mainly due to Richard Lion
Heart.

The king retired to Haifa for his health, for he was
suffering from the worst form of Syrian fever, and on the
9th of October following he set sail from Acre for
France. The citizens lamented his departure ; and he
left them hopes of his return. But he was destined only
to live for seven more years ; and after such victories,
and such long journeys, to fall before a little Norman
fortress in his own dominions. Wrecked in the Adriatic
by the winter storms, he tried to travel through Austria
in disguise, and being discovered near Vienna, was
imprisoned by Duke Leopold ; for thirteen months he
lay in a dungeon at Tyernstein on the Danube, while
none knew where he was. The Emperor, Henry VI,
hearing of his capture, removed him to Trifels, near
Landau, where—according to the popular romance—
Blondel, a gentleman of Arras, recognised his voice
singing a well-known air ; but another year passed by
before his ransom was paid, through the exertions of
Queen Eleanor and Pope Celestin; while Philip of
France invaded Normandy, and Earl John spread

daughter of King Amaury of Jerusalem, succeeded Guy in 1194, and
called himself Amaury II ; he died in 1205. His son by Isabel was
Amaury III, who died next year. Hugh I, son of Amaury II, by
Eschiva of Ibelin his second wife, ruled till 1218 : Henry I his son till
1253. He was followed by his son Hugh II, who died in 1267. The
succession then passed to Hugh III, son of Isabel, sister of Henry I, and
he died in 1284. His son John died in 1285, and Henry II brother of
the last ruled till 1324 A.D.

reports of his death. Barons and people were faithful to their hero; and the mock trial, in which he was accused of having made too easy a peace with Saladin, led to no result. It was too clearly due to enmity and envy, felt by princes who, like the Emperor and Philip, had done much less to help the Holy Land. The ransom asked was paid, and King Richard landed at Sandwich on the 20th of March, 1194. Five years later after recovering Normandy, he was stricken at Châlus by an arrow from the crossbow of Bertrame de Gourdon, and died in the arms of Berengaria, commanding with his last words that Bertrame should be spared.

On the 4th of March, 1193 A.D., Saladin also, the greatest of the Moslems, died, of fever, at the early age of fifty-six. They buried him at Damascus in the mosque courtyard, opposite the square building which had once been a cathedral, and where the "magic wall of glass" was a mosaic, erected of glass by Byzantine architects. Outside the little chapel of his sepulchre still stands the great lintel of the earlier temple, supported on mighty pillars, and bearing in Greek the motto :—

"Thy Kingdom, O Christ, is an everlasting Kingdom,
    And Thy dominion endureth throughout all generations."

Since Omar and Muhammad no Moslem like Saladin had arisen, and after him none other such arose; for though Bibars carried out his work, a century later, to its completion, the cruel Egyptian Sultan cannot be compared to one who was brave and just, merciful to all, tolerant even of Latin priests, and wisely prudent as well as determined and active. Among all who opposed him he found but one who was his equal, in Richard Lion Heart, the hero of the third Crusade.

Saladin's ambition did not stop at the redemption of Asia for Islam, for to his timid follower, who saw for the first time the winter sea near Ascalon, he said, "when by God's help not a Frank is left on this coast I will divide my dominions among my children, and bid them farewell, and sail on this sea to its islands, till not one unbeliever in God is left on this earth, or I will die in the attempt. And what is the most glorious of deaths? —that in God's path—then I will strive for the gate of that death." His parting words to Melek edh Dhâher his son were not less characteristic. "I commend you to the Most High, the giver of all good. Do thou His will, for that is the way of peace. Beware of bloodshed: trust not in that: for spilt blood never sleeps; and seek the hearts of thy people, and care for them; for thou art sent by God, and by me, for their good: try to gain the hearts of the emirs, the rulers, and the nobles: I have become great as I am because I won men's hearts by gentleness and kindness. Nourish no hatred of anyone, for death spares none. Be prudent in dealing with men, for God will not pardon if they do not forgive; but between Him and thee He will pardon, if thou dost repent, for He is most gracious."

Boha ed Dîn, his faithful secretary, who had been made Kadi of Jerusalem about 1188 A.D., gives us a detailed account of his last days, and of his patience and mildness. "Never before had his face shown such joy at seeing me," he writes, "and he pressed me in his arms

and his eyes filled with tears.   May God have mercy
on him . . .   On Thursday he sent for me once more,
and I found him seated in a summer house in the
garden with his little children round him.   He asked if
any one were awaiting audience, and on hearing there were
some envoys from the Franks . . .   he gave orders
for them to be brought in.   One of his little children—
the Emîr Abu Bekr—for whom he had a great affection,
and whom he used to pet and play with, was there also.
Now when the child caught sight of these folk with their
shaven chins, their close cut hair, and their strange
apparel, he was afraid and began to cry.   On this the
Sultan excused himself to the envoys, and dismissed
them without hearing what they had to say."*

The lassitude which precedes typhoid fever was even
then weighing on his energies, and on the next day he
caught a chill when riding out of Damascus to meet
the pilgrims from Mecca.   On the ninth day of the
fever he was unconscious for a time, and the Sheikh
Abu Jâfer, who watched beside him, repeated the Koran
Surahs by his bedside.

"I came," he told the chronicler, "to the words,
'He is the God beside whom there is no other God :
He knows both the seen and the unseen,' and I heard
him utter these words, 'It is true,' and this just as he
was passing away, it was a sign of God's favour.   Thank
God for it."   "I have been told," says Boha ed Dîn,
"that while the Sheikh Abu Jâfer read these words,
'There is no God but He, in Him I have set my trust,'

* Boha ed Dîn, II, Chaps. 172–182.

the sick man smiled ; his face lighted up ; and so he
went peacefully to God. Never since the death of the
four first Khalifs," he concludes, "never since that time
has the faith, or have the faithful, suffered such a blow
as that which lighted on them when the Sultan died."

Looking back to this heroic age we too can echo the
verse which Boha ed Dîn subscribes beneath his loving
account of Saladin's hard-spent life :—

> " So passed those years and men, and seem
> Both years and men to be a dream."

CHAPTER IX.

THE THIRTEENTH CENTURY FRANKS.

THE agreement reached by Saladin and Richard practically settled the Eastern question for almost a century. For fifty years the balance of improvement was on the whole in favour of the Christians. The great Moslem left no successor able to carry on his work; and, in spite of fluctuations, the Latin power increased, and their possessions spread further inland. The main features of the history of this period were, the increased influence of the pope and of the military orders, the conquest of Constantinople, and the new policy of Frederic II of Germany. The growth of trade, and of literature, in the East, was also very remarkable, till the great defeat at Gaza marked a change in the Christian fortunes, which then began to decay until, just a hundred years after Acre was won, it was again finally lost.

The truce which had been made by Saladin and Richard was to last three years from September, 1192, and allowed free trade to Christians. The Moslem dominions were divided among Saladin's heirs, and the period of rest, instead of strengthening their cause, was wasted in dissensions. Three of Saladin's sons ruled at Aleppo, Damascus, and Cairo, and Melek el Adel his brother in Mesopotamia. The sons fought, and many Emirs became independent, until finally the uncle became supreme ruler, and head of the Eyubite house. When the peace expired Pope Celestin III, now ninety years of age, preached a Fourth Crusade. Richard and Philip were too busy watching each other to listen, and letters to Sancho VII, King of Navarre, brought no response.* The Emperor Henry VI had been excommunicated, but making peace with the Pope he raised forty thousand men in Italy, who, aided by the Dukes of Saxony and Brabant, set out for Acre by sea. The first division on landing, without waiting—as Henry of Champagne advised—for the Saxons and Brabanters, marched into the Nâblus mountains where Melek el Adel defeated them, and then took Jaffa. About the same time Henry of Champagne died, falling with a balcony of his palace which gave way at Acre. Isabel was married soon after to a fourth husband — Amaury, brother of King Guy—who had succeeded to the throne of Cyprus. Her daughter Mary, by Conrad of Montferrat, was heiress to the kingdom of Jerusalem, and about 1210 A.D. wedded John of Brienne—the third titular king who never ruled in Jerusalem itself.†

The Saxons had been delayed, fighting Moors in Portugal. Reaching Acre they found Jaffa dismantled and Beirût taken by Moslems. Melek el Adel met them on the Kasimiyeh river, north of Tyre, and was in turn

---

* *Regesta*, Nos. 728, 752.
† Ditto, Nos. 741, 760.

defeated. He retired wounded to Damascus, and the Christians occupied Sidon, Latakia, Beirût and Gebal, capturing much warlike material and freeing many captives. Toron in Upper Galilee was attacked, and the walls mined, by forces under Conrad, bishop of Hildesheim. Chancellor of the Empire, but through sudden panic the army was broken up. All the shore towns as far as Ascalon remained however in the power of the Christians, and another three years' truce was made in 1198 A.D.

The Emperor Henry VI, resisted by Tancred, had meanwhile taken from him Naples and Sicily, and married Constance, last of the royal Norman race in Italy: he died while his army was still in Palestine. The Templars had again been accused of treachery in the Toron affair, and of a secret league with Melek el Âdel. The Germans, who rebuilt Jaffa, quarrelled with the Syrian Franks: some were massacred while drunk at the last named city, and hearing of the Emperor's death, the rest went home. Two short imperial reigns followed—that of Philip of Suabia, brother to Henry VI, lasting one year, and that of Otho IV, Count of Poitou for fourteen, before the accomplished Frederic II, son of Henry VI, acceded; and during this time neither England, France, nor Germany sent aid to Palestine. The aged Pope Celestin also died in 1198, and Innocent III was elected his successor at the early age of thirty-three, holding the chair of St. Peter for the unusual space of eighteen years. His energy in respect to Syrian affairs was great. He sent a ship-load of arms to help the

Templars and Hospitallers, whom he exhorted to vigilance in 1199, but owing to the truce no action was taken,* and his representations to the Kings of England and France were unheeded, as were his letters to Alexius of Constantinople. Germany was intent on the struggle of Otho of Saxony, the Papal nominee for the Imperial Crown with Philip of Suabia. France was for some months under interdict because of Philip's divorce of Ingeburge, sister of the Danish king. It was not till 1200 A.D. that further forces were sent, on the expiry of the truce.

This fifth Crusade was heralded by a miracle. A letter from heaven was found suspended on the altar of St. Simon of Jerusalem, exhorting Christians to observe the Lord's day.† A wonder working curé— Foulkes of Neuilly-sur-Marne—was also bidden by the young Pope to preach the Holy War. Thibaut IV Count of Champagne,‡ and Louis, Count of Blois and Chartres, related to both the French and English kings, brought a small force of two thousand five hundred knights, from Navarre and Champagne, and sent to hire ships at Venice. Their expedition led to unexpected results, but they never set eyes on Palestine at all.

The Greek emperor was eager to recover Cyprus, and Alexius wrote to the Pope in 1201 A.D., asking that Amaury II might be excommunicated if he refused to give it up, but this Innocent denied him.§ The

---

* *Regesta*, Nos. 760, 763.   † *Regesta*, No. 778.
‡ Brother of Henry of Champagne.   § *Regesta*, No. 782.

Greeks were growing ever weaker, and the Latins
ever stronger. The ambition of the Venetians, now
superior at sea to either Pisa or Genoa, pointed to
the conquest of Byzantium. The loss of Cyprus was
the first sign of the failing power of the emperors of
Constantinople. The Venetians had imitated their
Pisan rivals, in seeking to promote their trade by
treaties with Moslems, and had no great interest in
Jerusalem. When Count Thibaut asked for ships the
Doge Dandolo demanded eighty-five thousand silver
marks for fifty galleys and other vessels to carry
some thirty-five thousand men in all, and during the
delays which followed Count Thibaut died, and so did
Foulques, the preacher—already suspected of misuse of
funds committed to him.

Boniface of Montferrat, brother of the murdered
Conrad (accompanied by Baldwin, Count of Flanders,
brother-in-law of Thibaut), took command of the
small force waiting near Venice, but had no money
to pay for ships. The Doge proposed that the Crusaders should pay by capturing Zara, sixty leagues
from Venice east of the Adriatic, which the Hungarians had seized. Meanwhile Isaac, the dethroned
emperor whom Alexius, his brother, had expelled
from Byzantium, sent his son to Philip of Suabia,
who had married his daughter Irene. Philip being
at war with Otho, and unable to help, the Greek
prince went on to Venice to ask help of the embarking Crusaders. The Doge and his allies set out,
and having subdued Trieste, and pillaged Zara (which

offered no defence) on the 10th of November, 1202 A.D., were there overtaken by the son of Isaac—also named Alexius like his uncle. Caring nothing for the Pope's wishes, and unwilling to attack his allies of Damascus, Doge Dandolo led the new Crusaders on an expedition intended for the benefit of Venice only. By Easter, 1203, Corfu had submitted, and the fleet proceeded to Negropont, where the Greek prince was proclaimed emperor. Thence they sailed to Abydos, and on the 6th of July reached Byzantium.

The usurping Alexius was camped on the heights of Pera, but afraid to meet the Latins. Baldwin of Flanders· led the way : Galata was seized, and forces landed at Scutari. Flemish and Picard troops attacked Stambûl, and Boniface of Montferrat established a camp of Burgundians, Lombards, and men of Champagne, Piedmont, and Savoy. The defenders included the Danish and English mercenaries of the Varanger guard, but the resistance was feeble. Dandolo, the blind and aged Doge, whose ships blockaded the city, landed in triumph ; and Alexius fled, leaving Isaac free. The Pope declared in favour of the younger Alexius, who was crowned in Byzantium, but he distrusted the Crusaders who still delayed their voyage to Syria till the next Easter should come.

The year that followed was marked by desperate attempts to shake off the Latin yoke, during which the new emperor was strangled by rebels, and Isaac his father died. Constantinople was again besieged, and taken in four days, on the 10th of April, 1204.

A terrible sack of the city followed. St. Sophia was desecrated, and Justinian's body robbed of its jewels. The Franks and Venetians threw off the mask, and sought no Greek candidate for the throne. Baldwin of Flanders became the first Latin ruler of the great city, with a counsel of twelve Franks and twelve Venetians to advise him.

The astuteness of the Italians was shown by their arrangements. They took indeed half Constantinople —to be ruled by the laws of Venice—but they left to their allies the difficult task of defending the mainland. Bithynia in Asia, Roumania, Thrace, and Greece, formed Baldwin's kingdom ; other Asiatic provinces fell to the Count of Blois ; and Boniface of Montferrat had Crete, and the fief of Thessalonica ; but gave it up to Venice in return for grants in Asia Minor. These possessions were, however, only half conquered, and entailed struggles with Bulgarians and other fierce tribes. On the other hand, the Doge received not only a secure possession of the two great trading cities of the empire—Byzantium and Thessalonica— but also all the Cyclades and Sporades—islands easily protected by the Venetian fleet, and connected with Venice by possession of the Ionian group. The trading route with Central Asia was thus made safe, whatever might be the fate of the new Latin Empire. The Doge also claimed the Thessalian shore, and towns like Adrianople further north.

The Pope saw with satisfaction a Latin hierarchy established in the old seat of Greek schism, but did not scruple to accuse the supposed Crusaders of worldly aims. As regards the disestablished emperor—the elder Alexius—he fled from his prison to join the Turks, and died in a monastery. In 1206 A.D. the great Doge Dandolo died, and was buried in St. Sophia. Baldwin, defeated by Tartars and Bulgarians, disappeared, and Henry of Hainault, who succeeded him, ruled over the ruins of the land conquests ; but for a long time after the Venetians held the islands; and dukes of Paros, sires of Mycenæ, and princes of Naxos, became vassals of the proudest of Italian trading cities.

In 1217 the Imperial crown of Constantinople was given by Honorius III to Peter II of Courtenay, grandson of Louis VI of France, and married to Yolande heiress of the house of Baldwin of Flanders, who had followed his cousin, King Philip, to the third Crusade. He died within a year, but established a Frank dynasty, which endured for forty-four years till the rise of Michael Palæologus.

This conquest, while clearly shewing that the spirit of the age was no longer one in which crusades for a religious object roused the enthusiasm of Europe, was important in adding strength to the Latin cause in Asia.

The hopes of the Latins at Byzantium were for the moment extravagant. Kingdoms were gambled for, and Baghdad and Mosul assigned by throwing dice; but this was only a momentary elation after easy victory. It was, however, not only in Byzantium that the Latin power was newly established for even in

Armenia* the Pope and the Templars were for a time successful.

Boemund III, grandson of Raymond of Poictiers, and, by his mother's side, descended from the first conqueror of Antioch, was established in that city in 1164 A.D., and attacked Armenia ; but thirty years later the Armenian king, Leo II, seized him, and invaded his province ; and peace was only made when his daughter Alix wedded Rupon of the Mountain, nephew of Leo.   In May, 1199, Leo II wrote to Pope Innocent III, declaring his desire that all his kingdom should accept the Latin creed, deploring the weakness of the Christian States in the East, and asking help.   He announced that Rupon, his nephew, had been baptised the year before, when marrying Alix, and was chosen to be the heir of Boemund III, but that the Military Orders had declared for Boemund IV, brother of Alix.   The Pope in reply exhorted him to turn his arms against the Saracens.   At the same time the Catholicus of Armenia wrote to Innocent III a friendly letter, and in answer was commended for obedience to Rome.   Two years later Leo II accepted the presence of a Legate.   He invited the Templars to join his army against the Turks, sending a sum of some £8,000 for their acceptance, and promising castles and lands for them in Armenia after the war. He also gave free trade to the Venetians in his territories.

* *Regesta*, Nos. 755–6, 761, 785–6, 795, 798, 805, 817, 820, 838–9, 841–2, 842–3, 851, 862–3.   Thoros of Armenia was succeeded in 1175 by Rupon II, who was given Tarsus by Boemund III of Antioch ; he died in 1188, and Leo II, who succeeded him, had married a niece of Boemund.

The new alliance was not long peacefully continued, for in 1204 A.D. Leo II wrote again to Pope Innocent III, as to quarrels with the new Legate regarding the succession, and the secret agreements of the Templars. The aim of the Armenian intrigues was to make the heir of the throne Prince of Antioch, and for this reason the Templars were now expelled from the kingdom. An interdict was then pronounced, which led to peace being made for a time, though the Legate still opposed Prince Rupon's succession. Four years later the Latin cause prevailed, and Rupon was finally crowned by consent of Pope Honorius III on the 16th of December, 1220 A.D. He occupied Antioch from 1216 to 1219, and the principality was thus added to the Armenian kingdom. He, however, died in 1222, when Boemund IV recovered Antioch. The Knights Hospitallers were encouraged by grants in Armenia in 1210 A.D.; but Leo II refused to restore the Templars. In 1213 A.D. Innocent III threatened excommunication, unless the "intruding Greek clergy" were expelled, and the Latin Orders received into favour; but on the death of this Pope three years later a more conciliatory policy seems to have been thought advisable.

Through their establishment in Armenia the Latins came into closer contact with the Georgians* of the Caucasus; and great hopes were raised that a warlike Christian people might be thus induced to aid in attacking the Saracens on the north of Mesopotamia. In 1213 A.D. they attacked the now crumbling empire of

* *Regesta*, Nos. 868, 967.

Baghdad; but in 1221 their power was brought to nought by the Tartar victory at Tiflis. A temporary success three years later led them to promise help to the Emperor Frederic II; but, like the Armenian alliance, and the schemes for converting the Tartars themselves, this expectation failed when the new forces from Central Asia began to press upon the northern provinces of the Syrian kingdom.

During this period, while these various extensions of Latin power were being accomplished, the Franks in Syria were also becoming stronger ; but the country suffered from a terrible earthquake in 1201 A.D. Damascus, Tyre, and Nâblus were laid in ruins : the walls of Acre and Tripoli fell on the 20th of May ; and Hamath and Baalbek also suffered. At the same time a very low Nile in Egypt brought a fearful famine, followed by pestilence.* In consequence of these troubles, and of the war between Antioch and Armenia, and the invasion of the principality by the ever ready Sultan of Aleppo, many knights and barons left their lands.† John of Brienne brought with him only three hundred knights, and eighty thousand livres, for the maintenance of his small seaside kingdom. He was, however, popular with the Italians, being himself the brother of King Gauthier of Apulia. In 1204 the Pisans and Genoese made up their quarrels in Acre, but lay in danger of excommunication, such as fell on the Venetians, since both these States took example from the Doges, and made treaties

---

* *Regesta*, Nos. 787, 789.
† Ditto, 793, 794, 808, 825, 826–7, 836, 858.

with the Moslems who were then at peace with the Latins. The Pisans renewed their ancient understanding with Egypt, where the Venetians also were encouraged by Melek el Adel. The Venetians had a treaty in 1208 with Saladin's son at Aleppo. The jealousy of the three cities led to further quarrels in 1212 A.D., in Acre, where the quarters occupied by each community adjoined along the sea wall, east and west.

Pope Innocent III did not disdain to correspond even with infidels in the interest of the Christians.* In 1211 A.D. he wrote to Melek edh Dhâher, Sultan of Aleppo, in favour of the patriarch of Antioch; and in 1213 to Melek el Adel at Damascus to demand Jerusalem, having heard from the Templars that the Sultan was willing to make its neighbourhood a tributary Christian province. This, indeed, would appear to have been an agreement which the Moslem rulers were ready to make even much later, for the sake of peace, but Pope Innocent III became more violent and imperious as he grew older, and rejected any such compromise. He quarrelled with Armenia, and with his own Legate; he incited Simon de Montfort to persecute the Albigenses of Languedoc; he drove the Poles, Saxons, Norwegians, and Livonians, against the pagan Prussians of the Oder and Vistula; he supported Otho against Philip; and first instituted the Inquisition. His intolerance made heretics of the Vaudois, the Apostolics, the Popelicanes, and the Aymeristes, who agreed only in hatred of the Church of Rome. The peaceful policy of Frederic II was the

* *Regesta*, Nos. 852, 864.

exact reverse of that of Innocent III, and aimed at making the best of actual facts, while the Church still sought to dominate the Eastern sects, and trusted in shadowy alliances with Georgians and Tartars.

Within this Pontificate, in 1212 A.D., occurred the "Child's Crusade"—the most cruel delusion, and the most wicked fraud, witnessed during the two centuries of this period. France was at that time in a state of turmoil throughout. King John in England, after the great quarrel with the Pope, and the loss of all the Angevine possessions on the Continent, had taken sides with Flanders, and had defeated the French at sea; but the invasion of England was preparing. Languedoc was desolated by the wars against the Albigenses, and full of strange doctrines, and hatred of the Roman persecutors. The failures of the later Crusaders were attributed, not to the real causes—want of unity and of good judgment, or indifference to their professed objects—but to the impurity of their lives, and to their dissolute manners. Certain fanatical priests, successors of those who believed in the miraculous letter from heaven, and in the wonders wrought by the Curé Foulques, preached throughout France and Germany a new Crusade, in which the faith and prayers of children were to do what the arms of Templars and Hospitallers could not effect. The sea was to be dried up before them, and the Moslems to surrender the Sepulchre and the Cross. Fifty thousand of these innocents—both boys and girls—are said to have marched to Marseilles and Genoa, singing hymns and waving branches; and they were attended by a mob of

the lowest class, which robbed and maltreated them on
their road. Parents obeyed the preaching of the monks,
and credited their miracles and visions. The madness of
the people was turned to account by villainous traders.
Hugh Ferreus and William Porcus, merchants of Marseilles, embarked the children on seven ships, professing
to carry them, for love of Heaven, to Palestine. Their
trade was that of kidnapping for the Alexandrian
market. Two ships were wrecked, and all on board
went down : the fate of those sold in Egypt was worse ;
and none returned to their homes. The Pope built a
chapel on St. Peter's Isle, where the ships perished ; but
the kidnappers were finally hanged, not for this evil
deed, but on a charge of attempting to assassinate the
Emperor Frederic II.

Meanwhile John of Brienne was a widower ; and,
fearing that the truce with the Moslems would not
continue, he married, by advice of his barons and prelates, a daughter of the King of Armenia,* in 1214 A.D.
A Crusade was preached in France by Jacques de Vitry,
then an Augustin canon of Villebrouk in Brabant† : King
Philip Augustus gave a fortieth part of his revenue ; and
the submissive John of England promised to take the
Cross, but had no power over English barons—it was the
year before the signing of Magna Charta. The sixth
Crusade was led by Andrew II, son of King Bela of
Hungary, who ruled Dalmatia and Croatia, Bosnia and

---

* *Regesta*, No. 873.
† Bishop of Acre in 1217 ; he left Palestine in 1227 ; resigned two years
later ; was created cardinal and legate and titular patriarch of Jerusalem.
He died in 1240.

Galicia. It began by the attack on the Prussian pagans on the Baltic shores, and in 1216 Pope Innocent III died at Perugia while striving to make peace between the Pisans and Genoese in the interests of Syria. Their disputes in Acre were, however, not settled till six years later, after the Crusade was over.* In 1217 the Hungarians left Spalatro in Venetian ships, while others came from Brindisi, Marseilles, and Genoa. It was the largest army that had been assembled at Acre since that which defeated Saladin at Arsûf; but they were ill supplied with provisions; and Syria was suffering from dearth. No opposition was offered to their advance.

The empire of Saladin had indeed fallen on evil days. The great Tartar advance was impending: Melek el Adel had abdicated; and the provinces were ruled by his sons—at Baalbek, Damascus, Bozrah, and other cities. Melek el Kâmil, his eldest, was at Cairo; but his subjects were disaffected. In 1218 Melek el Adel Seif ed Dîn—Saladin's brother—died; and the fears of the Christians in Egypt led to a general panic and flight. The new Crusaders marched inland to Mount Gilboa, and, descending to the Jordan, bathed in the Sea of Galilee.† They then attacked Mount Tabor; but, finding a fortress on its summit, retired after two furious but vain assaults. A Turkish garrison had been placed there in 1212 A.D., but was withdrawn after this contest; the fortress was levelled by Melek el Adel's order, and the walls of Jerusalem also dismantled. In October a

---

* *Regesta*, Nos. 955-7.
† *Regesta*, Nos. 901, 913, 914, 924, 930, 936, 941, 946-8, 964, 969.

council was held in the camp at Acre, by the King of
Hungary : it was too late in the year for action, and the
storms discouraged the army in their camp south of
Tyre. King Andrew left his troops, for the winter, in
Palestine, and went to Armenia, where he obtained the
head of St. Peter, the arm of St. Thomas, and seven of
the waterpots from Cana of Galilee. He also probably
obtained useful information as to the Tartar advance.

When the spring-time returned a further force of
Frisians arrived, from Cologne and the Rhine, in 1218
A.D. Coming by sea they had fought the Moors, whose
power was now beginning to fail in Portugal. Leopold of
Austria was chosen commander of the army, but the
Legate was the moving spirit in the events that followed.
It was decided that the time had come for the con-
quest of Egypt, after which the rest of Palestine
would fall an easy prey, for the northern Moslems were
being attacked in rear by the Tartars in Persia. The
Crusaders assembled at Château Pelerin, the great
Templar castle, newly built on the shore west of Carmel, near the little fort of District, found there by King
Richard. Thence they proceeded to the Delta, and
besieged Damietta for seventeen months. The Duke of
Austria returned home, leaving John of Brienne in
command.

A remarkable incident of this year was the attempt
of St. Francis of Assisi to convert the Sultan of Egypt.
The pious founder of the Minorites went alone to see
Melek el Kâmil, who heard him preach the faith, and
sent him safely back. The opinion of a Cologne

professor—Oliver—supported the simple belief of St. Francis ; but he had not the saint's courage in enforcing his doctrine. Oliver wrote to the Sultan urging him to accept the true faith, and to restore the Holy City to the Christians. He also wrote to the Moslem learned— the Ulema—exhorting them to belief in Christ. These admonitions were due to the clemency, and tolerant character, of a highly cultured sultan, which bore fruit of a very different nature ; but in the war round Damietta we find, side by side, a true Christian preaching his Master in peril of martyrdom, and a legate of the Pope insisting on war when peace was offered. Melek el Kâmil offered, while the siege of Damietta continued, to give up Jerusalem : to free all Christian captives : and to pay a large sum towards the rebuilding of the walls. The legate refused, and gained a personal victory—to the disgust of John of Brienne—when Damietta was taken and sacked. The Duke of Bavaria joined with four hundred German knights ; and Italians from Milan, Pisa, and Genoa followed. But the new leaders refused to obey Cardinal Pelagius—the legate —and he was forced to send for King John of Brienne. He, however, persuaded the Templars and Hospitallers to support him, and the Christian army marched to Mansûrah, on the Damietta branch of the Nile, thirty miles from the sea. The force included Italians of Apulia and Sicily, Spaniards, Gascons, Germans, and French, with ships from Venice, Genoa, and Pisa : but it was August, and the Nile was rising, while rumours came of forces marching from Emesa, Bozrah, and

Damascus. An Egyptian fleet cut off the army from its base, and Cardinal Pelagius was forced to sue for peace. He became himself a hostage, with other principal chiefs. Damietta was again surrendered to the Moslems, and all the advantages offered by Melek el Kâmil were thus lost through the obstinacy of the Legate. Once more, as in King Amaury's time, the Delta was saved, not by Moslem courage but by Father Nile.

So ended the sixth Crusade, and so also the eighth was to end. The extremes of opinion in the thirteenth century are marked by a Church, on the one hand, which had permitted monks to preach the Child's Crusade, and which had refused the free offer of Jerusalem ; and by the policy of Frederic II on the other, which aimed at peaceful settlement, irrespective of religious prejudice. Thus the next incident in the history of Syria was an attempt which resulted in a Christian prince suffering excommunication when engaged in freeing the Holy City, and in that city itself being laid under interdict, when occupied by Christians.

The new Emperor Frederic II proved yet more contumacious towards the Popes—Honorius III and Gregory IX—than his father had been towards Innocent III. Frederic is said to have been an accomplished prince, a good Arabic scholar, and fond of artists and poets, many of whom were Moslems. He was politic and ambitious ; but if we may judge from his treatment of Yolande, was selfish in his aims, and

unreliable.   John of Brienne journeyed to France,
England, and Germany in 1224 A.D., to find Philip
Augustus dead, and his son Louis VIII at war with
Henry III of England. During the three years of
Louis' reign this war was waged in Poitou, and the
Pope stirred up the Lombards against the Emperor
Frederic. In Languedoc the Albigenses still were
fighting, and there was war in Spain with the Moors.
But Frederic met King John of Brienne at Brindisi, and
married Yolande his daughter, thus becoming heir of
the kingdom of Jerusalem.   Three years were lost in the
struggle with the Lombards, and it was now ten since
the sixth Crusade began ; but at length, in 1227 A.D.,
the emperor left Brindisi for the East.

The new Pope Gregory IX was old and obstinate,
and renewed the excommunication launched against
Frederic by Honorius III ; but the emperor chased
him from Rome, and wrote to Melek el Kâmil in 1228,
asking for Jerusalem, and received in reply an embassy
with presents.*   The Pope forbade the emperor to go
to Syria, but Frederic set out with fifty ships, and six
hundred knights, leaving most of his army in Sicily,
and arrived safely at Acre.

The Masters of the Temple and the Hospital owed
allegiance only to the Pope, they were at once forbidden
to aid the excommunicated emperor ; but against this
papal garrison in Syria reliance could be placed on the
younger Teutonic Order, already growing powerful, and

---

* *Regesta,* Nos. 992, 997–1001, 1008, 1015–16, 1022–3. 1025, 1040,
1043, 1053, 1061, 1070, 1079, 1081, 1083, 1088, 1094–5, 1099, 1101.

willing to help the German cause. Frederic's intentions were peaceful ; and in the winter of 1228 A.D. he met Melek el Kâmil south of Cæsarea as a friend. In Sicily he had already received the Moslem envoy—Fakr ed Dîn—when the philosophy of Averroes—the famous Moorish disciple of Aristotle born a century earlier at Kordova—was discussed, and problems in philosophy and geometry were sent by the cultured emperor to the Egyptian sultan. A peace was thus easily established ; to last ten years and ten months from the 20th of February, 1229 A.D. Jerusalem, and Bethlehem, and all the villages from Acre to Jaffa, were surrendered by Egypt, with Nazareth and Toron in Upper Galilee, and the fortresses of Jaffa, Cæsarea, and Sidon. The walls of Jerusalem were not to be rebuilt ; and the mosque was to be left in the city, with free worship for Moslems.

This agreement, which would now be thought a fair and final settlement of a bitter dispute, was accepted neither by Christians nor by Moslems. The emperor and the sultan were centuries before their time. The Moslems of Jerusalem cursed Melek el Kâmil : the Pope commanded the patriarch to lay an interdict on the Holy City. The Templars refused to admit Frederic into Château Pelerin, and proposed to the sultan his murder in the Jordan Valley—which letter Melek el Kâmil sent to his ally. Throned in the Holy Sepulchre church, which no Christian prince had entered for forty years, Frederic II placed the crown on his own head. The new territory in Galilee was given to the Teutonic order ; and when the interdict was placed on Acre, for such time as Frederic should remain in the city, he shut the gates, and flogged the monks in the streets during Holy Week.

The Papal army then marched on Naples, and Frederic returned to Europe. John of Brienne* had quarrelled with his terrible son-in-law, who had neglected Yolande, and he aided the Pope and the Lombards ; but Frederic defeated them, and all that Gregory IX could do was to command the faithful neither to eat, nor drink, nor speak with the apostate emperor. During this ten years' peace, however, the Christian possessions in Palestine increased almost to their ancient extent, and the truce was faithfully observed by the Moslems. In 1232 the Pope proposed to break it, and in the following February sent the Minorites as missionaries to convert Melek el Ashraf, the Sultan of Damascus, and the rulers of Baghdad and Cairo.† Other monks went to Iconium; and an envoy from the sultan was sent to Pope and Emperor, who now had entered into treaty together. The Dominicans and Franciscans preached peace in Europe, for new troubles began to loom in the far East.

* John of Brienne was elected Emperor of Constantinople in 1228, Baldwin de Courtney, the heir to the throne, being then a child : he married the sister of Yolande, and succeeded John in 1237.

† In this year, on 3rd of May, a contest was waged between the subjects of the Emperor and of Henry I of Cyprus. Richard Filangier, who was the Emperor's bailiff of Syria, met John of Ibelin and his knights at Hamsin (Casale Imbert), near Acre, and defeated them. John of Ibelin was bailiff in the name of the King of Cyprus, who claimed Jerusalem. Richard overran Cyprus, but was expelled next year (1233 A.D.), and John reasserted his claims in Palestine on behalf of his master. He died in 1236. Queen Alice of Cyprus, daughter of Isabel and of Henry of Champagne, and widow of Hugh I, claimed Jerusalem after the death of Yolande, and her third husband, Ralph of Soissons, was accepted as bailiff of the kingdom in succession to John of Ibelin. (Archer's *Crusades*, p. 384.)

The last year of the emperor's truce was the last of Christian peace and prosperity in Syria.

The masterful settlement made by Frederic had given rest for a while ; but the times were full of trouble. The young King of England was weak and incapable, the younger King (Louis IX) of France was hardly yet established on his throne, where his mother's regency was resented by intriguing barons. In Constantinople the Courtneys—successors of Baldwin of Flanders—were growing weaker, and the Greek and Bulgarian rebels were under the walls. The Pope and the Emperor quarrelled again as to Sardinia ; and Frederic was once more excommunicated, and marched on Rome, while Italy was rent by civil war. The Tartars were pushing west towards Russia, and Melek el Kâmil, the wise Egyptian sultan, died. So in January, 1240 A.D., the truce expired in a troublous time.

The Christians forthwith began to build the walls of Jerusalem, but David, the Emir of Kerak, fell upon them, and destroyed even the Tower of David, which Melek el Adel had left standing. New Crusaders set out to their aid, under Thibaut V, Count of Champagne, and King of Navarre—the troubadour. He was forbidden to go by both Pope and Emperor, but embarked at Marseilles, and found the princes of Damascus, Aleppo, and Hamath fighting each other. The Duke of Brittany raided to Damascus in this seventh Crusade, seizing camels and oxen, horses, asses, and buffaloes. The Duke of Burgundy and the Count of Bar, though mutually jealous, marched on Gaza before King

Thibaut, but there endured a defeat which led to the loss of all that Frederic's treaty had gained, and of the possessions in Galilee which had just been reconfirmed by a treaty with Sâleh Imad ed Dîn, Sultan of Damascus.* This reverse took place in consequence of the ill discipline of the army. The Count of Bar was taken prisoner to Egypt, and with him Amaury de Montfort, and many other leaders. King Thibaut was too late to help them, and retired on Ascalon and Acre. The Templars made a separate treaty with Damascus, and the Hospitallers with Egypt. Richard of Cornwall —following Thibaut to the East in despite of the pope— found none of the Franks ready to begin the war again. Amid these troubles Gregory IX died, in 1241 A.D., as did his successor Celestin IV, only fifteen days after he was elected. Innocent IV acceded in 1243.

The races which had fought so long for Palestine seemed all to be exhausted half a century after Saladin's death. Christians and Turks alike were divided among themselves, and the future lay with the Tartars and the Egyptians. The Kharezmians—a wild Turkic people east of the Caspian Sea—had conquered Persia under Sultan Muhammad in 1218, but after his defeat by Genghiz Khan were pressed westwards by the Tartar advance from Central Asia, and had crossed the Volga in 1236, invading Poland, defeating the Teutonic Order, and rousing terror even in England. The litany of the Latin Church now contained a new petition—"From the fury of the Tartars, good Lord deliver us!" As early

* Makrizi, see Bohn's *Chronicles of Crusades*, p. 536.

as 1228 A.D. the Sultan of Damascus had called them to
help him ; and in 1243 the Sultan of Egypt sought
their alliance against Damascus. They came in hordes
through Asia Minor and Syria, pillaging all the lands.
Twenty thousand horsemen of this great vanguard of
the coming Tartars ravaged the county of Tripoli, and
overflowed Galilee—terrible they were to Moslem and
Christian alike. Like the Scythians in King Josiah's
time, "their quiver was an open sepulchre." "The lion
is come from his thicket, and the waster of nations is on
his way : he is gone forth from his place to make thy
land desolate : thy cities shall be laid waste without
inhabitant." For they came from the ancient Scythian
home of Gog and Magog, and knew of neither Christ
nor Muhammad. The Christians fled from Jerusalem
as they came, with Templars and Hospitallers ; but they
rang the bells and lured them back. Seven thousand.
Christians returned, and all were massacred, even the
sick and aged were murdered. The tombs of Godfrey
and his successors were broken up for spoil. The
Sepulchre was violated and robbed. The holy relics
were burnt or broken in pieces.

This inroad of barbarians for a moment united Christendom and Islam in a common cause.* The Templars
called on Melek el Mansûr, Emir of Emesa, to help
them ; and the united army marched on Ascalon. But
the Kharezmians were at Gaza, where the Egyptians
joined them, and on the 17th of October, 1244, a disaster

---

* *Regesta*, Nos. 1119, 1123, 1125, 1127-8, 1133.

fell upon the Christians of Syria greater than even Thibaut's defeat, and on the same fatal field. They arrayed the battle with the Knights Hospitallers on the left, under Walter of Brienne, Count of Jaffa, and nephew of the King of Jerusalem. In the centre were the Templars, with the Patriarch bearing the Holy Cross : on the right were the Moslems under Melek el Mansûr : all the barons of Syria were with the Cross. For two days the battle was furiously waged, but at length the Moslems were driven back, and thirty thousand of the allies are said to have fallen. Only the Patriarch and the Prince of Tyre escaped, with thirty-three Templars, twenty-six Hospitallers, and three Teutonic knights. The Egyptians overran Palestine, occupying Jerusalem and Tiberias: the Kharez-mian hordes pillaged the Jordan valley and the Ascalon plains, and tied Walter of Brienne to a cross before the walls of Jaffa ; but the garrison refused even then to yield, and Walter was sent to Cairo—where so many Christian and Moslem prisoners now were taken—and there he was killed by the mob in the streets.

The Kharezmians were next induced to attack Damas-cus, which submitted ; but here they quarrelled with the Egyptians. The Moslem forces of Aleppo and Damas-cus joined the latter, and after two pitched battles the Kharezmians fled, and became dispersed in Asia Minor. Thus in 1247 A.D. the condition of Syria remained not very different from that which Richard and Saladin established. The plains from Jaffa northwards were still held by Christians, and the mountains and lands beyond the Jordan were possessed by Egyptian Moslems ; but this position resulted not from treaty but from conquest, and the Christians had lost their most experienced defenders, in the destruction of the Military Orders. Nejm ed Dîn of Egypt held the Holy City ; and a yet more terrible foe was to appear in Bibars. The history of the forty-four years that followed, down to the loss of Acre, is one of constant misfortune, and steadily decreasing territory.

Before considering this last half century of Latin occupation of Syria, we may turn for a moment to describe the social conditions of the better period, when Frederic II had established a ten years' peace, and when the trade of the East was not yet ruined by the Tartar outbreak. In many respects the Frankish society differed much, in the thirteenth century, from that described in the twelfth, before the kingdom was lost at Hattîn. The main new features were the growth of literature and knowledge, among both Christians and Moslems, which seemed at one time destined to lead to a better understanding between them ; the development of trade by the Italian cities ; and the increasing power of the Military Orders.

Respecting literature we have seen that the followers of Godfrey tore the Koráns in pieces, and burned the library of Tripoli, but that, in Saladin's times, the Frank nobles had learned Arabic, and had studied Arab books. In 1215 A.D. an Archbishop of Toledo even encouraged the translation of the Korán into Latin, and the Moslem

beliefs began to be well understood.*   But when this
learning led Frederic II to seek peace with Egypt the
popes began to set their veto on the study of the Arabic
tongue, and on the religious and philosophic writings
of the Arabs.   In Europe the knowledge gained in
Syria was thus forbidden for centuries after it was first
attained.

But it was not only Arab literature that attracted the
Latins.   The learning of the Jacobites was indeed the
source of Arab culture.†   When the great school of
Edessa was broken up by the Nestorian dispute, its
disciples gathered not only in Nisibis, but also in Tripoli.
They were students of Aristotle and Plato, and Abu el
Faraj—otherwise called Gregory bar Hebræus—was a
Syrian Jacobite whose works and studies in Tripoli
(between 1246 and 1259 A.D.) covered many scientific
subjects and remain in extant manuscripts.   His philosophic writings included : first, analectics, dialectics,
rhetoric, and sophistry ; secondly, cosmography, natural
history, and psychology ; and, thirdly, metaphysics.
They were founded on Aristotle, and were the basis of
much that became known later in Europe, when St.
Louis—taking example by what he saw in Palestine—
began to encourage the collection of books in libraries,
and the Benedictines began to learn the wisdom of the
East.   In other Syrian manuscripts of the same age are
found treatises on religion and religious history—the

---

* See Sir John Maundeville in 1322 A.D., Bohn's *Early Travels in
Palestine*, p. 200.   An earlier Latin translation dates 1143.

† Rey, *Colonies Franques*, pp. 166-171.   Bar Hebræus was a Jew by
race, and born at Malatiya in Armenia.   He became Bishop of Aleppo.

knowledge of God, the Creation, the nature of man, the elements composing the world, the phenomena of the atmosphere, the nature of birds, beasts, fishes, and reptiles—all no doubt very primitive in scope and in scientific character, yet representing that spirit of enquiry which arose with the great Greek genius whose mind still influences mankind, and which led Pliny to examine fossils, and to explain the true form of the world. In 1272 A.D. Bar Hebræus was still lecturing on Euclid and the Almagest of Ptolemy, and in addition he compiled chronicles of the highest value' for the history of his time.

Such knowledge spread among the seigneurs rather than the clergy; and whereas in the earlier age the authors of chronicles and pilgrim diaries are monks or priests, in the thirteenth century some of the most important memoirs and chronicles are due to nobles and knights. We have yet to consider the charming pages of Joynville, whose successors were the gouty old knight Sir John Maundeville,* and the Burgundian Bertrandon de la Brocquière. The account of the Tartars, by the good monk Rubruquis, is not more valuable than the travels of the layman Marco Polo. Villeharduin, who describes the conquest of Constantinople which he witnessed, was Marshal of Champagne, and became Marshal of Roumania. The increasing culture of laymen is one of the features of the thirteenth century; but it must not be forgotten that Vincent of

---

* Sir John Maundeville's work no doubt is largely based on Pliny, Marco Polo, and other authors for regions which he had not visited, but the account of Palestine appears to be original.

Beauvais, the Dominican, who was librarian to St. Louis and engaged in educating this king's children, was equally distinguished in France in the same age. His *Speculum Majus* appeared about 1250 A.D., and he attempted to bring together all the science of the times, treating of natural history, of arts, and of general history in all ages. It was on his return from Syria that St. Louis encouraged similar learned writers.

One of the great difficulties encountered by such enquiry lay in the multiplicity of alphabets and of languages to be learned. In addition to the Gothic capitals of monuments and the Gothic small text, the Greek uncials and minuscules were learned by men like William of Tyre. Syriac was written in the rounded Estrangelo and in the later Serta character. The Nestorian character and dialect, though connected, were not the same as the Syriac. The old Syrian script known as Kufic, and used near Damascus before the Moslem conquest, was unintelligible to the Crusaders in the time of William of Tyre, but the Latins became acquainted later with the flowing Neskhi writing of Saladin's age closely resembling the modern Arabic script. The Armenian and Georgian alphabets enshrined little but legends of saints and historical romance, but it became necessary later to understand the Uigur alphabet of the Mongols, in which letters sent from Mangu Khan to the Pope were written. The crabbed forms of later Jewish alphabets were perhaps known only to Jews, but names of Jewish pilgrims are written on the walls of Crusaders' churches — like that

of St. Samuel—by travellers who ventured into the
Latin Kingdom to visit the sacred cities of Jerusalem,
Hebron, Tiberias, and Safed, and to pray at the tombs
of prophets and rabbis ; while the Samaritans used the
Arabic letters in addition to their own most ancient
alphabet.

Literature flourished among Moslems as well as
among Christians. The geography of Edrisi was published at the court of Roger II of Sicily in 1154, and
though he only visited Asia Minor he tells us much of
Palestine. Ibn Jobeir was born in Spain in 1145 A.D.,
and at the age of forty travelled in Egypt and Arabia,
and by Mosul and Damascus to Acre. Yakût, the
Greek slave, educated at Baghdad, travelled in Persia
and Mesopotamia, and settled in Aleppo, dying in 1229
A.D. He had completed a dictionary of geography
(four years earlier) covering four thousand octavo pages.*
In 1177 A.D. was born at Tyre Reshed ed Din, who
studied the botany of Southern Syria and the Lebanon.
Ibn Beithar, a Spanish Moslem, visited Antioch and
Egypt in 1217 A.D., and settled under Melek el Kâmil
at Damascus : he also was busy with the flora of
the Lebanon. Kaswîni, the Arab Pliny, was Kadi of
Hillah, near Babylon, when he died in 1281 A.D. His
great work is divided into three parts : the first on
minerals, the second on botany, the third on zoology,
and his great authority was Aristotle.† His zoology
is faulty, but the spirit rather than the actual result

---

* Guy le Strange, *Palestine under the Moslems*, pp. 7–9.
† Rey, *Colonies Franques*, p. 185.

must be considered in estimating the culture of the age.

The commerce of the thirteenth century followed the same great routes—by the Caspian, by Baghdad, and through Egypt, already mentioned as explored much earlier by Italians, Greeks, and Jews, by Arabs, Indians, and Chinese. It must also be considered under the two heads of Christian and Moslem trade. The trade of Venice reached its height about 1200 A.D., but was interrupted by Tartar disturbances. The Genoese trade continued by the northern route till the fifteenth century; but the Pisan and Venetian gradually shifted to Egypt and reached India by the Red Sea. Of the Amalfi merchants we hear nothing in the thirteenth century, but the Marseilles* traders continued in Palestine down to 1260 A.D. at least: they aided Conrad of Montferrat to defend Tyre against Saladin, and helped in 1198 A.D. at Jaffa. They obtained free trade at Beirût, and possessions in Acre, and full rights in Cyprus and at Tyre, and they established a treaty with Venice in 1259 A.D.

The conquest of Constantinople and of the Greek islands gave the Venetians a more commanding position than was held by either their Genoese or their Pisan rivals; and some forty extant documents relate to their Syrian possessions in the thirteenth century.† Conrad of Montferrat confirmed their older rights. Leo II of Armenia granted them free trade in his kingdom.

* *Regesta*, Nos. 666, 697, 747, 855, 889, 965, 1014, 1045, 1052, 1071, 1109, 1283, 1297.

† *Regesta*, between No. 679 and No. 1481.

Melek el Adel promised them protection in Egypt, and Guy of Gebal gave them free trade, though Pope Honorius III took away their church at Tyre when they were excommunicated in 1216 A.D. They made treaties with Aleppo and with other Turkish cities, and renewed their Egyptian alliance with Kelaun in 1288 A.D., shortly before the fall of Acre. The papal ban thus only served to throw them more and more into intercourse with Moslems. They owned no less than eighty villages in the plains of Tyre, mostly purchased in the thirteenth century, and of these Marsilius Georgius, bailly of Syria, made a list in 1243 A.D.,* in which he speaks of the sugar cultivation, and names various Moslem rustics as their tenants.

The Genoese possessions are described in some fifty extant documents† after the battle of Hattin. They retained their privileges in Antioch and Tyre (where they helped against Saladin) and those of the "Gold Letters" of Jerusalem. Leo II of Armenia gave them free trade in the Gulf of Aiyas and at Tarsus, and other agreements were made in Cyprus, and at Beirût, Haifa, and Acre. There were Genoese residents in Damascus; and in 1290 A.D. they made a treaty with Kelaun in Egypt. Henry III of England wrote to a Genoese merchant of Damascus, in 1225 A.D, to provide scarlet and other gifts on his account for the Sultan.

The Pisans are found in the same sea coast cities— according to some forty other deeds, and documents,

---

* *Regesta*, No. 1114.
† Ditto, between Nos. 685 and 1503.

after the battle of Hattîn.* As early as 1208 A.D. they were in treaty with Egypt, though, like the other cities, not loth to break these alliances in favour of Crusaders attacking the Delta. They aided to recover Jaffa from Saladin, and were employed by King Guy at the great siege of Acre in 1189 A.D. Celestin III confirmed their rights in 1193, and they had quarters in Tyre and Antioch, and free trade in the Latin Kingdom, in Cyprus, and at Batrûn. Melek el Kâmil received their consul, and granted a funduk in Alexandria. Frederic II restored their lost properties, for good service rendered, and granted freedoms in Jerusalem, Acre, and Tyre; but their quarrels with the Genoese were of constant recurrence.

The trading ships which were built in Italian ports, for the transport of troops, pilgrims, and merchandise, probably resembled those which Felix Fabri describes in detail in the fifteenth century.† The galley in which he sailed was Venetian, with sixty benches, each for three rowers, to whom an archer was added in the ships of war. Its length was about one hundred and eighty feet, and its breadth forty-two feet at the mast. The truck of the mast was over ninety feet above the water. The ship had a beak for ramming other vessels, and a foresail. The rudder (which in Oriental ships was replaced by two long sweeps at the stern) was, in the Venetian galleys, single as now. The vessel, though broadly built, was swift, and the whole distance from Venice to Acre could

---

* *Regesta*, between Nos. 662 and 1518.
† *Felix Fabri*, Vol. I, Part I, pp. 125-163, English translation.

be covered in about a fortnight with fair weather. In
the high stern of the galley the "castle" was built in
three storeys, the steersman and the compass being
above the captain's cabin in the central storey, and the
treasury, and cabin for "noble ladies," below, reached
only by a hatchway.* Near the poop the boats were
hung, with companion ladders, and on the poop the flag
was hoisted. The kitchen was in this part, with a
cellar beneath, and a stable for live stock beside it.
The ship was provided with mangonels for throwing
stones. The mast had a square sail, and a cage above
for the outlook. Various sails were provided for change
of weather. The deck round the mast was called the
"market place" of the galley, being the only place of
meeting for passengers and traders. The merchandise
was stored along the sides, and over the deck was a
gangway, from stem to stern, for the officers who
ordered the rowers, who were galley slaves, chained to
their benches, but allowed to go on shore at the ports
to trade for themselves. The cabin in the body of the
ship was reached by a hatchway under the benches: it
ran from the castle to the prow, and was used both for
merchandise and for travellers ; but was only lighted
from the deck. The berths touching each other were
arrayed with the head to the ship's sides ; and the
passengers' chests were placed at their feet, by the central
gangway. The hold beneath the cabin contained the
ballast of sand, in which the passengers buried their

---

* The total number on board would not have exceeded four hundred
persons.

bottles of wine, and other provisions, for coolness—as in
the Greek ships of the time of Justinian.   The well for
the bilge water appears to have given great annoyance
to the land's-men in the berths, as did the smell of pitch
on timbers and sheets.   The altar was by the mast, and
the pilgrims stood there singing hymns as the ship left
port, and made processions round the mast in other
cases.   The captains were men of wealth and station ;
and pilots, acquainted with the whole course, were
carried.   Charts were in use, and a second compass by
the mast.

The lot of the galley slave was a hard one : they
were divided into three classes, and included Greeks,
Albanians, Illyrians, and Slavs, with a few Turks and
Saracen captives.   They were incited to their hard
labour with " shouts, blows, and curses."   They were
wretchedly fed, and slept on their benches, unprotected
from weather.   When not pulling they gambled with
dice and blasphemed.   They were terrible thieves, and
sometimes dangerous mutineers ; but each and all had
some small venture under his bench, for harbour trade ;
and they could speak Turkish and Greek, as well as
Italian, enough for such a purpose.   The sailors and
cabin boys belonged to a better class of freemen : there
were also trumpeters, barbers, doctors, surgeons, and
clerks on board.   The administration of justice was
strict, but the punishments were not severe.   In cases
where horses and mules were carried they stood on
deck above the cabin, to the discomfort of those who
could not sleep for their stamping.   The food was

coarse, and vermin abounded ; while the presence of a few violent characters among the passengers destroyed all hope of rest, in the long undivided and dark cabin, where they were closely packed : while the bilge water was pumped out from its midst. The petty thefts of the rowers, and the rolling up of beds each morning, were other troubles of these unhappy passengers. Nor were they able to sleep on shore, in the islands visited, for the inns were of evil repute, and the lives of strangers often in danger. The hardships encountered during storms, when the waves dashed over the rowers, and flooded the cabin, must often have made the pilgrims prefer even the toils and dangers of the long land journey to the East.

Turning next to the native trade of Syria which enriched the Italians, it is to be noted that the Arab trade with India, from Alexandria and Aden, already brought Chinese products to the West in the sixth century A.D.,* having been established by the Romans four hundred years earlier, when silk first became known in Italy. In the eighth century the Arabs visited Canton,† and Chinese fleets then reached Aden and the Persian Gulf, bringing silk and porcelain and other merchandise. In the ninth century Ibn Khordadbeh had described the double monsoon of the Indian Ocean, of which Hippalus had taken advantage under Augustus. In the

---

* Cosmas, quoted by Priault, *India and Rome*, pp. 129–219 ; *Antoninus*, p. 31, English translation.

† Rey, *Colonies Franques*, pp. 193–234. The Moslems are noticed in China under the Tang dynasty within a century of the Hegirah. (Williams, *Middle Kingdom*, Vol. II, p. 285.)

twelfth and thirteenth centuries this Arab trade flourished, as it had done under the great khalifs, and the Chinese were met at Sumatra. Chinese snuff bottles, with quotations from poets who wrote in the "Flowery Kingdom" between the eighth and thirteenth centuries, have been found in Egypt and in Cyprus.* In 1137 rich gifts of Chinese silks were made to the Kaaba at Mecca, and the Arabs appear to have been still visiting China.

Rakkah on the Euphrates was the point of junction of the caravans from east and west—the first coming from Mosul, the latter from Iconium in Asia Minor by Edessa, or from Aleppo, Antioch, and Aiyas. The line from Rakkah to Damascus lay through the Jewish settlement at Palmyra. The Italian treaties with the Moslems placed all the products of this commerce in Italian hands for transport to Europe; but it passed through many Jewish trading settlements further east— as already explained—before reaching the Euphrates marts. In 1184 Ibn Jobeir speaks of the rich merchants of Damascus, who sent caravans to the Latin Kingdom. At Acre there were merchants of Mosul established as vassals of the Templars. In 1268 an agreement was made between these Mosul traders and the Genoese† at Acre, concerning a dispute in which an Italian ship had been seized. The trade between Aleppo and Antioch existed before the twelfth century, and Greek merchants were thus in relation with Moslems. In the Edessa

---

* Williams, *Middle Kingdom*, Vol. II, p. 27.
† *Regesta*, Nos. 1362, 1381.

Principality the Jacobite Syrians monopolised the trade ; and from the Euphrates fords the caravan routes extended to Tarsus and Iconium ; and slaves were brought to Aiyas from Georgia, Russia, and Armenia, with spices, cloth, and silk embroidered with gold—as described by Marco Polo in the thirteenth century. The pilgrims to Mecca, allowed by their Prophet to trade during their journey, communicated between Asia Minor, Damascus, and the western ports of Arabia, while Damascus was also in communication with Suez and Akabah, where ships from Yemen were met. Ibn Batuta describes Chinese junks* by that name (in the fourteenth century) as coming to Arabia. The Egyptian caravans came through the Sinaitic desert to Kerak, or by Gaza and Hebron to meet at Damascus.

The Arab traders, settled in Syria itself, were the intermediaries of this foreign commerce, with whom the Franks communicated. In their stores were found carpets of Baghdad and Persia, ivory and perfumes, sandal wood, musk, and aloes, civet and spices, and glass from the Irak regions. Chinese porcelain is mentioned in the Assizes of Jerusalem as coming from " the Paynims " ; and Ibn Batuta says it was much prized in Syria as early as the tenth century. It continued to be brought to Damascus in the fourteenth century. Pearls from the Persian Gulf were also bought by the Franks ; and precious vases of painted marble from Mecca, and enamelled pottery, with damascined copper, and Damascus blades. The apothecaries dealt

---

* Rey, *Colonies Franques*, p. 203.

in opium, rhubarb, tamarind, gums, cantharides, and cardamoms, in myrrh and balm, in attar of roses, orpiment, scammony, and senna.   There were electuaries of citrons, and sherbets and syrups in their shops, aromatic vinegar and myro-balsamum.   The matahassep inspected the wares of the grocers, and the sherbets, so that according to the Assizes nothing "that was not good might be sold," and perhaps to prevent the sale of poisons.

Another important trade with Siberia brought various furs to Syria and Europe.   Boats from the Volga came to Derbend on the Caspian, with skins of red and white foxes.   The furriers had a street in Jerusalem,[*] and sold skins of the ermine, marten, otter, beaver, wild cat, and squirrel.   Minever was the skin of the Siberian squirrel, brought to the port of Aiyas across Armenia.   Ibn Batuta, Marco Polo, and Abu el Feda, speak of the fur trade with the invisible inhabitants of the "Land of Darkness" in the high latitudes of Siberia ; and legends of its long arctic nights go back to the time of the Pseudo-Callisthenes.[†]   Sir John Maundeville repeats three stories, relating how the voices of men, the neighing of horses, and the crowing of cocks, might be heard where nothing could be seen—in the winter darkness ; and in these Mongolian deserts the sands were said to lap like the waves of the sea, in a region still terrible for its dust storms.

---

[*] William of Tyre : Rey, *Colonies Franques*, p. 209.
[†] Yule's *Marco Polo*, II, p. 415 ; Sir John Maundeville in Bohn's *Early Travels*, p. 258.

Among the Syrian products were feathers of the ostrich from the eastern deserts, and salt from the Dead Sea, and the alkali plant from the plain to its north. The helmets were adorned also at times with plumes of peacock feathers—white, or green with purple eyes.

The Syrian industries were highly important, because in many instances they gave the models of later European art. When the Arabs conquered Persia, in the seventh century A.D., they found in existence an art which, though partly of Greek or Byzantine origin, was mainly based on the old civilisation of Babylon and Assyria. Thus, for instance, the cloisonné enamels, which were famous in later times in Damascus and Persia, trace back to a Persian or Assyrian art, of which a specimen exists in the British Museum. The Arab khalifs encouraged such art, and it spread with Islam to Egypt, Spain, and Syria. The faïence work with which the Dome of the Rock is adorned was of Persian origin, and traced back to the wonderful coloured tiles of Susa,. dating from 400 B.C. This art began to show its influence on the ceramic work of France even in the twelfth century, when Arabic letters were imitated on the enamelled tiles of St. Antonin.

In Antioch, Hebron, Tripoli, Damascus, and Acre, glass was made in the twelfth century.* It was a very early discovery, either in Syria itself or in Egypt. Lamps, cups, bowls, and bottles were manufactured of gilded and enamelled glass, at some of the towns noted, even in the eleventh century ; and heraldic animals—

* *William of Tyre*, XIII, 3.

lions, eagles, and martichores—were represented in the ornament. The Venetian glass took its origin in the imitation of this Syrian art ; and the materials were brought from Syria. The Damascus inlaid metal work— still an extant industry—was also imported to Europe, and became the source whence the idea of copper plate printing arose. The gold and silver smiths of Syria wrought after Byzantine models, and their work found its way to churches such as that of Namur, where a cross made at Acre still exists, adorned with cloisonné work, representing figures of St. Mark, St. John, St. Matthew, St. Peter, St. Paul, and the angel Gabriel, with Greek texts in red enamel, and turquoises, rubies, and other stones.*

Syria had been the first country in which silk was spun in Justinian's time ; and it continued to be manufactured at Damascus in the twelfth century,† as well as at Tyre, Tripoli, Antioch, and Tarsus, with taffeta, satin, and sendal. In 1283 there were at least four thousand workers in silk and cloth in Tripoli alone. The inventories of St. Paul's in London, and of the Cathedral of Canterbury, include notices of silk vestments from Antioch, of embroidered work from Tarsus, and sendals from Tripoli. In Syria and Cyprus cotton was also made into cloth and buckram—a material noticed in the Assizes. Camelots or camel-hair stuffs were also highly prized in the thirteenth century—such as Joyn-ville bought at Tortosa ; and tyretaine or tartan took its

* Rey, *Colonies Franques*, p. 232.
† Ditto, p. 214.

name from Tyre. Carpets used by Franks and natives alike* came from Asia Minor, Baghdad, and Persia. Soap was made as now—from olive oil and alkali. Salt was manufactured in the salt pans—such as those of the Tour des Salines, which still remain on the shore close to the Crocodile river. Iron was also mined in the Lebanon near Beirût, while Asia Minor supplied other metals in abundance. Such a review of Oriental trade not only shews us the prosperity which grew out of the conquest of Syria, but it also serves to explain the rapid growth of art and commerce in Europe, which followed that conquest.

The defence of the country, and the maintenance of the Italian trade, became the duty of the great Military Orders. The Templars were thought to aim at the possession of the whole country as the property of their Order, but they found rivals, with whom they even sometimes actually fought, in the Knights Hospitallers; while through the influence of Frederic II the Teutonic Order became important in the thirteenth century, and took his side against the Pope in the great quarrel of his reign. The Templars in this age had eighteen fortresses, of which the most important were Tortosa in the north, and Château Pelerin built under Carmel in 1218 A.D. They were especially strong in the county of Tripoli where Château Blanc—north of the capital—was their great castle. They had fourteen commanders in Syria besides those in Cyprus and Armenia : they acted not only as guards and guides to pilgrims, but also as

* *William of Tyre*, V, 23.

bankers: though, according to Joynville, it was not always easy to recover money deposited with them. They did not scruple to make alliances, not only with schismatic Christians, but even with Moslem princes. They took the side of Bibars in 1274 A.D. against the King of Cyprus, and interceded with Kelaun in 1282 for the King of Armenia, concluding a ten years' truce with that Sultan of Egypt. Some forty extant documents relate to their history and possessions in Syria, after the battle of Hattîn down to the fall of Acre.* In 1195 they obtained property near Nicosia in Cyprus, from Amaury II ; and the next year were warned by the Pope to keep the peace with the prior of the Holy Sepulchre. Three years later they were excommunicated by the Patriarch of Jerusalem, for retaining certain funds, but Innocent III settled the quarrel. Their adventures in Armenia have been already noticed : the Pope took their part against Leo II, the Armenian king, who accused them of siding with the Sultan of Aleppo against his cause.

The Order spread also along the shores of Asia Minor,† where the Pope confirmed their holding of the port of Satalia. In 1216 Frederic II recognised their right to build ships at Marseilles, and to bring pilgrims from Spain and other countries. In 1228 the Master swore obedience to the Patriarch of Jerusalem. Immediately after the third Crusade a great quarrel with the Hospital had arisen about lands near Margat. At

---

* *Regesta*, between No. 676 and No. 1447.
† Ditto, No. 815.

this time the Templars had nine thousand manors, and the Hospitallers nineteen thousand (including European possessions)*: the boundaries of their lands near Margat were not finally fixed till about 1243 A.D.,† the year of the Kharezmian invasion, when peace was a vital necessity between the Orders. Yet in 1262 they had to settle another dispute as to villages in the plains east of Acre.‡

The more popular Order of the Knights of St. John—or Hospitallers—established their principal seat at Krak des Chevaliers north-east of Tripoli, where the Grand Master abode after the battle of Hattîn. About one hundred and twenty contemporary documents relate their history during this later period.§ Among their important castles were Margat north of Tortosa, Château Rouge in the Sharon plain, Belvoir south-west of the Sea of Galilee—which long resisted Saladin, and Gibelin, now Beit Jibrîn, east of Ascalon. They owned in all one hundred and eighty-two villages in

---

* The English possessions of the Templars (see Archer's *Crusades*, p. 180) included the old Temple outside Holborn Bars, whence they removed in 1185 to the Temple on the Thames. Hugh de Payen had been received by Henry I in Normandy in 1128, and Stephen gave Temple Cressing in Essex to the Order about 1150. Queen Matilda gave them Temple Cowley, near Oxford. Henry II gave them Waterford and Wexford, and John gave Lundy Island. The chief English house of the Hospitallers at Clerkenwell was founded by Jordan Briset in 1110. Stephen gave them Little Maplestead in Essex, Shandon in Herts, and Shengay in Cambridgeshire. The small English Order of St. Thomas of Acre (Stubb's *Lectures on Mediæval History*, pp. 182–5, quoted by Archer, *Crusades*, p. 183) was founded by William, chaplain of Ralph de Diceto at Acre, in honour of Thomas à Becket. They were attached to the Templars, and had a red and white cross. They had a Hospital in Acre, and survived to the fourteenth century in Cyprus.

† *Regesta*, No. 1111.
‡ Ditto, No. 1318.
§ Ditto, between No. 679 and No. 1493.

Palestine, during their most prosperous time, lying in the shore plains or in the foot hills to the east: they had twelve commanders in Syria, besides those in Cyprus and Armenia, where they superseded the Templars.

In 1199 A.D. the Order took charge of the Island of Marâkieh and of the City of Homs, ceded by Boemund IV of Antioch, who was afraid of the Assassins living in this region,* whom the Hospitallers watched, but who became tributary later to the Templars. In the next year they made a special alliance with the Bishop of Acre, who allowed them to build a chapel in the city, and promised to do justice on their enemies, and to be at peace with themselves† ; but in 1203 A.D. we find them quarrelling in Cyprus with the Bishop of Nicosia.‡   The first Norman Emperor of Constantinople—Baldwin— attracted them in the following year by a grant of land in Neocastro,§ and their possessions steadily increased through places bequeathed by private owners in their wills, or through agreements with the Syrian princes and seigneurs in return for their services. The humble brethren became some of the proudest landowners in the country as time passed by.

So in 1207 they obtained Kefr Lâm and the Salt Pans north of Cæsarea, and a large grant further south, including villages in the low hills and the Castle of Plans west of Samaria‖ where traces of their presence

* *Regesta*, 759.
† Ditto, 771.
‡ Ditto, 790.
§ Ditto, No. 796.
‖ Ditto, Nos. 818–819.

still remain; while in the Antioch Principality they
obtained the town of Gabala, and soon after half of
Château Blanc north of Tripoli.* Leo II of Armenia
promised them half of Laranda near Iconium, if it
should be conquered. Hugh I of Cyprus gave them
lands near Paphos in 1210 A.D.; and in the same year
Prince Rupon, nephew of Leo II, joined the Order.
Four years later they advanced £7,000 for the marriage
of Leo II's daughter to King John of Brienne, and obtained further privileges in consequence†; and in 1218
others from Andrew of Hungary.‡ In 1231 they obtained rents in Antioch from the products of fisheries,
tanneries, and vineyards.§ In 1232 their disputes with
the Templars were settled by the Archbishop of Nazareth, and other prelates‖; and three years later the two
Orders agreed as to the water for mills on the River
Belus near Acre. They settled other properties with
the Teutonic Order soon after, and in 1243 received the
custody of Ascalon from Frederic II.¶ In 1255 they
obtained the fortress on Tabor,** and their possessions
round Acre, and eastwards in Lower Galilee, steadily
increased with the increase of Christian power before
the battle of Gaza. In 1259 nineteen villages were
handed over to them by the Archbishop of Nazareth,
for an annual payment of about £5,000.†† Sir Joseph

---

* *Regesta*, 820 829, 843, 844, 845.
† Ditto, Nos. 869, 870, 877, 878.
‡ Ditto, No. 908.
§ Ditto, No. 1032.
‖ Ditto, Nos. 1039, 1062.
¶ Ditto, No. 1112.
** Ditto, No. 1230.
†† Ditto, Nos. 1282, 1286.

de Cancy, who wrote letters to Edward I of England, was the treasurer of the Order at this time in Palestine, being an English knight of a good Yorkshire family.

As the final catastrophe approached, the sales to this Order became yet more important. In 1261 A.D. they bought the town of Arsûf, near which they had long held lands in the plain of Sharon.* Villages near Tyre were granted in 1269 : and further properties in Cyprus.† In 1289, just before the final struggle, the Master of the Hospital wrote to summon his knights to the Holy Land after the losses suffered at Tripoli.‡

The Teutonic Order rose, as already said, out of the Hospital, and the date of its independent existence is uncertain. The German Hospital was, however, founded in Jerusalem in 1128 A.D. It was not till the thirteenth century that these knights became important. In 1192 they were established at Acre, and they obtained lands in the Lebanon above Beirût, in Galilee, and in the Jordan Valley. Nearly a hundred villages belonged to them in later years. Upwards of ninety documents exist concerning their affairs.§ Having lost the German Hospice in Jerusalem, the Teutonic knights began to build one near the east wall of Acre, which, during the siege, King Guy had promised to grant them, the Master of the Order of St. John granting lands near the town ‖ and Pope Celestin III promising them the Papal protection.

* *Regesta,* Nos. 1302, 1313, 1371.
† Ditto, Nos. 1366, 1370.
‡ Ditto, No. 1493.
§ Ditto, between Nos. 696 and 1492.
‖ Ditto, Nos. 699, 700.

In 1195 Henry of Champagne gave them equal rights
with the two older Orders, and land near Jaffa; and
further properties were acquired not far from Acre,
where they were accepted by the Templars as regu-
larly established in 1198 A.D.* In the first year of
the new century Boemund IV granted them free trade
in Antioch. Lands in Upper Galilee and near Tripoli
followed,† and half the spoil of Damietta was granted
in 1220,‡ with a large purchase (confirmed by John of
Brienne) of all the principal villages between Acre and
Safed, which Frederic II again confirmed six years
later. They had also a house in Tyre, and gardens
at Sidon.§ Montfort, their great castle in the mountains north-east of Acre, was built in 1229, and in
the same direction they held Château du Roi at
Màlia, built about 1220, and Château Jiddin, which
retains its name, close by. Montfort stood on a high
narrow ridge south of Wâdy el Kurn, and was the
seat of the Grand Master, and the treasure house of
the Order. The foundations of its walls and towers
alone remain for the greater part of its extent.

In 1240 a treaty with the Sultan of Damascus secured
their wide lands in Galilee, which included Safed, and
extended to Chorazin north of the Sea of Galilee.‖ In
1256 further villages were granted in the plains north of
Acre, and others in the Sidon hills (called the Land of

* *Regesta*, Nos. 720, 740.
† Ditto, Nos. 772, 828, 839.
‡ Ditto, Nos. 930, 933, 934, 940, 974, 978.
§ Ditto, Nos. 954, 986.
‖ Ditto, Nos. 1026, 1104.

Shouf), by the Seigneur of Beirût and the Seigneur of Sidon*; and five years later they rented a large number of villages in the same Land of Shouf for £105 yearly, paying a capital sum of £2,000 to Julian lord of Sidon. They, however, quarrelled with the Bishop of Hebron about property in Acre, and the dispute continued for twenty years till 1273 A.D., when the Order was excommunicated, but absolved by the Legate.† They, too, gathered in 1289 for the final defence of Acre. The Order had also its lands in Germany, and fought the Tartars in Poland. The Cartulary of their possessions is still preserved in Berlin.

The final loss of Syria differently affected the fortunes of these three great Orders. The Templars, who were immensely rich, and whose treachery was suspected on account of their known relations with Moslem princes, became the scapegoats of the great disaster, and were everywhere abolished as an Order about 1315 A.D. The Knights of St. John retained their good name for valour and benevolence—in Cyprus, Rhodes, and Malta. The Teutonic Order, or Knights of St. George, had obtained the provinces of Livonia, Culm, and part of Prussia, and became a Lutheran Order at the Reformation in Germany. In an age when the power of popes was less, and the prejudices of the people less strong, the Templars—whose policy was one of peaceful relations with the Moslems—might perhaps have been recognised as the best friends of

---

* *Regesta,* Nos. 1250, 1256, 1300-1.
† Ditto, Nos. 1207, 1388, 1390.

Syria, and of European culture. They expiated at the stake the crime of tolerance. Their records are destroyed; and only their beautiful churches remind us in Europe of the Dome of the Rock at Jerusalem, which was their original sanctuary.

CHAPTER X.

St. Louis.

In telling the story of the eighth Crusade (including
that which led to the conquest of Byzantium) we rely
on one of the most charming biographies ever penned.
The perfect knight and Christian gentleman, who was
hereafter to be known as St. Louis, was happy in the
choice of a friend. For him the Sieur de Joynville
wrote a loving memoir, and for him the good and brave
monk Rubruquis journeyed to far-off Karakorum north
of China. The results of his wars in Palestine were
meagre, and in Egypt the cowardice and insubordina-
tion of his dissolute soldiers brought disaster on the
cause; but the fair fame of King Louis IX of France
was not dimmed by such misfortune, and to the end he
held the hearts of honest and gentle friends.

St. Louis was not yet thirty years of age when the
news of the terrible inroad of the Kharezmians reached
Europe. He had acceded as a boy of eleven, under
the regency of his mother Blanche of Castile, who was
hated, as a Spaniard and a woman of independent
character, by the scheming barons of France. From
her he learned never to lie or break his word, to be
temperate in diet, to be chaste in life and speech, to

defend the poor against the rich, and the peasant against
the tyranny of priests: though his zeal unfortunately
led to the burning of many heretics, for the good—as
he believed—of their souls. He was modest in speech,
hating argument, never contradicting, and humbly holding that the faith must be simply accepted by laymen who were without controversial knowledge. He
was a king after the Pope's heart save in one particular,
that he refused to confiscate the property of those
excommunicated by French prelates. In the forest of
Fontainebleau, and the woods of Vincennes, where he
loved to hunt, St. Louis would seat himself under the
green oaks in summer, to hear the woes of his meanest
subjects, dressed in camlet or tyretaine, with black
mantle of sendal, while his great lords were decked in
cloth of gold and embroidered coats. In his boyhood
a rebellion of the barons, headed by his father's uncle—
the Count of Boulogne—brought many dangers on his
mother and himself; but the people loved him; and as
he passed with his guards from Mont Clery to Paris
the crowds prayed aloud for his life and prosperity.
Count Thibaut of Champagne aided him against
Mauclerc, Count of Brittany, whom St. Louis forgave,
after defeating him by such aid; and the great friend of
his life was John Sieur de Joynville, who was "not his
subject," but rose to be high steward of Champagne.
The country of his ally was wasted by the barons; and
in 1230 A.D. Henry III of England attempted to recover
Gascony, but was defeated by St. Louis, who thus
became inured to war at the early age of fourteen.

Seven years later, when he attained his majority, he
was safely established on the throne, and maintained
unquestioned authority till death, becoming the arbiter
of peace between other princes in Europe.   Early in his
reign St. Louis had received from John of Brienne a
present of the Crown of Thorns, and from Baldwin of
Constantinople a portion of the True Cross.   For these
precious relics the beautiful Sainte Chapelle was built
in 1242–47 and consecrated in 1248 A.D., and it remains
among the earliest and most unchanged of French-
Norman churches.   It was perhaps the possession of
these relics which first turned the thoughts of the king
to his wars in Palestine.

In 1244 St. Louis lay dangerously ill in Paris, and
was thought to be dead ; when the crisis was past he
asked for a crucifix, and his mother's joy at his recovery
was turned to grief seeingt hat he had taken the cross.
In the following year an Œcumenical Council was summoned at Lyons, where the Pope had taken refuge, to
consider the terrible news of the Kharezmian inroads,
and of the dangers in Syria.   There were two policies in
the East—that of the Pope and that of the Emperor—
the first seeking alliance with the Tartars, and pointing
to the conquest of Egypt which threatened Syria from
the south, the other aiming at alliance with the Sultan
of Cairo against the new invaders from the North.
These policies arose from the events of the previous
years, and from the internecine hate of Guelph and
Ghibeline, then rending Italy, where the great republics
sided with the Pope against Frederic II, while St. Louis

vainly strove to make peace. The Pope refused at Lyons to allow help to be sent to the Emperor against the Tartars; and sent brother John Plano Carpini to the great ruler, Mangu Khan,* whom he exhorted not to war against or persecute the Christians, but to be baptised. In 1246 Mangu Khan replied to Innocent IV—who unable even to maintain himself in Rome thought to give orders to the ruler of nearly all Asia—advising Christians to submit to his power; and two years later other letters in Mongolian reached the Pope. Baidshu, the Tartar Prince of Persia, challenged the Holy Father to wage war if he chose, yet in the same year—1247 A.D—the Constable of Armenia wrote to Henry II of Cyprus, to say the Tartars were Christians, a totally misleading statement which encouraged the papal party in a useless policy. In 1249 fictitious letters were circulated in Europe, according to which a Tartar prince, David—descended from one of the Magi, Belthasar—consoled the Emperor Frederic II for the Mongol victories, and promised aid, dating from the River Chobar and "the presence of the kings of Gog and Magog." The personal names and the bad geography alike attest the falsehood of such epistles, yet they were greedily received as confirming the popular delusion.

Innocent IV also wrote in 1245 A.D. to Ismâil, Sultan of Damascus, who merely acknowledged that he had received the monkish ambassadors. Melek es Sâleh of

---

* *Regesta*, Nos. 1134, 1138, 1140, 1142-3, 1147, 1150, 1155, 1163, 1186.

Egypt wrote to the Pope to say he had conquered the
Tartars near Emesa, and to set forth the Moslem faith.
This was on the occasion of the Kharezmian defeat, but
the sultan was as little able to convert the Pope as the
missionaries sent to him were able to convert the sultan.
This sultan—who was the son of Melek el Kâmil—
understood the enmity of the Pope to Frederick II, for
he wrote to Innocent IV again next year refusing to
make any truce with him against the emperor his
friend. He deplored the destruction of the Holy
Sepulchre, and promised to punish the offending
Kharezmians, to give up the keys of the church, and
to rebuild and adorn it; but in 1248 he received news
from Frederic of the hostile expedition setting out with
St. Louis. The Emir of Kerak—Melek en Nâsir—also
refused the Pope's invitation to become a Christian, and
set forth his Moslem beliefs. In these various missions
and diplomatic communications three years were wasted,
and not till 1248 A.D. did St. Louis leave Europe, embarking late, on the 23rd of August, at Aigues Mortes.

Meanwhile the brothers of St. Louis—Robert, Count
of Artois; Alfonse, Count of Poitou; and Charles,
Count of Anjou—took the cross, with Hugh, Duke of
Burgundy, William, Count of Flanders, and others,
among whom was John de Joynville, then not more
than twenty-five years of age. He hired a small ship,
and brought twenty knights, after the celebration of
the birthday of his little son at Easter, when he made
amends to all of his vassals who had suffered any
wrong. He tells us of the birthday feast, the songs and

drinking ; of the mortgage on his property ; of the pilgrimages he made to churches near his home, when he
first received his scrip and pilgrim's staff, going barefoot in his shirt to the holy places.

"But as I was journeying," he says, "from Bliecourt
to St. Urban, I was obliged to pass near to the castle of
Joynville. I dared never to turn my eyes that way, for
fear of feeling too great regret, and lest my courage
should fail on leaving my two fine children, and my fair
castle of Joynville which I loved with all my heart."

Passing through the disturbed country where robbers
lay in wait for merchants and pilgrims, Joynville embarked at the Rock of Marseilles in August, and set out
in a fair breeze, while monks and priests sang Veni
Creator on the castle of the galley. He suffered much
from sea-sickness, and had to be supported in the procession by which a fair wind was invoked off the coast
of Barbary, of which he gives the following characteristic
account :—

"A very discreet churchman called the dean of Mauru
came forward and said 'Gentlemen, I never remember
any distress in our parish . . . but that God and
His Mother delivered us from it . . . when a procession had been made three times with devoutness on
a Saturday.' Now this day was a Saturday, and we
instantly began a procession round the masts of the
ship. . . . Immediately afterwards we lost sight of
the mountain, and arrived at Cyprus the third Saturday
after we had made our procession."

At Limasol, in Cyprus, St. Louis had already arrived

on the 21st of September, where news came of
Turkoman raids near Antioch ; and six hundred bowmen were sent on to Boemund's aid. Melek es Sâleh
was besieging Aleppo, and soon after returned ill to
Egypt. The King of Armenia had made a truce with
the Tartars, whose prince was reported to have been
baptised. The Templars and Hospitallers advised
peace with Egypt, but only roused indignation against
themselves. The French army, given up to drink and
luxury, began at once to suffer from the autumn fever of
Cyprus, and no less than 250 knights died. In the
winter the Count of Poitou set out, on 7th December,
from Aigues Mortes, to join his brother ; and about this
time Melek es Sâleh died in Egypt. From England
also came the Earls of Salisbury and Leicester, the
former—grandson of Rosamund the Fair—having been
deprived of his lands by Henry III, who, though only
about forty, was too doubtful of his throne, and too
indolent, to take the Cross.

During this time, while stores were being collected in
Cyprus, where gigantic piles of wine casks, and heaps of
wheat and barley sprouting green, were raised to the
amount of two years' rations, there came Tartar envoys
to St. Louis offering alliance. An embassy was sent
in return with presents, concerning which more must be
said later.

After Whit Sunday, 1249 A.D., the fleet of St. Louis
set sail for Egypt, and reached Damietta in four days.
A landing was effected in spite of the Egyptian army,
and the oriflamme planted in Egypt. Rumours of the

sultan's death discouraged his army, and Damietta was found to be deserted early in June.* The troubles that followed began with commissariat frauds, and exactions on the suttlers which discouraged them from feeding the army, the immorality of which was shocking to the king.† Towards the end of the year, after five months of skirmishing, the French army, delayed by the Nile floods, had only penetrated thirty miles inland, and was attacking Mansurah, which was defended by Bibars, commander of the memluk guards of the new Sultan El Muaddem.‡ The town was reached by damming a branch of the Nile: in the fighting that followed St. Louis was nearly captured, and his brother, the Count of Artois, was killed. In the end of February, 1250, the sultan met the Christian army, which, on the 19th of December, had advanced as far as Ashmûn, between the Damietta and Bolbitic branches of the Nile, twenty miles north of Cairo. The advance was badly planned, as the main body with the king was separated by the river from the Duke of Burgundy—east of the Damietta branch. The forces were also suffering from famine and scurvy; and on the 5th of April a retreat was ordered, which degenerated into a rout when the Turks fell on the rear of the army. The king was ill with dysentery: the sick, left on shore for transport by the galleys, were massacred; and St. Louis, anxious to help them, was left behind by his cowardly soldiers, and captured. A

---

* *Regesta*, No. 1180.

† Joynville, in Bohn's *Chronicles of the Crusades*, p. 396.

‡ He succeeded his father Melek es Sâleh Eyûb 23rd November, 1249, and reached Cairo on 24th February, 1250.

truce followed, while the question of ransom was de-
bated ; and thus the last Crusade against Egypt was
frustrated, like all former attempts, by the climate,
by the diseases due to heat, bad water, and bad food, by
the intricate system of irrigation channels which inter-
sected the country between the river mouths, and by the
annual rise of the Nile.   The advance from the sea has
always been dangerous and difficult, in marching on
Cairo, and the city only became vulnerable when, in the
present century, the Suez Canal enabled an army to
reach it east of the Nile.   Even Napoleon found it impossible to keep his hold on the country reached from
so dangerous a base as that on the Mediterranean.

Joynville himself, from his ship, witnessed the flight
of the army, and found the stream held below by
Moslem ships, which cut off the supplies of the force
coming from Damietta.   His small galley was captured,
and flinging his jewels and relics into the Nile he tried
to swim away with a Saracen, who was bent on making
a valuable prisoner.   Weak and helpless he was drawn up
into a Moslem ship, and his life saved by his captor's
assuring the crew that he was the king's cousin.   " I
felt," he says, " the knife at my throat, and had already
cast myself on my knees on the ground, but God
delivered me from this peril by aid of the poor Saracen,
who led me to the castle where the Saracen chiefs were
assembled."   Here he was stripped of his coat of mail,
but kindly treated, being ill with malarial fever, of which
a native doctor cured him.

The negotiations which were set afoot for the ransom

of the King and his barons were complicated by the
intrigues of Bibars. In Egypt the military power constantly usurped the rights of the sultans, and the last of
Saladin's dynasty—itself of military origin—was about
to fall a prey to the commander of the memluks.
Joynville witnessed some of the cruelties which made
Bibars hateful in later times, including the murder of
his chaplain, and of the sick. He saved the life of a little
boy, who was the son of Lord Montfaucon de Bar, by
never leaving hold of his hand ; and brought him safely
to the mud enclosure where the barons of France were
held prisoners. They refused to surrender any of the
castles in Palestine for ransom, in spite of threats of
losing their heads, and St. Louis was menaced with
torture. At length a sum of five hundred thousand livres
was agreed on for ransom of the army ; and this seems
to have astonished the sultan, who was no doubt accustomed to haggling for his prisoners. " By my faith," he
said, "the Frenchman is generous and liberal, when he
does not deign to bargain about so large a sum of money,
but has instantly complied with the first demand. Go
and tell him from me that I make him a present of
one hundred thousand livres."

The prisoners were now taken down the Nile on four
galleys to Damietta, where Queen Margaret of Provence
was awaiting the birth of her second child amid all the
terrors of war and of her husband's captivity. And here
they landed before Ascension Sunday, at the sultan's
summer house, only to witness his murder by his memluks, called *Buheiri* or " chosen youths," and knights of

the *Hauleka* or " guard."   These emirs being invited to a
feast rose on him, and one who bore his sword cut off his
fingers.   El Muaddem thus wounded fled to a tower,
which was set in flames with Greek fire.

" When the sultan saw the fire gaining ground on all
sides, he descended to the lawn of which I have spoken,"
writes Joynville, "and fled to the river ; but in his flight
one of the Hauleka struck him a severe blow on the ribs
with a sword, and then he flung himself, with the sword
in him, into the Nile.   Nine other knights pursued and
killed him while in the water near the side of the
galley."

According to another chronicler of the age,* the cause
of the dispute was the distribution of St. Louis' ransom.
It was strange that the captive should thus witness the
death of his captor, but for the moment it seemed that
a general massacre of the prisoners would follow.   The
emirs, however, agreed to the terms of the sultan, if
half the ransom were paid before the French left
Damietta, and the other half in Acre, the sick and
munitions of war and provisions of the army being
retained as security.   The agreement was to be ratified
on the part of the Moslems by an oath by the " triple
divorce," and on the king's side by his hope of Paradise.
St. Louis refused to swear,† though urged by the aged
Patriarch of Jerusalem, who was bound so tightly that
his arms were swollen, and who was willing to take all

---

* See note in Bohn's *Chronicles of the Crusades,* p. 448.
† King Richard also (see Boha ed Din) was excused swearing to Saladin,
this not being a royal custom.   He gave his hand only.

the consequences on his conscience. Finally, it appears that the simple promise of the king was accepted.

The Turkish emirs in Egypt do not appear to have been very strict Moslems. They greatly admired the fortitude of St. Louis, and are even said to have thought of making him their sultan. They also drank wine in excess, and were mainly intent on securing money. Their religious advisers consulted the Korân, and argued that the king's death would be allowed by its teaching; but the emirs contented themselves with murdering all the sick, destroying the war machines, and making a general bonfire of the French stores, which burned for three days. St. Louis on his galley was taken again up the stream, and it is doubtful what would have been his fate but for the valour of certain Genoese bowmen, who suddenly left their galley, and boarding that on which the king was prisoner bent their bows against the Saracens. The Count of Poitou, however, remained as a hostage, and the agreement was duly observed by St. Louis, who borrowed money from the Templars to complete the total of two hundred thousand livres payable before leaving Damietta.

The Earl of Salisbury had been slain at Damietta early in the war, and such barons as had been freed were so eager to leave Egypt that they refused even to wait till the Count of Poitou was free. The Counts of Brittany, Flanders, and Soissons set sail, leaving St. Louis and his two brothers behind. Joynville himself completed the total of the ransom, by the high-handed method of breaking open the Templars' cash box—

which the brethren remembered against him. Meanwhile the queen suffered all the torments of anxiety, and alarm, expecting every day to become the mother of the unhappy John Tristan—so named from the troubles of his birth—the second son of St. Louis. Fearing a sudden Saracen attack she besought the old knight who guarded her to promise that he would behead her if the Saracens came, and received the comforting assurance "that he would cheerfully do so, and that he had before thought of it in case such an event should happen." She was forced to buy up all the provisions in Damietta at her own expense, to feed the Pisans and Genoese, who threatened to desert the town because of famine ; and within a few days after the birth of John Tristan she set sail with St. Louis in the early spring of 1250 A.D.[*] On this voyage Joynville, who was on the king's ship, witnessed a curious incident, which shews how little the French were worthy of their brave and gentle leader. St. Louis one day asked " what his brother the Count of Anjou was doing. . . . When the king was told that he was playing at tables with Sir Walter de Nemours, he arose hastily, though from his severe illness he could scarcely stand, and went staggering to where they were at play, when seizing the dice and tables he flung them into the sea, and was in a violent passion with his brother for so soon thinking of amusing himself by gaming, forgetful of the death of his brother the Count of Artois, and of the great perils from which the Lord had delivered them. But Sir Walter de Nemours

* *Regesta*, No. 1190.

suffered most, for the king flung all the money that lay on the tables after them into the sea."

The Poictiers edition of Joynville's Memoirs contains at this point* a passage omitted by a later editor, respecting the Templars' attempt to retain the money which he had lodged with them at Acre. By threatening to expose the Order Joynville recovered it, and adds : " I took good care in future not to trouble these monks with the keeping of my cash." Only some hundred knights remained with St. Louis, out of two thousand eight hundred whom he had led from Cyprus; and his brothers, the Counts of Anjou and Poitou, went home, while he remained with any who would stay, intent on doing something that might strengthen the Syrian Christians. Joynville gives a picture of his own meditations as to what course to adopt, and the passage seems to explain the charm which St. Louis exercised over so many.

"While I was thus meditating," he says, " the king leant on my shoulders, and held my head between his hands. I thought it was Sir Philip de Nemours, who had been fretting me all the day for the advice which I had given the king, and said to him, ' Sir Philip, do leave me quiet in my misfortune.' As I turned round the king covered my face with his hands, and I then knew it was the king, from an emerald on his finger. I wished to make some reparation,- as one that had improperly spoken ; but the king bade me be silent, and continued, ' Now, Sieur de Joynville, tell me how you, who are so young a man, could have the courage

* Bohn's *Chronicles of the Crusades,* p. 460.

to advise me to remain in these countries, contrary to the opinion of all my greatest nobles.' I replied that if I had advised him well he should follow it ; but if the contrary, he ought to think no more on what I had said. ' And will you remain with me here if I should stay ? ' ' Yea, certes,' answered I ; ' were it at my own or at another's expense.' The king said that he was pleased with the advice I had given, but ordered me to tell this to no one."

These gallant gentlemen stayed, therefore, while the cowards, drinkers, and dicers sped home, and Joynville's heavy expenses were paid by St. Louis. The news of the misfortunes of the army was received with grief in Europe, but the Emperor's assurances of sorrow were little credited by Joynville. King Henry III was asked to take the Cross ; but few of the English acceded to the call "because of the extortions of the Roman court," which was then powerful in England, where so many benefices of the Church were given by the Pope to Italians. The Holy War was desolating Germany, and in 1250 Frederic II died at Naples, and his son was excommunicated. From Flanders and Picardy disorderly mobs, called Pastoureaux, advanced on Paris, led by a certain Jacob, with a lamb painted on a banner, mocking the monks and clergy, and rioting at Bourges, where they were dispersed. Amid these troubles Queen Blanche, the mother of St. Louis, died, and the news reached him in Palestine in 1253, to his great grief. "On my presenting myself," says Joynville, " he extended his arms and said, ' Ah, Seneschal, I have lost my mother. ' "

An alliance was offered to the king by the Sultan of
Damascus, but declined because the captive nobles had
not as yet been rescued from Egypt, including many
knights of the Temple and Hospital.* The treaty with
Egypt left to the Christians in Palestine the towns of
Jaffa, Arsûf, Cæsarea, Château Pelerin, Haifa, Tell
Keimûn (east of Carmel), Nazareth, Safed, Belfort, Tyre,
and Sidon ; and St. Louis spent his time and money in
rebuilding the walls of the chief fortresses in the plains.
The Egyptians were meanwhile at war with Aleppo,
and the widow of a Tartar khan sent to summon St.
Louis to obedience. The embassy of Rubruquis was
then despatched, and meanwhile three years were spent
in Palestine, till all the king's funds were exhausted. In
1251 and 1252 Sidon, Haifa, and Cæsarea were rebuilt,
and the walls of the latter still remain. Baniâs was
also seized, but the Turks drove out the Teutonic
knights soon after. At Easter time, in 1252, a treaty
was made with Egypt, by which Gezer, Beit Jibrîn,
Darum, and Jezreel were given up to the Moslems.
The Turks and Tartars from Aleppo advanced to the
borders of Egypt, and wasted Tripoli, and Krak—the
chief fortress of the Hospitallers. Thus, after so much
useless misery and bloodshed, the policy of Frederic II
prevailed over the Papal policy of Tartar alliance, and
St. Louis left in 1254, after six years of struggle and
suffering, a Palestine which was neither stronger nor
weaker than when he first approached its shores.
Frederic II had done more, and Richard of England

* *Regesta,* Nos. 1191-5, 1199.

had accomplished much more, than St. Louis could effect when deserted by his mutinous army.

Joynville's chronicle of the incidents of the three years spent in Palestine is discursive, but full of interest. He gives an account of an embassy from the "Old Man of the Mountain," or sheikh of the Assassins, to St. Louis. The peculiarities of this secret society have been already noticed. They were at this time tributaries of the Templars, and aimed at independence through the king's consent. The envoys claimed that Frederic of Germany, the King of Hungary, and the Sultan of Egypt, had all been friends with the Assassins. Their boasting was little regarded by the Masters of the Temple and Hospital, who knew them well, and ordered them within fifteen days to bring more humble messages from their sheikh. The presents then sent included a ring, a shirt, a crystal figure of an elephant, and figures of men in amber and crystal set with gold, in a case which filled the room with perfume. Very friendly messages were sent with these by the sheikh, and the king in return sent, by Father Yves, gold cups, vessels of silver, and scarlet robes. The king's envoy reported that the Assassins were followers of Àly, and that they cursed their children if afraid to go to battle without armour. Father Yves was also shewn a copy of the "Gospel of Peter" in the sheikh's house—an apocryphal work, no doubt taken from Maronites who had quoted it in 1099 to Godfrey, when he passed through the Lebanon. Only two or three tattered leaves of this work—recently discovered—are now

known, which relate the events of the Crucifixion. The
Old Man of the Mountain, speaking of this gospel,
explained his views as follows : " In the beginning of
the world the soul of Abel, after his brother Cain had
murdered him, entered the body of Noah, and the soul
of Noah on his decease went into the body of Abraham,
and after Abraham it entered the body of St. Peter, who
is now under the earth." We have seen already that
this doctrine of metempsychosis really formed part of
the exoteric teaching of the Assassins, and of other
sects ; and Joynville's account is therefore easily understood, though Father Yves appears to have been puzzled
at such beliefs among followers of Àly.

During this period Joynville obtained leave to visit
Tortosa north of Tripoli, where was St. Luke's portrait
of the Virgin,* and which many pilgrims then frequented.
He relates that while St. Louis was still in Egypt a
poor demoniac was brought before the Altar of Our
Lady in Tortosa, " and as his friends who had brought
him were praying to Our Lady to cure him and restore
his senses, the devil whom the poor creature had in his
body replied, 'Our Lady is not here but in Egypt,
whither she is gone to aid the King of France and the
Christians, who land this day on the Holy Land to
make war on the pagans, who are on horseback to
receive them.' What the devil had uttered was put
down in writing ; and when it was brought to the legate,
who was with the King of France, he said that it was
on that very day that we had arrived in Egypt ; and I

* See *Jacques de Vitry*, p. 20, English translation.

am sure" (Joynville adds) "that the good Lady Mary
was of the utmost service to us."

Joynville was charged to buy some camlets—or
camel-hair cloth—for the king at Tortosa, to be given
to the cordeliers in France ; and an amusing incident
arose on his return to Acre, with the camlets and a few
relics given by the Christians to himself.

"You must know," he writes, "that the queen had
heard that I had been on a pilgrimage, and had brought
back some relics. I sent her by one of my knights four
pieces of the camlets which I had purchased ; and when
the knight entered her apartment she cast herself on
her knees before the camlets that were wrapped up in a
towel ; and the knight, seeing the queen do this, flung
himself on his knees also. The Queen, observing him,
said, 'Rise, sir knight, it does not become you to kneel,
who are the bearer of such holy relics.' My knight
replied that it was not relics, but camlets, that he had
brought as a present from me. When the queen and
her ladies heard this, they burst into laughter, and the
Queen said, 'Sir knight, the deuce take your lord for
having made me kneel to a parcel of camlets !'"

Queen Margaret was, however, a forgiving woman, for
she wept much when a little later the news of her mother-
in-law's death came from France, following the many
letters in which Queen Blanche had begged her son
to come home to see her. Yet there had been such
jealousy between the mother and the wife of St. Louis
that, at one time, he could only meet the latter by stealth.
Joynville's consolation of his master in this sorrow was

stoical. "Whatever grief the valiant man suffers in his mind, he ought not to shew it on his countenance, nor let it be publicly known, for he that does so gives pleasure to his enemies and sorrow to his friends."

At length the walls of Sidon, Cæsarea, and Jaffa were finished, and the king prepared during Lent to return to his masterless kingdom in 1254 A.D. On the eve of St. Mark after Easter the wind held fair, and the king and queen embarked. "The king," says our chronicler, "told me he was born on St. Mark's day; and I replied that he might well say he had been born again on St. Mark's day, in thus escaping from such a pestilent land, where he had remained so long." At Cyprus they fell in with a sea fog, and stuck fast on a sandbank, and the divers reported the ship to be injured in the keel. But St. Louis would not desert the vessel, which had nearly six hundred persons on board, and it weathered a furious gale which followed, and reached the port of Hyères, in Provence, after ten weeks spent at sea. The Queen vowed a silver ship to St. Nicholas for her safe return to France; and the vow was paid, the ship being represented with figures of the king and queen, their children, and the sailors, also in silver, and with ropes of silver thread.

The further history of St. Louis was unconnected with Palestine; but the influence of his Eastern experience was felt in France, where he not only established just laws, and put down the scandals of official corruption, but also gathered learned men, and collected manuscripts

in the monasteries, and gave to his cities privileges like
those which the Italians enjoyed in the East, so securing
their loyalty, and curbing the power of his barons.   His
brother Charles, Count of Anjou, who deserted him in
Palestine, was given the crown of the Two Sicilies by
the Pope, and killed Manfred, the natural son of
Frederic II, at Benevento in 1266 A.D.   His honour was
further stained by the execution of Conradin, son of the
Emperor Conrad IV, in Naples, which was avenged by
the Sicilian Vespers in 1282 A.D.   But St. Louis took
no part in these struggles of the papal party against the
heirs of Frederic II, and peacefully strengthened and
enlarged his dominions.   He lived for sixteen years
after his return from Syria, attaining the age of fifty-four.
In 1270 A.D. he again took the cross at St. Denys, and
sailed on the 5th of July for Tunis, in Genoese ships.
Landing his army near Carthage, he strove to wrest this
province from Bibars, the Egyptian sultan ; but the
summer heat overcame his soldiers, and he himself was
stricken down with fever, and died on the 25th of August.
His advice to his son (given at Fontainebleau during
one of his illnesses) shews us the spirit of his rule : " Fair
son, I beseech thee to make thyself beloved by the
people of thy kingdom ; for in truth I should like better
that a Scot fresh from Scotland should govern the
subjects of my realm well and loyally, than that thou
shouldst rule them wickedly and reproachfully."

On this last expedition Joynville did not accompany
his friend and master, pleading the disorders which had
arisen in his estates during the six years of his absence

in Palestine. He had been constantly with St. Louis for twenty-two years, and survived him for forty-five, attaining to the great age of ninety-two as Seneschal of Champagne. He saw the prosperous reign of the son, and the stormier days of the grandson, of St. Louis, and penned his memoir in 1309 A.D., publishing it after the death of the latter in 1315 A.D., when Louis X, great grandson of the saint, became king. He saw the Templar Order destroyed, and lived at least a quarter of a century after the final loss of Acre. But he never forgot the friend of his youth, as his closing words may shew us:

"I was on a certain day in my chapel of Joynville when I thought I saw him resplendent with glory before me. I was very proud to see him thus in my castle, and said to him, 'Sire, when you shall depart hence I will conduct you to another of my castles that I have at Chevillon, where you shall also be lodged.' Methought he answered me with a smile: 'Sieur de Joynville, from my affection for you I will not, since I am here, depart hence so soon.' When I awoke I bethought myself that it was the pleasure of God, and his own, that I should lodge him in my chapel, and instantly afterwards I had an altar erected to the honour of God and of him."

More surely than by papal canonisation, or by the relics of his consecrated skull in Paris, the memory of St. Louis was so preserved—enshrined in the faithful heart of this brave and gentle knight, who has left to us the true story of his life.

CHAPTER XI.

The Tartars.

ST. LOUIS was the first of European kings to obtain real knowledge of the Tartars from their own country; and in order to understand the history of the last forty years of Latin rule in Syria, we must look back to consider what had happened in Central Asia early in the thirteenth century. The power of the Christians waned from year to year, after the Kharezmian inroad, and the struggle for Syria was one between Egypt and the Tartars, in which the Latins played only a minor part. After the return of St. Louis the Papal policy prevailed until the loss of Acre, and the Christians sided with the Tartars against Bibars; but in the end the Egyptians proved the strongest, and Islam prevailed against Christian and Mongol alike.

The term "Tartar" (less correctly written "Tatar") appears to mean a "nomad." Under this title were included the Mongols (from the Kirghiz Steppes and Khokand to the Sialkoi Mountains), the Kalmuks, the Kalkas, the Eleuths on the Ili River, and the Buriats in southern Siberia. The Kalkas dwelt in the Altai Mountains and in the Gobi desert south of this chain.

The Tartar tribes thus covered a mighty stretch of cold
and arid desert, east of the Turkish regions (which
stretched from Lake Balkash to the Caspian) and
north of Thibet and China. Their ancient capital,
Karakorum, was near the centre of Mongolia, three
thousand miles from Baghdad, and here, according to
the ancient Uigur legend, a beam of heavenly light fell
on a tree on the mountain, and from it were born five
boys the forefathers of the Mongol race. The Mongols,
or *Kukai Mongol,* " the heavenly race," as Genghiz Khan
called his people, were of the same stock as the Turks
of the Oxus region and Kirghiz Steppes to the west,
but had grown into a distinct race differing both in
type and in language. The Turks—Uzbek, Kirghiz, and
Uigur—were lean and angular, with rosy faces and
hooked noses, resembling the ancient Hittites of the
Syrian monuments. The Mongols, or Tartars, were
stout and thick-set, with high broad shoulders and squat
figures, swarthy and ugly, with short broad noses and
pointed projecting chins—more like the Manchus and
the Mongols of China than like Turks. They lived in
wild and barren lands, enduring cold, which was severe
for the latitude, and where no shelter could be found,
and so became inured to hardship, and accustomed to
long unending journeys. The dialects spoken over the
whole Mongolian region differed little from each other,
and had a recognisable connection with the Turkish language. The original beliefs of the Tartars were similar
to those of the earliest Mongols, whose civilisation we
trace up to the dawn of history in Chaldea and Armenia.

It was an animism which regarded all natural phenomena as due to the acts of spirits which abode in
mountain and river, in trees and stones, in fire and
water, with adoration of the sun, the moon, the stars,
the winds and the heavens and earth.

We have already seen that the legend of Prester John,
in the twelfth century, was founded on the conquests of
the Khitan prince Ung Khan.* The Khitai were a
Turkic people, whose home was west of Lake Balkash,
but who, in the tenth century, were powerful throughout
Central Asia and in China. In 1177 A.D. Pope Alexander III wrote to the supposed Prester John, as King
of the Indians,† to say that he had heard he was a
Christian, and to teach him the Catholic faith ; but the
Khitan empire was then approaching its end, and never
came into contact with the Christian kingdom in Syria.
Genghiz Khan—a Mongol of the Altai Mountains—
raided on the Khitai from the east, while the Kirghiz
attacked them from the northern steppes. He is said to
have married a daughter of Ung Khan to his son, and
from this marriage sprang Mangu Khan, who thus
might claim Western Turkestan by right of his mother.
In 1218 A.D. Genghiz Khan left his camp in the Altai
Mountains, and spent the summer on the Irtysh River,
which flows north into Siberia, east of the Kirghiz Steppes
and north of Lake Balkash. Here he was joined by
the Uigurs, and began his western raids in the time of

---

* See *Journal Royal Asiatic Society*, North China Branch, No. X, 1876,
"Notices of Mediæval Geography and History of Central and West Asia
from Mongol and Chinese Sources." E. Bretschneider, M.D.

† *Regesta*, No. 544.

Frederic II of Germany. The Kin Tartars had risen in China against the Khitai, as early as 1115 A.D., and their dynasty lasted till 1234 A.D. They were of the Manchu stock, and friendly to the Mongols, sending ambassadors to Genghiz Khan in 1220.* The aim of Genghiz Khan was to establish his sway in the west, and in 1221 he crossed the Caucasus, taking Derbend and defeating the Georgians at Tiflis. He was opposed not only by the Christians of Eastern Armenia, and the wild Alans and Ases of the Caucasus, and the Circassians, but also by the Kipchaks, a nomad Turkish people north-east of the Caspian, whom he again attacked two years later, and penetrated into Russia, raiding on the Bulgarians of the Volga.

In 1236 a yet more serious outbreak of the Tartars under Batu, grandson of Genghiz Khan, against Russia and Persia took place, while the Kharezmians were driven from their homes and let loose on Palestine. The campaigns lasted till 1243 A.D., and the Mongols ravaged Northern and Southern Russia, the Caucasus, Poland, Silesia, and Moravia. In 1241 they invaded Hungary, but returned eastwards two years later. The famous "Golden Horde" was established on the Volga by a son of Genghiz Khan. Southern Russia and Lesser Armenia became subject to the great Khan at Karakorum as their suzerain. Mangu Khan succeeded his grandfather, and it was to him that St. Louis sent envoys in 1250 A.D. The devastating struggle of Pope and Emperor: the struggle with Rome in England:

* *Chinese Recorder*, VI, p. 83.

the failure of France in Egypt : the power of the
Moslems in Spain, so weakened Europe that it became
more and more difficult to give help to the Holy Land.
The great hope of the Papacy lay in the conversion of
the Tartars ; and zealous monks were sent by St. Louis
and by various popes, down even to the close of the
thirteenth century, to bring news from the interior of
Asia, and to attempt the Christianising of its rulers.
While St. Louis was preparing for war in Cyprus
envoys came from a Tartar khan, with Friar Andrew
de Longtumal, whom the Pope had previously sent to
the East. In return two Dominicans were despatched—
one of whom was apparently Brother Andrew. It
was stated that this khan had become a Christian,
but this appears to have been false.* The monks were
accompanied by a large train of persons, bearing a tent
to be used as a chapel, embroidered inside with pictures
of the Annunciation and Passion. The khan in question was, however, only one of the provincial rulers, and
the mission failed, the monks returning to Acre and
thence—not finding the king, who was at Cæsarea—to
France.

In May, 1253, the Franciscan brother William de
Rubruquis, also sent by St. Louis, set out from Constantinople to visit Mangu Khan ; and to him we owe the
first important account of the Tartar civilisation. He
crossed the Black Sea to the Crimea, then held by
Greeks trading with the north for ermine and other
furs, and so reached the mouth of the Don. The

* *Rubruquis*, p. 95·(Pinkerton), and *Joynville*, p. 385 (Bohn's edition).

people of Asov and Georgia were then independent of
the Tartars, and the South of Russia was peopled by
Alans, who were Greek Christians, on the Volga, and by
pagans and Moslems. The superstitions of the Crimea
seem, however, to shew a strong Tartar element in the
old Comanian population, which retained the Scythian
customs of burial described by Herodotus, and which
was allied with the Latin emperors of Constantinople.

The Mongols proper were first encountered on the
Volga, where a certain Sartak had been reported a
Christian. Here Rubruquis found a Knight Templar
from Cyprus, and a Nestorian priest named Coiat. The
interview with the Mongol chief was a strange one, the
monks in their best vestments bearing a missal, a bible,
and a psalter, on cushions, and carrying the cross before
them. The Tartars were camped in felt huts, with
numerous wagons, and were seated drinking koumiss—
the fermented mare's milk famous from the days of
Herodotus. The king's letter, with translations in
Syriac and Arabic, was presented, and by the aid of the
Templar and of certain Armenian priests was rendered
into Turkish. The envoys were sent on to Sartak's
father, the famous Batu, a brother of Mangu Khan, but
it became at once apparent that none of these Tartar
leaders were Christians. Batu was camped on the east
bank of the Volga, in an *ordu* or city of felt cabins of
great extent. He had already been visited by Plano
Carpini, the monk sent by Pope Innocent IV, eight
years earlier. He received Rubruquis in a great assem-
bly, seated with his wife on a broad throne gilt over,

with three steps.   The lesser wives surrounded the throne, and koumiss was handed in cups of gold and silver set with gems (the spoils of recent conquests).   Rubruquis was forced to kneel on both knees before this magnate, and learned that he must travel two thousand five hundred miles to the east, to present himself to the great suzerain Mangu Khan, whose empire he entered on crossing the Volga.

This wonderful journey he safely accomplished, riding —though a stout and heavy man—long distances every day, and fasting duly.   For two months, from the middle of September to the middle of November, the way led across the Kirghiz Steppes to the north shores of the Issyk Kul—an average daily ride of twenty-five miles.   After a rest of a fortnight the travellers hurried on, crossing snowy tracts in December, and reached Karakorum by the end of the year, having marched about forty miles each day.

The capital of Mangu Khan was apparently a small town, but the Court was large.   In one street or bazaar were Moslem merchants, in another Chinese artificers. The population included many strangers—Hungarians, Alans, Ruthenians, Georgians, and Armenians—some of whom, no doubt, were captives.   A Frenchwoman from Metz, named Pascha, had married a Ruthenian, and was an attendant of the Tartar queen.   A French goldsmith of Paris, named William Bouchier, had been brought from Belgrade, and was busy with his art in Karakorum, fashioning wonderful silver fountains, for wine and koumiss, in the Khan's palace.   His son was interpreter for Rubruquis. A clerk named Raymond, from Acre, had come the year before from the Legate to greet Mangu Khan—as he said—and was sent back with a Mongol envoy charged to bring a full account of western countries to his master.

The professed creed of the country was neither Christian nor Moslem—though all religions were tolerated—but that species of corrupt Buddhism which preserved much of the ancient paganism of Central Asia. The shamans wore the yellow robes, and shaved the head, like Buddhists. They taught the doctrine of a single deity and an immortal soul; but Mangu Khan's actions were determined by their calculation of eclipses, and by divination with mutton bones. The Armenians and Nestorians at the Court had great hopes of his conversion, but Rubruquis was shrewd enough to see that the Khan only sought popularity with all. Mangu, indeed, explained his own beliefs very clearly to the pious and fearless monk, at one of their interviews, in these words :—

"We Mongols believe that there is but one God, through whom we live and die, and we have an upright heart towards Him" (but) "God who hath given to the hand divers fingers, so He hath given many ways to men. He hath given you the Scriptures, and the Christians keep them not." "He hath given to us shamans, and we do that which they bid us, and we live in peace."

The accounts of popular superstition scattered through Rubruquis' narrative are interesting as shewing the real beliefs of the Mongols. They were a subtle and crafty

people, whose object was dominion ; and they were not
unwilling that the Christians of the West should regard
them as possible allies. But the ancient paganism,
which had preceded the appearance of Buddhist and
Christian missionaries in their midst, was not extinct.
On the walls of the huts felt images—the Tartar penates
—were fastened, and libations of koumiss were offered to
the Fire, the Water, the Wind, and the Spirits of the
dead. Great importance was ascribed to not treading on
the threshold in entering the palace, and this was a very
ancient and widespread superstition. It is still common
among Moslems, especially as regards mosques, and it
is noticed in the Bible : for the priests of Dagon " lept
over the threshold."* Rubruquis' companion was forbidden the Court, because " he stumbled at the threshold
of the house."

The object of Rubruquis would seem to have been
either to baptise, or to witness a baptism, of Mangu Khan.
Batu reported that he came to ask for an army to aid the
Christians but this he denied, saying that he had been
sent by St. Louis because Sartak was reported to be a
Christian, and that otherwise no letters would have been
sent to the khans. It seems, however, that he had secret
instructions, and was very anxious to be able truthfully
to report a conversion. Other Christians were equally
eager to effect this triumph of the Faith, and an Armenian
monk assured Rubruquis that at Easter he expected to
baptise Mangu Khan. All that really took place, however, was a Nestorian Church ceremony, at which he

* I Sam. v; 8 ; Zeph. i, 9. *Rubruquis* (Pinkerton, pp. 66-67).

and his queen were present. The khan was perfumed
with incense, and blessed by the priests; his attention
was roused by a Bible which the Franciscans carried.
The second wife, who was ill, was induced to kiss a silver
cross, and gave meat and drink to the monks; she was
also dosed with rhubarb, and recovered her health ; but
as to the conversions all that Rubruquis could say was,
" I saw a silver bason brought, but whether they baptised
her or not I know not."

A very remarkable controversy was ordered to be
publicly carried on between advocates of various religions,
in presence of judges appointed by the Khan. The first
debate—which, like the rest, was ordered to be without
contentions or injurious words, or tumult—was between
the Franciscan and a Chinese, who was driven to assert
that no God was omnipotent—which the Saracens received with shouts of ridicule. The next was between
Nestorians and Saracens. The arguments led to no
result ; but, "the conference ended, the Nestorians and
Saracens sang together with a loud voice, . . . and
after that they all drank most plentifully.'

The account given by Rubruquis of the Nestorians
may be tinged with prejudice, yet, considering the
character of the Oriental clergy, it is also possible that
it is true. He accuses their monks and priests of being
usurers and drunkards, and says that some had many
wives like the Tartars. Yet it was from the earlier
Nestorians and Jacobites that much of the rude civilisation of Central Asia was derived. Rubruquis speaks of
the Mongol writing, which was in vertical instead of

horizontal lines; and there were already three scripts in Mongolia—the Indian alphabet brought by Buddhists, the Arabic brought by Saracens, and a development of the Syriac brought by Nestorians.* The latter missionaries had penetrated even to China before 650 A.D., and taught letters to the Uigurs—a Turkish tribe—who were the chief scribes of Mangu Khan's Court. The Uigur alphabet was in use all over Central Asia, as far east as Manchuria, and an extant MS. of the fifteenth century in Vienna, preserves in this writing a Tartar poem of the eleventh century, concerning the duties of mankind, called the *Kudatku Bilik*, or "blessed knowledge." In the reign of Kubla Khan, the brother and successor of Mangu (1259 to 1294 A.D.), the Buddhists perfected this Uigur alphabet for the necessities of Mongol speech; and the vertical writing which Rubruquis observed is a mark of the Syriac origin of the script (such an arrangement being not unusual in Syria in earlier ages among Greeks and Jacobites alike), though the influence of Chinese methods may also be suspected.

The return journey of Rubruquis led from the Volga through Armenia, and Asia Minor, to Iconium. He met in Georgia four preaching friars from Provence, bearing the Pope's letters to Mangu Khan, and missed on the road Haithon, King of Armenia, who also travelled in 1254 and 1255 A.D. to see Batu and Mangu Khan, proceeding from Cilicia to Kars and Derbend, and thence to the region of the Kara-Khitai, near Lake Balkash. The elder Polo (father of the famous Marco) was also in

* Taylor, *Hist. of Alphabet*, Vol. I, pp. 297–311.

Mongolia during the time of Rubruquis' journey.
Haithon appears to have been successful in his endeavours
to strengthen the Christian cause in Syria and Armenia :*
for Mangu Khan promised him peace and acceptance of
the Christian faith, if he would acknowledge him as
suzerain. He professed to send Hulagu to Jerusalem to
restore the Sepulchre to the Christians, and to dethrone
the khalif. Haithon also made peace with the Sultan
of Iconium, and with Batu Khan (who had promised not
to destroy Christian churches), for which services he
was much commended by the Pope. The letters
which Rubruquis brought back to St. Louis, from Mangu
Khan, denounced the former envoys to Cyprus as im-
postors, and invited the king to become his vassal, and
so enjoy peace and friendship.

This strange correspondence was continued by Pope
Nicholas IV half a century later. He wrote, in 1288 A.D.,
to Argun, the Tartar prince,† by the Bishop of Barsauma
(a Jacobite), exhorting him to receive baptism, which
he undertook to do on reaching Jerusalem. The Tartar
queens were exhorted at the same time to cherish the
faith. In the year following the Franciscans, who were
zealous in preaching among the Tartars, were sent by
the same Pope to Kubla Khan ; and in 1291 (the year
of the loss of Acre) Nicholas IV admonished a Tartar
princess to convert the brothers of Argun. It appears
that the son of the latter was expected to be about to

---

* *Regesta*, Nos. 1211, 1215, 1456, 1475, 1477, 1479, 1489, 1491, 1515, 1516, 1517.
† Son of Abagha and grandson of Hulagu.

receive baptism, but the success of the Moslems put an
end to all these hopes.

In Anatolia Rubruquis found only about a tithe of the
population to be Moslems, the majority being Armenians
and Greeks. The sultan had a Georgian wife, and
another who was Greek, and a third who was Turkish.
There were many Venetians and other Franks in
Iconium. The sultan was a tributary of the Tartars,
like the King of Armenia, having been overcome in one
of the earlier expeditions to the West. The opinion of
Rubruquis appears to have been that future Crusades
should be by the land route through Asia Minor, and
that no reliance could be placed on any treaty with
Tartars.

The travels of Marco Polo, who lived twenty-six years
in the lands of the Khan, are more famous than those of
Rubruquis. His father Nicolo, and his uncle Maffio, set
out from Venice in 1250 A.D., and came back safely nineteen years later. Marco went with them, at the age of
nineteen, on their second expedition, and returned in
1295 A.D. They went first to Bokhara beyond the Oxus,
and were chosen as interpreters of a mission to Kubla
Khan, bearing also letters from the new Pope Gregory X,
handed over by monks who were afraid to venture into
Mongolia, and who remained with the Templar Master
in Armenia. A whole year was occupied in crossing a
distance equal to that which Rubruquis traversed in
three months, the reason being that floods and snow
delayed their journey. Marco Polo was, however, far
better fitted for the task of exploration, being able to

write and read four languages spoken among the Tartars.
He also travelled much further—to China, India, and
Java; and his account of the countries he visited gives
evidence of the widespread trade of the age, which
enriched Genoa and Venice.*

In Armenia he describes the people as degenerate
and drunken. Here he saw the petroleum of the Baku
wells, which furnished material for the Greek fire. In
the Kurdish mountains he notes the manufacture of
buckram from cotton, and the silk factories. Among
the mingled peoples of Mosul—Arabs, Nestorians,
Jacobites, and Armenians, who fled from the Tartars
in Persia—he mentions muslins, silks, and cloth of gold;
and at Baghdad velvets, damask, pearls, and other
precious things. In Persia caravans were journeying,
and the artificers in the towns wrought in gold and silk:
the country was well tilled, and full of wine and fruits.
East of Persia Marco Polo entered the Tartar dominions,
and found mines of turquoise. From Ormuz came spices
and pearls and ivory, and here he notices the Assassins,
and the junks which had come from China. Among
the wild populations of Eastern Persia he found traders
with balas-rubies, lapis-lazuli, silver, copper, and lead.
At Samarkand, west of the Pamirs, were fair gardens
and a Church of St. John. In Kashgar the soil was
fertile, and vines, fruits, cotton, flax, and hemp were
cultivated. Crossing the great Gobi desert to Karakorum, Marco Polo found the rich Tartars clothed in
sable and ermine and cloth of gold : " they are hardy,"

* Yule's *Marco Polo*, 2 vols. London, 1871.

he says, " active, brave, but somewhat cruel ; will continue two days and nights on horseback armed, exceed-
ing patient, and obedient to their lords." The khan was
regarded as a deity, and his birthday was the great feast
of the year, when rich presents were given, and processions of elephants paraded his treasures. Christians,
Jews, Moslems, and Buddhists were alike commanded to
pray, after their own rites, for the health and good fortune
of the khan.

The service of the empire was conducted along roads
with regular posts. Corn was stored against dearth.
Coal was dug from the mountains, and used for fuel,
while about the same time the people of Newcastle (in
1272 A.D.) obtained their first licence from Henry III
to open coal mines. The coal seams of the Tien Shan,
north of the Gobi, have been seen burning in our own
times by the Russians.* The Tartar cycle of twelve
years is described by Marco Polo, and was imported into
China. It would seem that the early Mongol civilisation,
which existed in Media before the rise of the Semitic
peoples—in the earliest known historic age—was never
entirely lost, and it had flourished among the Khitai,
from whom the Mongols derived their arts and literature.

These accounts have carried us almost as far away
from Syria as Marco Polo himself went ; but without
some insight into the conditions of Tartar life it is difficult rightly to understand the events that followed. It
is clear, on the one hand, that the Mongols were not
wholly savage, nor wholly ignorant of Western civilisa-

---

* Williams, *Middle Kingdom*, Vol. I, p. 215.

tion. They not only knew the Christians, but had become acquainted with three Churches—the Latin, the Armenian, and the Nestorian : they were in contact with the Jews—both Rabbinical and Karaite—with the Moslems, and with the northern Buddhists, who had recently penetrated into Mongolia in the thirteenth century, from China and Thibet. Their highest religious conceptions were the unity of God, and the immortality of the soul. They could write and read, and encouraged trade and arts ; and the justice and strength of their great khans, Genghiz, and his grandsons Mangu and Kubla, united many Tartar and Turkish tribes into a single almost irresistible force. Three years after the return of Rubruquis Hulagu, brother of Mangu Khan, crossed through Persia and besieged Baghdad. In 1258 A.D. he put to death El Mustasim, the last of the Abbaside khalifs, and no Moslem ruler claimed to be khalif from that time for two centuries and a half, until the Osmanli sultan Selim I assumed the title. The Arab khalifate had been but a shadow for two centuries before it finally disappeared, but its death blow was dealt by the Tartars. Yet while Marco Polo was in Mongolia the attempt to conquer Syria failed, and he returned to find the Moslems owners of all the Holy Land. He went home by Trebizonde and Constantinople, and was unrecognised at first, so thoroughly Tartar had he become in a quarter of a century ; but, with his father and uncle, he lived long after in Venice, and after his Genoese captivity dwelt rich and honoured in his native city, while his book of travels circulated

in Latin and Italian through Europe. By the year
1260 A.D., or nine years before Marco Polo left Venice
with his father, the summit of Mongol success had been
reached; and though a second attempt to conquer
Syria was made in 1280, the Mongols did not again
reach Palestine itself.

After the capture of Baghdad Hulagu advanced
across the Euphrates, having been joined by his
Armenian vassal. The Preceptor of the Templars fore-
saw their approach as early as 1256,* and four years
later they attacked Aleppo and Damascus, and advanced
to the borders of Egypt. Hulagu was, however, forced
to return to Baghdad to put down a revolt, and left
Ketboga ravaging Sidon and threatening Acre, after
having demolished the churches and mosques of
Damascus; but Bibars was already advancing from
Egypt to drive back the invaders. On the 3rd of September, 1260, Sultan Kutuz defeated the Tartars at Ain
Talut two months before he was himself murdered by his
memluks.

During this invasion the Christians were divided
among themselves. The Pisans and Genoese quarrelled
in Acre, the Greeks were at enmity with Venice, and the
Templars and Hospitallers were also striving with each
other. The Legate wrote, in 1260 A.D., to inform all
Christian princes of Hulagu's conquests—at Aleppo,
Hamah, and Emesa, and of the flight of the Damascus
sultan to Egypt. The princes of Antioch and Tripoli

---

* *Regesta*, Nos. 1251, 1263-4, 1269, 1288, 1289, 1290, 1294, 1295,
1298-9, 1303, 1325.

had yielded before March of that year; but Tyre and Acre held out, and the castles of the Templars, the Hospitallers, and the Teutonic knights. "Help was sorely needed," the Legate wrote, for the Tartar prince threatened the Christians "in a letter full of blasphemies." It was somewhat humiliating to the Papal Court that so little could be expected from an Europe torn with wars of Guelphs and Ghibelines, and that all the Pope could do was to send Franciscan missionaries, hoping to soften the hearts of Tartar conquerors. The Military Orders were led by men of experience, who knew the East, and who for a century had counselled peace with Egypt; but their advice was neglected by popes who continued to believe in the possibility of regaining Palestine for Christendom by aid of baptised Mongols and Armenians; and the final result was the loss of even that part of the Holy Land which King Richard and St. Louis had saved to the Franks. In the end of the year 1260 A.D. Pope Alexander IV congratulated Hulagu on his supposed conversion to the Christian faith, and recommended him to see the Patriarch of Jerusalem. He had already written, three years earlier, to the Turkish Sultan of Iconium, who was said to be about to be baptised, and who had received a Pentateuch, with the Prophecies of Isaiah and Jeremiah, the Epistles of St. Paul, and the Gospels of St. Matthew and St. John; but the Turks were weak, and not likely to aid the Franks, preferring to raid on the now ruined province of Antioch whenever they found a fitting chance. In 1258 the Pope also besought the Legate to make peace

between the Pisans, Genoese, and Venetians, and to obtain
satisfaction for injury done to the brethren of St. Mary
of Jehoshaphat. These well-meaning attempts led to
little result, but the popes remained infatuated with a
belief in their power of stemming the great movements
of the time, by moral forces, while more and more
the Christian influence waned, leaving the Moslems
of Egypt to fight out the quarrel for Syria with the
Mongols.

The common danger served, however, to bind the
three great Military Orders together ; and the three
Masters signed an agreement, on the 9th of October,
1258 A.D., concerning their various quarrels in Palestine,
Cyprus, and Armenia, and promised peace and concord
in future. The Legate was obliged, two years later, to
counsel that pilgrims—especially Frisian women—should
not be endangered by being allowed to come to the
Holy Land. A messenger of the Templars was sent to
Henry III in England, to give news of Hulagu's conquests, and travelled with the utmost speed, reaching
London from Acre in thirteen weeks. He gave a
terrible account of the Mongols, whose women, he said,
fought like men, being expert with the bow. The
Venetians, Pisans, and Genoese were meantime disputing as to their property and towers in Acre, and
refused to obey the Legate's decisions. In the following
year the Master of the Temple sent messengers to Spain,
France, and Germany, to relate the peril of the Christians, complaining of the heavy losses of the Order, and
of the non-arrival of Genoese merchants on whom he

depended. It was during these troubles that the Seigneur of Sidon sold most of his lands to the Teutonic Order. The Templars also complained that the Prince of Antioch, the King of Armenia, and the " King of Russia," were leagued with the Tartars. In 1263 A.D. a further appeal was sent to Henry III, by the Masters of the three Orders, the Legate, and the Seneschal of the kingdom, to say that, having broken the truce, Bibars was occupying all the country, while advancing on the Tartars, and that little remained beyond the port of Acre. But Henry III was unable to send help : all his power was wanted at home in the war with his barons. The battle of Evesham was not fought till two years later, and it was seven before any help came from England. Meanwhile the ruin of the Latins was well-nigh completed by the cruel ravages of Bibars.

CHAPTER XII.

THE LOSS OF ACRE.

WHEN El Muaddem fell under the memluks' knives in sight of St. Louis in 1250 A.D., a sultana named Shejr ed Dur, widow of his nephew Melek es Sâleh Nejm ed Dîn --son of Melek el Kâmil—had a young son the heir to the throne. Shejr ed Dur married a Turkoman emir named Ezz-ed-Din Aibek, and they became together the guardians of the young sultan, who was called Melek el Mansur Khalîl. But the new Turkoman regent proved cruel and ambitious. His murder of the Emir Fâris ed Dîn was followed by a demand for the hand of a princess of Mosul, and this roused the jealousy of Shejr ed Dur, through whose favour he had become powerful. She sent for a certain emir, Seif ed Dîn, who slew the Aibek in her presence ; but she was not allowed to reign alone, and was murdered in turn, and a son of the Aibek proclaimed sultan. Kutuz—the bravest of the Egyptian emirs— and Bibars, who had defended Egypt against St. Louis, were thus the military rivals to whom the nation looked for a future leader, and the latter was unhindered by any scruples in pursuit of his ambition. He stabbed Kutuz while hunting, and the army proclaimed him sultan in 1260, when the possibility of a new advance of Hulagu made such a soldier necessary for the safety of Egypt. He climbed to power by very different means to those which Saladin had used, and his career was disgraced by violence and cruelty. But his success was constant and justified the proud titles which accompany his name on the inscriptions carved on conquered castles of the Franks—"father of victory and pillar of the faith." The state of Europe favoured his career, for civil war raged in England and in Germany, and Italy was ruined by the quarrel with the Pope. Eudes of Nevers and a few other knights took the cross, but the defence of the Holy Land was mainly left to the three great Orders. The Normans in Constantinople were weak and poor, obliged to raise money by selling relics, and to enter into treaty with Michael Palæologus, who took Constantinople while the Latin army was away on the shores of the Black Sea. In 1262 Baldwin fled, and Michael became emperor in Byzantium, restoring a Greek dominion which lasted for nearly two centuries.[*]

In the same year Bibars attacked the Christian possessions in Palestine, ravaging Antioch, and burning the church at Nazareth. In 1255 the strong position of Mount Tabor had been given to the Hospitallers, after the destruction of the monasteries by the Saracens[†] in order that they might build a fortress on the summit

---

[*] The negotiations of Michael Palæologus with the Pope for union of the Churches failed, and seem to have had a political object in protecting him against Charles of Anjou (see *Gibbon*, Ch. lxii.)

[†] *Regesta*, No. 1230.

within the ten years of truce with the Moslems. In
1263 Bibars laid waste the surrounding villages, including Nain, and destroyed this fortress.* He also threatened Acre; and suspicions arose that he was secretly
allied to the Genoese and to the Seigneur of Tyre.

In 1265 the Archbishop of Tyre endeavoured to make
peace between the Venetians, Genoese, and Pisans in
face of these new dangers,† and the Christians asked aid
of the Tartars to defend Cæsarea against Bibars; but
the city fell to the Moslems, and Arsûf was also taken
after forty days' siege. Alphonso of Arragon and the
King of Armenia sent envoys to the conqueror, who
had gone on pilgrimage to the mosque at Jerusalem.
The spirit of Islam was roused by his success, and by
the strict austerity of his manners: for he forbade the
drinking of wine in his army, which attacked Tyre and
Tripoli and Acre. Safed, one of the strongest of the
remaining castles, was besieged, and its walls breached.
All the prisoners taken were slain, except one Templar
who turned renegade, and one Hospitaller sent to bear
the news to Acre.‡ In the following year the Holy
War was preached, and a tax laid on Moslems for its
purposes. Jaffa was surprised, Kerak was subdued, and
the army of Bibars marched on Tripoli.

In 1267§ A.D. we find the Christians expecting the
immediate loss of Tripoli, and the Patriarch of Jerusalem begging the Templars to send money to Acre for

---

* Robinson, *Bib. Res.*, II, p. 360.
† *Regesta*, No. 1341.
‡ Belfort, held by the Templars since 1240, was lost in 1268 A.D.
§ *Regesta*, Nos. 1346, 1347, 1348, 1354, 1357, 1363.

the defence of the Holy Land, asking them to promote peace between the Venetians and Genoese, to prevent the poor and feeble from coming out as pilgrims, and hoping for a new Crusade from Europe. In May he wrote again to describe the desolation wrought by Bibars in the plain of Acre, the death of John of Brienne, and the attack on Safed, asking help from the three Orders. In August Pope Clement IV wrote to Abagha—the Tartar prince—to praise him for a supposed conversion, and to announce that the kings of France and Navarre were taking the cross, and that help was to be sent to Jerusalem. But the hopes of the Christians in the East were sinking, and Philip de Montfort, lord of Tyre, wrote, in April, 1268, to St. Louis, asking him to receive his son and heir as a vassal for fiefs in France. The answer, which was favourable, was not written till December.

The Christians now began to desert Antioch, which Bibars besieged and took on the 18th of May, 1268 A.D. Seventeen thousand Christians are said to have been slain, and those who remained were sold as slaves. The priests and monks were murdered, the churches were destroyed. Bibars himself wrote to Boemund VI, Prince of Antioch, in bitter and scornful language, to announce his victory, and that he had ruined the churches of St. Paul and St. Cosmas, had slain all the citizens, and had taken the neighbouring towns—Shakif Talmis and Shakif Kefr Deina.* The news sped to France, and St. Louis appeared in the Parliament at

* *Regesta*, No. 1358.

the Louvre bearing the crown of thorns ; but his policy, as we have seen, was to draw off the invaders by an attack on Tunis, and the French army never again appeared in Palestine. The Tartar Abagha was fighting the Turks in Asia Minor, and a proposed treaty with the Venetians and Genoese who were to send a fleet of fifteen galleys and fifteen transports for a year came to nothing. Money failed, and the Pope imposed a tithe for three years; but meanwhile Bibars strengthened his position by further conquests.

At last appeared Prince Edward of England, the son of Henry III, whose courage and warlike ability had been shown at Evesham, and who had restored his father to the throne by the defeat of Simon de Montfort. He was the last Crusader; but his presence in England was sorely needed, for Henry was old and feeble, and the land was full of rioters and robbers. On the 4th May, 1270 A.D., he set sail at Portsmouth, to join St. Louis in Tunis. James of Arragon had conquered the Moors, and gathered forces in Castille, Catalonia, and Portugal. He also set out, though the Pope regarded him with little favour; but he was wrecked off Languedoc, and only a few Arragonese reached Acre. Charles of Anjou was hindered by revolts in Naples and Sicily, after the execution of Conradin; and when Prince Edward reached Tunis he found St. Louis already dead, and a treaty effected. Disappointed on every side, he still went on to the East, but had with him only three hundred knights and five hundred Frisians, his little host altogether numbering not more than twelve hundred fighting men. The Templars, Hospitallers, and Teutonic knights joined his force; but the army did not amount to more than 7,000 at most, even including five hundred Papal troops sent in Italian ships. It was, however, strong enough to drive back Bibars from Acre, and to march on Nazareth, which was pillaged, and all the Moslems found there slain.*

Bibars did not scruple to use the dagger of the Assassin against this last defender of the Holy Land, and the attempt was made at Acre in June, 1272; but the murderous Anzazim, sent by the Old Man of the Mountain, failed: for Prince Edward wrested the knife from his hand, after being wounded in the arm, and Latimer, an English knight, slew the Assassin. The prince was then thirty-five years of age, and at the early age of seventeen had married his first wife, Eleanor of Castile. She reached Palestine with him, in the spring of 1271 A.D., and had witnessed his victory over Bibars near Nazareth, wintering with him in Cyprus, and returning to Acre on the following year. To her devotion he owed a life destined to last for another thirty-five years: for the Assassin's dagger was poisoned, and Eleanor sucked the poison from the wound. "For when," says Speed, "no medicine could extract the poison, she did it with her tongue, licking daily, while her husband slept, his rankling wounds, whereby they perfectly closed, yet she herself received no hurt; so soveraigne a

---

* Other reconnaissances were made to St. George (*El Khudr*) east of Acre, and even as far south as Kakun in the plains of Cæsarea beyond Château Pelerin.

medicine is a wife's tongue, anointed with the virtue of lovely affection."*

The English army was wasted with sickness, and without hope of aid from Europe ; and Prince Edward concluded a truce with Bibars for ten years, ten months, and ten days—the last peaceful period enjoyed by Christians in Syria. On his way home he heard at Messina, in Sicily, of the death of his eldest son John, and of his father's death which happened on the 16th of November, 1272. He did not, however, reach England till the 2nd May, 1274, and his whole energies were occupied henceforth by the conquest of Wales, and the war in Scotland; thus Palestine was left without any further hope of aid from Europe; yet the king continued to take interest in the affairs of the East down to the last days of Christian resistance.

Even while opposing Edward Bibars gained further successes. In April, 1271, as the English were approaching Palestine, he wrote to the Master of the Hospital† to say that Krak—the chief fortress of the Order east of Tripoli—had fallen; and the breach he made in its walls still remains, built up with smaller masonry when the castle was restored as a Moslem stronghold. Upon its rampart an ornate Arab text records this restoration as follows :—

" In the name of God merciful and pitying, the repair of this castle has been ordered in the reign of our

---

* The genuineness of this story is of course doubted by modern writers, though why it should have been invented is not clear.

† *Regesta*, No. 1374.

‡ Rey, *Colonies Franques*, p. 128.

master the Sultan, the conquering king, the wise, the just, the champion of the Holy War, the pious, the defender of frontiers, the victorious, the pillar of the world and of the faith, the father of victory Bibars."

In May of the same year, 1271, Bibars also wrote once more to Boemund, Count of Tripoli, boasting that he had taken Akkar, the strong fortress in the mountains south-east of that city.* Abagha, the Tartar, wrote to Prince Edward on the 4th of September, proposing alliance against the Moslems, and acknowledging the English envoy John le Parker; but the treaty with Bibars put an end to these schemes. In the year after King Edward's access on the Master of the Hospital wrote to the Count of Flanders, to describe the misery of the Holy Land, and the lack of money—that which the new King of France had sent by order of the Pope being expended. In 1274 A.D. Pope Gregory X assembled a Council at Lyons, at which the Patriarchs of Jerusalem and Constantinople were present, with a thousand archbishops and bishops. Envoys were sent by the Emperors of East and West, by the Kings of France and of Cyprus, and by the Tartars, some of whom are said to have been baptised by the Pope. A tithe was ordered, to defray expenses in Palestine during the ten years' truce; for now the loss of territory began to tell on the resources of the barons, and on the funds of the Military Orders.

In the year that followed many other letters were exchanged,† and many sales of property were effected.

---

* *Regesta*, No. 1377, 1380, 1383, 1387.
† Ditto, Nos. 1401-1405, 1407, 1409, 1423.

King Edward I wrote on the 26th of January to Abagha,
who professed a desire to be baptised, asking him to
defend the Christians, but saying that nothing was
settled as to his own return to Palestine.   Pope
Gregory X confirmed an alliance between the three
Military Orders at Lyons, on the 13th of March.   Hugh
Revel, Master of the Hospital, wrote on the 30th of
September to Edward, to say the ten years' truce with
the Christians still held, but that war had broken out
between Bibars and the Tartars ; two days later the
Master of the Templars in Acre reported that money
was much needed by the Order, for the fortification of
the castles and towns still held, and entreating the king
to order a " general passage " of troops from the West,
on account of the threatening dangers.   The Patriarch
of Jerusalem, and the Bishop of Bethlehem, and Balian,
the Constable of the Kingdom of Jerusalem, wrote to
Rudolph, Emperor of Germany, for aid, because the
Christians were weak, and the Saracens wasting Armenia.
The King of Bohemia wrote to Bibars about the same
time on a very different subject.   He sent (as did other
Christian princes) a friendly message, and presents of
beaver fur, asking for one of the fingers of St. Catherine
of Mount Sinai, or for a little of the oil which was
said to distil from her bones, in the coffin shewn in the
monastery.   In November, 1276, John Vassal and James
Vassal brought messages from Abagha, the Tartar, to
the Kings of Sicily and of England and to the Pope,
and these envoys appeared in London.   In 1278, on the
1st of April, Pope Nicholas III sent Franciscan monks

in return to Abagha, reminding him of his promise to help, should a new army arrive from Europe, and to receive baptism. But no such army ever again set out for the East.

In 1275 A.D. Humbert of Romanis, general of the Preaching Friars, endeavoured to stir up again the ancient spirit. He lamented the sins of the Western Christians, their fear of toil and danger, their dislike of leaving home, their pleading of family ties, their evil language and bad example, their lack of hope, and the coldness of their faith. But the Crusader spirit was dead in Europe, and Palestine was left to its fate. Bibars observed his truce, and was busy fighting in Nubia, and in Armenia ; and so active were his movements that often when supposed to be in his palace in Cairo he suddenly appeared in Damascus or Aleppo. After having defeated the Tartars in the North, he laid heavy taxes on Damascus, where he died in 1277 A.D. He was hated and feared in the later years of his severe and cruel rule. He was crafty, tyrannical, and pitiless, and is said to have slain two hundred and twenty-four emirs. Kelaun, one of the memluks or slave guards of the sultans, usurped the throne of Egypt two years later, and carried on the war against the Tartars. He is said to have had spies in various parts of Europe, and had an ambassador at Seville. His difficulty in reducing the Christian seaports lay in having no fleet, and this saved the remainder of the Christian possessions for the whole period of his reign.

There were about this time three claimants for the

throne of Jerusalem, the first being Mary of Antioch, descended from King Amaury's daughter Isabel, the second her nephew the King of Cyprus, and the third Charles of Anjou,* who bought the title of Mary for the sum of four thousand livres Tournois, payable yearly. He also married, on the 20th of January, 1278, Margaret, a granddaughter of John of Brienne. The sum agreed was, however, not duly paid, at least for four years after 1285 A.D.

In 1276 Bibars gained a victory over Abagha's brother at Emesa (La Chamelle); but on the death of Bibars the Tartars, the Armenians, and the Georgians advanced again from the North. Kelaun met them at Emesa, and the result, though not apparently decisive, led to the retreat of the invaders in 1280 A.D. Several letters exist which refer to these first years of Kelaun's reign, and to the interest which King Edward continued to take in Palestine.†

On the 23rd July, 1278, Pope Nicholas III wrote a long letter to the Bishops of Sidon and Beirût, as to injuries sustained by the Bishop of Tripoli. A riot appears to have occurred against this ecclesiastic, led by the Bishop of Tortosa, and twelve Templars were killed. Boemund, Count of Tripoli, took the part of the assailants, and appears to have given the Templars' Hospice to the Saracens, for which cause the Bishop of Tortosa was summoned to Rome. The dispute, however, was settled through the influence of the Master of the

---

* *Regesta*, Ncs. 1411, 1422, 1486.
† Ditto, Nos. 1424-5, 1432, 1436, 1442, 1445, 1446, 1448.

Hospital.* King Edward was especially favourable to the latter Order, and an account of the war between the Templars and Boemund was sent to him, by one of the brethren from Acre, in September, 1279, when it was pointed out that the quarrels of the Saracens among themselves—on the death of Bibars—gave a good opportunity for active attack. The vicar of the Patriarch of Jerusalem wrote, in the autumn of 1286, to report famine and locust swarms, and fearing that the truce with the Saracens would be broken next spring : an offer of aid had then been received from the Tartars. In the following autumn the Master of the Hospital wrote again to King Edward, to say the Tartars were coming, and that the fortress of Margat was well provided ; but they were again defeated, as the Master announced next spring.

Another correspondent of Edward's was Sir Joseph de Cancy, who has been already noticed as treasurer of the Hospital—an Englishman from Yorkshire. He had been in Palestine for thirty-four years† at Acre, and seven extant agreements bear his signature. On the 31st May, 1281, he wrote to describe the battle of Emesa on the 30th of the preceding October,‡ and King Edward's reply was dated the 20th of May in the next year. Sir Joseph reported that neither the Hospitallers, nor Boemund VII of Antioch, nor the King of Cyprus

---

* The dispute was an old one. The Pisans and Genoese fought at Acre in 1249. The Venetians, Pisans, and Templars fought the Genoese and the Hospitallers from 1258 to 1260.

† *Regesta*, Nos. 1164, 1159. ‡ Pal. Pilgrim Text Society, 1888. The advance of the Tartars had been stemmed by their defeat in 1260 at Ain Talut by Sultan Kutuz, but they had now recovered.

(Hugh III) had been able, as intended, to join the
invaders: for Kelaun held the road by which the
Christians might have advanced from Tripoli on Emesa,
and the army from Cyprus had not arrived. The forces
of Kelaun are stated to have been fifty thousand horse
in three battalions, opposed by forty thousand in three
Tartar divisions, including one thousand Georgians and
an Armenian contingent, with three thousand Turks from
Asia Minor. The Armenians attacked from the west, and
repulsed the Moslems ; and the battle raged till night-
fall, resulting in a Tartar victory ; but the disorderly
hordes fell upon the spoil, and Kelaun forced them to
withdraw. The darkness closed in without either side
having secured a final decision, and the Tartars and
Armenians retreated, losing many men and horses on
the march. Abagha himself was marching further east
through the desert to Damascus, but appears to have
been also obliged to retire. Kelaun rallied his army at
the Lake of Kadesh, south of Emesa, where the Templars went to spy out his forces, under pretext of giving
presents. His losses appear to have been also heavy,
and he returned to Egypt, levying taxes in Syria, and
preparing for further expeditions. Great consternation
existed among the Moslems of Hamah and Emesa, who
fled, expecting a further Tartar inroad, and fifteen emirs
who deserted in the battle were put to death. The
Turkomans took this occasion to harry Armenia, and
the Hospitallers sent one hundred horsemen, fifty
knights, and fifty Turkopoles, to aid the king. Palestine itself was desolated by lack of rain and pestilence,

and provisions from Sicily were denied. Sir Joseph concludes :—

"And know, Sire, the Holy Land was never so easy of conquest as now, with able generals and store of food: yet never have we seen so few soldiers, or so little good counsel in it. May your worthy and royal Majesty flourish for all time, by increase of good for better. And would God, Sire, that this might be done by yourself, for it would be accomplished without fail if God would give you the desire of coming here. And this is the belief of all dwellers in the Holy Land, both great and small, that by you, with the help of God, shall the Holy Land be conquered, and brought into the hands of Holy Christendom."

King Edward's reply "to his dearest in Christ, and faithful secretary, brother Joseph de Chauncy," gave no hope of such assistance. "For the rest," he wrote, "we have received with cheerful hand your New Year's gift of jewels, which you have sent to us—to wit, two Circassian saddles, and two saddle cloths ; and two gerfalcon's hoods, and four falcon's hoods, for which we return you our abundant thanks. Wishing you to know that we have not considered these presents as small, because we have weighed the goodwill of the giver more than the gifts themselves in this case. Nor indeed do we at present want any more hoods, as by reason of arduous matters of our kingdom, which intimately concern us, we do not as yet wish to keep more falcons than we already have . . . and because we much wish that you should be near us, for our solace and

convenience, we will and require you that you hasten
your arrival in England, by the best and quickest means
you can. . . . Given at Wocester on the 20th of
May in the tenth year of our reign."

The "arduous matters of our kingdom" so noticed
related to Wales, for in the same year Llewellyn was
overthrown on the 11th of December, and the first
Prince of Wales—the infant Edward who could speak
no English—was presented to the Welshmen. The
wars in Scotland began four years later, and continued
till long after the fall of Acre. After such discouragement the Military Orders made peace with Kelaun,* and
the King of Armenia swore, by the Trinity, the Cross,
and the Gospels, to become the vassal of Egypt, under
pain of journeying thirty times barefooted and bareheaded to Jerusalem, if he failed of his word. Margat
had already been taken by assault, and the limits of the
Christian possessions dwindled year by year.

The agreement of the Templars stipulated that a truce
of ten years and ten months should begin on the 15th of
April, 1282, and they surrendered to the Egyptians all
Syria, and the mountain of the Assassins—thirty-seven
"cantons" in all, conquered by Bibars, including
Latakia, Arca, Margat, and Château Blanche. The
limit of Syrian Christendom on the north was thus
marked by the town of Tripoli, and the Templars.
promised to build no new castles. Another agreement
was made by Kelaun, on the 3rd of June, with the
Princes of Acre, Sidon, and Château Pelerin—which

* *Regesta,* Nos. 1447, 1450.

latter castle now marked the southern border of the small strip between Carmel and Tripoli, which was all that Bibars had left to Christendom. The church of Nazareth was allowed to remain, with six houses for clerics and pilgrims, but the border was drawn at Caymont, Haramis, and Mansurah—at the east end of the Carmel ridge, and the document acknowledges the loss of all save seventy-three "cantons" round Acre, Haifa, and Carmel, and fifteen near Sidon. The Christians in this case also promised not to rebuild any ancient fortress, or make any new one. Three years later Kelaun called on the Count of Tripoli to dismantle Marakieh—a castle on an island north of Tortosa,* and the châtelain, to the horror of all, stabbed his son for wishing to receive lands in exchange. This castle was abandoned and demolished, leaving Tripoli defenceless on the north.

The breathing time was spent in further correspondence with the West, and with the Tartars.† A letter was addressed in 1285 by Argun, Khan of the Mongols, to Pope Honorius IV, and to the Kings of France and Sicily—dated according to the Tartar cycle of years already noticed—which proclaimed the khan's friendship for Christians, and invited a further alliance against Egypt, which was to be conquered by the united armies of Europe and of the further East. But almost at the same time the King of Armenia (Leo III) made a ten years' truce with Kelaun, in which all the towns up to

---

* Marâkieh was built by the Hospitallers in 1260.
† *Regesta*, Nos. 1456, 1457, 1458, 1460, 1470.

the Taurus are mentioned as belonging to the latter.
On the 18th of July also Margaret, the lady of Tyre,
made a similar ten years' agreement, in which the
boundary between the Moslem and the Christian lands
is described in detail. The exact line can be drawn on
the map from this document, coinciding nearly with the
ancient border of the fief of Tyre, while further north
the Lebanon remained in the hands of the Christians as
far as Tripoli, but the plains of Baalbek and the castle
of Belfort were in the country held by Kelaun. The
line ran from Jedeidah west of Belfort to Maron, which
was on the border, and garrisoned by both parties.
Toron was given up to Egypt, and Kanah was also on
their side of the line. Thence the border ran south to
Beit Lif; and Montfort, the castle of the Teutonic
knights, was also held by the Egyptians. The west
slopes of the Nazareth hills formed the limit further
south, leaving only a strip of plain about eight miles
east of Acre. Carmel remained Christian, and Château
Pelerin ; so that a strong base still existed, if any
forces could have been mustered in Europe to land at
Acre—the key of Syria.

These treaties did not, however, include any mention of the County of Tripoli. The Templar castle of
Margat was demolished on the 25th of May, 1285, and
in 1287 Kelaun besieged Latakia, when an earthquake
destroyed the tower of the Pisans and the lighthouse.
After the fall of this town the Egyptians advanced on
Tripoli itself, and though Boemund had offered submission the town was attacked. The Templars, and

the Seigneur of Gebal to the south, had plotted together to possess themselves of this important port, but the agreement failed. Boemund died soon after, and his mother and sister disputed the succession. Kelaun set up seventeen siege machines against the walls ; and after thirty-five days of fighting, mining, and Greek fire throwing, the city fell. Seven thousand Christians were slain, women and children were taken for slaves, Tripoli was demolished, and its famous silk industry was ruined. The time had long gone by since it had been possible to settle the Eastern question by making peace with Egypt. The fair terms offered by Melek el Kamil, and accepted by Frederic II, had been rejected ; and for half a century the Papal policy had prevailed against the advice of Templars and Hospitallers and against the opinion of men like Rubruquis and St. Louis. The talk was still of converting Tartars, and baptising khans ; though two things must ere now have become clear— first, that the Tartars were insincere, and, secondly, that they were not as strong as the Moslems. The loss of Palestine may mainly be traced to the prejudice of the Popes, and to their fatal quarrel with the empire. In 1288 we still find the Nestorians sending news of supposed conversions to Rome, and, as already explained, Nicholas IV continued to correspond with Argun down to the fall of Acre. In 1289 he was still exhorting Haithon II of Armenia, to obedience and perseverance, by the Minorite brethren.*

On the 22nd of August, 1289, the Master of the

* *Regesta,* Nos. 1477, 1490, 1493-1499.

Hospital wrote from Acre to describe the heavy losses
of the Order in the siege of Tripoli; and on the 9th of
September the Pope sent four thousand livres Tournois
towards the redemption of captives, the making of warlike machines, and the repair of the walls and ditches of
Acre.   On the 13th of the same month he wrote again
to the Patriarch of Jerusalem, to say he had ordered
twenty galleys to be armed for use in the Holy Land;
and sent sixteen thousand livres left by the will of his
predecessor Adrian V.   On the 30th of September he
wrote to Edward I, to say that Argun, the Tartar emperor, had promised to accept the Christian faith, and
to aid in recovering Palestine for Christendom; but in
October of the same year the Legate wrote from Acre,
to the abbot of St. Mary of Jehoshaphat, to say that
since the fall of Tripoli the abbey had nothing to rely
on but its possessions in Calabria.   The Greeks had long
since obtained possession of the original church, which
in the twelfth century had owned so many villages in
Palestine.

Jerusalem itself would now have been hardly recognised by the Christians, few of whom had seen it since
the time of Frederic II.   New chapels had arisen round
the Templum Domini, which had been in Moslem hands
since the days of Saladin.   In 1213 A.D. cloisters had
been built on the west side of the great enclosure, and
in 1256 a porch had been added to the Templars'
church on the south—the Templum Salomonis.   Kelaun
himself appears to have erected the minaret on the rock
at the north-west angle of the enclosure; and an inscrip-

tion bearing his name records the rebuilding of the outer
wall on the south-east. The Hospice of the Templars,
outside the Damascus Gate, built to receive pilgrims
about the time of Saladin, was falling in ruins: the
Church of St. Lazarus, outside the wall further west,
was destroyed, and only a few Franciscans held on, amid
many dangers, to their religious duties in Jerusalem.
The thoughts of Europe were intent, not on the recovery
of the Holy City, but on the impending fate of Acre.

After the fall of Tripoli attempts were made to patch
up another truce for two years, two months, and two days.
The Legate—who was the titular Patriarch of Jerusalem
—was violently opposed to this treaty, and insulted the
Moslem merchants, and threatened to excommunicate
the Military Orders when they offered reparation for the
injury. Yet in such concessions lay the only hope of
peace. James of Sicily had made a pact with Kelaun,
and so had the Genoese. The Pope allowed the Augustine brothers to sell their property in Acre to the Hospital; but on the 15th of October, 1290, he wrote to
recommend a French captain, and to exhort the knights
of Syria to vigilance. He was still commending Tartar
envoys to Edward I of England.*

The final quarrel arose no doubt out of the treatment
of the Moslems by the Legate. It was reported that a
Christian woman had been surprised by her husband,
with a Moslem lover, in the gardens of Acre. The report
roused popular fury, and a general massacre of Moslems
followed. The ten years' truce made by the Templars had

* *Regesta*, Nos. 1502, 1504, 1505, 1506, 1507.

not yet expired, but Kelaun had died, and, as Joynville
tells us, all such agreements became null unless renewed
by the successor of a sultan.   Melek el Ashraf,* Kelaun's
successor, wrote in March, 1291, to the Master of the
Temple, to say that he would avenge the murder of
the Saracens by the hirelings of the Pope, and would
come forthwith against the city.   Kelaun had commanded that his body should not be buried till Acre
was taken, and his son hastened to obey, appearing
before the city with a mighty force on the 5th of April.
On the 18th of May the town was stormed, and on the
25th the new sultan sent the news to Haithon II of
Armenia demanding tribute.   Tyre opened its gates
after the loss of Acre, and Tortosa, Beirût, and Sidon
were taken.†   Haithon II sent the heavy news to
Edward of England before the 15th of June.   The
Pope was still writing to the Tartars, who were still
promising to be baptised, while in Cairo, Damascus,
Aleppo, Edessa, and Iconium the Christian churches
were being destroyed, and on Carmel all the hermits
had been massacred, with those in the caves of Lebanon
and Judea, and in the monastery of Sinai.   Few indeed were the survivors who fled to Europe after this
terrible catastrophe, when the three Military Orders,
unaided from without, strove manfully to retain the last

---

* *Regesta*, No. 1508.

† Beirût, lost on the 6th August, 1187, had been regained by Amaury II
of Cyprus in 1197, and fell finally about the end of July, 1291.   Tortosa,
taken by Saladin in 1188, fell on 3rd August, 1291.   Sidon was taken
by Saladin in 1187, and retaken from Melek el Ádel in 1197, retaken by
Saracens in 1249, and recovered in 1253, when St. Louis rebuilt it.   The
Templars bought it in 1260, but abandoned it in 1291 after the fall of
Acre and the surrender of Tyre.

foothold of the Christians in the East. The Pope, indeed, sent one thousand six hundred Italians, in twenty Venetian galleys, to aid the town, but the troops, arriving in 1290 A.D., were found to be mere vagabonds, who, being unpaid, pillaged Christians and Moslems alike. The force which finally gathered at Acre included only nine hundred knights, and eighteen thousand foot soldiers, of whom five hundred came from Cyprus. The force sent by Kelaun, just before his death, was led by seven emirs, each of whom had four thousand horse and twenty thousand foot, according to the chroniclers. With such proportions, though the Egyptians had no fleet, the fate of the city was certain.

St. Jean D'Acre as it was called, from the Knights Hospitallers' church, was, at the time of its capture, a rich and considerable city. In it were still to be seen the palaces of the kings of Jerusalem, and of the princes of Galilee and Antioch, with houses of the lieutenants of the kings of France and Cyprus, of the great barons of Cæsarea, Tripoli, and Jaffa, of the seigneurs of Beirût, Tyre, Sidon, and Tiberias. Even its churches were fortified. The men of Naples and Cyprus, of France and England, the Italian traders, and even the Tartars, had their streets and quarters in the city. The Guelph and Ghibeline factions quarrelled often within its walls, and bloody fights took place at times between Venetians and Genoese. It was the home of the Legate, and the last abode of the three great Military Orders.

The ancient town, built by Phœnician traders some

twenty centuries before the Christian era, and noticed
in Egyptian tablets of the reign of Amenophis III,
stood on a rocky reef jutting out at the north end of
the shallow bay of Carmel. To the south the green
malarious gardens, full of palms and fruit trees, hid the
course of the Belus, which flows into the Mediterranean
south of the port. Fertile plains stretched northwards
from the walls to the Ladder of Tyre : on the south were
the broad sands, on which the quiet waves were lapping
in the spring-time ; and behind them rose the sand dunes,
covered with dry grasses, on the edge of the marshy
plains where Saladin had camped. The long dark
chain of the Galilean hills rose eastwards to Safed, and
behind them was the snow-streaked dome of Hermon.
As the sun sinks down in the West and the steel blue
shadows creep over the plain, and up the Galilean slopes,
a deep pink flush enflames the upper ridges of those
rocky mountains, and long after these have sunk into
darkness it still tinges the Hermon snows, five thousand
feet higher above the sea. The night was creeping over
the Christian kingdom, and soon would fall ; for the
hosts—gathered from Syria and Arabia, from beyond
the Euphrates and from Egypt and the Red Sea shores
—hemmed in the last great fortress of the Latins.

The twelfth century city was nearly square—about
three-quarters of a mile across—but a great suburb of
triangular shape had now grown up on the north, and
was known as Mont Musard. A wall divided this
suburb from the older town, being the old north wall of
the city ; and on this was the Castle towards the centre.

On the land side there was a double wall to both town and suburb. The little harbour, with its two moles on the south, was closed by a chain from the "Tower of Flies,' which stood on a rock on the west side of the entrance ; and there were two small docks on the west side of the harbour. The Hospice of the Knights of St. John was in the north-west part of the old town ; and to the south of this was the Church of St. Michael. The Templars' house was at the end of the promontory, close to the sea, in the south-west angle of the city. The Hospice of the Teutonic Knights was north of the harbour, near the eastern inner wall, and the Patriarchate stood between this and the port. The brethren of St. Lazarus had a property between the two Hospices of St. John and of the Teutonic Order ; and the north-east quarter near the Castle was called St. Romain. The Church of St. Andrew was west of the port, and east of the Temple : traces of its buildings might still be seen in the eighteenth century, but hardly anything is now left of the Latin buildings that once adorned the town, which in size was about equal to Jerusalem. Other churches were named from St. Stephen, St. Martin, St. Peter of the Pisans, St. Bartholomew, St. Laurence, St. George (of the Teutonic Order), St. Anne, St. Samuel, Our Lady of Tyre, Our Lady of the Knights, Our Lady of Provence, Our Lady Latin, St. Sepulchre, and the Holy Spirit. The Church of St. John, near the middle of the city, is now a mosque. The Hospice of St. John to its north has become the Serai. The quarter of the Venetians lay along the harbour, and adjoined that of the Pisans, which extended along the south-west part of the town towards the Temple. The Genoese were established next, on the west sea face. In Mont Musard there were many streets and houses and churches. The Butchery of the Templars was in this suburb, or northern quarter, and a lodge of the Hospital and another of St. Lazarus. The churches of St. Thomas à Becket, St. Catherine, of the Trinity, the Magdalen, St. Giles, St. Antony, and St. Denys, were in Mont Musard ; and the Franciscans lived near its eastern wall.

The famous tower Maledictum was at the salient of the outer wall, where that which surrounded Mont Musard joined the older fortification. The English tower, or king's new tower, was on the north face of the salient, west of the Maledictum, and on the east face were three other towers, of the Patriarch, the Bridge, and St. Nicholas. The inner wall on the east had the Bloody Tower at its north-east corner, and south of this the Pilgrim's Tower and the German Tower. The quarter within—including the Patriarchate—was called St. Cross. The old north wall of the city had two towers east of the castle ; and west of the same were four, namely, that at the Gate of Nôtre Dame, and going west those at the gate of the Hospital, the new gate, and St. Michael's gate. The outer wall of Mont Musard had also six towers : that at the sea-end, in the extreme north-west angle of the city, being the Devil's Tower. This rampart was divided into two custodies : that of the Templars to the north, and of the Hospitallers to the south.

Such, according to an ancient extant plan of the city, was St. Jean d'Acre on the day of its capture, after a siege of forty-three days. The Moslems brought rams and catapults against the walls, and made cats of the Lebanon cedar, and of oaks from the Nazareth woods. Stones, logs, and arrows, were hurled at the defenders from numberless machines of war. Twice the Templars counselled a parley, and the advice was rejected, cries of treason being as usual raised against the wisest of the Syrian Orders. The garrison dwindled to half its numbers, through disaffection and desertions. After a month's siege, on the 4th of May the Saracens advanced to the attack, well armed and bearing shields of gold. The Gate of St. Antony, in the inner angle, west of Maledictum, where the Cyprian troops were stationed, was besieged with machines of war. Scaling ladders were raised against the wall, but the night fell, leaving the Teutonic Order in charge of the point of attack. During this night the King of Cyprus, who like others despaired of the town, embarked with all his men. On the morrow the furious assault continued, and the fanatic Hajjis from Mecca lined the ditch with their bodies. The merchants and effeminate citizens, who had so long lived in luxury in this great port of Italian trade, began to tremble for their fate ; but the Templars and Hospitallers held out stoutly on the walls, though the rams began to breach the ramparts. At length the Moslems retreated, baffled by their stubborn courage.

Many attacks were made during the two weeks that followed. At last, on the 18th of May, a desperate

sortie was driven back, and the Masters of Temple
and Hospital were both wounded. Only a thousand
men remained at the Gate of St. Antony, and the
Templars retreated to their strong Hospice close to
the sea. In the middle of a storm of hail and rain,
such as sometimes breaks over Palestine in May, the
Moslems fought their way into the town, but the
resistance was stubbornly maintained from street to
street. The city was sacked, and the Christians were
burned in their churches; but William of Clermont,
Master of the Hospital, still remained faithful at his
post by the Gate of St. Antony, and defended the
northern quarter from the Hospice of his Order. He
died, by an arrow, while still on horseback encouraging
his knights.

Meantime the legate had embarked on a ship, and
received the fugitives who crowded to it; but the storm
had lashed the waves, and the vessel sank with all on
board. A terrible scene of misery followed, when noble
ladies came down to the shore, carrying their jewels, and
praying the rude boatmen to row them away—offering
all they had, promising even to marry the sailors who
would save them, if only they could escape to Tyre or
to Cyprus. Sad descendants were they of the proud
baronesses who had walked the halls of their palaces in
cloth of gold, and paced the roofs of the fair houses of
Acre, in crowns rough with gems. The port was seized,
and no vessels could go out: the city was in flames: the
women were ravished in the streets. The great tower of
the Temple was mined, after several days of parley and

of resistance, and knights and ladies perished in its ruins, as it toppled on the streets below. With the fall of this tower fell the Christian kingdom, which Godfrey had won two centuries before, when, in the seventh generation after him, the knights of the great Orders perished in hopeless discharge of duty ; and the feudal system was swept away, by the sword of Islam, when the last church in Acre had crumbled in its smouldering ashes, and the ramparts of the city had been levelled to the ground. Within a month of the fall of Acre the cause of Islam had triumphed from Edessa to Cairo, and the soul of Kelaun could rest in peace. The three years struggle which Richard Lion Heart had carried to success against Saladin saved Acre for Christendom during a century, but the ruin of the Christian cause was symbolised by the fallen tower, where the bodies of brave knights and noble ladies lay crushed and buried under the stones of the Temple.

CONCLUSION.

LOOKING back over the two centuries of this well marked episode in history various things seem to become clear. In the first place, the conquest of Palestine was not due solely to a sudden religious mania, seizing on popes and princes as well as on their subjects. It was an event which, like all others, was brought about by various causes acting in one direction. The Turkish cruelties roused a flame of indignation in Europe, and made practicable what had before been preached in vain; but besides this popular wrath, which would perhaps have died away had it not been fostered by those in power, there were other reasons to be found in Papal policy, in Norman ambition, in the restlessness of a still savage European population; and there was the trade of the Greeks and of the Amalfi merchants, which Turkish barbarism had ruined. Pressure of population, and the energy of the Scandinavian race, lay at the roots of a movement which has sometimes been regarded as due solely to fanaticism.

In the second place, it is also clear that the Latins in the East were not mere freebooters raiding from time to time on Asia. Their early leaders were statesmen as well as soldiers, who were able to control their own wild followers, and to direct their energies to useful ends. They were tolerant rulers, whose policy was the true policy of justice and equal law: who built up strong states in the conquered lands, and stood above the prejudices and hatreds of their age. Under their direction a mighty commerce was developed, which enriched Italy and educated Europe. Under their laws the Holy Land enjoyed a measure of peace and prosperity greater than any western country enjoyed in the same age. When Kelaun carried out the work of Saladin to its conclusion the night settled down on Asia, and the unhappy Arabs exchanged the tolerant rule of the Franks for a bitter Egyptian bondage. It was Europe, not Asia, that profited most by the Crusades, and by the occupation of Syria. When Christians and Moslems came to know each other better friendly relations were established, which enabled the traders of the West to pursue their calling even after the kingdom was lost. For a century all Palestine and Syria were held by generations of Aryans who were born and lived and died in the East. For another century after that Syria and the plains to the south were still ruled by the great Orders, whose experience taught them how to deal with Oriental vassals.

In the third place, however, it is clear that the disunion of Islam was the reason why the native races were unable to resist this strong current from the West. It is remarkable that no great Arab ruler appeared during the centuries of the Crusades. The sultans and generals of the Moslems were Turks, Kurds, or Persians. The Arab khalifs were mere shades—religious figure-heads whose political influence was null. The Arab race seems to have been exhausted in the times of Omar, of El Mamun, and of Harûn er Rashîd; and the Seljuk conquest put an end forever to Arab supremacy. When Saladin united Sunnee and Shiàh in a common cause the native strength became greater than that of the Latins; and the weakening of Europe by internal quarrels brought disaster on Syria. The citizens of Acre were the victims of the great struggle between the Pope and the Emperor. The conquests of Bibars were made easy by the hatreds of *bianchi* and *neri*, of Ghibelines and Guelphs.

Fourthly, it is clear that two policies antagonistic to each other grew out of the conditions of the race struggles of Asia, and out of the division that severed the educated and superstitious—the liberal and the prejudiced—in Europe. There was, on the one hand, the policy of the empire, which was content to make peace with Islam, and to regard Jerusalem as being what it really was—the Holy City of Christendom, which was valued only as a place of pilgrimage, not as an earthly possession. There was, on the other hand, the policy of the Church, which refused to compromise, and which aimed at destroying a religion far too deeply impressed on Asiatics for it to be possible that they should relinquish the teaching of Muhammad for the dogmas of Rome. The popes indeed despaired, in the thirteenth century, of either converting Moslems, or of bringing Eastern Churches into the fold of what they—

like the Greeks—called the Catholic Church. They turned their attention to the Tartars, whom they so long strove to convert. But Buddhism was as obstinately opposed as the creed of Islam to that form of Christianity which they taught to be the only Truth. Regarded from a purely lay stand-point it is clear that the Latins took the wrong side in the Asiatic struggle. They over-estimated the power of the Tartars, and they under-estimated the power of the native Moslem races. If the policy of Frederic II had prevailed, the exclusion of Christians from Palestine, during the five centuries that followed the loss of Acre, might perhaps have been avoided, and the lot of Asia would have been happier.

The history of Palestine and of Western Asia after 1291 A.D. was a long episode of increasing barbarism. Some attempt was made in 1363 to recover what the Latins had lost, when the King of Cyprus burnt Tripoli, Tortosa, and Latakia, and made a truce with Egypt, which gained for him half the rights of trade in Tyre, Beirût, Acre, Jerusalem, and Damascus. Christian churches were rebuilt in Bethlehem, and Nazareth, and over the Holy Sepulchre ; but future troubles were then gathering in the rise of the Osmanlis, and in the conquests of Timur. Beiazid Ilderim (1389–1402 A.D.) defeated the French and their allies under Sigismund of Hungary, and overran Servia and Bulgaria. The new Turkish dynasty was not of pure blood, for, as already noticed, the sultans of Iconium had long been wont to marry Greeks and Georgians, and their heirs were often of mixed descent. The vices of Oriental despotism

were early observed in these half-bred sultans.   Timur,
a descendant of Genghiz Khan on the mother's side,
made Samarcand his capital in 1369 A.D.   In 1392 his
troops swam the Tigris and took Baghdad.   Through
Georgia he advanced to Moscow, which the Uzbeks had
conquered in 1313 A.D., while at the same time establishing his rule in Delhi.   He attacked and defeated
Bajaset (Beiazîd) at Angora, and invaded Syria, taking
Aleppo and Damascus in 1402 A.D.   The sufferings of
the eastern Christians were terrible.   At Sivas four
thousand are said to have been buried alive, and a
pyramid of ninety thousand heads was erected at
Baghdad.   In Ispahan seven thousand children were
trampled under the hoofs of Tartar horses—such, at
least, is the statement of history ; but these incursions
had no permanent effect on the history of Western Asia,
and the Turks recovered twenty years after the defeat
at Angora.   The Osmanli family, founded by Othman,
the Kharezmian vassal of the Sultan of Iconium in
1288 A.D., had established themselves at Broussa and
had threatened Constantinople before Timur appeared.
The conquest of the city was delayed by the Tartar
onset, but only for a time.   In 1453 its crumbling walls
were attacked, and Constantine Palæologus was subdued by Muhammad II.   In 1518 Syria fell to Selim I,
and the tide of Osmanli success flowed steadily to the
reign of Muhammad III (the close of the sixteenth
century) : with Selim the title of khalif was re-assumed,
by one who could not trace descent from Muhammad,
but who possessed the claim of *Hâmi el Haramein*,

"guardian of the two sanctuaries" of Islam. The condition of Palestine then resembled almost exactly that which had prevailed in Godfrey's time, before the conquest by the Latins.

Before this rising tide of barbarism the Franks gradually retreated. Suleiman II took Rhodes from the Knights Hospitallers. Cyprus—where the Venetians had bought the rights of Catherine Cornaro, heiress of the Lusignan house—fell to Selim II. The Turkish conquests were stayed only when John Sobiesky defeated Muhammad IV before Vienna on the 13th of September, 1683 A.D. The travellers' accounts, from the fifteenth to the seventeenth centuries—such as those of Bertrandon de la Brocquière, and Henry Maundrell—abundantly testify to the decay of civilisation under the Osmanlis. The trade of Venice, which was at its height in 1200 A.D., was injured by the conquests of Genghiz Khan, but still continued by the Caspian long after. The Genoese, however, deserted this route in the fifteenth century, after Timur had ruined western Asia, and the Venetians prospered by developing the southern trade with Egypt.* In 1574 the English made a treaty with Murad III, and Queen Elizabeth founded the Levant Company in 1583 A.D. But none of these trading enterprises brought any revival of the prosperity of Palestine, where all the evils of foreign tyranny and internal dissension continued to be felt. It

---

* The Genoese and Venetians struggled for ascendancy at Constantinople in the fourteenth century. The Genoese defeated their rivals, and gained a naval victory in the Bosphorus in 1352.

was Europe—not Syria—that profited most by the Latin conquest: that learned from an ancient civilisation, and applied its lesson at home: that became acquainted with wider knowledge than existed in the West, and experienced in the government of men of varying belief and race. How little Asia was impressed by Europe we may see from the language of Syria in our own times; and by the same means we may judge of the impress of Arab civilisation on the West. It was but natural that this should be the case, because Asia was the home of ancient culture, while Europe was still barbarous. The oldest civilisations known to history are those of Chaldea, Palestine, and Egypt. The art and science of Babylonians was handed down to the Persians, and civilised the Greeks. From such an origin sprang the culture of the early days of Islam, when the torch of knowledge was kept alight by the Arabs during the darkest of dark ages in Europe. The Latins knew well how to rule, and how to fight ; but in all other respects they were pupils of the Arab, who had himself been a pupil of the Persian and the Byzantine, and even of the subtle Hindoo.

The effect of Godfrey's conquest on Europe was already great in the twelfth century, and became greater in that which followed. The Crusades carried away the most turbulent classes in the West, and left the quiet traders to grow rich at home. Many great seigneurs were ruined by the heavy expenses of these wars ; and the Communes, which first appeared in Syria, gained strength later at home. The power of kings increased, and the states of Europe were consolidated into king-doms. The Moslems of Spain grew ever weaker, while the power of Islam was crushed for a time in its home, till John of Arragon conquered Valentia and Murcia in the end of the thirteenth century. The trading cities of Italy became free, and the German towns obtained privileges during the struggles with the papacy. St. Louis, who came home with the experience gained in Syria, did much to strengthen the bourgeois class in France, and to encourage learning and art. The "new and detestable" Communes not only preserved the peace, and upheld the rights of the newly rising middle class, which began to claim justice from its peers, but they also strengthened the king against the power of the clergy, and of the barons alike. Universities also arose, to study new learning of Eastern derivation. Paris gave education to the Greeks sent by Latin patriarchs to learn the Roman creed, and Greek books were brought to France in 1255 A.D. Bologna and Salamanca became famous centres of learning, and Oxford humbly followed them in its early obscurity.*

---

* The school of Salerno, tracing to the eleventh century, decayed in the thirteenth. Bologna had a privilege from the Emperor Frederic I in 1158. Paris dated from about 1150. Naples was founded by Frederic II in 1224, but Salamanca was not recognised as a leading university till 1311. The German universities date later, Prague having a Bull from the Pope in 1347, and Vienna in 1365, while the other German universities belong chiefly to the Reformation period. Oxford, supposed to originate in migration of English students from Paris in 1167, is only first noticeable in 1170 as of local reputation for schools. Cambridge claims the *studium generale* from 1318 by Papal Bull. (See *Universities of the Middle Ages*, H. Rashdall, 1895, and *Quarterly Review*, April, 1896, pp. 449-463.) The influence of the Moslems in Spain on European civilisation has already been noticed (Chap. I), but that of the Syrians and Egyptians seem to have been more important.

The countries nearest Palestine were the first to feel the influence of learning and commerce, and the Lombard trade in London arose under Edward I.

The Papal power waxed and waned with the fortunes of the Holy Land; but the increased knowledge of the Latins led to its final ruin. With Innocent III (1198 to 1216 A.D.) it reached its summit, when the Military Orders ruled in Palestine, though Gregory VII claimed temporal power over all Europe before the first Crusade. In 1316, under Boniface VIII, after the loss of Syria, it had fallen again from its pride. The Pope could no longer levy taxes, or order expeditions, when Europe ceased to be willing to take the cross for the defence of the Holy Land. The degradation of the Church in the fourteenth century is attested in the " Revelation of St. Bridget," which is of acknowledged authenticity—according to Benedict XIV.

" The Pope," says this outspoken document, " is a murderer of souls : he destroys and flays the flock of Christ : he is more cruel than Judas—more unjust than Pilate. All the Ten Commandments he has changed to this one—money, money ! "*

Europe became full of murmurings against the Church which no longer owned the Holy Land ; but priests still monopolised almost every profession—as lawyers, notaries, collectors of taxes, and even as merchants.

* We must not forget the attacks of Piers Ploughman on friars, monks, absolution, &c., in Langland's work before 1399, the complaints of the Good Parliament as to Roman encroachments and the "sinful city of Avignon " in 1376, the year before Wycliff was summoned as a heretic, or the contemporary complaints of Chaucer about pardoners and summoners from Rome. (See Jusserand's *Literary History of the English People,* pp. 272–6, 375, 420.)

But meanwhile the new knowledge was spreading far and wide. Aristotle, translated from Arabic, was championed by Thomas Aquinas, by the Dominicans, and by other learned Orders, though at times denounced by popes and councils. Homer and Virgil became known, and yet more precious foundations of science were laid, in the study of mathematics, astronomy, and other exact subjects, which the Syrian Jacobites had preserved, and taught to the Latins, or which an Emperor like Frederic II received from the Moslems of Egypt. It is often said that Europe owed most of this culture to the Moors in Spain ; but it must not be forgotten that universities first appeared in France and Italy soon after the conquest of Palestine by the Christians, and only a century later in Spain. From Christians of the East the Latins would accept knowledge which, when taught by Saracens, they would in the twelfth century have distrusted. It was not only learning, trade, and art that profited by intercourse with the ancient East, even agriculture owed much to the contact. The maize came to Italy, the damson took its name from Damascus, and the shalot from Ascalon* ; but yet more, the foundation of the Renaissance was laid through the conquest of Syria ; and the Reformation was hastened by knowledge gained in the Holy Land.†

* The Oriental plane was brought by the Templars to Ribstone.
† Versions of Plato, Aristotle, Hippocrates, Galen, &c., are ascribed to Honain, a Nestorian physician at Baghdad, who died as early as 876 A.D. Leo Pilatus taught Greek in Florence as early as 1360. The communications between the later Byzantine emperors and Italy gave an impulse to Greek literature which was also encouraged by the Medicis. The fall of Constantinople to the Turks drove many scholars to the West. The Vatican library was founded by Pope Nicholas V about 1450 A.D.

Meanwhile, however, the wisest of the Syrian Orders became the scapegoat for the sins of Europe. The Templars had fought bravely in a forlorn hope at Acre, and did good service later in Greece, but they were hated and distrusted, envied for their wealth, and accused of atheism and nameless crimes. In October, 1307 A.D., they were summoned home to France, and the Grand Master arriving from Cyprus was imprisoned. Fifty-seven knights were burned alive, and died suffering their torments with constancy. In 1314 A.D. the Grand Master was burned with three others, and is said to have summoned Philip of France and the Pope to meet him, in four months and in forty days respectively. King and Pope both died within the time of their summons, but the Order was dissolved for ever. The Bull of Clement V (" Faciens Misericordiam "), issued in 1312 A.D. at the instigation of Philip le Bel, made the most absurd charges against the Templars. There were more than a hundred articles of accusation, among which were, the renunciation of Christ, the Virgin, and the Saints ; spitting on the Cross ; the adoration of " a certain cat," and criminal offences. It was said that they worshipped an idol—" that is a head with three faces, or with one, or with a human skull," round which they hung their girdles to consecrate them. The charges against the French Templars (in the chronicle of St. Denys) are equally strange, and included secret infidelity, a treaty with Egypt to betray the Christians, treachery to St. Louis and at Acre, and misuse of public funds. Their supposed idol Baphomet was described as "an old skin with carbuncles for eyes." The dead Templars were said to be burned, and their ashes eaten by the novices. Even the old accusation which had served against Manicheans and Jews was brought against them, for they were believed to eat new-born babies, and to anoint Baphomet with the fat of their victims. Such were the monstrous means by which popular suspicions were diverted from king and Pope, against a valiant and useful Order, whose rich possessions the great conspirators shared between them.

But popular condemnation was not so easily averted. Dante had married Gemma de Donati in the year of the fall of Acre, and the Divina Commedia appeared not many years later. He first dared to represent a pope in Hell,* and, though driven from his home and threatened with the stake, his voice was never silenced. The knowledge of Homer and Virgil which he attained was then new knowledge in Europe. The very circles of his Inferno found their prototypes in the " Book of Enoch," which Jacobites and Copts preserved, and which—with the Gospel of Peter—was rendered into Greek by the Egyptian hermits.†

It has already been noted that the china and metal work of Europe, from the twelfth century downwards, owed its beauty to Arab and Byzantine influence ; and that Venetian glass was only a copy of the older Syrian manufacture. Painting and sculpture, wood cutting and the art of copper-plate engraving, are equally traced to

---

* *Inferno*, iii, 56, xix, 55, 71.
† *Times*, 2nd December, 1892.

the East. Bank notes were used in China in the ninth
century, and block printing in the tenth. The Arab
numerals alone made possible the calculations of later
mathematics. Roger Bacon was able to draw a map of
Central Asia in the reign of Henry III ; and with him
appeared at Oxford lenses and gunpowder. He suffered
as a wizard in prison, and died the year after the fall of
Acre. In Italy Byzantine painters appeared, on the
conquest of Constantinople in 1204 A.D. ; and schools
of art were founded by them at Siena and Pisa. Cima-
bue, the father of Italian painting, was born in 1240,
and painted his most famous picture thirty years later.
The influence of the art which was then adorning Bethlehem with glass mosaics, and covering the chapels of
the Jordan monasteries with frescoes, is only too plainly
visible in the stiff forms of the first Italian masters.
The gloomy imagination of Orcagna, in the fourteenth
century, was fed by the Eastern love of terrible subjects, such as were painted on the walls of the Jerusalem
churches. Even Raphael places the Templum Domini
behind the figures in his " Marriage of the Virgin," and
the arid rocky ravine of Gethsemane seems to have been
familiar to more than one early Italian painter.

These are but illustrations of the well-known connection that exists between the growth of civilisation in
Europe and the knowledge of older culture attained in
the East. They serve to show that Europe profited by
the Crusades, not only as regards art and commerce, but
also as regards science and freer thought. The first
Crusaders were ignorant men ; Frederic II was an

elegant scholar. The army of Godfrey burned the "detestable" libraries of Syria : the later emperor sought to learn from Moslems. The Church waxed proud and rich, when the Duke of Jerusalem, and the kings who followed became vassals, not of France or of Germany, but of Rome. Yet the influence of Eastern philosophy was fatal to the superstitions of Europe.

All this civilisation transported to the West was slowly lost in the East. No new Bible, not even a new Korân, was produced by the Arab race ; and knowledge was despised by the Turk. In our own times we see perhaps the first signs of a new awakening ; and the tide sets once more from Europe to the shores of Acre and to the Nile. For more than thirty years the old County of Tripoli and Seigneurie of Beirût have now been ruled by Christians. Cyprus has passed to the nation which conquered it under Richard Lion Heart ; and Englishmen have done what St. Louis failed to do in Egypt. Tunis has fallen to the race of that great Christian monarch ; and the commerce of the West, in Syria and Asia Minor, presses once more upon the Turkish Empire. The Holy Land is fuller of pilgrims to-day than it ever was in the best times of Latin rule ; and even Damascus cannot now resist the inroads of Western enterprise. A happier time may be in store for Syria than any it has known as yet ; but we must not forget that much of what we now enjoy is due to the brave and wise rulers who founded the kingdom of Jerusalem, and to the men of science and learning who taught to them the secrets of the East, and preserved the fruits of earlier human thought and labour, during centuries when all was dark in Europe. The Crusades were no wild raids on Palestine, resulting only in misery and destruction. The kingdom of Jerusalem was the model of just and moderate rule, such as we boast to have given to India, under somewhat similar conditions ; but the benefits of these two stirring centuries have as yet been mainly enjoyed in the West, and a debt due by the Frank has still to be paid in the East.

INDEX.

THE END.

BY THE SAME AUTHOR.

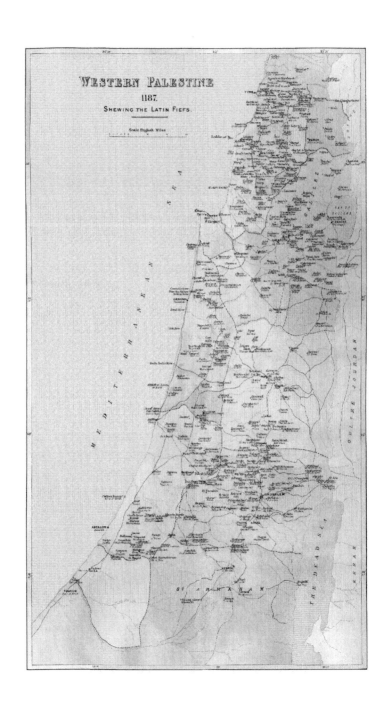

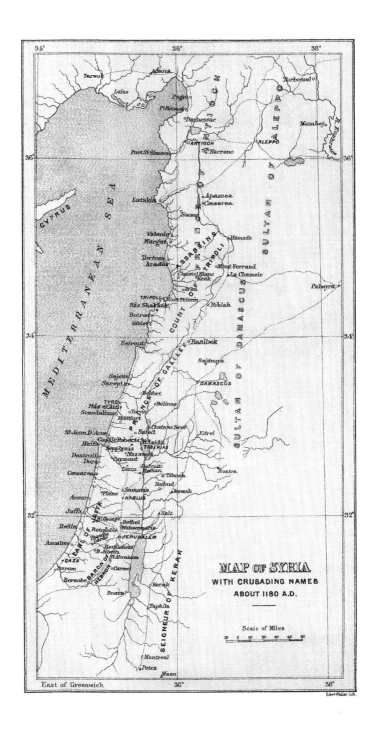

MAP OF SYRIA

WITH CRUSADING NAMES

ABOUT 1180 A.D.

Scale of Miles

East of Greenwich

Edwd Weller lith.

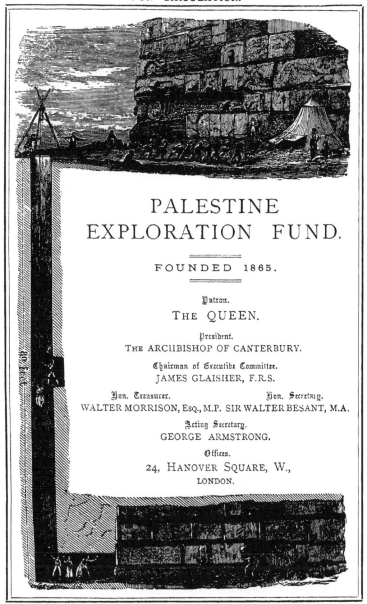

PALESTINE EXPLORATION FUND.

FOUNDED 1865.

Patron.

THE QUEEN.

President.

THE ARCHBISHOP OF CANTERBURY.

Chairman of Executive Committee.

JAMES GLAISHER, F.R.S.

Hon. Treasurer.   Hon. Secretary.

WALTER MORRISON, Esq., M.P. SIR WALTER BESANT, M.A,

Acting Secretary.

GEORGE ARMSTRONG.

Offices.

24, HANOVER SQUARE, W.,

LONDON.

The illustration on this frontispiece represents SIR CHARLES WARREN'S exploration of the south-east corner of the Haram, or Temple, Wall, at Jerusalem. The lower portion of the wall at this place is hidden by an accumulation of nearly 80 feet of débris; through which a shaft was sunk to where the foundation stones rested on the solid rock, where the small vase and inscriptions were found.

For the Information of Subscribers.

SUBSCRIPTIONS ARE EARNESTLY DESIRED
FOR CARRYING OUT THE OBJECTS OF THE SOCIETY.

1. Those who subscribe a guinea or $5·00 a year are entitled to receive

> Post free the "QUARTERLY STATEMENT," which is the JOURNAL of the Society, containing Reports of work done by its Agents, and a record of discoveries made in the Holy Land ; as well as much valuable information bearing on Scriptural Subjects.

> Post free on application a Presentation volume.

> The Maps and Books published by the Society at greatly reduced prices.

2. Those who subscribe half-a-guinea or $2·50 annually receive the "QUARTERLY STATEMENTS" free, and are entitled to the Books and Maps at the reduced price.

The reduction in price is only granted by application at the Head Office, 24, Hanover Square, W.

Cheques, Money Orders, and Postal Orders payable to the order of Mr. George Armstrong, Acting Secretary of the Fund. Money Orders may be made payable at Charing Cross. All Cheques and Orders may be crossed Coutts & Co.

All subscriptions and donations are recorded in the "QUARTERLY STATEMENT."

PALESTINE EXPLORATION FUND,

24, Hanover Square, W.,

London.

THE

Palestine Exploration Fund.

A Society for the accurate and systematic
investigation of the Archæology, the Topography, the Geology
and Physical Geography, the Manners and Customs
of the Holy Land, for Biblical Illustratioh.

PUBLICATIONS OF THE SOCIETY.

1. THE SURVEY OF WESTERN PALESTINE.

This magnificent work consists of "THE MEMOIRS," in 3 vols.; "THE NAME
LISTS," 1 vol.; "THE SPECIAL PAPERS," 1 vol.; "JERUSALEM,"
1 vol.; "THE FLORA AND FAUNA OF PALESTINE," 1 vol. In all
seven volumes, with "THE MAPS," great and small.

The last two volumes, "JERUSALEM" with 50 plates in a Portfolio, and "FLORA
AND FAUNA," can be had separately. The complete set consists of the
following seven uniform volumes 4to. For terms apply to the Secretary, 24,
Hanover Square, W.

THE MEMOIRS. Being the Notes taken in the Field, and
written to accompany the sheets of the great Map, by Lieut.-Col. CONDER,
D.C.L., LL.D., R.E., and Major-Gen. Sir H. H. KITCHENER, C.M.G., A.D.C.,
R.E. With additions, historical and archæological by the Editors. In
3 volumes, Illustrated by many hundreds of Plans and Sketches made
specially for the work.

THE NAME LISTS: Transliterated from the Arabic, with
translation by Lieut.-Col. CONDER, and edited by the late Prof. PALMER. 1 vol.

THE SPECIAL PAPERS on the Archæology, Topography,
&c., of the Country. 1 vol.

THE JERUSALEM VOLUME. A complete account of the
Excavations and Researches in Jerusalem, with a portfolio of Fifty Plates. By
Major-Gen. SIR CHARLES WARREN, K.C.B., G.C.M.G., F.R.S., R.E. In
the same volume a history of the Architectural Monuments in the City, and an
Account of his own and the German Researches, and Excavations in the City,
by Lieut.-Col. CONDER, R.E., also an abstract of M. CHARLES CLERMONT-
GANNEAU's Researches and Excavations in the year 1874-5. 1 vol.

Publications of the Society—*continued.*

THE FLORA AND FAUNA OF PALESTINE.
Richly Illustrated. By the Rev. Canon Tristram, F.R.S., LL.D. 1 vo.

THE MAPS, great and small.

2. ## THE RECOVERY OF JERUSALEM: with Fifty
   Illustrations. By Maj.-Gen. Sir Charles W. Wilson, K.C.B., and Maj.-Gen. Sir Charles Warren, K.C.B. Price to Subscribers, 16*s.* Non-subscribers, 21*s.* Demy 8vo.

3. ## TENT WORK IN PALESTINE. New Edition. By
   Lieut.-Col. Conder, D.C.L., R.E. Price to Subscribers to the Fund, 4*s.* 6*d.* Non-subscribers, 6*s.*, 8vo.

   "A popular account of the Survey of Western Palestine, freely illustrated by drawings made by the author himself. This is not a dry record of the sepulchres, or a descriptive catalogue of ruins, springs, and valleys, but a continuous narrative full of observations upon the manners and customs of the people, the Biblical associations of the sites, the Holy City and its memories, and is based upon a six years' experience in the country itself. No other modern traveller has enjoyed the same advantages as Lieut.-Col. Conder, or has used his opportunities to better purpose."

4. ## HETH AND MOAB. By Lieut.-Col. Conder, D.C.L., R.E.
   Price to Subscribers to the Fund, 4*s.* 6*d.* Non-subscribers, 6*s.*, 8vo. New and Revised Edition.

   "Under this title Lieut.-Col. Conder gives a narrative as bright and as full of interest as 'Tent Work,' of the expedition for the *Survey of Eastern Palestine.* How the party began by a flying visit to North Syria, in order to discover the Holy City— Kadesh—of the children of Heth ; how they fared across the Jordan, and what discoveries they made there, will be found in this volume."

5. ## ACROSS THE JORDAN ; being a Record of Explorations
   in the Hauran. By Gottlieb Schumacher, C.E., with Map, Sections, and a hundred and fifty Illustrations. Price to Subscribers to the Fund, 4*s.* 6*d.* Non-subscribers, 6*s.*, 8vo. An instalment of the Survey of Eastern Palestine.

6. ## THE SURVEY OF THE JAULAN. By G. Schu-
   macher, C.E. With Map, Special Plans, and a hundred and fifty Illustrations. Price to Subscribers to the Fund, 4*s.* 6*d.* Non-subscribers, 6*s.*, 8vo. An instalment of the Survey of Eastern Palestine.

7. ## MOUNT SEIR. By Prof. E. Hull, M.A., LL.D., F.R.S.
   Price to Subscribers to the Fund, 4*s.* 6*d.* Non-subscribers, 6*s.*, 8vo.

   "This is a popular account of the Geological Expedition conducted by Prof. Hull for the Committee of the Palestine Fund. The part which deals with the Valley of Arabah will be found entirely new and interesting."

Publications of the Society—*continuea.*

8. **SYRIAN STONE LORE.** New Edition. By Lieut.-Col.
CONDER, D.C.L., R.E. Price to Subscribers to the Fund, 4s. 6d. Non-subscribers, 6s., 8vo.

> "This volume, the least known of Lieut.-Col. Conder's works, is, perhaps, the most valuable. It attempts a task never before approached—the reconstruction of Palestine from its monuments. It shows what we should know of Syria if there were no Bible, and it illustrates the Bible from the monuments."

9. **THIRTY YEARS' WORK :** By SIR WALTER BESANT, M.A.
Price to Subscribers to the Fund, 2s., by post 2s. 3d. Non-subscribers, 3s. 6d., by post 3s. 9d., 8vo.

> "This work is a popular account of the researches conducted by the Society during the thirty years of its existence."

10. **ALTAIC HIEROGLYPHS AND HITTITE IN-SCRIPTIONS.** By Lieut.-Col. CONDER, D.C.L., R.E. Price to Subscribers to the Fund, 3s. 6d. Non-subscribers, 5s., 8vo.

> "This book is an attempt to read the Hittite Inscriptions. The author has seen no reason to change his views since the publication of the work."

11. **THE GEOLOGY OF PALESTINE AND ARABIA PETRÆA.** By Prof. E. HULL, M.A., LL.D., F.R.S. With Illustrations and coloured Maps. Uniform with "The Survey of Western Palestine." Price to Subscribers to the Fund, 12s. 6d. Non-subscribers, 21s., 4to.

12. **NAMES AND PLACES IN THE OLD AND NEW TESTAMENTS AND APOCRYPHA, with references to Josephus, and their Modern Identifications.** By GEORGE ARMSTRONG. Price to Subscribers to the Fund, 3s. 6d. Non-subscribers, 6s., 8vo.

> "This is an index to all the names and places mentioned in the Bible and New Testament. Full references are given to the passages in which they occur. The modern names are given with notes, &c., and the identifications adopted are those that will be found on the new map published by the Society."

13. **THE HISTORY OF JERUSALEM** (R. Bentley & Son, 8, New Burlington Street). By SIR WALTER BESANT and PROFESSOR E. H. PALMER. Price to Subscribers to the Fund, 5s. 6d. Non-subscribers, 7s. 6d., 8vo.

> "The 'History of Jerusalem,' which was originally published in 1871, and has long been completely out of print, covers a period and is compiled from materials not included in any other work, though some of the contents have been plundered by later works on the same subject. It begins with the siege by Titus and continues to the fourteenth century, including the Early Christian period, the Moslem invasion, the mediæval pilgrims, the Mohammedan pilgrims, the Crusades, the Latin Kingdom, the victorious career of Saladin, the Crusade of Children, and many other little-known episodes in the history of the city and the country."

Publications of the Society—*continued.*

14. THE BIBLE AND MODERN DISCOVERIES. New and cheap Edition, revised. With Map, Illustrations, and Index. Price to Subscribers, 5*s*. Non-subscribers, 7*s*. 6*d*., 8vo.

" This work, written by a Member of the Executive Committee of the Palestine Exploration Fund, is an endeavour to present in a simple and popular, but yet a connected form, the Biblical results of twenty-two years' work of the Palestine Exploration Fund. The writer has also availed himself of the discoveries made by the American Expeditions and the Egyptian Exploration Fund, as well as discoveries of interest made by independent travellers.

" The Bible story, from the call of the Abraham to the Captivity, is taken, and details given of the light thrown by modern research on the sacred annals. Eastern customs and modes of thought are explained whenever the writer thought that they illustrated the text. This plain and simple method has never before been adopted in dealing with modern discovery.

" To the Clergy and Sunday School Teachers, as well as to all those who love the Bible, the writer hopes this work will prove useful. He is personally acquainted with the land ; nearly all the places spoken of he has visited, and most of them he has moreover sketched or painted. It should be noted that the book is admirably adapted for the School or Village Library."

15. PALESTINE UNDER THE MOSLEMS. By GUY LE STRANGE. With Map, Illustrations, and Index. In one Vol. Price to Subscribers to the Fund, 10*s*. Non-subscribers, 16*s*., 8vo.

" For a long time it had been desired by the Committee to present to the world some of the great hoards of information about Palestine which lie buried in the Arabic texts of the Moslem geographers and travellers of the Middle Ages. Some few of the works, or parts of the works, have been already translated into Latin, French, and German. Hardly anything has been done with them in English, and no attempt has ever been made to systematise, compare, and annotate them.

" This has now been done for the Society by Mr. Guy le Strange. The work is divided into chapters on Syria, Palestine, Jerusalem, and Damascus, the provincial capitals and chief towns, and the legends related by the writers consulted. These writers begin with the ninth century and continue until the fifteenth. The volume contains maps and illustrations required for the elucidation of the text.

" The Committee have great confidence that this work—so novel, so useful to students of mediæval history, and to all those interested in the continuous story of the Holy Land—will meet with the success which its learned author deserves."

16. LACHISH (Tell el Hesy). One of the five strongholds of the Amorites. An account of the excavations, with view of the Tell. Plans and Section, and upwards of 270 Drawings of the objects found. By Professor FLINDERS PETRIE. Price to Subscribers to the Fund, 6*s*. 6*d*. Non-subscribers, 10*s*. 6*d*., 4to.

17. AN INTRODUCTION TO THE SURVEY OF WESTERN PALESTINE. Its Waterways, Plains, and Highlands, with reference to Map No. 6. By TRELAWNEY SAUNDERS. A few Copies left. Price to Subscribers, 3*s*. 6*d*., demy 8vo.

Publications of the Society—*continued.*

18. **THE CITY AND THE LAND.**—2nd Edition, with Plan of Jerusalem According to Josephus. A Series of Seven Lectures on various points connected with the Objects and Work of the Palestine Exploration Fund, which were delivered in Hanover Square in May and June, 1892. (1) Ancient Jerusalem ; (2) The Future of Palestine ; (3) Natural History of Palestine ; (4) The General Work of the Fund ; (5) The Hittites ; (6) Tell el Hesy (Lachish) ; (7) The Modern Traveller in Palestine. By (1) Major-General Sir Charles W. Wilson, K.C.B.; (2) Lieut.-Col. Conder, D.C.L., R.E. ; (3) Canon Tristram, F.R.S. ; (4) Sir Walter Besant, M.A. ; (5) The Rev. William Wright, D.D. ; (6) Professor Flinders Petrie, D.C.L. ; and (7) Canon Dalton, C.M.G. Price of Single Lecture to Subscribers to the Fund, 6*d.*, and that of the Volume, 2*s.* 6*d.* Non-subscribers, 1*s.* and 3*s.* 6*d.*, 8vo.

19. **THE TELL AMARNA TABLETS, including the one found at Lachish.** Translated from the Cuneiform Characters by Lieut.-Col. C. R. Conder, D.C.L., LL.D., M.R.A.S., R.E. The letters, numbering 176, are from Palestine and Syria, were written about 1480 B.C. by Amorites, Phœnicians, Philistines, &c., to the King of Egypt, to Generals and other Officials, and include those from Jabin, King of Hazor, Adonizedek, King of Jerusalem, and Japhia, King of Gezer, Contemporaries of Joshua, referring to the Hebrew Conquest and naming 130 towns and countries. Price to Subscribers to the Fund, 3*s.* 6*d.* Non-subscribers, 5*s.*, 8vo. New and revised Edition now ready. ^

20. **ABILA, PELLA and NORTHERN 'AJLÛN (of the Decapolis).** By G. Schumacher, C.E. These are three records of special surveys, with Maps and many Illustrations, bound in one volume. The ruins of Abila and Pella are of great extent, including Temples, Basilicas, Theatres, Paved Roads, &c. Northern 'Ajlûn : 220 square miles of this important tract of country were surveyed, plans and drawings made of the important ruins of Gadara, Capitolias, Arbela, &c., and two great fields of Dolmens noted. Price to Subscribers to the Fund, 4*s.* 6*d.* Non-subscribers, 6*s.*

21. **A MOUND OF MANY CITIES, Tell el Hesy Excavated.** By F. J. Bliss, M.A., Explorer to the Fund. With upwards of 250 Illustrations. Price to Subscribers to the Fund, 3*s.* 6*d.*, by post, 3*s.* 9*d.* Non-Subscribers, 6*s.*, by post, 6*s.* 3*d.*

22. **JUDAS MACCABÆUS AND THE JEWISH WAR OF INDEPENDENCE,** with Map, by Lieut.-Col. Conder, D.C.L., R.E. Price to Subscribers to the Fund, 3*s.*, by post, 3*s.* 3*d.* Non-Subscribers, 4*s.* 6*d.*, by post, 4*s.* 9*d.* New Edition. Just issued. This Book gives the history of the Jews from the fall of the Kingdom of Judah to the end of the Maccabæan War. It bridges over the period between the Old and New Testament.

23. **THE LATIN KINGDOM OF JERUSALEM, 1099 to 1291, A.D.** By Lieut.-Col. C. R. Conder, LL.D., M.R.A.S., R.E. This work which is an account of Palestine, Syria, and Western Asia during the rule of the Franks, in the time of the Crusades, has a special interest at the present time, when attention is called to the condition of the Turkish Empire by recent events—the condition of the Orientals being almost the same as that when Europe intervened in the Eastern question in the days of Godfrey de Bouillon and of King Richard Lionheart. Price to Subscribers to the Fund, 5*s.* 6*d.* To Non-Subscribers, 7*s.* 6*d.* [*Ready in January.*

24. **INDEX TO THE QUARTERLY STATEMENTS, 1869-1892 inclusive.** Price to Subscribers to the Fund (in paper covers), 1*s.* 6*d.*, by post, 1*s.* 8*d.* ; in cloth, 2*s.* 6*d.*, by post, 2*s.* 9*d.* Non-Subscribers, 2*s.*, by post, 2*s.* 2*d.*, and 3*s.*, by post, 3*s.* 3*d.*, 8vo.

THE QUARTERLY STATEMENT. A Journal of Palestine Research and Discovery. The first number was issued in 1869. Free to Subscribers to the Fund. Non-subscribers, 2*s.* 6*d.* Cloth cases, Green or Chocolate, for binding the four parts, 1*s.* and 1*s.* 6*d.* Back Numbers of the Quarterly Statement can be had, apply at 24, Hanover Square, W.

A complete set of the books, 2–24, can be had by Subscribers to the Fund at the reduced price of £5 12s. 6d. on application to the Secretary, 24, Hanover Square, W. Carriage paid to any part in the United Kingdom only.

Branch Associations of the Bible Society, all Sunday Schools within the Sunday School Institute, the Sunday School Union, and the Wesleyan Sunday School Institute, will please observe that by a special Resolution of the Committee they are allowed to purchase the books, maps, &c. (by application to the Secretary only) at reduced price.

Subscribers to the Fund are supplied with all Books, Maps, Photographs, Slides, &c., at the reduced prices direct from the Office, 24, Hanover Square, W.

Photographs.

A VERY LARGE COLLECTION.

UNMOUNTED 10d.   MOUNTED 1s. each.

A NEW CATALOGUE OF PHOTOGRAPHS,

Arranged alphabetically according to the Bible names of places, with notes and references. Subscribers, 6d. Non-subscribers, 1s.

PHOTOS of Inscription from Herod's Temple and Moabite Stone, with translations, also of Jar found at the foundation of the S.E. corner of the wall of the Temple Area, 80 feet below the present surface, and fac-simile of the Siloam Inscription, with translation, sent direct from the Office, 24, Hanover Square, W., to Subscribers for 7d. each, post free.

LANTERN SLIDES of the Bible places mentioned in the Catalogue of Photos can be had by Subscribers to the Fund on application to the Office. A large assortment to choose from. Price 1s. each, uncoloured.

SEAL OF "HAGGAI, THE SON OF SHEBANIAH." Casts in metal of this Signet, 2s. each.

INSCRIBED TABLET, found at Lachish. Casts of this Tablet, 2s. 6d. each.

ANCIENT HEBREW WEIGHT, from Samaria. Casts of this Weight, 2s. 6d. each.

INSCRIBED WEIGHT OR BEAD, from Palestine. Casts, 1s. each.

Address—THE SECRETARY,

Palestine Exploration Fund, 24, Hanover Square, W.

MAPS Published by the Society.

1. **OLD AND NEW TESTAMENT MAP OF PALESTINE.** In twenty sheets (*see* key map). Embracing both sides of the Jordan, and extending from Baalbek in the north to Kadesh Barnea in the south. Reduced from the surveys of the Palestine Exploration Fund and other sources. Scale, ⅜ of an inch = 1 mile. In twenty-one sheets and a cover. Showing modern names in black and all the latest identification of the Old Testament and Apocrypha names in red. The New Testament, Josephus, and the Talmudic names in blue. The Tribal Possessions tinted in colours. Price to Subscribers to the Fund, 23s. Non-subscribers, £2. Postage to all foreign countries, 1s. extra.

The same map can be had mounted on Cloth, Rollers, and varnished for hanging. Size, 8 feet by 6 feet. Price to Subscribers to the Fund, £2 4s. Non-subscribers, £3 3s.

The same map, mounted on Cloth, to fold in three parts in a neat portfolio. Price to Subscribers to the Fund, £2 4s. Non-subscribers, £3 3s.

The same map can be had mounted in any form to suit Subscribers, plus the additional cost of mounting.

NOTE.—A copy of "Names and Places" (No. 14) can be had with this Map by Subscribers for 2s. 6d.

2. **MODERN MAP OF PALESTINE.** In twenty sheets. Embracing both sides of the Jordan, and extending from Baalbek in the north to Kadesh Barnea in the south. Reduced from the Surveys of the Palestine Exploration Fund and other sources. Scale, ⅜ of an inch = 1 mile. With modern names only. In twenty sheets and a cover. Price to Subscribers to the Fund, 23s. Non-subscribers, £2. Postage to all foreign countries, 1s. extra.

The same map can be had mounted on Cloth, to fold in three parts in a neat portfolio. Price to Subscribers to the Fund, £2 4s. Non-subscribers, £3 3s.

The same map can be had mounted in any form to suit Subscribers, plus the additional cost of mounting.

3. OLD AND NEW TESTAMENT MAP OF

PALESTINE in 12 sheets. Scale ⅜ of an inch = 1 mile. This 12-sheet map consists of sheets 5–7, 9–11, 13–15, 20–22 (*see* key map to the sheets), which include the whole of Palestine from Mount Hermon in the north to Kadesh Barnea in the south, and the districts beyond Jordan as far as they are surveyed. The modern names are in black, and all the latest identifications of the Old Testament and Apocrypha names in red; the New Testament, Josephus and the Talmudic names in blue, the tribal boundaries are printed in colours. To Subscribers to the Fund, 12*s.* 6*d.* To the public, 21*s.* Postage to all foreign countries, 1*s.* extra.

The same map can be had, mounted on Cloth, Rollers, and varnished for hanging, size 4½ feet by 6¾ feet, price to Subscribers 23*s.*, to the public £1 11*s.* 6*d.* ; Mounted on cloth to fold in two parts, in a neat case, price to Subscribers 24*s.*, to the public £1 12*s.* 6*d.* ; Mounted on cloth to fold in two parts, in a neat portfolio, price to Subscribers 24*s.*, to the public £1 12*s.* 6*d.* ; or mounted in any other form desirable (cost of mounting extra).

4. MODERN MAP OF PALESTINE in 12 sheets. Scale

⅜ of an inch to a mile. (*See* key map.) This map has only the modern names on it. Price to Subscribers to the Fund, 12*s.* 6*d.* Non-subscribers, 21*s.*

Any single sheet of the maps can be had separately, price to Subscribers to the Fund 1s. 6d. ; mounted on cloth to fold in the pocket, suitable for travelling, 2s. ; to the public, 2s. and 2s. 6d. (See key map.)

A copy of "Names and Places," an Index to all the names in the Bible and New Testament, with full references, can be had by Subscribers to the Fund, with the maps, at the reduced price of 2s. 6d.

5. THE GREAT MAP OF WESTERN PALESTINE,

on the scale of one inch to the mile, in twenty-six sheets, with a portfolio. Price to Subscribers to the Fund, £2 2*s.* Non-subscribers, £3 3*s.*

The same map, mounted on Rollers for hanging, size 7 feet by 13 feet. Price to Subscribers to the Fund, £3 17*s.* 6*d.* Non-subscribers, £5 5*s.*

Any single sheet of the Great Map (see Key Map to the sheets on next page), can be had separately, 2s. each. The three sheets, Nos. 13, 16 and 17, containing the new Railway from Jaffa to Jerusalem. Price 2s. each, or 5s. 6d. the three. Non-subscribers, 2s. 6d. or 7s.

MAPS—*continued.*

6. THE REDUCED MAP OF WESTERN PALESTINE

showing WATER BASINS IN COLOR, AND FIVE VERTICAL SECTIONS, showing the natural profiles of the ground, according to the variations of the altitude above or below sea level. In six sheets and a wrapper. Scale ⅜ of an inch = 1 mile. Price to Subscribers to the Fund, 7s. 6d. Non-subscribers, 13s. Postage to all foreign countries, 1s. extra.

> The same map, mounted on Rollers for hanging. Price to Subscribers to he Fund, 12s. 6d. Non-subscribers, 18s.

> The same map, mounted on Cloth and in a neat case, 10½ in. by 8 in. Price to Subscribers to the Fund, 12s. 6d. Non-subscribers, 19s. 6d.

7. PLAN OF JERUSALEM (modern) showing latest discoveries

in red. Scale, 18 inches = 1 mile. Price to Subscribers to the Fund (on Cloth), 2s. Non-subscribers, 2s. 6d.

8. PLAN OF JERUSALEM, according to Josephus. The

Modern Walls of the City, &c., are shown in black. The course of the Walls, &c., according to Josephus, with names in red. To this has been added a series of Contour lines of every 25 feet. Price to Subscribers to the Fund, 1s. Non-subscribers, 1s. 6d.

9. THE SECTIONS of the Country north and south, and east

and west, on two sheets. Price 2s. (Western Palestine only.)

Application for Maps should be made to—

THE SECRETARY,

Palestine Exploration Fund,

24, Hanover Square, W.

or of—

EDWARD STANFORD,

26 and 27, Cockspur Street,

Charing Cross, London.

DIAGRAM Shewing the extent of the Old and New Testament Maps and the Great Map of Western Palestine published by the Palestine Exploration Fund.

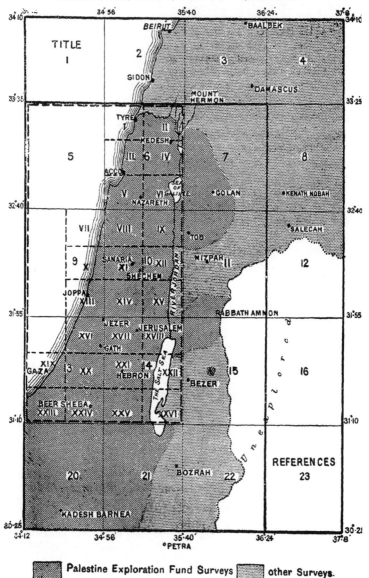

Palestine Exploration Fund Surveys   other Surveys.

The Old and New Testament Map in 20 Sheets, scale three-eighths of an inch to the mile, consists of Sheets 1—16 and 20—23.

The Old and New Testament Map in 12 sheets, scale three-eighths of an ch to the mile, consists of Sheets 5—7, 9—11, 13—15, 20—22.

The Great Map of Western Palestine scale one inch to the mile, consists of Sheets I—XXVI.

The Survey of Palestine.

Consists of the following four Volumes, uniform in size and appearance with The Memoirs of the "Survey of Western Palestine," 4to :—

THE SURVEY OF EASTERN PALESTINE.
(In one Volume).

By LIEUT.-COL. C. R. CONDER, D.C.L., LL.D., R.E.

This Survey, commenced by Lieut.-Col. Conder, and stopped by order of the Turkish Government, consists of 500 square miles.

The country is full of interest, and abounds with ruins of places Biblical and Classical. Among these ruins are most wonderful fields of dolmens and stone circles. Many drawings of these are given, and there are also special plans of all the most important ruins in the district surveyed.

The map of the Survey, reduced to the scale ⅜ths of an inch = 1 mile, the same as that of the Map published by the Fund, is added to the volume.

All Lieut.-Col. Conder's drawings and plans, numbering more than 350, are inserted.

The Memoirs supplied by Lieut.-Col. Conder were printed under his supervision. Among them are descriptions, with plans and drawings, of Heshbon, Amman (Rabboth Ammon), 'Arak el Emir (the Castle of Hyrcanus), the Persian building formerly considered a Byzantine Church, and other interesting remains.

THE FAUNA AND FLORA OF SINAI, PETRA, AND THE WÂDY 'ARABAH.

By H. CHICHESTER HART, B.A., F.L.S.

Mr. Chichester Hart accompanied Professor Hull in his Geological Expedition through Sinai and Palestine in 1883 as Naturalist. This volume is the outcome of the journey. It contains :—

A. An Analysis of the Fauna and Flora of Sinai, with general remarks on its botany and that of the Dead Sea Basin. Insecta. Mollusca. Reptilia. Aves and Mammalia.

This volume is illustrated with Maps and Plates, which are produced (without colour) in the same style and equal to those in Canon Tristram's "Flora and Fauna of Palestine."

THE ARCHÆOLOGICAL RESEARCHES IN PALESTINE.

(In two Volumes).

By Charles Clermont-Ganneau, LL.D.,
Membre de l'Institut, Professor au Collège de France.

Many years have elapsed since the drawings made for this expedition were placed in the hands of the Committee by M. Clermont-Ganneau. They are most exquisitely drawn by M. Lecomte, and are chiefly of architectural value. It is most desirable that they should no longer be withheld from the world. The only possible way of publishing them is by subscription in this manner.

The illustrations are upwards of 1,000 in number.

The Committee have found it necessary to arrange for the publication of the Researches in two volumes, instead of one volume, as originally intended. Vol. II., which is devoted to Palestine, is published in advance for the reasons stated in the Prefatory Note. Vol. I. treats of Jerusalem and neighbourhood, is well forward, and, when ready, will be sent out to the first 250 Subscribers, free of any further charge.

The edition is limited to 500 sets.

The Subscribers to the first edition (250 copies) of the "Survey of Western Palestine" are entitled to receive these volumes at the reduced price of £7 7s. 0d. No copies will be disposed of under the price of £7 7s. 0d. the set.

The first 250 Subscribers are entitled to the reduction in price, whether they be Subscribers to the first work or not; but the price will be £12 12s. to all subsequent Subscribers, unless they are Subscribers to the "Survey of Western Palestine."

Three volumes are ready and have been issued to Subscribers, in order of application.

An Illustrated Circular giving further particulars will be sent, post free, on application.

Application should be made to the Secretary, at the office of the Fund,

24, HANOVER SQUARE, W.

THE NEW — RAISED MAP - OF PALESTINE.

Constructed from the Surveys of the Palestine Exploration Fund,
and other sources, by

GEORGE ARMSTRONG

(OF THE SURVEY PARTY),

Acting Secretary to the Fund.

Scale $\frac{3}{8}$ of an inch to one mile or $\frac{1}{168960}$, being identical
with that of the Map.

PUBLISHED BY

The Palestine Exploration Fund,

24, HANOVER SQUARE, LONDON, W.

THE RAISED MAP OF PALESTINE

Is constructed on the basis of the recently issued Old and New
Testament Map. It embraces the whole of Western Palestine, from
Baalbeck in the North, to Kadesh Barnea in the South, and shows
nearly all that is known on the East of Jordan.

The natural features of the Country stand out prominently, and
show at a glance the relative proportions of the mountains, heights,
valleys, plains, &c.

Names are given to the coast towns and a few of the inland ones ;
other towns are numbered to correspond with a reference list of
names.

The seas, lakes, marshes and perennial streams are coloured blue, the Old and New Testament Sites are marked in red, the plains green, the rising ground, hills and mountains in various tints, the olive groves and wooded parts of the country stippled in green, and the main roads are shown in a thin black line.

—————◦◦◦◦◦◦◦◦◦◦◦◦—————

Casts in Fibrous Plaster, Coloured and Framed.
Price to Subscribers to the Fund, £10 10s.
To the Public £13 13s.

The Map measures 7 feet 6 inches by 4 feet, and is on view at the Office of the Fund, 24, Hanover Square, W.

PHOTOGRAPHS OF THE RAISED MAP, 8 ins. by 4 ins., 1s. each.

A NEW EDITION OF THE COLLOTYPE PRINT
of the Raised Map, 20 ins. by 28½ ins., now ready. Price to Subscribers, 2s. 3d.; Non-Subscribers, 3s. 3d., post free.

❧ ◉◉ ❧

LANTERN SLIDES OF THE RAISED MAP,
PLAIN, 1s. 3d.; COLOURED, 2s. 9d. each, post free.

The Secretary, 24, Hanover Square, W.

—◆◆◆—

SUBSCRIPTION FORM.

To the Secretary,

Please send me One Set of Books Nos. 2--24 as noted in list of publications, for which I enclose a Cheque for £

*Signature*_____

*Address*_____

Cheques and Money Orders to be made payable to the order of Mr. George Armstrong, Acting Secretary to the Fund. All Cheques and Orders should be crossed "Coutts & Co."

Palestine Exploration Fund,
24, Hanover Square, London, W.

Harrison and Sons, printers in ordinary to her majesty, st. martin's lane, london, w.c.

Printed in Great Britain
by Amazon.co.uk, Ltd.,
Marston Gate.